THE CAMBRIDGE COMPANION TO
LOGICAL EMPIRICISM

If there is a movement or school that epitomizes analytic philosophy in the middle of the twentieth century, it is logical empiricism. Logical empiricists created a scientifically and technically informed philosophy of science, established mathematical logic as a topic in and a tool for philosophy, and initiated the project of formal semantics. Accounts of analytic philosophy written in the middle of the twentieth century gave logical empiricism a central place in the project. The second wave of interpretative accounts was constructed to show how philosophy should progress, or had progressed, beyond logical empiricism. Since the 1980s, a new literature has arisen that examines logical empiricism in its historical, scientific, and philosophical contexts, in the belief that its philosophical significance has not been adequately judged, to the detriment of contemporary philosophy. This *Companion* provides informative overviews and further advances this reconstructive project. The essays survey the formative stages of logical empiricism in Central Europe and its acculturation in North America; discuss its main topics, achievements, and failures in different areas of philosophy of science; and assess its influence on philosophy, past, present, and future.

Alan Richardson is professor of philosophy at the University of British Columbia.

Thomas Uebel is professor of philosophy at the University of Manchester.

OTHER VOLUMES IN THE SERIES OF
CAMBRIDGE COMPANIONS

continued after the Index

The Cambridge Companion to
LOGICAL EMPIRICISM

Edited by

Alan Richardson
University of British Columbia

Thomas Uebel
University of Manchester

CAMBRIDGE
UNIVERSITY PRESS

CAMBRIDGE UNIVERSITY PRESS
Cambridge, New York, Melbourne, Madrid, Cape Town,
Singapore, São Paulo, Delhi

Cambridge University Press
32 Avenue of the Americas, New York, NY 10013–2473, USA

www.cambridge.org
Information on this title: www.cambridge.org/9780521791786

First published 2007

Printed in the United States of America

A catalog record for this publication is available from the British Library.

Library of Congress Cataloging in Publication Data

The Cambridge companion to logical empiricism / Alan W. Richardson and
Thomas E. Uebel, editors.
p. cm. – (Cambridge companions to philosophy)
Includes bibliographical references and index.
ISBN-13 978-0-521-79178-6 (hardback)
ISBN-13 978-0-521-79628-6 (pbk.)
1. Logical positivism. I. Richardson, Alan W. II. Uebel, Thomas E. (Thomas
Ernst), 1952– III. Title. IV. Series.

B824.6.C36 2007
146'.42–dc22   2006035760

ISBN 978-0-521-79178-6 hardback
ISBN 978-0-521-79628-6 paperback

Contents

Contributors

STEVE AWODEY is Associate Professor of Philosophy at Carnegie Mellon University. A logician and historian of logic, he is among the editors of the *Collected Works of Rudolf Carnap* and the author of *Category Theory* (Oxford, 2006). Together with A. W. Carus, he has coauthored numerous articles on Carnap, including most recently "Carnap's Dream: Gödel, Wittgenstein, and Logical Syntax" (*Synthese*).

A. W. CARUS is the author of numerous papers on Carnap as well as the forthcoming book *Carnap in Twentieth-Century Thought: Explication as Enlightenment* (Cambridge).

RICHARD CREATH is Professor in the Department of Philosophy and in the School of Life Sciences and Director, Program in History and Philosophy of Science at Arizona State University. He is the author of numerous articles on Carnap and Quine; the editor of *Dear Carnap, Dear Van* (California, 1990); and most recently co-editor of *The Cambridge Companion to Carnap* (Cambridge, forthcoming). He is also the general editor of the forthcoming *Collected Works of Rudolf Carnap* (Open Court).

MICHAEL FRIEDMAN is Frederick P. Rehmus Family Professor of Humanities at Stanford University and author of *Foundations of Space-Time Theories: Relativistic Physics and Philosophy of Science* (Princeton, 1983); *Kant and the Exact Sciences* (Harvard, 1992); *Reconsidering Logical Positivism* (Cambridge, 1999); *A Parting of the Ways: Carnap, Cassirer, and Heidegger* (Open Court, 2000); and *Dynamics of Reason* (CSLI, 2001), as well as co-editor of *Kant's Scientific Legacy in the Nineteenth Century*

(MIT, 2006) and *The Cambridge Companion to Carnap* (Cambridge).

MARIA CARLA GALAVOTTI is Professor of Philosophy of Science at the University of Bologna. Her publications include *Philosophical Introduction to Probability* (CSLI, 2005). She also is co-editor of *Stochastic Causality* (CSLI, 2001); *Probability, Dynamics and Causality. Essays in Honour of Richard C. Jeffrey* (*Erkenntnis* 45, 1996); and *Cambridge and Vienna. Frank P. Ramsey and the Vienna Circle* (Springer, 2006).

GARY L. HARDCASTLE is Assistant Professor of Philosophy at Bloomsburg University. He is editor of *Logical Empiricism in North America* (Minnesota, 2003) and *Monty Python and Philosophy* (Open Court, 2006) and author of articles in journals and collections.

DIETER HOFFMANN is Professor and Research Scholar at the Max Planck Institute for the History of Science, Berlin. His publications include *Science under Socialism. East Germany in Comparative Perspective* (Harvard, 1999) and *Quantum Theory Centenary. The Pre- and Early History* (Berlin, 2000) and numerous articles in journals and collections.

THOMAS MORMANN is Professor in the Department of Logic and Philosophy of Science of the University of the Basque Country UPV/EHU in Donostia–San Sebastian, Spain. His publications include *Rudolf Carnap* (Beck, 2000) and an edition, in German, of Carnap's *Pseudoproblems in Philosophy and Other Early Anti-Metaphysical Writings* (Meiner, 2004).

ELISABETH NEMETH is Professor of Philosophy and Head of the Department of Philosophy at the University of Vienna. She is the author of *Otto Neurath und der Wiener Kreis: Wissenschaftlichkeit als revolutionaerer Anspruch* (Campus, 1981) and numerous articles. Her edited volumes include *Encyclopedia and Utopia. The Life and Work of Otto Neurath* (with Friedrich Stadler; Kluwer, 1996).

GEORGE A. REISCH is an independent scholar and an editor at Open Court Publishing Company. His publications include *How the Cold War Transformed Philosophy of Science* (Cambridge, 2005), and he is coeditor of *Monty Python and Philosophy* (Open Court, 2006).

ALAN RICHARDSON is Professor of Philosophy and Distinguished University Scholar at the University of British Columbia. He is author of *Carnap's Construction of the World* (Cambridge, 1998) and coeditor of *Origins of Logical Empiricism* (Minnesota, 1996) and *Logical Empiricism in North America* (Minnesota, 2003).

THOMAS RYCKMAN is Lecturer in Philosophy of Science and Philosophy of Physics at Stanford University. He is the author of *The Reign of Relativity: Philosophy in Physics 1915–1925* (Oxford, 2005) and of articles in journals and collections.

FRIEDRICH STADLER is Professor at the University of Vienna, Head of the Department of Contemporary History, and Founder and Director of the Vienna Circle Institute (Institut Wiener Kreis). His publications include *Studien zum Wiener Kreis* (Suhrkamp, 1997), translated as *The Vienna Circle* (Springer, 2001), and his edited volumes include *Scientific Philosophy* (Kluwer, 1993), *History of the Philosophy of Science* (Kluwer, 2001), and *Vienna Circle and Logical Empiricism* (Kluwer, 2003).

DAVID STERN is Professor of Philosophy at the University of Iowa. He is the author of *Wittgenstein on Mind and Language* (Oxford, 1995) and *Wittgenstein's* Philosophical Investigations: *An Introduction* (Cambridge, 2004) and an editor of *The Cambridge Companion to Wittgenstein* (Cambridge, 1996) and *Wittgenstein Reads Weininger* (Cambridge, 2004).

THOMAS UEBEL is Professor of Philosophy at the University of Manchester, England. He is the author of *Overcoming Logical Positivism from Within* (Rodopi, 1992) and *Vernunftkritik und Wissenschaft* (Springer, 2000), co-author of *Otto Neurath: Philosophy between Science and Politics* (Cambridge, 1996), editor of *Rediscovering the Forgotten Vienna Circle* (Kluwer, 1991), and coeditor of *Otto Neurath: Economic Writings. Selections 1904–1945* (Kluwer, 2004).

THE CAMBRIDGE COMPANION TO
LOGICAL EMPIRICISM

Introduction

If there is a movement or school that epitomized or typified analytic philosophy in the middle of the twentieth century, it was, by all odds, logical empiricism.[1] Logical empiricists such as Hans Reichenbach, Rudolf Carnap, Carl G. Hempel, and Herbert Feigl had, by 1950, influenced the major fields of analytic philosophy. They had been instrumental in creating a scientifically and technically informed philosophy of science, in establishing mathematical logic as a topic in and a tool for philosophy, and in creating the project of formal semantics. Logical empiricism provided an importantly new understanding of the nature of empiricism and a new rejection of metaphysics. Accounts of analytic philosophy written in the middle of the twentieth century give logical empiricism a central place in the project, often repeating for analytic philosophy the revolutionary rhetoric of early logical empiricism.

Because of this importance of logical empiricism in establishing the project of analytic philosophy, philosophical innovations both within and outside the analytic tradition in the 1960s and 1970s often were at pains to distance themselves from one aspect or another of logical empiricism. Karl Popper's philosophy of science, for example, distanced itself from concerns about the meaninglessness of metaphysics, whereas Thomas Kuhn's historical philosophy of science distanced itself from the formalism and

---

[1] Throughout this book "logical empiricism" is understood to be synonymous with "logical positivism," or even "neopositivism," unless it is clear in context that a distinction is being drawn. Some logical empiricists thought the names had different reference, but most did not; in any case, by the middle of the 1930s, "logical empiricism" was the preferred term for leading representatives of both camps. Thus, we have chosen it rather than the more well-known but more misleading "logical positivism."

ahistorical approach to philosophy of science that had become associated with logical empiricism. Similarly, in philosophy of language, Saul Kripke's semantics of modal logic and "new theory of reference" enforced a turn toward metaphysics in formal semantics, whereas Donald Davidson and W. V. O. Quine, each in his own way, moved semantics away from formalism and toward a naturalistic empiricism. Such moves away from (what were understood to be) central commitments of logical empiricism, whether explicit or implicit, were widely noted and embraced. By the 1970s, logical empiricism had few advocates, and the project became firmly associated with a set of discarded philosophical doctrines and methods. Further afield, the positivism associated with logical empiricism was widely decried in European philosophy and in the social sciences as too narrowly scientistic and, thus, able neither to illuminate the business of social science nor to serve as a proper basis for philosophy. The first wave of interpretative accounts of logical empiricism had placed it at the heart of analytic philosophy, and the second, therefore, was constructed to show how philosophy should progress or had progressed beyond logical empiricism.

Since roughly the early 1980s a new literature has arisen that is less argumentative with or dismissive of logical empiricism, a literature that seeks to understand the place of logical empiricism in its historical, scientific, and philosophical contexts. This work proceeds in important ways on both sides of the Atlantic Ocean as scholars reconsider the origins of logical empiricism in Europe in the early twentieth century and its transmission to North America and throughout the world with the rise of fascism in Europe in the 1930s. This work has engaged not only philosophers but also intellectual historians, historians and sociologists of science, and researchers in intellectual migration and exile from Europe in the twentieth century. The purpose of this volume is to provide an entry into this new literature on the reappraisal of logical empiricism as well as suggestions for further reading.

This new work in the reappraisal of logical empiricism seeks to be more fair and disinterested than previous work – it is designed neither to sign up recruits nor to induce an act of intellectual homicide nor yet to preside over a funeral. Nevertheless, the work is not antiquarian. It agrees with both the early promotional and the later critical literature in finding logical empiricism central to analytic philosophy in the twentieth century. It is based, however, in the sensibility that the philosophical significance of logical empiricism has not been adequately judged and that this is to the detriment of contemporary philosophy generally. The work this volume introduces, then, seeks to be both historically accurate and philosophically informed; throughout an eye will always be open to questions of the significance of logical empiricism to contemporary projects in philosophy – and to projects that might be available for tomorrow's philosophers to take up.

Logical empiricism, whatever else it might be or have been, was a movement or program for philosophy that developed in Central Europe. A number of scientifically minded philosophers and philosophically minded scientists came together in various places throughout Europe to reflect on the current state of scientific and philosophical knowledge. The projects characteristic of logical empiricism developed primarily in Vienna and Berlin. The Vienna Circle, a group of researchers who met regularly from the mid-1920s to the mid-1930s under the leadership of Moritz Schlick, then the Chair for the Philosophy of the Inductive Sciences at the University of Vienna, counted among its junior members Rudolf Carnap and Schlick's student Herbert Feigl, and Hans Hahn, Philipp Frank, and Otto Neurath amongst its founders. In Berlin the Society for Scientific Philosophy was led by Hans Reichenbach and counted among its members and associates, besides Walter Dubislav and Richard von Mises, his student Carl G. Hempel. Connections were drawn also to various other centers of intellectual life in Europe in the 1920s and 1930s, such as Prague (where both Frank and Carnap worked at various times) and Warsaw (then home to the leading group working in mathematical logic, including Alfred Tarski).

Reflection upon the list of names appearing above indicates that the logical empiricists numbered among themselves several of the leading philosophers of the twentieth century – and they had substantial contact with other leading philosophers and scientists (Bertrand Russell, Ludwig Wittgenstein, Albert Einstein, Niels Bohr, Kurt Gödel, W. V. Quine, Karl Popper, David Hilbert, Hermann Weyl, et al.). Nonetheless, it was characteristic of the logical empiricists to stress the communal nature of philosophical research and the belief that philosophical results belonged to the community. For this reason, among other more quotidian ones, the editors have not chosen to organize the volume by individual philosopher, featuring a chapter on Schlick, one on Neurath, etc. We have, rather, chosen a topical approach, in our belief that one achieves a better sense of the group's own philosophical self-understanding by studying the topics they investigated and the methods they employed than by reading a set of quasi-biographical-cum-quasi-philosophical remarks.

Logical empiricism was a philosophy centrally concerned with science. Even when their interests moved them into areas such as semantics and metaethics, the logical empiricists sought both to understand and to promote the scientific understanding of the world. Science was, to their minds, both the locus of our best knowledge of the world and the source of hope for a brighter, less obscure and obscurantist future for philosophy. The Vienna Circle chose the term *"wissenschaftliche Weltauffassung"* – scientific world-conception – when, in 1929, they published their manifesto. Logical empiricism offered a scientific conception of the world in two senses, in fact: it offered a conception of the world that was deeply informed by science, and in doing so it sought to bring philosophy into the fold of genuinely scientific disciplines. Logical empiricism's form of scientific modernism flourished perhaps most brightly in Central Europe between the world wars and apparently lost its idealistic shine as it temporarily assumed a dominant role in post–Second World War North American philosophy (a role it never attained in Britain).

To reflect the importance of science as topic, method, and ideal among the logical empiricists, the essays in this volume are most centrally concerned with topics in general philosophy of science and in the philosophy of the special sciences. Where, for example, semantics is discussed, it is discussed in its central application for the logical empiricists – the question of the meaningfulness of scientific theories and their relation to evidential reports. Similarly, the elimination of metaphysics and the verification criterion of meaning are discussed here not as central dogmas of logical empiricism but in their contexts as part of the historical narrative of the logical empiricists' attempts to find a nonmetaphysical form of philosophy that could illuminate and reflect how science achieves knowledge of the world. Attention to then-contemporary science and its relations to then-contemporary philosophy is necessary to illuminate the philosophical moves characteristic of logical empiricism, including, of course, their joint sense that theirs was a philosophy entirely without doctrines, much less dogmas.

The volume is, thus, divided into thematic sections. The first section, "The Historical Context of Logical Empiricism," features essays that situate logical empiricism in the contexts of its development, first in Europe and then in the United States. Friedrich Stadler's essay examines the principal place of origin of logical empiricism, the Vienna Circle. Dieter Hoffmann's essay details the place of logical empiricism in the Berlin Society for Empirical/Scientific Philosophy. George Reisch looks at the development of logical empiricism in North America from the 1930s onward. These essays all bring new historical scholarship and historiographic subtlety to the question of the historical career and significance of logical empiricism.

The second section of the book examines some of the large issues in general philosophy of science that animated the work of the logical empiricists. Michael Friedman's essay examines the career of the notion of an a priori element in knowledge in logical empiricism; he points out the many twists in the understanding of the a priori and the lingering significance of it in mature logical empiricist philosophy of science. Maria Carla Galavotti's essay examines a project that many would think to be the heart of mature logical empiricism, the foundations of probability theory and the theory of confirmation, topics absolutely central to the logical empiricist's account of the structure and basis of scientific knowledge. Thomas Mormann examines another set of issues central to all logical empiricist theories of science: their account of the nature and structure of scientific theories. Throughout the essays in this section, the logical empiricist concerns with elucidating the place of conventions in scientific theorizing, answering questions of the relations of scientific theories to sensory evidence, and illuminating the logical structure of theories as well as other central issues in the general approach to philosophy of science within logical empiricism are examined from various angles.

The following section, "Logical Empiricism and the Philosophy of the Special Sciences," speaks to specific themes in the logical empiricist understandings of particular scientific disciplines. Steve Awodey and A. W. Carus offer an account of the particular nature of logical empiricist concerns with the foundations of mathematics and logic, an extraordinarily rich field both technically and philosophically, given the prominence of logic in the methods employed by the logical empiricists throughout their philosophy. Another rich field is mined by Thomas Ryckman in his detailed account of the philosophy of physics offered by logical empiricism, a philosophy both inspired by and seeking to explain the revolutionary developments in relativity theory and quantum mechanics in the early twentieth century. Logical empiricism is famous (or infamous) for its interventions in the methodology of psychology, the topic of Gary Hardcastle's essay. Thomas Uebel offers an account of the philosophy of social science embedded in the project of the physicalistic unity of science pursued especially by Otto Neurath in the 1930s and 1940s. Elisabeth Nemeth considers the hitherto scarcely explored relations between logical empiricism and contemporaneous history and sociology of science.

The final section of the book considers the relations between logical empiricism and some of its main critics. David Stern illuminates the vexed relations between the logical empiricists and Ludwig Wittgenstein through an examination of Wittgenstein's claim in the early 1930s that Carnap had plagiarized his work. Richard Creath examines the significance of the Carnap-Quine dispute regarding analyticity, the single most important episode in the turn of analytic philosophy from logical empiricism. Alan Richardson's essay details some historical puzzles surrounding the relations of Thomas Kuhn's historical philosophy of science and logical empiricist philosophy of science.

The editors would like to thank many people and institutions without whom this volume would not have been possible. The volume was substantially aided by a workshop sponsored by the International Society for History of Philosophy of Science (HOPOS) and the Vienna Circle Institute and held at the University of Vienna. Early encouragement was offered also by the late Cambridge University Press editor Terence Moore. Research assistantship was ably provided at various stages by University of British Columbia graduate students Alex Harmsen, Michael Waters, Stephen Friesen, and Roger Clarke; funding for these students was provided by the Social Sciences and Humanities Research Council of Canada, the UBC Hampton Research Fund, and the UBC Humanities and Social Sciences Large Grant fund. The contributors were notable for their good will and patience throughout this project. Deeply grateful to them, each editor also absolves the other for all faults that remain in the work.

FURTHER READING (IN ENGLISH)

Bibliographies of members of the Vienna Circle, the Berlin Society, and selected associates are given, along with short biographies in Stadler (2001, pp. 610–865).

Extensive bibliographies of Anglo-American analytic philosophy during logical empiricism's heyday are featured in Ayer (1959, pp. 381–447) and in Richard M. Rorty (ed.), 1967. *The Linguistic Turn. Essays in Philosophical Method*. Chicago: University of Chicago Press. Rev. ed. 1992, pp. 375–407.

EARLY MOTIVATING LITERATURE FROM
(AND ABOUT) THE LOGICAL EMPIRICISTS

Hahn, Hans, Otto Neurath, and Rudolf Carnap. 1929. *Wissenschaftliche Weltauffassung. Der Wiener Kreis*. Vienna: Wolf. Trans. by P. Foulkes and M. Neurath as "Scientific World-Conception: The Vienna Circle" in O Neurath (ed. M. Neurath and R. S. Cohen), *Empiricism and Sociology*. Dordrecht: Reidel, 1973, pp. 299–318.

Feigl, Herbert, and Alfred O. Blumberg. 1931. "Logical Positivism." *Journal of Philosophy* 28: 281–96.

Reichenbach, Hans. 1935. "Logical Empiricism in Germany and the Present State of Its Problems." *Journal of Philosophy* 33: 141–60.

Nagel, Ernest. 1936. "Impressions and Appraisals of Analytic Philosophy in Europe," *Journal of Philosophy* 33. Repr. in Nagel. 1956. *Logic without Metaphysics and Other Essays in the Philosophy of Science*. Glencoe, IL: Free Press, pp. 191–246.

RETROSPECTIVE ACCOUNTS OF THE DEVELOPMENT
AND SIGNIFICANCE OF LOGICAL EMPIRICISM

Frank, Philipp. 1949. "Introduction: Historical Background." In his *Modern Science and Its Philosophy*. Cambridge, MA: Harvard University Press, pp. 1–52.

Jorgensen, Jorgen. 1951. "The Development of Logical Empiricism." *Foundations of the Unity of Science*, volume 2, number 9. Chicago: University of Chicago Press pp. 845–946 of volume 2 of the combined edition: Neurath, Otto, Rudolf Carnap, and Charles Morris (eds.), *Foundations of the Unity of Science*. Chicago: University of Chicago Press, 1970.

Kraft, Viktor. 1953. *The Vienna Circle*. New York: Philosophical Library (orig. 1950).

Ayer, Alfred Jules. 1959. "Introduction." In A.J. Ayer (ed.), *Logical Positivism*. New York: Free Press, pp. 3–28.

Carnap, Rudolf. 1963a. "Intellectual Autobiography." In Paul Arthur Schilpp (ed.), *The Philosophy of Rudolf Carnap*. LaSalle, IL: Open Court, pp. 3–84.

Feigl, Herbert. 1969. "The Wiener Kreis in America." In D. Fleming and B. Baylin (eds.), *The Intellectual Migration*. Cambridge, MA: Harvard University Press.Cambridge, MA: Harvard University Press Repr. in Feigl, *Inquiries and Provocations* (ed. R. S. Cohen). Dordrecht: Reidel, 1981, pp. 57–93.

Achinstein, Peter, and Steven F. Barker (eds.). 1969. *The Legacy of Logical Positivism*. Baltimore: Johns Hopkins University Press.

Suppe, Frederick. 1977. "The Search for a Philosophical Understanding of Theories." In F. Suppe (ed.), *The Structure of Scientific Theories*, 2nd ed. Urbana: University of Illinois Press, pp. 3–241.

Hanfling, Oswald. 1981. *Logical Positivism*. Oxford: Blackwell.

Gadol, Eugene T. (ed.). 1982. *Rationality and Science*. Vienna: Springer.

Menger, Karl. 1994. *Reminiscences of the Vienna Circle and the Mathematical Colloquium* (ed. B. McGuinness and A. Sklar). Dordrecht: Kluwer

RECENT HISTORICAL SCHOLARSHIP

Haller, Rudolf (ed.). 1982. *Schlick and Neurath Centenary. Grazer Philosophische Studien 16–17*.

Rescher, Nicholas (ed.). 1985. *The Heritage of Logical Positivism*. Lanham, MD: University Press of America.

Proust, Joelle. 1989. *Questions of Form. Logic and the Analytic Proposition from Kant to Carnap*. Minneapolis: University of Minnesota Press (orig. 1986).

Zolo, Danilo. 1989. *Reflexive Epistemology. The Philosophical Legacy of Otto Neurath*. Dordrecht: Kluwer (orig. 1986).

Coffa, Alberto. 1991. *The Semantic Tradition from Kant to Carnap. To the Vienna Station* (ed. L. Wessels). Cambridge: Cambridge University Press.

Spohn, Wolfgang (ed.). 1991. *Hans Reichenbach, Rudolf Carnap: A Centenary. Erkenntnis 35*.

Uebel, Thomas E. (ed.). 1991. *Rediscovering the Forgotten Vienna Circle. Austrian Studies on Otto Neurath*. Dordrecht: Kluwer.

Bell, David, and Wilhelm Vossenkuhl (eds.). 1992. *Science and Subjectivity*. Berlin: Akademieverlag.

Sarkar, Sahotra (ed.). 1992. *Rudolf Carnap Centenary*. Synthese 93 nos. 1–2.

Uebel, Thomas E. 1992. *Overcoming Logical Positivism from Within. Neurath in the Vienna Circle's Protocol Sentence Debate*. Amsterdam: Rodopi.

Oberdan, Thomas. 1993. *Protocols, Truth, Convention*. Amsterdam: Rodopi.

Salmon, Wesley, and Gereon Wolters (eds.). 1993. *Logic, Language and the Structure of Scientific Theories*. Pittsburgh/Konstanz: University of Pittsburgh Press/Universitätsverlag.

Stadler, Friedrich (ed.). 1993. *Scientific Philosophy: Origin and Developments*. Dordrecht: Kluwer.

Cirera, Ramon. 1994. *Carnap and the Vienna Circle. Empiricism and Logical Syntax*. Amsterdam: Rodopi.

Cartwright, Nancy, Jordi Cat, Lola Fleck, and Thomas E. Uebel. 1996. *Otto Neurath: Philosophy between Science and Politics*. Cambridge: Cambridge University Press.

Giere, Ronald N., and Alan W. Richardson (eds.). 1996. *Origins of Logical Empiricism*. Minneapolis: University of Minnesota Press.

Nemeth, Elisabeth, and Friedrich Stadler (eds.). 1996. *Otto Neurath: Encyclopedism and Utopia*. Dordrecht: Kluwer.

Sarkar, Sahotra (ed.). 1996. *The Legacy of the Vienna Circle: Modern Reappraisals*. New York: Garland.

Richardson, Alan W. 1998. *Carnap's Construction of the World*. Cambridge: Cambridge University Press.

Friedman, Michael. 1999. *Reconsidering Logical Positivism*. Cambridge: Cambridge University Press.

Friedman, Michael. 2000. *A Parting of the Ways: Carnap-Cassirer-Heidegger*. Chicago: Open Court.

Fetzer, James (ed.). 2000. *Science, Explanation and Rationality. Aspects of the Philosophy of C. G. Hempel*. Oxford: Oxford University Press.

Stadler, Friedrich. 2001. *The Vienna Circle: Studies in the Origins, Development, and Inflence of Logical Empiricism*. Vienna: Springer (orig. 1997).

Bonk, Thomas (ed.). 2003. *Language, Truth and Knowledge. Contributions to the Philosophy of Rudolf Carnap*. Dordrecht: Kluwer.

Hardcastle, Gary L., and Alan W. Richardson (eds.). 2003. *Logical Empiricism in North America*. Minneapolis: University of Minnesota Press.

Parrini, Paolo, Wesley Salmon, and Merrilee Salmon (eds.). 2003. *Logical Empiricism. Historical and Contemporary Perspectives*. Pittsburgh: University of Pittsburgh Press.

Stadler, Friedrich (ed.). 2003. *The Vienna Circle and Logical Empiricism. Re-evaluation and Future Perspectives*. Dordrecht: Kluwer.

Awodey, Steve, and Carsten Klein (eds.). 2004. *Carnap Brought Home. The View from Jena*. Chicago: Open Court.

Reisch, George. 2005. *How the Cold War Transformed Philosophy of Science: To the Icy Slopes of Logic*. Cambridge: Cambridge University Press.

Creath, Richard, and Michael Friedman (eds.). 2007. *Cambridge Companion to Rudolf Carnap*. Cambridge: Cambridge University Press.

For further individual essays, see also journals like *Philosophy of Science, British Journal for the Philosophy of Science, Studies in the History and Philosophy of Science, Perspectives on Science, International Studies in the Philosophy of Science, Synthese, History and Philosophy of Logic, Journal of the History of Philosophy, British Journal for the History of Philosophy, Journal of Philosophy, American Philosophical Quarterly, Canadian Journal of Philosophy, European Journal of Philosophy, Philosophy and Phenomenalogical Review, Pacific Philosophical Quarterly, Philosophical Topics, Grazer Philosophische Studien,* and, last but not least, *Erkenntnis.*

Part One: The Historical Context of Logical Empiricism

1 The Vienna Circle
Context, Profile, and Development

INTRODUCTION. THE COLLECTIVE DIMENSION: EMERGENCE AND DEVELOPMENT OF THE VIENNA CIRCLE

The so-called Vienna Circle of logical empiricism first came to public attention in 1929 with the publication of a manifesto entitled *Wissenschaftliche Weltauffassung. Der Wiener Kreis* (The Scientific World-Conception. The Vienna Circle). Published for the Ernst Mach Society, this influential philosophical manifesto – dedicated to Moritz Schlick, the titular leader of the Vienna Circle – was signed by Rudolf Carnap, Hans Hahn, and Otto Neurath, who may be regarded as its editors and, with Herbert Feigl, its authors (Mulder 1968). The name "Vienna Circle" was originally suggested by Otto Neurath, who wanted to evoke pleasant associations with the "Vienna woods" or the "Viennese waltz" by alluding to the local origin of this collective (Frank 1949, 38).

The plan for this publication was set in motion when Moritz Schlick, who had come to Vienna in 1922 to take up a professorial appointment previously held by Ernst Mach and Ludwig Boltzmann (and Adolf Stöhr) and had founded the Vienna Circle in 1924, received a lucrative offer from the University of Bonn at the beginning of 1929. The threatened departure of Schlick was to be prevented by a joint official declaration of solidarity by the members of the Vienna Circle, the Ernst Mach Society (of which he was the head from 1928 to 1934), and further sympathizers with the cause of scientific philosophy. After receiving a letter from his supporters

If not otherwise indicated in the references, this paper is based on Stadler (1997; 2001). It was translated by Camilla Nielsen.

dated April 2, 1929, Schlick after long reflection and with a heavy heart decided to remain in Vienna "out of attachment for Austria", even though the Viennese ministry reacted rather passively. The following summer semester of 1929 Schlick spent at Stanford University as a visiting professor while in Vienna his supporters worked on the manifesto, which was presented to the scientific community at large at the Conference on the Epistemology of the Exact Sciences in Prague from September 15 to 17.

This publication and the conference, organized jointly by the Ernst Mach Society and the Berlin-based Society for Empirical Philosophy, marked the beginning of the *public phase* of the Vienna Circle, during which the Circle established international contacts first in France and then in the English-speaking world although it remained marginalized within Central European academia. Schlick, like Wittgenstein, did not particularly appreciate the content and wording of the manifesto because of its "ballyhoo style" (Mulder 1968, 390). Even so, as a representative of the Circle's "moderate wing" and chair of the Ernst Mach Society until its forced dissolution in 1934, Schlick backed the collectivist efforts of some of his colleagues, just as he supported the project of starting the journal *Erkenntnis* in spite of philosophical differences with the editors Reichenbach and Carnap.

The term scientific "world-conception" (*Weltauffassung*) intended to signal a sharp contrast with the metaphysically informed German "worldview" (*Weltanschauung*) and to stress its scientific orientation. The preface of the manifesto underlined the Circle's principles of this-worldliness, practical relevance, and inter-disciplinarity. Among the intellectual precursors named were Leibniz, Bolzano, Berkeley, Hume and Mill, Comte, Poincaré and Duhem, along with Frege, Russell and Whitehead, Wittgenstein, and even the American pragmatists. The Circle's work was further contextualized by reference to Vienna's "liberal tradition" and adult education movement; influences and orientations ranged from the liberalism of Carl Menger's marginal utility economics to Austro-Marxism. Notably, the manifesto's diction of enlightened cultural struggle was explicitly connected to "endeavours toward a new organization of economic and social relations, toward the unification of mankind, toward a reform of school and education". Thus the goal was to "fashion intellectual tools for everyday life, for the daily life of the scholar but also for the daily life of all those who in some way join in working at the conscious re-shaping of life" (Carnap, Hahn, Neurath 1929/1973, 304–5). The main theoretical elements of the scientific world-conception – empiricism, positivism, and logical analysis of language – meanwhile were to be applied for work on the foundational problems of arithmetic, physics, geometry, biology, psychology, and social science. Traditional system-building philosophy was to be dethroned as "queen of the sciences", and in its place a more practical, this-worldly orientation was promoted. This approach culminated in the slogan "The scientific world-conception serves life and life receives it" (ibid., 318).

The manifesto concluded, following some general references to the relevant literature, with a bibliography of members of the Vienna Circle – Gustav Bergmann, Rudolf Carnap, Herbert Feigl, Philipp Frank, Kurt Gödel, Hans Hahn, Viktor Kraft, Karl Menger, Marcel Natkin, Otto Neurath, Olga Hahn-Neurath, Theodor Radakovic, Moritz Schlick, and Friedrich Waismann – and of "authors affiliated to the Vienna Circle" – including Walter Dubislav, Kurt Grelling, Hasso Härlen, Eino Kaila, Heinrich Loewy, Frank P. Ramsey, Hans Reichenbach, Kurt Reidemeister, and Edgar Zilsel. Lastly, Albert Einstein, Bertrand Russell, and Ludwig Wittgenstein were listed with their most important writings as the "leading representatives of the scientific world-conception".

This self-portrayal reflects, as it were, the Vienna Circle at "half-time" and must be updated, as I have argued, on the basis of independent sources and more recent studies, in terms of the concept of the Circle's "core" and "periphery". Applying the criterion of regular participation at the Circle's Thursday evening meetings yields a core group comprising at least 19 persons: Gustav Bergmann, Rudolf Carnap, Herbert Feigl, Philipp Frank, Kurt Gödel, Hans Hahn, Olga Hahn-Neurath, Bela Juhos, Felix Kaufmann, Viktor Kraft, Karl Menger, Richard von Mises, Otto Neurath, Rose Rand, Josef Schächter, Moritz Schlick, Olga Taussky-Todd, Friedrich Waismann, and Edgar Zilsel. A list of at least 16 visitors and collaborators from Austria and abroad constitute the periphery: Alfred J. Ayer, Egon Brunswik, Karl Bühler, Josef Frank, Else Frenkel-Brunswik, Heinrich Gomperz, Carl Gustav Hempel, Eino Kaila, Hans Kelsen, Charles Morris, Arne Naess, Willard Van Orman Quine, Frank P. Ramsey, Hans Reichenbach, Kurt Reidemeister, and Alfred Tarski.

According to existing sources, Ludwig Wittgenstein and Karl Popper were not personally present in the Schlick Circle, but they did maintain intensive contacts with various members of the Vienna Circle.

It is to be noted that already before World War I the "first Vienna Circle" had emerged in Vienna as a sort of *proto-circle* (see Frank 1949; Haller 1985; Uebel 2000b). From 1907 to 1911 the later Vienna Circle members Philipp Frank, Hans Hahn, Otto Neurath, and Richard von Mises discussed in Vienna coffeehouses the "crisis of philosophy" that followed the so-called second scientific revolution, triggered off by the work of Ernst Mach, Ludwig Boltzmann, Max Planck, and Albert Einstein. The members of this early group were interested in overcoming metaphysical philosophy through a synthesis of empiricism and symbolic logic, helped by the French conventionalism of Abel Rey, Pierre Duhem, and Henri Poincaré, by David Hilbert's method of axiomatization, which had rendered geometry a system of implicit definitions, and by Russell and Whitehead's *Principia Mathematica*. Their version of scientific philosophy was intended as an anti-aprioristic theory of science, even though various forms of neo-Kantianism were still to exert an influence on the Vienna Circle in its heyday. (On the neo-Kantian legacy in the Vienna Circle see Richardson 1998 and Friedman 1999.) Thus one already finds in the first Vienna Circle a modernist empiricism combined with Russellian logicism, a holistic theory of science enriched by conventionalism as a response, on the one hand, to the metaphysics of what Frank called "school philosophy" and, on the other hand, to dialectical materialism (in particular Lenin's *Materialism and Empirio-Criticism*, 1908). Already here we can recognize the predilection for monism and methodological nominalism, a conception of science that continued to develop after World War I as the unified science of physicalism.

Following the war-related interruptions and delays of this innovative development, the *constitutive phase* of the Vienna Circle extended until about 1924. It began in the academic year 1921–2 when the mathematician Hans Hahn, who had returned to a chair in Vienna, laid the institutional groundwork at the University of Vienna by playing a crucial role in bringing about Schlick's appointment to Vienna in spite of protests by the local philosophers. Hahn and his colleague Kurt Reidemeister also laid the intellectual groundwork by drawing attention to Ludwig Wittgenstein's *Tractatus Logico-Philosophicus*. Until his death, Hahn also was one of the most adamant representatives of the so-called left wing with Frank, Neurath, Carnap, and Zilsel. The Circle's *non-public phase* began with the regular discussion meetings in Boltzmanngasse 5 that were led by Schlick from the winter semester 1924–5 onwards. It was in this period that the initial contacts with Wittgenstein took place and Carnap moved to Vienna at the behest of Schlick. The *public phase* was ushered in with the already mentioned publication of the manifesto and the first international appearance of the group as the Vienna Circle in Prague in 1929. Its end was protracted, extending from the dissolution of the Ernst Mach Society after February 1934 and continuing through a first wave of the emigration (which began still earlier with Herbert Feigl in 1931 but started in earnest with Otto Neurath in 1934) and the death of Hahn later in 1934 up to Schlick's murder on the steps of the University of Vienna in June 1936. One significant offshoot of the Vienna Circle during this period was the "Mathematical Colloquium" established by Karl Menger. From 1928 to 1936 this colloquium represented an important parallel initiative, partially overlapping with the Circle and developing its own dynamic, as was also the case with the Heinrich Gomperz Circle after 1934. (Both will be discussed further below.) The early 1930s also marked the beginning of the intensive communication by the young Karl Popper with members of the Vienna Circle, even though he was never personally invited by Schlick to attend the Circle's meetings.

The phase that followed Schlick's violent death can only be described as an *imitative phase* with sporadic meetings in Vienna around Viktor Kraft, Friedrich Waismann, Edgar Zilsel, Karl Menger, and Heinrich Gomperz, lasting until the so-called *Anschluss* of Austria to Hitler's Germany in 1938, which marked the final disappearance of the Vienna Circle in its country of origin. From our wider perspective we can therefore note a certain simultaneity in the processes of internationalization and local disintegration from the early 1930s onwards, resulting in the expulsion and virtual destruction of logical empiricism (the Vienna Circle, the Berlin Society for Scientific Philosophy, and the Prague group around Frank) in Austria, Germany, and the Czech Republic.

The changes that affected science during these years in terms of politics, worldview, and theory and the concomitant transformation that resulted from emigration to the Anglo-American world first became noticeable with the publication of the influential article "Logical Positivism: A New Movement in European Philosophy" in the *Journal of Philosophy* by Herbert Feigl and his friend Albert Blumberg (who had written his dissertation under Schlick). Here the new Wittgenstein-inspired anti-Kantian synthesis of empiricism and logic was presented as follows:

The new logical positivism retains the fundamental principle of empiricism but, profiting by the brilliant work of Poincaré and Einstein in the foundations of physics and Frege and Russell in the foundations of mathematics, feels it has attained in most essentials a unified theory of knowledge in which neither logical nor empirical factors are neglected. (Blumberg and Feigl 1931, 282)

This trend was reinforced mainly by the Unity of Science movement promoted by Neurath, Carnap, and Charles Morris and their efforts to create an *International Encyclopedia of Unified Science* between 1934 and 1941. Five international congresses were organized: an initial preparatory one in Prague (1934), as well as two in Paris (1935 and 1937) and one each in Copenhagen (1936), Cambridge, England (1938), Cambridge, Massachusetts (1939), and Chicago (1941). All of these had at least parts of their proceedings published. Their contributions often featured cross-references to the house journal of early logical empiricism, *Erkenntnis*, produced by the Hamburg publishing house Felix Meiner Verlag until 1938 with Rudolf Carnap and Hans Reichenbach as editors in exile from 1933 onwards. (Thereafter, for a brief period, it appeared as the *Journal of Unified Science* published by the Dutch Van Stockum & Zoon.) In addition, two book series were continued which had been started in the heyday of the Vienna Circle: "Schriften zur Wissenschaftlichen Weltauffassung" (Writings on the Scientific World-Conception) running to 11 volumes edited by Moritz Schlick and Philipp Frank and published by the Viennese Springer Verlag between 1929 and 1937, and "Einheitswissenschaft" (Unified Science) running to seven monographs edited by Otto Neurath with the Viennese publisher Gerold & Co. (as of the sixth issue: Van Stockum & Zoon, The Hague). The "Library of Unified Science" started by Neurath in Dutch exile still managed to produce three books with Van Stockum & Zoon between 1939 and 1941.

THE SOCIAL AND INSTITUTIONAL CONTEXT:
FROM THE FIRST VIENNA CIRCLE TO
THE SCHLICK CIRCLE AND
THE ERNST MACH SOCIETY

As noted, the project of rendering philosophy scientific already was placed on the agenda by the young revolutionaries in the first Vienna Circle. Drawing on their contemporary philosophical background (Brentano, Meinong, Husserl, Schröder, Helmholtz, Hertz, and Freud) they attempted a synthesis between Mach's empiricist program and French conventionalism. Frank, the successor to Einstein's chair in physics in Prague, gave an authentic reconstruction of this early (and long neglected) history of logical empiricism. Metaphysical "school philosophy", even Kant, could be countered with Nietzsche, Mach, and Boltzmann, but there remained a rift to be bridged between modern empiricism and symbolic logic. At this juncture Abel Rey (1907), Henri Poincaré (1908), and Pierre Duhem (1906) provided crucial contributions. Frank described the synthesis of Mach as follows:

According to Mach, the general principles of science are abbreviated economical descriptions of observed facts; according to Poincaré, they are free creations of the human mind which do not tell anything about observed facts. The attempt to integrate the two concepts into one coherent system was the origin of what was later called logical empiricism. (Frank 1949, 11–12)

This anti-Kantian turn in theory of science was completed by following the lead provided by Einstein's special and general theories of relativity, which Moritz Schlick (1917) addressed in philosophical terms that found Einstein's explicit approval, and by Russell and Whitehead's *Principia Mathematica* (2nd ed. 1925). Einstein's theory

seemed to be an excellent example of the way in which a scientific theory is built up according to the new ideas of positivism. The symbolic or structural system is neatly developed and is sharply separated from the observational facts that are to be embraced. Then the system must be interpreted, and the prediction of facts that are observable must be made and the predictions verified by observations. (Frank 1949, 18–19)

The conception of observation implied here was part of the theory of scientific theories outlined by Frank. Later it was explicitly developed

with the help of Percy Bridgman's "operational definitions" (1927).
A physical theory does not directly describe the "world in itself"
but only its structure, a view that was also formulated by Schlick in
his *General Theory of Knowledge* (1918/25). Yet while the fact that
the idea of an *experimentum crucis* as a criterion of truth was
rejected by this methodologically holist conception of science,
efforts continued to develop an alternative to metaphysical vitalism
by means of a causal approach that allowed for a probabilistic
orientation (Frank 1932). Together with Richard von Mises, Frank
thus ushered in *The Fall of Mechanistic Physics* (1935) and the
probabilistic turn in the theory of the natural sciences. With his
frequentist and objective conception of probability (1928), his
interpretation of Mach, and his history of the empiricist approach
to science, Mises (who held the first chair for applied mathematics
in Berlin) made sure that, even in its heyday, "positivism" was not
reducible to a narrowly normative theory of science fully char-
acterizable by verificationism and value-neutrality (1939).

The "real founder" of the Vienna Circle (Frank 1934) was no
doubt the mathematician and logician Hans Hahn. In his later
publications such as "The Crisis of Intuition" (1933) and "Superfluous Entities (Occam's Razor)" (1930) he aptly described the thematic range of logical empiricism. For his student Karl Menger, he
was an important influence in both the Schlick Circle and the Ernst
Mach Society (Menger 1980, ix–x). Like his brother-in-law Neurath,
he, too, did not shirk from appearing in public as a speaker on topics
concerning scientific philosophy and adult education and as a political commentator advocating the democratization of the University
of Vienna and the Viennese school reform movement.

Otto Neurath, a veritable polymath, offered important impulses
to the early group with his interdisciplinary orientation (history,
economics, sociology, logic, and mathematics) and his ability to
contextualize philosophy of science in a socio-critical sense. Thanks
to his untiring work as organizer and historiographer of the Vienna
Circle, there is no lack of accounts of the early and classical Vienna
Circle. His nonreductionist, holistic, and naturalistic philosophy of
science places him in the tradition of Duhem and Quine. Decidedly
empiricist and antimetaphysical in orientation, his concern lay largely with the construction of unifying principles and multiple connections between individual scientific disciplines, an "encyclopedia

of unified science", that sought to avoided the hierarchical "system" of unified science (1938, 1938a).

Once note is taken, in addition, that still prior to World War I another later member of the Vienna Circle, Viktor Kraft, had laid the foundation for a critical realism with hypothetico-deductive methodology in his book *Weltbegriff und Erkenntnisbegriff* (The Concept of World and and the Concept of Knowledge, 1912), then we find before us the main theoretical elements of the logical empiricism of the interwar years. After World War I this prototype was further enriched and refined by the linguistic turn and the reception of Wittgenstein's *Tractatus*, by Carnap's large-scale attempts at systematization (from *Aufbau* to *Syntax*), the American neopragmatists (P. W. Bridgman, John Dewey, Charles Morris), and the Polish school of logicians centered around Alfred Tarski. An important role was played by the communicative network between Vienna (around Schlick), Berlin (Reichenbach), and Prague (Frank, as of 1931 Carnap). Efforts to popularize the ideas of this movement assumed institutional form in the Ernst Mach Society (1928–34), while publication activities were intensified with the journal *Erkenntnis* and the two book series, and internationalization was promoted by the already noted international conferences. Among the results of the latter were the transdisciplinary publications of the *International Encyclopedia of Unified Science*, guided from 1938 mainly by Neurath and after 1945 by Carnap and Morris, with a total of 19 monographs, reprinted as *Foundations of the Unity of Science* (Carnap, Morris, and Neurath 1955).

So much for the external developments, which can be understood only by considering the socio-political background of the time, the transition from democracy to totalitarianism, and the specific contexts in the individual European countries. I shall now turn to the internal theoretical dynamic that characterized the Vienna Circle and its periphery in the interwar years and to the Circle's place amidst contemporary Enlightenment movements. But it must not be forgotten that the Vienna Circle emerged during an extraordinary high point of intellectual life in Central Europe, before the Nazi seizure of power and destruction of this creative milieu. This alone suggests that the Circle's development cannot be detached from its socio-cultural context and that its pluralist self-understanding as well as its perception from the outside were at least partly conditioned by external events. Any abstraction from these basic conditions inevitably simplifies the understanding of the Vienna Circle and logical empiricism.

In the *constitutive phase*, Schlick's appointment to the chair for natural philosophy at the University of Vienna in 1922 was crucial for the further development of logical empiricism. Immediately after arriving in Vienna and together with Hahn, Schlick organized an informal discussion circle while he continued to work on the second edition of his *General Theory of Knowledge* (1925), which was still committed to a kind of scientific realism. Nonetheless, he presented himself as a successor of Ernst Mach, to whom he dedicated his first lecture on natural philosophy in the winter semester of 1922/23. Schlick's Enlightenment-inspired view of science bridged their philosophical differences, as also became evident in Schlick's leadership of the Ernst Mach Society, which popularized the Vienna Circle in the field of adult education.

During the same period, the congenial Hahn promoted modern logic and mathematics, especially with seminars on the *Principia Mathematica*. Kurt Reidemeister, whom Hahn had brought to Vienna as associate professor for geometry, played an important role by introducing the *Tractatus* in one of his seminars. This reception was continued in Schlick's discussion circle, in which Hahn, Neurath, Kaufmann, Waismann, Feigl, and later Carnap participated. After Reidemeister received a call to Königsberg (today's Kaliningrad) as full professor, he organized there (as a continuation of the Prague conference of 1929) the Second Conference on Epistemology of the Exact Sciences (more on this below).

Thus we note that both the intellectual and institutional foundations were laid for the formation of the Vienna Circle in the form of the circle around Schlick by the end of 1924 and early 1925. On the one hand, there was the theoretical framework derived from Frege, Russell/Whitehead, and Wittgenstein, enriched with Mach's and Boltzmann's antimetaphysical worldview and complemented by Duhem's and Poincaré's conventionalism. On the other, there was Schlick's institutional position as *Ordinarius*, his professorial chair, which served as a center for discussing "scientific philosophy".

It was Schlick's students Friedrich Waismann and Herbert Feigl who had first suggested creating a regular "evening circle" to their teacher. Here not just acclaimed scholars and guests from abroad were to participate but also students and graduate students. This composition reflected in a very typical way the pluralism and egalitarism of the Circle, even though admission was gained only by Schlick's personal invitation. In the first years, the participants included – in addition to Feigl, Waismann, and Hahn – Carnap, Juhos, Neider, Schächter, Zilsel, (the secondary teacher) Neumann, the mathematician Menger, Gödel, Bergmann, Löwy, Radakovic, Kaufmann, and sometimes also Schlick's Viennese colleagues Karl Bühler and Robert Reininger; the younger generation was represented also by Brunswik, Rand, Natkin, and Hollitscher. This composition reflects the open network character of Viennese logical empiricism already in the 1920s, which was reinforced from 1930 onwards. In the Circle's public phase, the guests from abroad included Ayer, Hempel, Nagel, Quine, Tarski, Kaila, Naess, Reichenbach, Dubislav, Grelling, Härlen, Blumberg, Petzäll, Tscha Hung, and Geymonat.

The institutionalization of the Schlick Circle in the prepublic phase can be described as an ongoing discussion forum, moving between Wittgenstein's *Tractatus* (1922) and Carnap's *The Logical Structure of the World* (hereafter *Aufbau*, 1928). The "Vienna Circle" emerged from the Schlick Circle that met regularly every Thursday evening from the winter semester of 1924/25 onwards in the philosophy library of the Mathematical Institute in Boltzmanngasse 5, for which Waismann was responsible. In 1925 Carnap spent a short time in Vienna (his first visit) and circulated the first version of the *Aufbau* in the Circle. With Schlick revising ever more his position as expounded in the *Theory of Knowledge*, Wittgenstein's linguistic turn seems increasingly to have gained ground. By contrast, from the beginning of the Circle, Neurath emphasized the philosophy-free "scientific world-conception", much to Schlick's dismay, and its social relevance in the Enlightenment discourse of modernity. The controversy over the very context in which philosophy was practiced thus also figured in the Schlick Circle, even if Carnap did not allow the personal political, largely leftist allegiance to play a role in the discussions. This is reflected in the exegesis of the *Tractatus* when its "mysticism of silence" was met with skepticism by Carnap, Neurath, and Menger. Themes such as Carnap's axiomatics, Ramsey's definition of identity, the foundations of mathematics and probability theory, even the problem of other minds were on the agenda of this "republic of scholars". According to Feigl, the first volumes of *Erkenntnis* partly reflect the results of these discussions, and in spite of differences – for instance, rational reconstruction (Carnap) versus ideal-language philosophy (Wittgenstein) – there is discernible a common, identity-creating self-understanding of a philosophical reform movement. Feigl himself prefered a critical realism like that of the early Schlick, and with Kraft – and later with Popper on the periphery – the option of critical or constructive realism with a hypothetico-deductive methodology saw further development.

The increased theoretical differentiation, anticipating the tolerance principle later elaborated by Carnap, also led to a separate logical platform, the already mentioned Mathematical Colloquium. Its founder Karl Menger had returned to Vienna in the fall of 1927 from Amsterdam, where he worked as L. E. J. Brouwer's assistant. In Vienna he became associate professor for geometry (succeeding Reidemeister) and was active as a mathematician and member of the Schlick Circle up until his emigration in 1937. Menger once described his famous student Kurt Gödel as an interested but silent figure in the Schlick Circle. Both took a critical stance to Wittgenstein and the manifesto of 1929, which provides a plausible motivation for their pronounced involvement in the equally publicly oriented Colloquium, inspired by Alfred Tarski's guest lectures. Thereby the semantic turn was introduced into the philosophy of science as a serious alternative to the previous linguistic turn. At the same time, exchanges with the Polish school of logicians ("anti-irrationalism") were intensified by Circle members and continued up to the phase of emigration and exile.

The nonpublic phase up to 1929 can accordingly be summed up as follows. The essential elements of the philosophical conception of the first Vienna Circle were further developed and enriched by the contributions of Wittgenstein and Carnap. With the manifesto's "scientific world-conception" and soon the idea of a physicalist unified science as endorsed mainly by Carnap and Neurath, there obtained a real alternative to the traditional opposition between philosophy and science. An interesting addition to this intellectual history is the account given by Philipp Frank, who saw the new philosophy as directly related to the political developments of the period after World War I, namely, the emergence of new democracies in Europe and their defensive stance as a result of the emerging authoritarianism (Frank 1949, 26). This corresponds to the preface to Carnap's *Aufbau* (1928), where the author's solidarity with the progressive socio-cultural reform movements was made explicit. Yet the desire to gain a distinctive profile for the group was strong enough that it no longer sufficed for Circle members to participate in the conventional philosophical societies and journals, like that of the Philosophical Society of the University of Vienna or in the *Annalen der Philosophie* or *Die Naturwissenschaften*. This led to the takeover of *Annalen* and its renaming as *Erkenntnis*, edited by Carnap and Reichenbach on behalf of the Society for Empirical Philosophy in Berlin and the Ernst Mach Society in Vienna, as one of the results of the "rise of scientific philosophy", as Reichenbach chose to call it in retrospect (1951). (See also Haller and Stadler 1993 and Danneberg, Kamlah, and Schäfer 1994.)

The beginning of the *public phase* (in the fall of 1929) coincided with the climax of the Thursday evening discussions, as reflected in the number of participants and the intensity of the meetings. The next break occurred in 1934, following Feigl's emigration (1930) and Carnap's call to Prague (1931), Hans Hahn's early death, and the dissolution of the Ernst Mach Society and Otto Neurath's emigration, both of the latter due to the new authoritarian Dollfuss regime following the civil war that erupted after February 12th of that year.

Something that is widely ignored in many histories of the Vienna Circle is that neither the idea of a physicalistic unified science nor the verification principle was universally accepted for significant lengths of time. The Circle's pluralism of views and perspectives increased over time. For instance, the influence exerted by Wittgenstein decreased at the beginning of the 1930s on Hahn, Neurath, Carnap, and Frank, but not on Schlick and Waismann (and Schächter to a certain extent). Meanwhile, the Berlin group with Reichenbach and Hempel and especially the Warsaw group of logicians around Tarski gained in influence, mostly on Carnap (as evident in his *Logical Syntax*, 1934), but hardly on Schlick and Waismann. This trend was reinforced by the dissemination of P. W. Bridgmann's *Logic of Modern Physics* (1927) and the publication of Popper's *Logic of Scientific Discovery* (1934), which at the time was not perceived as an alternative position to those held in the Vienna Circle, except by Neurath (1935). The "turning point in philosophy" (Schlick 1930) appeared final, even though a considerable continuity with the aims of the first Vienna Circle remained and new challenges had to be faced, such as quantum physics (Frank 1949, 47).

The pluralism of the mature Vienna Circle is reflected in various positions on the problem of the foundations of empirical science (protocol sentence debate), on methodological issues like verification versus falsification and induction versus deduction, and on the foundations of logic and mathematics (especially the roles played by metalogic and metalanguages). The fact that in spite of a plurality of differentiated positions it became possible for a common international and transdisciplinary forum to emerge in 1934 with the *Encyclopedia of Unified Science* again documents the overwhelming convergence of views in a large reform project (which became transatlantic with the inclusion of American pragmatism). This Enlightenment-inspired vision was able to accommodate a theoretical heterogeneity which ranged from the empiricist and physicalist orientation of Neurath to the originally phenomenalist orientation of Kaufmann (see the essays in Stadler 1997a), yet still seemed able to create a common instrumentarium in symbolic logic or Charles Morris's semiotic.

Aspects of the Vienna Circle's philosophy were further developed by Kraft and von Juhos and Schlick's students such as Hans Neider and Walter Hollitscher in Austria (where they influenced Paul Feyerabend), Ludovico Geymonat in Italy, Josef Schächter in Palestine (later Israel), and Tscha Hung in China. Through Carnap the intellectual transfer of ideas took place primarily to Quine (see Creath 1990). In addition, Ernest Nagel, on his visit to Europe, also attended to the new philosophy with critical interest and later developed it further in the United States, in particular as an author for the *Encyclopedia* (Nagel 1939). Eino Kaila (in Vienna during 1934 and 1936) contributed to the influence of logical empiricism in Finland, where it found a critical reception among his students, an influence evident still in Georg Henrik von Wright and Jaakko Hintikka. In Norway (Oslo), Arne Naess, the last surviving participant of Schlick's Circle, addressed the Viennese tradition in his dissertation titled *Erkenntnis und wissenschaftliches Verhalten* (1936) and elaborated in the vein of Neurath, Carnap, and Brunswik, long before he himself became a pioneer of ecological philosophy. In reminiscences Naess strongly emphasized the Circle's tolerant style of discussion and its critical attention to language (1993). In

England Alfred J. Ayer played a similarly important role to Quine's and Nagel's in the United States, particularly with his influential *Language, Truth and Logic* (1936). With its verificationist focus and stress on the dualisms of fact and value and of analytic and synthetic statements, Ayer's book is partly responsible for the popular image of logical positivism as dominated by the ideas of the early Wittgenstein, an image which obscured the theoretical substance and social relevance of what later he called a "Revolution in Philosophy" (1957).

That the common framework of identification did not exclude irreconcilable individual differences can be seen in the strong controversies between Carnap and Neurath regarding the "semantic turn" that took place towards the end of World War II or in the differences between Schlick and Reichenbach over the interpretation of the theory of relativity and Richard von Mises and Reichenbach over the theory of probability early in the interwar period.

THE CULTURAL MILIEU OF THE VIENNA CIRCLE: "RED VIENNA"

The history of the Vienna Circle and its periphery becomes more understandable when it is historicized in connection with the intellectual movements of "late Enlightenment". Here, in particular, the Ethical Movement, the Monist League, and the Freethinkers merit mention. These movements constituted the social background and fertile soil for the Ernst Mach Society as the adult education wing of the Vienna Circle. Yet these associations of logical empiricism must be viewed in the context of the tension between socialism and liberalism that dominated Viennese reform culture as a whole. These associations can be characterized by way of the concentric and overlapping circles around the Schlick Circle (for more on this see Stadler 1982).

This collective embedding was complemented by the individual involvement in the Viennese adult education movement on the part of Vienna Circle members, some of whom were motivated not only philosophically and politically but also by a desire to secure their existence, since the Circle's place in academia could only be described as partial and fragile. (Against the backdrop of the growing "conservative revolution" at the University of Vienna and the growing anti-semitic and anti-democratic trends leading up to the *"Anschluss"* in 1938, the Jewish background and the enlightened and even social-reformist orientation of most members became a parameter for their social integration or marginalization. See the essays in Stadler 2004.) Another motive for participation was the fact that concentration on purely academic ties was seen by most members of the Schlick Circle as unsatisfying, either because of the already alluded to authoritarian university climate or because of their self-understanding as scholars in the service of general well-being with the slogan "knowledge for all".

All the late-Enlightenment movements shared a basic humanitarian and cosmopolitan outlook, an orientation based on progress and reason as well as a social reform and personal responsibility. These groups, which were organized in the "Freier Bund kultureller Vereine", an umbrella association founded in 1919, were active in theory and practice in propagating an antimetaphysical, evolutionary world image, giving an ethical thrust to everyday life with a socio-liberal motivation. (For more on this background, see Stadler 1981.) The personal and programmatic overlap with the Ernst Mach Society and Otto Neurath's Social and Economic Museum is explained by this. Neurath increasingly distanced himself, however, from the often vulgar materialistic and Darwinist graspings towards a scientific philosophy and world view. These movements for humanism, pacifism, and life and social reform as well for a kind of "scientism" that advocated the sharp separation of faith and knowledge, church and state, all featured a sizable Jewish membership and had been a feature of Vienna's intellectual life since the turn of the century. After 1918 the workers movement played a stronger role as ally for these reform and Enlightenment movements, with repercussions for the general social situation of the Vienna Circle. The participation of Schlick, Carnap, Feigl, Kraft, and Neurath in these organizations documents their catalyzing function, even though in the end Schlick found a more adequate platform in the Ernst Mach Society, and Neurath commented on the shallow monism of the Freethinkers. The public presentation of the manifesto in 1929 can thus also be seen as a further development and autonomization of the "scientific world-conception" from existing forms of popular scientific and proletarian "worldviews".

Turning to the Circle's antagonistic setting within the University of Vienna, the growing marginalization must be seen in a larger context. This was the dominance of a rightist-conservative front that opposed all forms of liberalism (e.g., the school of marginal utility), empirical social research (e.g., the Bühler school and the group around Paul Lazarsfeld and Marie Jahoda), psychoanalysis (around Sigmund Freud), pure theory of law (around Hans Kelsen), and Austro-Marxism (Friedrich Adler, via Max Adler to Otto Neurath). This cultural struggle was characterized, on one side, by the leadership of an academic elite who based themselves on the doctrines of political Catholicism and German nationalism (and tolerated alliances with National Socialism), who perceived the union of "fascism and universalism" (around Othmar Spann) as a viable alternative to "Jewish science" (*verjudete Wissenschaft*), and who, in consequence, sought to achieve control of the university by pursuit of an appropriate appointment policy. The establishment of an authoritarian corporative state in 1934 aggravated this ideologization of the university, until from 1938 onwards National Socialist university professors and students were able to violently and very quickly streamline the "German-Austrian" path. Illustrative cases for the consequences of this appointment policy to the clear detriment of the representatives of scientific philosophy are provided by the difficulties encountered in the appointment of Schlick, the career obstacles experienced by Viktor Kraft and Karl Menger, the failed *Habilitation* of Edgar Zilsel, and the dismissals of Heinrich Gomperz and Friedrich Waismann. The most shocking example of and symptom for the marginalization of the Vienna Circle in the Austrian capital is the reaction to the murder of Moritz Schlick on the steps of the university by one of his former students (from personal motives), in particular the virtual legitimation of this act by most of the Austrian press with the reference to the "deleterious and negative philosophy" of Schlick, the "friend of the Jews". (For extensive documentation, see Stadler 2001, 866–909.) In 1937 Schlick's chair was filled by a representative of Catholicism and has, since then, even after 1945, never been filled by a representative of the tradition of Mach, Boltzmann, and Schlick, thus illustrating the postwar fate of the Circle in the Second Republic. (See the essays in Heidelberger and Stadler 2003.)

These same representatives of the University of Vienna also took a similarly negative stance toward the school reform movement of "Red Vienna", which was also actively supported by the psychology professors Karl and Charlotte Bühler, and not least by their student Karl Popper. It does not surprise us, then, to find Vienna Circle members active in the Vienna adult education programs, especially Hahn, Neurath, Waismann, and Zilsel, who taught there regularly. (The last was a full-time secondary school teacher up until his dismissal in 1934.) Hahn, in his role as head of the Union of Socialist University Teachers and member of the Vienna Municipal School Board, also actively promoted university and school reform in newspaper articles, appealing for a close cooperation between both areas of education, and soon found opposition within the university. It was, we may note, mainly the marginalized movements between liberalism and socialism outside of the university that sought the renewal of school and university – in other words, the cultural-intellectual movements of late Enlightenment cited earlier as socio-cultural field of reference for the Vienna Circle. The motives for this social engagement, remarkable for a philosophical group, are to be found in the self-understanding of the Circle members that connects with the social reformist orientation tradition of Ernst Mach himself and his friend Josef Popper-Lynkeus. The founding of the Ernst Mach Society and of Neurath's Social and Economic Museum were but a consequence of this political outlook. (Yet the school reform and adult education movement, as already alluded to, also offered employment that compensated for the lack of it in the university, as in the cases of Feigl, Zilsel, and Waismann.)

It may also be noted that in their adult education or in other public engagements, members of the Vienna Circle did not offer academic philosophy. Rather, the entire spectrum of natural and social sciences was dealt with at the level of most recent research, albeit from a philosophical perspective. This is reflected in the lectures of the Ernst Mach Society as well as in the three lecture series organized by Karl Menger between 1933 and 1936. This type of activity was no longer pursued after emigration, since in their respective host countries a suitable public composed of workers and the liberal bourgeoisie and an appropriate framework for popularization efforts seemed to be missing (see Thurm and Nemeth 2003). Neurath meanwhile opposed simplifying popularizations, and in his Social and Economic Museum from 1925 to 1934 instead developed a method of visualization under the name "Viennese Method of Picture Statistics" or "ISOTYPE" (International System of Typographic Picture Education), which since has become part of the international picture language. Neurath's slogan "words separate – images connect" was to allude to the fact that everyday and scientific communication could also take place via symbols and visual arguments.

The goal of his picture statistics with a socio-critical thrust was to depict social and economic facts by means of simple figure symbols. Any given number of things was to be represented by a corresponding number of symbols, with the same type of symbol always being used for the same type of object. The design and layout for this picture language were invented by the Dutch artist Gerd Arntz, a representative of figurative constructivism in the artistic avant-garde of the Weimar Republic (Rheinische Gruppe progressiver Künstler). Thematically unified exhibitions of related tableaux were produced by interdisciplinary teamwork, with a separate social scientific department and Neurath's second wife Marie Reidemeister leading the "transformation" of data into their visualization. Neurath's work on pictorial communication reflects not only its origin within the Viennese workers movement, but also the debt of the scientific world-conception to the tradition of Comenius, Leibniz, and the great French *Encyclopédie*. It must be remembered that Neurath originally planned for the *Encyclopedia of Unified Science* not only some 260 monographs but also 10 pictorial thesauri that were to employ his method of visualization in the service of unified science. For a variety of reasons, this plan was never realized.

SCIENTIFIC COMMUNICATION WITHIN AND AROUND THE VIENNA CIRCLE: THE SCHLICK CIRCLE, THE MATHEMATICAL COLLOQUIUM, THE GOMPERZ CIRCLE, AND POPPER

In the Vienna Circle proper around Schlick, a certain pluralization and differentiation, in terms of both form and content, can be detected from the beginning and was reflected in the later congresses and publications. The high point of the discussions appears to have been around 1930, before the Wittgenstein reception began to recede and the controversies over the physicalist unified science, protocol sentences, and verificationism led to a transformation but also a diffusion of the original program of a "scientific world-conception".

The valuable questionnaire on the "Development of the Theses of the Vienna Circle", compiled by Rose Rand at Neurath's behest and put to Schlick, Waismann, Carnap, Neurath, Hahn, and Kaufmann between November 1932 and March 1933, very clearly documents how this polarization emerged in response to the *Tractatus* (Carnap, Neurath, Hahn, and Frank versus Schlick, Waismann, and in part Kaufmann), but also an increasing individualization of views, leaving a number of questions unanswered (see Stadler 2001, 323–7). Thus no consensus was found on Waismann's Wittgensteinian "Theses", on the role and function of philosophy and of language generally, on reality and metaphysics, on the notion of truth and on atomic sentences, protocol sentences, physicalism, definitions, metalogic and metalanguage, etc. During this particular phase, much more common ground is found concerning the nature of a sentence (proposition) and its meaning, especially empirical ones, the method of verification, the nature of laws, etc.

The lasting (and growing) influence of the Circle's Berlin and Warsaw associates (Reichenbach, Hempel, Tarski) and the challenge issued by the young Popper accelerated this process of theory differentiation, as confirmed by the relative outsider Kraft (1973, 17). Karl Menger recalled as particularly significant the discussions about the tolerance principle, the protocol sentence debate, and the method of confirmation, accompanied by a prolonged *"Methoden-streit"* (Kaufmann 1936), a methodological dispute about unity or diversity in the sciences. With the input from students and foreign visitors, discussions of the Viennese reform program for philosophy were further enlivened.

In sum, a minimal basic consensus sufficed to furnish the Vienna Circle with a foundation for fruitful discussions of concrete methodological problems and the foundations of empirical and formal science, discussions which in turn issued in a plurality of proposals and solutions. Newly published original documents preserve in a fragmentary way Rand's documentations, which included analyses of the positions of individual members, and the detailed protocols of the discussions in the Vienna Circle during 1930–1 about, among other topics, Gödel's results, Bohr's quantum theory, and Carnap's metalogic, which allow for a much more adequate picture of logical empiricism in the period of its culmination (see Stadler 2001, 241–327). They render obsolete all previous characterizations of the Vienna Circle as a homogenous, (anti-) philosophical school. The problems addressed in the Vienna Circle were not dealt with exhaustively and continue to be discussed still today. In addition, a closer look at the periphery of the Vienna Circle enriches the picture of logical empiricism in a decisive way. Here I can present only two examples of this.

As already noted, the mathematician Karl Menger, son of the famous political economist Carl Menger, returned to the Vienna Circle in 1927 and soon founded his Mathematical Colloquium, which lasted from 1928 to 1936. As a leading representative of the Vienna school of topology Menger played a decisive role in inviting Tarski to Vienna and in laying the groundwork for the career of the young Kurt Gödel, who became a member of his group. Its revolutionary work was documented regularly in the *Ergebnisse eines Mathematischen Kolloquiums* (1931–7) (see Dierker and Sigmund 1998). Also meeting in the Institute of Mathematics on Vienna's Boltzmanngasse, the Colloquium dealt with symbolic logic, mathematics, and the mathematically oriented social sciences and economics. The list of participants, which included, among others, Abraham Wald, John von Neumann, Gustav Bergmann, Alfred Tarski, Hans Thirring, Hans Hahn, Karl Popper, and Olga Taussky, reflects the high quality of the work of the Colloquium. With some 120 meetings the Mathematical Colloquium can be considered as a parallel Vienna Circle and laid the foundations for the well-known Vienna School of Mathematics. That this school was able to find fertile ground for further development in the United States in particular is indicative once more of the transformation of logical empiricism through "forced migration".

In addition and in parallel to the efforts of the Ernst Mach Society, Menger also sought to popularize the "new logic" in three series of public lectures which were published at the time: *Krise und Neuaufbau in den exakten Wissenschaften* (Crisis and Reconstruction in the Exact Sciences, 1933), *Alte Probleme – Neue Lösungen in den exakten Wissenschaften* (Old Problems – New Solutions in the Exact Sciences 1934), and *Neuere Fortschritte in den exakten Wissenschaften* (Recent Progress in the Exact Sciences, 1936). The Second Conference for the Epistemology of the Exact Sciences in

Königsberg in September 1930, organized by Kurt Reidemeister, had proved decisive for the foundational dispute in mathematics. The established controversies about logicism, intuitionism, and formalism were interrupted by discussion remarks made by Gödel, who presented there for the first time his incompleteness theorem, which led to the collapse of Hilbert's program and traditional logicism. His contribution on "The New Logic" to the first of the public lecture series (1933) introduced Gödel's revolutionary works to a larger public.

Thus Menger played an important role for the Vienna Circle both in organizational terms and as an innovative scholar within its core and on its periphery. As his approach was characterized by conventionalist skepticism viz-à-vis foundationalism, verificationism, and the absolutist distinction of analytic and synthetic statements, Menger can be said to have dealt with central elements of logical empiricism as a counterpart to Otto Neurath. As a critic of Wittgenstein (whose attendance at lectures given by Brouwer and arranged by Menger in Vienna in March 1928 proved decisive for his return to philosophy) and as inventor of the principle of tolerance, Menger developed his pragmatic-conventionalist position in the form of an "implicationist viewpoint" (Menger 1979, 12).

Turning to the controversial relation between Karl Popper and the Vienna Circle, we may note that Popper's self-portrait is the only source for the now traditional characterization of himself as the "outsider". His "Intellectual Autobiography" contains the section "Logical Empiricism is Dead: who is the perpetrator?" which discusses the so-called Popper legend. According to this "legend", Popper was a positivist as an adherent of the empiricist criterion of meaning and a member of the Vienna Circle. Popper's attempt to distance himself sharply from the Circle may be regarded as a response to Viktor Kraft's "Popper and the Vienna Circle" in the same volume of the *Library of Living Philosophers* (Schilpp 1974): Kraft had identified a sort of asymptotic approximation between Popper and the Vienna Circle. Popper's arguments can, however, be largely relativized on historical and content-related grounds. First, as described above, there was no homogenous Vienna Circle with an undisputed program and verificationism at its center. For instance, on the basis of his own holistic theory of science Neurath (1935) criticized in very clear terms both verificationism and Popper's falsificationism as "pseudo-rationalism", a criticism Popper never directly responded to. (Compare the interview with Popper in Stadler 2001, 474–97.) Second, the Popperian positions of epistemological and scientific realism and hypothetico-deductive methodology can also be found in Kraft, Feigl, Menger, Kaufmann, and others. Methodological pluralism was an inherent feature of the Vienna Circle. Third, there was a dynamic development of programmatic issues and theses since the manifesto, extending all the way to the *Encyclopedia of Unified Science* with its more liberal understanding, even questioning, of the verificationist criterion of meaning by recourse to a pragmatic notion of metaphysics based on "Occam's Razor". The symmetrical logical difficulties of verification and falsification as well as the foundational problem of the empirical sciences led on both sides to conventionalist solutions with a strongly rational (Popper) or empiricist trend (Neurath). (A. J. Ayer even saw the demise of common-sense thinking in Popper's *Logic of Scientific Discovery*.)

If we contextualize Popper's main work, *The Logic of Scientific Discovery* (1934), we arrive at a differentiated picture of "normal science", containing elements of convergence and disagreement that obtain from both perspectives. (In passing we may note that the so-called positivism dispute in German sociology in the 1960s between Popper and Hans Albert on one side and Max Horkheimer and Theodor W. Adorno on the other only led to the further ideologization and obfuscation of the relation between Popper and rival conceptions. See Dahms 1994.) While working on his manuscripts *Die beiden Grundprobleme der Erkenntnistheorie* (The Two Fundamental Problems of Epistemology, published 1979) and *Logic of Scientific Discovery*, Karl Popper was engaged in sometimes intense discussions with Kraft, Feigl and Carnap, even Schlick, and sought contact as well with other Circle members (Frank, Hahn, Kaufmann, Menger, Richard von Mises, Waismann). Schlick and Frank invited Popper to have his *Logic of Scientific Discovery* published in their series "Schriften zur wissenschaftlichen Weltauffassung". Finally, immediately after its publication, Carnap and Hempel (unlike Neurath and Reichenbach) wrote very positive reviews.

The fact that Schlick did not want to have the young Popper in his Circle, either for personal or philosophical reasons (his critique of the linguistic turn), cannot distract from the fact that Popper had close contacts with individual members of the Vienna Circle and so may be located on its periphery. Notable here are the Mathematical Colloquium and the circle around Heinrich Gomperz. Immediately after World War I, the historian of philosophy Gomperz formed a circle for creative discussion in his home. This group, known as the "Socratic Circle", discussed topical issues of politics, economics, science, philosophy and psychoanalysis. Ever since he abandoned his *Weltanschauungslehre* (Theory of Worldviews, 1905/8), Gomperz, a former student of Mach's, moved towards a semiotically oriented neopragmatism and epistemological monism with a historico-genetic methodology, influenced in this development by the Vienna Circle. This became manifest in his loose cooperation in the Unity of Science movement after his emigration to the United States at the University of Southern California, for instance, in his *Interpretation: Logical Analysis of a Method of Historical Research* (1939) for Neurath's *Library of Unified Science*. In parallel to Schlick, Gomperz organized discussion meetings in the 1930s with the participation of Kraft, Hahn, Carnap, Neurath, and Zilsel, about which, however, we have only fragmentary knowledge. (For more on this see Stadler 2001, 451–74.)

In a wider perspective, Gomperz and Popper can be integrated within an ideal-typical "Austrian philosophy". (For more on Austrian philosophy, see Haller 1979; on Gomperz and Popper, see Seiler and Stadler 1994.) The following count as essential common traits of this tradition: methodological nominalism (linguistic anti-essentialism), the theoretical critique of depth psychology (Sigmund Freud and Alfred Adler), epistemological fallibilism, a hypothetico-deductive realism with an objectivist conception of truth, and, finally, an evolutionary approach to both language and theory. In this perspective, both Gomperz and Popper, as teacher and student, stand on the periphery of the Vienna Circle (I discount Popper's strictly anti-inductivist position), equidistant to the doctrines of logical empiricism, whose reception varied strongly as a result of the different biographical and historical ruptures and/or continuities.

In any case, the dominant Popper-centered accounts of the relation of critical rationalism and logical empiricism (Hacohen 2000; Oeser 2003) require complementation by an account from the perspective of the Vienna Circle. To reach beyond mere myths, a more complete account would demand the relativization of their intellectual interplay in biographical and doctrinal terms, as was recently dramatized in the case of Wittgenstein versus Popper. (On "Wittgenstein's poker", see Edmonds and Eidinow 2001.) The case of Popper and the Vienna Circle presents an analogous model of interpretation to the case of Wittgenstein and the Vienna Circle and should take into account the at least symmetric, if not weightier, significance of the group in relation to the individual.

THE VIENNA CIRCLE AND LOGICAL EMPIRICISM – ELEMENTS OF A REEVALUATION

Summing up our findings, we have isolated the following elements for a reconstruction and reassessment in light of current research, a reassessment which calls into question the pejorative image of logical positivism that is at least partly due to its association with the so-called received view of scientific theories in the 1950s. (For recent evaluations see the essays in Bonk 2003 and Stadler 2003c.)

    a) In terms of philosophical reflections of scientific methodology, we find – on the basis of a shared commitment to "scientific philosophy" within an Enlightenment context – a wide spectrum of approaches ranging from inductivism, deductivism, and methodological holism including ties between science and art (as exemplified by the Bauhaus involvement).

    b) As regards scientific communication, we find that it was primarily international, multilingual and multiethnic – with the majority of the members of the Vienna Circle stemming from a Jewish background – and committed (with the exception of Schächter) to an enlightened collective identity variously based on liberalism or socialism.

    c) Looking at the scientific (self-) organization, we find a strong interaction between academic and extra-academic scientific culture, which, after the forced transfer of logical empiricism to an Anglo-Saxon world dominated by pragmatism, led to both an analytic philosophy of science and, after some delay, to an empiricist "social epistemology".

d) Considering the composition of the Vienna Circle and its periphery, we also find a notable presence of female scholars (Olga Hahn-Neurath, Rose Rand, Olga Taussky-Todd), untypical for academic science of its day, and the creative coexistence of various generations.

e) Finally, the Vienna Circle also represents typical examples of scientists who emigrated. In the 1930s and 1940s both Great Britain and the United States provided exile to former members whose philosophies sometimes underwent a significant transformation because of the forced migration to in the Anglo-American world and the interaction with the philosophies of science already existing in the host countries. (See essays in Stadler 2003, 2003a, and Hardcastle and Richardson 2003.)

The conventional picture of emigtation that is limited exclusively to the year 1938 with successful acculturation in England or America fails to take into account the very varied temporal, personal, and socio-cultural conditions of this process, since it usually focuses on the successful biographies of Carnap, Feigl, Frank, or Bergmann, and underestimates the already existing transatlantic patterns of communication between the logical empiricist and the English and American philosophy of science. Yet this ongoing exchange of ideas also influenced the complex history of reception of Vienna Circle philosophy, and logical empiricism generally, with all its failures and successes. In any case, the early internationalization with the concurrent departure from "German philosophy" influenced the intellectual process of emigration just as much as the lack of reemigration (a fate very different from that of the Frankfurt School).

The quantitative scale of the emigration of the Vienna Circle documents the losses for the countries of origin. From the core of the Vienna Circle with its 19 members, 13 had emigrated by the start of World War II, not so much for a variety of political, economic, or philosophical reasons, but first and foremost because of the surge of racism and anti-Semitism in Austria and Germany. The list of those forced into exile from Vienna, Berlin, and Prague reads like a Who's Who of modern philosophy of science: Gustav Bergmann (1939, USA), Rudolf Carnap (1936, USA), Herbert Feigl (1931, USA), Philipp Frank (1938, USA), Kurt Gödel (1939, USA), Walter Hollitscher

(1939, UK), Olga Hahn-Neurath (1934, Holland), Felix Kaufmann (1938, USA), Karl Menger (1937, USA), Richard von Mises (1933, Turkey; 1939, USA), Otto Neurath (1934, Holland; 1940, UK), Rose Rand (1939, UK), Josef Schächter (1938, Palestine), Olga Taussky (1937, UK; 1947, USA), Friedrich Waismann (1937, UK), Edgar Zilsel (1938, UK; 1939, USA). Of the periphery of the Vienna Circle, the following should also be named: Karl Bühler (1939, Norway; 1940, USA), Ego Brunswik (1936, USA), Josef Frank (1934, Sweden; 1941, USA), Else Frenkel-Brunswik (1938, USA), Heinrich Gomperz (1935, USA), Carl G. Hempel (1934, Belgium; 1940, USA), Marcel Natkin (1930, France), Karl Popper (1937, New Zealand; 1946, UK), Hans Reichenbach (1933, Turkey; 1938, USA), Ludwig Wittgenstein (1929, UK). Viktor Kraft and Heinrich Neider resorted to the so-called inner emigration. Bela Juhos was able to survive the Nazi period in relative economic independence.

The six international congresses for the unity of science mentioned above also served as an institutional platform for scientific communication and contacts before the final cultural exodus (see essays in Stadler and Weibel 1995). The fact that Thomas Kuhn first published his *Structure of Scientific Revolutions* (1962) in the *Encyclopedia of Unified Science* and that Paul Feyerabend first published his essay "Against Method" (1970) in Feigl's *Minnesota Studies in the Philosophy of Science* points to the long-forgotten innovative potential of logical empiricism in exile. Many former Vienna Circle members were able to continue their work in philosophy and theory of science without any great interruption after arriving in the United States, even if under different conditions and in different contexts. A significant if again often overlooked example is Philipp Frank, who joined the discussion circles at Harvard from 1940 on and subsequently founded and headed the Institute for the Unity of Science from 1947 until 1958 in connection with the American Association for the Advancement of Science. Thematic and personal connections extend from there to the Boston Center for the History and Philosophy of Science, initiated and directed by Robert S. Cohen and reflected in pertinent publications as well as in the renowned series *Boston Studies in the Philosophy of Science* (Reidel/Kluwer). In 1953, meanwhile, Herbert Feigl founded the Minnesota Center for Philosophy of Science at the University of Minnesota, which still exists as a leading center for interdisciplinary philosophy of science. The founding of the Pittsburgh Center for the Philosophy of Science by Adolf Grünbaum, the renowned philosopher of science who was forced to flee Germany as a child, may also be considered in the context of the reception of logical empiricism. The social science wing of the philosophy of science was further cultivated at the Graduate Faculty of the New York New School for Social Research, where Felix Kaufmann promoted a convergence of logical empiricism, phenomenology, and pragmatism. An independent branch of phenomenological research was initiated by Gustav Bergmann in Iowa at the state university's Department of Psychology, where he established a local tradition of critical reception of doctrines associated with the Vienna Circle (Bergmann 1954). Finally and with an eye to the legacy of the Mathematical Colloquium, when we speak about the continuity of the exceptional scientific achievements typical of the transfer of knowledge "from the Vienna Circle to Harvard Square" (Holton 1993a), the work of Kurt Gödel or Oskar Morgenstern at the Institute for Advanced Study in Princeton should not be forgotten.

For the short period of two decades a creative and reform-minded philosophical movement was able to establish itself in Central Europe as the Vienna Circle, which even after it was forced into exile continued to influence the philosophy of science either directly or indirectly. (The present pragmatic and historical turn in the philosophy of science also, in addition to the linguistic turn, belongs to its intellectual legacy.) And in spite of the fact that the remigration of its former members into its country of its origin did not take place or even was prevented (notwithstanding the significant impulses received after 1945 from those forced into exile; see Pasteur and Stadler 2004), we can note even there a belated revival of the Circle's scientific culture, which made a lasting contribution to philosophical modernism. (For the activities and publications of the Vienna Circle Institute in Vienna since 1991, see http://www.univie.ac.at/ivc/.)

2   The Society for Empirical/ Scientific Philosophy

First of all I have to say that I very much regret that you almost always write only about the Vienna Circle, so that it almost appears as if this entire philosophical movement had originated only in Vienna and Prague. Our Berlin group was just as active as the Vienna Circle, and within the movement there was never any doubt about this. Not only because a large part of the scholarly work of [the movement] was written in Berlin – along with my works there were those by Dubislav, Grelling; Herzberg also belongs here and a few younger [authors] – organizational work was also performed in Berlin. Every two or three weeks our Society for Scientific Philosophy brought together a group of 100 to 300 people for lectures and discussions; all of our problems were discussed thoroughly in my seminars and colloquia, and, last but not least, *Die Erkenntnis*, surely the most important link in the chain of our organizational work, was founded in Berlin and edited from there. This Berlin Circle has now been dispersed by the Hitler government, but it lives on as a virtual unit. Especially now that our work has been hit so hard by the political developments, it is important to me that this work is at least mentioned in the history of our movement.

(H. Reichenbach to E. v. Aster, Istanbul, June 3, 1935, Archive of Scientific Philosophy, University of Pittsburgh, Reichenbach Papers (hereafter ASPP) HR-013-39-34. Translation by the author.)

Thus Hans Reichenbach in a letter written during the summer of 1935 to his colleague Ernst von Aster in Giessen, by way of comment on his book *Die Philosophie der Gegenwart* (The Philosophy of the Present, 1935). The fact that in his Turkish exile

Reichenbach was still keen to point out the independence of the "Berlin Circle" is also demonstrated by other parts of his correspondence at that time. In January 1936 he wrote to Ernst Cassirer:

That you intend to deal with the Vienna positivism in your work seems to me very important. . . . In this connection it would be very valuable to distinguish very clearly between my own work and that of the Vienna colleagues. Because *Die Erkenntnis* was jointly edited, many people have assumed that I am a part of the Vienna Circle. This is neither historically nor factually correct. (H. Reichenbach to Ernst Cassirer, Istanbul January 19, 1936, ASPP, HR-013-41-72)

Although both passages were already written about 70 years ago, the assessment of the Berlin Circle around Reichenbach and its classification in the history of philosophy and science has changed only in part. In the older, standard literature on logical empiricism, if the Berlin Society is mentioned at all, it is generally seen as part of or as an appendix to the Vienna Circle (e.g., Kraft 1950 or (much improved!) Stadler 1982, 207–13); in the more recent literature, it is largely obliterated by the focus on the Vienna Circle (e.g., Stadler 1997). But it is not only Reichenbach's remarks that indicate the need to distinguish between the Berlin and the Vienna groups, for such a differentiation is also suggested by the circumstances that led to the establishment of the Society for Empirical (later: Scientific) Philosophy in Berlin and its history. While the Berlin Society, the center of activity for Reichenbach and his followers, entertained close relations with the Viennese neopositivists, there also exists ample evidence of its local and, importantly, independent roots in the tradition of positivistic philosophy in Berlin. One differentiation from the Vienna Circle springs from the fact that members and the sympathizers of the Berlin Society were recruited from very different fields. Its intellectual spectrum was widespread and very inhomogeneous. Moreover, the Society avoided a highly specific theoretical framework for its foundation as well as for its activities, unlike the Vienna Circle. Berliners would furthermore point to their interdisciplinary orientation and the strong emphasis of the logic of science as a differentiating characteristic.

THE FOUNDATION OF THE BERLIN
SOCIETY FOR EMPIRICAL PHILOSOPHY

The Society was founded on February 27, 1927, when about 60 to 70 persons came together in the home of Count Georg von Arco to establish the local Berlin chapter of the International Society for Empirical Philosophy. Count Arco was one of the distinctive pioneers of wireless telegraphy, a man of wide intellectual interests as well as having a left-wing and pacifist political orientation (Fuchs 2003). At that time he was the technical director of the Telefunken Company, Germany's leading company for telecommunications, particularly in the increasingly important radio technology. Besides Arco, the physicians or psychoanalysts Max Deri, Alexander Herzberg, and Reginald Zimmermann as well as the philosopher Joseph Petzoldt signed the circular for the Society's foundation (Oscar and Cecile Vogt Papers, University of Düsseldorf (hereafter OCVP), No. 62). Petzoldt, a teacher at a Berlin classical high school and associate professor for philosophy at the Technical University Berlin-Charlottenburg, was the most important exponent in Berlin of a positivistic philosophy oriented towards Mach (see Dubislav 1929). Petzoldt was the leading figure in the foundation of this Society. Friedrich Kraus, the physician and head of the II. Hospital of the Charité, and Oskar Vogt, the brain researcher and director of the Kaiser Wilhelm Institute for Brain Research, also belonged to the core of the charter members (see Satzinger 1998). They formed the first board of the newly founded Society: Kraus as chairman, Arco and Vogt as vice-presidents, and Petzoldt as secretary general (see Anonymous 1927; Mühsam 1927). A circular explained its goals as follows:

Philosophical interests and creative philosophy have once again bloomed mightily in Germany after the war. But the field is dominated by narrowly logical tendencies, restricted to the pure analysis of concepts, and apriorist theories of knowledge, mystical-religious currents, romantic historical constructions. By contrast, there is little evidence of empirical philosophy cautiously evaluating the results of the individual sciences. Yet there is a great deal here awaiting evaluation, for example, the new results of atomic research and the theory of relativity, the science of heredity, brain research, Gestalt and developmental psychology, psychoanalysis and psychopathology. For this reason the undersigned decided to found a local chapter of the International Society for Empirical Philosophy, of which anyone may become a member who cares about the development of philosophy based upon scientific experience. The local section will seek to advance these developments by organizing lectures on philosophically significant problems in science as well as publishing articles in the *Annalen der Philosophy*. This journal, edited by Prof. Vaihinger and Dr. R. Schmidt, one of the most read and best in the field of philosophy, will dedicate a considerable portion of its space to our local section. (OCVP, No. 62)

The newly founded Society followed in a direct line from earlier interdisciplinary associations which had also considered it necessary that scientists of the most diverse disciplines work collaboratively on a modern world picture to be able to take recent advances in scientific knowledge into account. Efforts of this kind can be traced back to the second half of the nineteenth century and were prominent from then onward through the period in which Germany enjoyed great achievements in the realm of natural science and technology. Coping with this task pushed the great and well-established systems of natural philosophy to the limits of their ability and intelligibility. It was against this intellectual and cultural background that a series of associations were founded during the second half of the nineteenth century. Although their aims were mostly broadly ideological, a large part of their membership was recruited from different fields of science, which rendered them interdisciplinary associations as well. A good example is the *Deutsche Freidenkerbund* (German Free Thinkers' Association), established in 1881 under the presidency of Ludwig Büchner, and the *Deutsche Gesellschaft für ethische Kultur* (German Society for Ethical Culture), founded in 1892 after an American model (see Daum 1998, 210–20). Among the leading members of the latter was the astronomer Friedrich Wilhelm Foerster, as well as the philosophers Georg von Gyzicki, Friedrich Jodl, and Ferdinand Tönnies. The activities of this group, which can be viewed as the first "club for ideologically engaged German positivism" (Lübbe 1965, 44), took place chiefly in Berlin. It had close, in part even personal, connections with the Monist League, which, founded in 1906, played the most important role in a philosophical and ideological sense. Its inspiration and leading representative was the Jena biologist Ernst Haeckel; some of those scholars who worked in the Monist League, for example, Count Arco, Petzoldt, and Herzberg, also are found among the membership lists of the Society for Scientific Philosophy.

PETZOLDT'S PIONEERING EFFORTS

The Berlin Society for Empirical Philosophy had a direct predecessor in the Society for Positivistic Philosophy, which was founded by Petzoldt in 1912[1] but lasted only a few years. In a letter to his intellectual mentor Ernst Mach, Petzoldt characterized his society as an "organization of intelligent persons" that does not "conduct an eclectic philosophy but works from a unified perspective ... many of the members thereby serve notice of their discontent with prevailing philosophy by joining. It is extremely inspiring that so many researchers of the highest caliber are found among the first members. They thus throw down the gauntlet to vague philosophies still in the clouds" (J. Petzoldt to E. Mach, Berlin, September 1, 1912. Petzoldt Papers, Archive of the TU Berlin (hereafter PP-TU), Pe 42a-65).

This pride in the membership of "first rank" scientists was not at all exaggerated, for the membership list included among others the Russian physician Vladmir M. Bechterev, the physicist Max von Laue, and the Austrian engineer and social reformer Joseph Popper-Lynkeus, as well as honorary members Albert Einstein, Sigmund Freud, Felix Klein, Ernst Mach, Wilhelm Roux, and Hugo Seeliger (see PP-TU, Pe42a-65). This list of names, but also the effort of the society to establish a regular connection as a special section of the Society of Natural Scientists and Physicians (PP-TU, Pe42a-65), makes clear the lasting interest in a philosophical and ideological penetration of contemporary scientific processes.

Until his death in the summer of 1929, the high school teacher and adjunct professor Joseph Petzoldt was the leading proponent of positivism of a Machian orientation and a driving force in all efforts to establish this direction of philosophical thought in Berlin, including giving it an institutional context. Born on November 4, 1862, in Altenburg (Thuringia), he studied mathematics and physics at various German universities (Ohmann 1930) and took his Ph.D. in 1891 at the University of Göttingen with a treatise "Maxima, Minima, and Economics" (Petzoldt 1891). From 1891 on, he taught at the Kant-Gymnasium in Berlin-Spandau, while simultaneously and repeatedly trying to launch an academic career. His *Habilitation* at the University of Berlin ran aground in the face of resistance from

---

[1] The declaration for the foundation of the society is published in Holton (1993, 13–14).

the three "mandarins" in philosophy: Wilhelm Dilthey, Friedrich Paulsen, and Carl Stumpff. Only in 1904, and with "great effort," as he wrote in retrospect, was he able to habilitate at the Technical University of Berlin-Charlottenburg, where he served at first as a privatdozent. Efforts to get an professorship in Vienna (as a successor of E. Mach) and Leipzig were also disappointed. In 1922 he was appointed as an associate professor at the Technical University, to teach in a modest capacity and, of course, in addition to his school duties (PP-TU, Pe 4). On April 1, 1925, he was granted an official teaching contract for "philosophy with particular attention to natural science and technology" with the proviso "to represent the instructional area in a weekly 4-hour lecture and to select the topics accordingly" (Anonymous 1925). He died on August 1, 1929, in Berlin.

Even if Petzoldt was one of the first philosophers at a technical university in Germany (H. Petzoldt 1984, 84), his biography makes clear that natural scientifically oriented philosophy, and in particular positivism, had to overcome many obstacles placed in its way by academic philosophy and in the end was unable to establish itself at universities or even technical colleges. Meanwhile, against the background of the stormy ascent of natural science and technology, as well as revolutionary changes in their foundations, especially in physics, scientists were very interested in the corresponding subject-related philosophical and epistemological reflections. One extraordinary example is the Berlin physicist and founder of quantum theory Max Planck, who reflected on such topics in a philosophically naive, but very popular, manner in a couple of papers and talks (Planck 1933). But the neohumanistic orientation of the universities could not meet this need in a professional way, or did so only unsatisfactorily. Forums had to be established outside the university, for which Berlin, as a world center of natural scientific research, had at its disposal a particularly large number of potentially interested scientists.

Indicative of this effort is Petzoldt's attempt to bring together the adherents and sympathizers of positivist doctrines by establishing the Society for Positivistic Philosophy. However, it seems that this society also was unable to do justice to the philosophical demands of natural science and technology, for in 1921 it merged with the Kant Society and established within it a special group for positivistic philosophy. Its work did not find much resonance among mathematicians and specialists in other disciplines and so did not lead to a lasting cooperation between natural scientists and philosophers.

Signs of a fundamental change came with the founding in February 1927 of the local chapter of the International Society for Empirical Philosophy, which at first, however, remained handicapped by a rather one-sided Machian orientation. This became apparent in Petzoldt's lecture at the opening session on May 6, 1927, in which he acknowledged his indebtedness to the views of Mach and Avenarius. There can be little doubt that he intended to place the philosophical accents in such a way that his philosophy and the newly founded Society would gain unlimited access to all of the modern scientific developments. Thus he claimed that

empirical philosophy cannot dispense with rational thought, and if we call ourselves a Society for Empirical Philosophy, that does not mean that we want to renounce knowledge that stems from pure thought, i.e. rational thought. Rational and empirical thought are not absolute, mutually exclusive opposites; rather, both are indispensable components of cognition, of our research and knowledge. ... We are not lumpers (*Summalisten*), and if people have so christened our great master Ernst Mach, then this rests on ignorance and misunderstanding. (Petzoldt 1927, 146)

This new coloration of Petzoldt's philosophy was to be taken seriously, even if it remained within the realm of a basically positivist orientation. However, it may be doubted whether Mach would have followed Petzoldt's conceptual notation in which simplicity, absence of sensuous intuitability (*Unanschaulichkeit*), and nonsensuousness (*Nichtsinnlichkeit*) hold true as basic qualities of concepts (Petzoldt 1926, 88). By comparison, Mach stipulated that "the concept of the physicist has a definite capacity for reaction that enriches a fact with new sensory elements" (Mach 1922, 164). Whereas Petzoldt summarized his views in the formula "perception is sensation plus concept" (Petzoldt 1927, 267), Mach would reduce the conceptual features to the elements of sensation (Mach 1965, 136).

In any case, Petzoldt's formulations amounted to a compromise whose transitional character did not escape the broader public. On March 4, 1927, the *Vossische Zeitung* posed the question of the renaissance of positivism in the Berlin Society. On June 30 it reported with reference to Petzoldt's opening lecture on a "deficiency in empirical ways of thought" because the speaker "glimpses above all a biological foundation of all knowledge in the positivist manner" (Anonymous 1927; Mühsam 1927). A similar unease was felt by other members and sympathizers of the Society. While Petzoldt wanted to address the philosophical needs of the natural sciences by a cautious modification of Mach's views, in the Society a far more thorough-going process of reevaluation began. The entry of, and various lectures given by, members from other intellectual traditions in particular led to a liberation from the clutches of Machian positivism, and by its heterogeneity guaranteed the Berlin group its autonomy within the movement of logical empiricism.

REICHENBACH TAKES OVER

The turning point for this development was the appointment of Hans Reichenbach as an extraordinary professor "for epistemological issues in physics" at the University of Berlin in 1926 (see Hecht and Hoffmann 1982). In the following years he gathered a group of talented and engaged students that included Carl Gustav Hempel and Martin Strauss, who later became active members of the Society. Initially, though, Reichenbach appears to have had reservations about it. Although in the fall of 1927 he gave a talk at the Society "on the philosophical foundation of mathematics," he was not yet a member. His reservations are also reflected in correspondence with A. Herzberg during the next year, when they discussed future lectures. Reichenbach would accept an invitation only if he was paid an honorarium, for to remain equitable "with regard to other societies" he could not give lectures in "such a famous society like yours" without one (H. Reichenbach to A. Herzberg, Berlin, September 14, 1928. ASPP, HR-015-29-03). In the last session of 1928, on December 14th, he finally presented a talk entitled "Causality or Probability," but in the meantime he had established a much closer relation with the Society. In a letter to Rudolf Carnap he reported: "The foundation of your Verein Ernst Mach is a very fine thing ... we have already a similar one here in Berlin with the Society for Scientific Philosophy. ... Recently Dubislav and I were integrated into its board, where we, together with Herzberg, have the real power" (H. Reichenbach to R. Carnap, Berlin June 30, 1929,

ASPP, HR-013-39-34). This transformation of the Society was speeded up and completed with the death of Joseph Petzoldt in the summer of 1929. The most obvious expression of this was the change of its name to the Society for Scientific Philosophy in 1930, which went back to a suggestion from David Hilbert.

The work of the Society is reflected in its membership lists and the lectures held under its aegis. Besides those already mentioned (Arco, Kraus, Herzberg, Reichenbach, Vogt), Walter Dubislav was a core member of the Berlin group, serving until 1933 as secretary general and subsequently as its last president. Other members included the logician Kurt Grelling and younger people like Victor Bargmann, Olaf Helmer, Carl Gustav Hempel, and Martin Strauss. In addition, a number of prominent personalities from the scientific life of Berlin were more or less closely connected to the Society. In particular the psychologists Kurt Lewin and Wolfgang Köhler, the psychoanalyst Lily Herzberg (née Wagner, wife of A. Herzberg), the airship engineer Adolf von Parseval, and the mathematician Richard von Mises were active in its leadership and in its lecture activities. We should also mention in this regard the radio engineer Count Arco, the psychoanalyst Carl Müller-Braunschweig, the astrophysicist Erwin Finlay-Freundlich, as well as the physicists Fritz London and Lise Meitner, who were sympathetic to the Society and pursued similar goals. Despite the diversity of the scientists carrying on the work of the Society, representatives of the logic of science dominated, along with the protagonists of psychology and psychoanalysis. The Society represented a scientific elite, for almost all of the above-mentioned persons were occupants of university chairs and held leading positions in various of Berlin's scientific institutions, or at least were experienced and recognized specialists.

This character of the Society also becomes clear in the lecture program.[2] This was not only broadly diversified and unusually large – annually some 10 to 20 events were held – but in addition recorded the foremost persons of Berlin scientific life as well as leading scholars from outside. Lectures were given by the biologists Max Hartmann and Richard Goldschmidt, the physicists Ludwig

---

[2] The most compete list of the lecture program can be found in Danneberg and Schernus (1994, 478–81) or Hecht and Hoffmann (1991, 58–9).

von Bertalanfy and Bernhard Bavink, and the physical chemist Wilhelm Ostwald as well as the psychologists Alfred Adler, Max Dessoir, and Kurt Sternberg. A concentration is noticeable in the area of psychology and "logical empirical" philosophy. It is indicative of the pluralism of the Society that at the evening lectures, outspoken opponents of a positivistically oriented philosophy gave presentations – names like Hans Driesch, Karl Korsch, and Julius Schaxel may suffice as examples.

It is difficult to characterize the theoretical framework of the Society in general terms, for it was very open and avoided specific theoretical maxims or philosophical systems. The general profile of the Berlin Society was highly interdisciplinary, finding a place for discussions of ideas from very different fields, origins, and persons (Reichenbach 1936, 144). In this way the space was created for the reception of intellectual traditions like that of the Friesian School, through the mediation of Dubislav and Reichenbach (Hecht and Hoffmann 1987) and, of course, Kurt Grelling (Peckhaus 1994, 53–73). Receptivity to these traditions helps to explain the high value that was put on probability and statistics in the philosophical debates of the Berlin Society. Reichenbach's method of "analysis of science" provides a point of reference with regard to which we can integrate the diverse kinds of influences. This is remarked upon in Reichenbach's letter to his colleague von Aster (from which we have already quoted above):

I have deliberately remained independent until now from every philosophical system, because I do not see the point of our movement in the development of a system but in methodical work. . . . I have therefore concentrated consciously on the solution of certain individual problems, because I saw that without their prior resolution a comprehensive system in our direction is not at all possible. My works are also much more closely entwined with positive science than those of Carnap. I wanted to show in important examples how one can use analytic scientific methods – which were propagated by me already in 1920 (in *Relativity Theory and A Priori Knowledge*) to arrive at philosophical discoveries. I would like to gather these together into a system at a later time. (H. Reichenbach to E. v. Aster, Istanbul, June 3, 1935, ASPP, HR-013-39-34)

Natural scientific activity serves in this context as a process of division of labor in which experimenter, theoretician, and natural philosopher work together (Dubislav 1933, 2), such that philosophical considerations are not auxiliary products for the physicist but "the conceptual subsoil from which his work first becomes possible" (Reichenbach 1979, 381). With regard to the functional goal of natural philosophy, Reichenbach expressed himself clearly. He saw its task in the solution of a series of epistemological questions "that in part already played a role in the older philosophies, in part have only been recognized in our time" (Reichenbach 1979, 381; 1931, 3). He formulates as its fundamental condition the "insight into the capacity for development of basic philosophical terms" (Reichenbach 1931, 8). Reichenbach negated neither the intrinsic value of philosophical investigations nor their function in determining ideology (Reichenbach 1930, 39).

A comparison of the views of Petzoldt and Reichenbach demonstrates that, with this stance, the Berlin Society achieved a significant philosophical gain in knowledge and was able to shed Machian positivism. Both felt chiefly indebted to relativity theory, both considered the solution of the problem of induction as a central task of empiricism, and both agreed in their denial of any possibility of apriorism; nevertheless, their positions were irreconcilable. The Society became a partner to be taken seriously by physics and mathematics in Berlin only when it could demonstrate research findings, achieved through the assumption of the method of scientific analysis, that were significant for foundational discussions in the early decades of the twentieth century. Reichenbach's contribution to the philosophical understanding of the theory of relativity corresponded to one generally accepted in the Berlin community. It distances itself in its philosophical preliminaries from the Machian tradition in that instead of reducing the context of cognition (*Erkenntniszusammenhang*) to the immediate certainty of sensation complexes, it examines the relation between theory and empiricism, into which a certain amount of epistemology enters (Reichenbach 1979, 15).

The goal of the method of analysis of science consists in differentiating the epistemological assumptions of a given natural scientific theory from its factual physical claims, thereby portraying the development of both. Reichenbach found the means for this in a particular form of axiomatization that is a logical reconstruction of the structure of physical theories guided by epistemological interests. Reichenbach distinguished axioms, coordinative definitions (*Zuordnungsdefinitionen*), and mathematical definitions. The empirical assumptions of a theory are concentrated in axioms as the basic experiential propositions, while mathematical definitions set forth their theoretical portions. Both are mediated by coordinative definitions that convey a relation between mathematical definition and reality. Since definitions are neither true nor false, a concept defined by the definition is not at all a physically interpretable proposition. It becomes so only in the unity of empirical experience, coordinative definition, and mathematical concept formation, and herein lies for Reichenbach one of the decisive epistemic innovations of Einstein's theory.

Yet it is also the main problematic point of Reichenbach's epistemology, which culminates in Einstein's question, "Why do the individual concepts that occur in the theory require a special justification if they are indispensable only in the context of the logical net of the theory and the theory of the whole is preserved?" (Einstein 1955, 503). It was this empiricist, antitheoretical orientation that led Einstein to decline membership in the local Berlin chapter of the International Society for Empirical Philosophy in 1927 (A. Einstein to J. Petzoldt, March 3, 1927, Albert Einstein Archive, The Jewish National and University Library Jerusalem, No. 19-061-1). Later he also did not take an active part in the work of Reichenbach's Society for Scientific Philosophy. A lecture to be given by Einstein announced in 1932 did not take place (Anonymous 1931), even though he had supported Reichenbach's call to the University of Berlin (Hecht and Hoffmann 1982) and the two maintained a good personal relationship (letter of M. Reichenbach to G. Kröber, Pacific Palisades, August 27, 1978; personal archive of the author).

Another Berlin colleague of Reichenbach's was the mathematician Richard von Mises, though his concrete relation to the Society is still unclear. Certainly, he stood in lively and personal contact with the leading members of the Society, but he was neither a formal member nor did he present talks there. His role seems to have been mainly that of a mediator or "ambassador" between the groups in Berlin and Vienna (see Stadler 1990, 7ff.). By contrast, Kurt Grelling played an important role in the Society itself, in particular during its final period (as will be discussed below). Although he too cannot be found on the list of lecturers, he was very active and belonged to the inner circle of the group around Reichenbach (see Peckhaus 1994, 61–4). One of the reasons was that his empiricist point of view and his work in logic possessed a specific meaning for the general orientation of the Society and the work of Reichenbach in particular. Similar considerations hold for Walter Dubislav, who was deputy head of the Society. Dubislav's attempt to provide a foundation for mathematics and physics on the basis of principles of logic and a general theory of science lay at the heart of the Society's philosophical ambitions.

The significance of men like Joseph Petzoldt, Walter Dubislav, Kurt Grelling, Richard von Mises, or Count Georg von Arco and Friedrich Kraus, however, cannot be measured by their special philosophical and scientific achievements or failures alone, nor in systematic or school-building activities. It lies above all in their involvement in forms of organization in which the effects of a worldview were thought to have prepared the way for a blossoming of science, technology, industry, and culture. Thus they created the conditions that made possible peak performances of philosophy of science and logic in a time of far-reaching changes, as well as helping to smooth the way for an opening up of academic philosophy to this process.

Still, it is a fact that attempts to build a bridge between the sciences and local academic philosophy succeed only in the most unusual cases. The results of the research undertaken by people like Reichenbach or Dubislav – results which without doubt constituted epistemological progress beyond *"Naturphilosophie"* – were scarcely noted by the prevailing academic philosophy. Part of the reason probably lies in the fact that the Society's influence in Berlin, and in Germany in general, lasted less than a decade. On the other hand, the processes of professionalization and institutionalization of intellectual disciplines came into play here. Since the Industrial Revolution, the broad stream of traditional philosophical activities and influences had become more limited, and philosophy directed its epistemological claims in the first place only to particular practical life situations (from which they were sometimes extended to other problems). As it happens, Reichenbach's scientific philosophy even provides a mirror image of this, since it tied the character of scientific philosophy solely to its contact with mathematics and natural science.

EXCHANGES WITH THE VIENNA CIRCLE

Stressing the philosophical independence of the Berlin Society does not mean, of course, that its connection with the Vienna Circle is depreciated. The joint editing of the journal *Erkenntnis* (Danneberg and Schernus 1994, 391–481) was but one example of the many relations between the Berlin Society and the Vienna Circle and of the broad consensus with regard to the philosophical orientation in Berlin, Vienna, and Prague. Moreover, both groups profited mutually from lectures, visits, and other activities. On July 5, 1932, Carnap spoke in Berlin on "Overcoming Metaphysics," and on February 21, 1933, Otto Neurath spoke on "The Basic Problem of Physicalism" (see Kamlah 1985, 228); both men, as well as other associates of the Vienna Circle like Philipp Frank, visited Berlin very often, just as the "Berliners" von Mises or Reichenbach periodically traveled to Vienna. Students were recommended to visit Berlin or Vienna to complete their studies (see, e.g., Reichenbach to Carnap, Berlin, June 24, 1927, ASPP HR-015-30-24). Thus C. G. Hempel studied in the winter term of 1929/30 in Vienna and gave some reports about his impressions to his teacher in Berlin (see C. G. Hempel to H. Reichenbach, Vienna, December 15, 1929, ASPP, HR-014-28-12). Another example of the close relationship between both groups were the efforts of Philipp Frank to appoint Reichenbach to the newly founded chair for Natural Philosophy at the German University in Prague in 1928. This failed, not only for financial reasons but also because Reichenbach, as he confessed later, considered the scientific atmosphere of Berlin and the "Berlin Circle" too important for his own career and wanted to contribute to the development of scientific philosophy in Berlin. In his place Rudolf Carnap was appointed in 1931. Last but not least, there were the famous joint meetings on "Epistemology of Exact Science," held for the first time in September 1929 in Prague as part of the fifth "Conference of German Physicists and Mathematicians" – the result of suggestions and initiatives by Reichenbach – and continued in 1931 in Königsberg.

THE DISSOLUTION OF THE BERLIN SOCIETY

The inauguration of the Nazi regime of terror resulted in the expulsion of many scientists and a general impoverishment of the entire intellectual life in Berlin. This fact was directly reflected in the activity of the Society for Scientific Philosophy. Many of its members had already left Germany during the first months of the Hitler dictatorship for racial or political reasons, in practice initiating a process of self-dissolution that lasted for a couple of years. Although the last recorded lecture was held by Alfred Adler on May 23, 1933, the correspondence of Reichenbach and his friends and students gives some evidence that the Society still existed until around 1935/36. C. G. Hempel noted in March of 1935: "The Society continues to try and pull through, of course experiencing a significant loss of membership, particularly among the non-Aryans. Nonetheless there were still a few nice lectures" (C. G. Hempel to H. Reichenbach, Brussels, March 18, 1935, ASPP, HR 013-15-09). From the beginning Reichenbach, who had already emigrated to Turkey, was under no illusions about the character of the Nazi regime and its consequences. On February 23, 1933, he wrote to his colleague Kurt Lewin:

as you already know from the newspapers, the situation appears bleak for us; but it seems it will get much worse, as the new government has now made it their aim to suppress all progressive cultural organizations. Because the realization of the economic goals of the National Socialists is now hindered because of their alliance with Hugenberg, they will turn to the cultural arena. ... Under these conditions we must be especially cautious with our "Scientific" [Society]. Undoubtedly you will recall how Korsch's lecture resulted in our being forbidden to hang posters around the university advertising upcoming lectures. Back then we were able to get that overturned. Today, however, such a lecture as Korsch's would result, in the very least, in being denied the use of lecture hall. (H. Reichenbach to K. Lewin, Berlin, March 23, 1933, ASPP, HR-014-54-09)

Although Reichenbach had just received a grant of 3,000 Marks from the Berlin Academy of Sciences for his research, in the spring of 1933 he resolutely pursued his emigration. Because of the Civil Service Law and denunciations, he resigned his professorship in May 1933. A few weeks later he accepted an invitation by the Turkish government and emigrated to Istanbul, where he received a professorship for philosophy at the university. In 1938 he moved on to the United States, where he could build up a new circle of influence and helped to shape the very discipline of the philosophy of science.

In Berlin Walter Dubislav, who together with A. Herzberg had managed the activities of the Society since 1927, took over as chair of the Society. In this capacity he sent this request to Oscar Vogt in the summer of 1933:

Professors Hans Reichenbach and Kurt Lewin, both of the University of Berlin, already have changed or plan to change their residencies to universities abroad by accepting appointments there. They remain foreign members of the board. We nevertheless have to replenish our board with resident scholars. Therefore I would like to ask you to become a member of the board of our Society. (OCVP, No. 62)

Dubislav chaired the Society up to his emigration to Prague in 1936, where he hoped to be appointed to the chair previously held by Carnap (see, e.g., the letter of Ph. Frank to H. Reichenbach, Prague, undated, 1937, ASPP, HR-013-12-16), but before that could happen he died under suspicious circumstances in September 1937 (see the reports in the Prague press: Anonymous 1937; 1937a). By that time many other leading members of the Society had also left Berlin, for instance, von Mises and London. If it was comparatively easy for such prominent scientists to establish themselves outside of Germany, others were not so fortunate. For example, all traces are lost for some, chiefly younger, scholars, in the confusion of exile, wartime, and the postwar period. In particular, the trail of Alexander and Lily Herzberg fades in postwar England. Martin Strauss joined the anti-fascist resistance before he also left Germany in 1935 for Copenhagen and Prague, where he finished his Ph.D. with Philipp Frank in 1938; afterwards he had to flee again from the Nazis and went to England, where he survived the war as a teacher at a London college. Later he came back to Germany and began in East Germany a (not very successful) academic career in physics (see Hoffmann 2004). Probably the most tragic fate befell the logician Kurt Grelling, who succeeded in fleeing Berlin in 1939 to Brussels and Paris, but who was deported to Auschwitz after the occupation of France and was murdered there in 1942 (see Thiel 1984, 233; Peckhaus 1994, 64–9).

It was Grelling who after the flight of Dubislav once again tried to wake up the Society from its "Sleeping Beauty's rest" (Dornröschenschlaf) (K. Grelling to H. Reichenbach, Berlin, January 16, 1936, ASPP, HR-013-14-06). Thus he reported to Reichenbach in spring 1937: "you may be interested in hearing that over the last few months I have organized two private working groups on logic and established a new Berlin Circle where we are discussing logical questions and problems in theory of science" (K. Grelling to H. Reichenbach, Berlin, March 14, 1937, ASPP, HR-013-14-02). Nothing more is known about this new Berlin Circle, and it must be assumed that it remained a mere "episode" – not least because this kind of philosophy no longer had a place in Nazi Germany. This was given explicit and official expression on the occasion of the dedication celebration for the Heidelberg Philipp-Lenard Institute in December 1935 by L. G. Tirala:

The so-called Vienna Circle, a club of mostly persons of a foreign race, largely of Near Eastern and oriental race, announces a new logic that distinguishes itself thoroughly from Aryan logic. This "Vienna Circle," with which Einstein was sympathetic, claims that there is no [substantive] logic, that formalist calculating thought is primary, and that [substantive] logic is secondary. One hears the Near Eastener, who computes until reality disappears. (Tirala 1936, 55)

It is true that not all the members of the Berlin group could or had to emigrate. The brain researcher Oskar Vogt, for example, worked on until 1937 in his Institute in Berlin-Buch, but then resigned his directorship for political reasons and withdrew to a private research institute in the Black Forest. Yet the fact seems to be symptomatic that no philosophical activity from Oskar Vogt and other members of the former Berlin Society who remained in Germany during this period can be found. It is arguable that greater still than the gain for the philosophical "community" in the Anglo-Saxon host countries was the loss that the philosophical life of Berlin – and Germany as a whole, even Central Europe in general – suffered from the destruction of the Society for Scientific Philosophy (and related groups affiliated with it) during the Nazi period.[3]

[3] I would like to thank Thomas Uebel for helpful comments on style and content, and I am particulary indebted to Mark Walker, who helped with my English.

3 From "the Life of the Present" to the "Icy Slopes of Logic"

Logical Empiricism, the Unity of Science Movement, and the Cold War

> The scientific world-conception is close to the life of the present. Certainly it is threatened with hard struggles and hostility. Nevertheless there are many who do not despair but, in view of the present sociological situation, look forward with hope to the course of events to come. Of course not every single adherent of the scientific world-conception will be a fighter. Some glad of solitude, will lead a withdrawn existence on the icy slopes of logic.
>
> From the Vienna Circle's manifesto, *Wissenschaftliche Weltauffassung*
>
> (Carnap, Hahn, and Neurath 1929/1973, 317)

Logical empiricism of the 1930s was quite different from logical empiricism as it thrived in the 1950s. This later version is better known in part because it was codified by Thomas Kuhn's influential book *The Structure of Scientific Revolutions* (1962). Kuhn attacked "that image of science by which we are now possessed" (1962, 1) – an image of theories as logically transparent structures reaching from observations to abstract theory and changing in time by acquiring or modifying concepts and statements. This image of science went hand in hand with logical empiricism's interests in the logical structure of theory and procedures such as explanation and confirmation.

Yet the project that Kuhn attacked was itself very young. Kuhn wrote *Structure* in the late 1950s after a transformation had taken place, specifically, a narrowing in the scope, of the values and goals of logical empiricism. For Kuhn, logical empiricism was a philosophy of science concerned mainly with logic and using logic to understand science. But only two decades before, logical empiricism was engaged with progressive, modern trends in science, social life, education, architecture, and design. Originally logical empiricism was in the business of social enlightenment (Scott 1987; Galison 1990, 1996; Uebel 1998).

This chapter will answer two questions: How did logical empiricism so drastically and so rapidly transform, and Why did this change take place? I will argue that the transformation consisted mainly in the decline and disappearance of Otto Neurath's Unity of Science Movement. Not well known precisely because it fell from view, this Movement was the public, pedagogic, and scientific voice of logical empiricism. Not unlike the Ernst Mach Society through which the Vienna Circle promoted its ideas to the public in Vienna, the Movement was a broad, international forum designed to promote the social and scientific agenda of logical empiricism.[1] It included annual International Congresses for the Unity of Science and publications including the *International Encyclopedia of Unified Science* (for which Kuhn's *Structure* was originally commissioned), a short-lived English incarnation of *Erkenntnis* (titled the *Journal of Unified Science*), regular announcements and short articles appearing in journals such as *Philosophy of Science* and *Synthese*, and coverage in newspapers and popular magazines such as *Time*.[2] Neurath oversaw most of these projects, while he edited the *International Encyclopedia* with the assistance of Rudolf Carnap and the American pragmatist Charles Morris.

Logical empiricism came to America joined to the Unity of Science Movement. The two were largely welcomed (and not usually distinguished) in the socialist milieu of the famous New York intellectuals. For a few years before the Second World War philosophers of science in America – émigrés as well as natives – were

[1] On the Ernst Mach Society, see Stadler (2001, 328–34), which contains extensive historical information about the Vienna Circle and the Unity of Science Movement. Valuable essays about the ongoing "rediscovery" of logical empiricism may be found in Uebel (1991). Other recent publications addressing the political and social aspects of logical empiricism and the Unity of Science Movement include Reisch (1994), Cat et al. (1996), Galison (1990; 1996), Cartwright et al. (1996), Friedman (2000), Uebel (2004), Dahms (2004).

[2] International Congresses were held in Prague, 1934, Paris, 1935, Copenhagen, 1936, Paris, 1937, Cambridge, England, 1938, Cambridge, Massachusetts, 1939, and Chicago, 1941. For popular writings about the Movement, see Kaempffert (1937; 1938) and *Time* (1939).

socially and politically engaged in ways that answer the second question posed above: the Unity of Science Movement died because its methods, values, and goals were broadly sympathetic to Socialism at a time when America and its colleges and universities were being scrubbed clean of red or pink elements. The apolitical logical empiricism of the 1950s, that is, was a newborn child of the cold war.

To support these claims, I will rely in part on the research of Ellen Schrecker (1986) to document how difficult life was for left-leaning academics during the cold war. Then I will examine how Rudolf Carnap, Charles Morris, and Philipp Frank (who helped lead the Movement after Neurath's death in 1945) experienced various political pressures of the cold war. These leaders knew that Neurath, his Unity of Science Movement, and even the idea of unifying the sciences had dubious political reputations in cold war America.

THE EMIGRATION OF LOGICAL EMPIRICISTS AND LOGICAL EMPIRICISM

When logical empiricists emigrated to the United States from Vienna and Germany in the 1930s, the main philosophical parts of logical empiricism – strict empiricism, rejection of the synthetic apriori, the identification and elimination of metaphysics, and its view of philosophy as a tool of analysis and not a source of knowledge – were joined to a constructive scientific project that Neurath called "unified science." As Neurath, Carnap, and Hans Hahn put it in the Vienna Circle's manifesto, *Wissenschaftliche Weltauffassung*, "the goal ahead is *unified science*. The endeavour is to link and harmonize the achievements of individual investigators in their various fields of science. From this aim follows the emphasis on *collective efforts*, and also the emphasis on what can be grasped intersubjectively" (1929/1973 306). While the circle aimed to reform philosophy and counteract overspecialization in science, other movements in Europe were modernizing architecture and education and promoting social and economic planning using scientific tools (Galison 1990). The Vienna Circle reached to these groups, to other "living movements of the present," for they were also driven by "the spirit of the scientific world-conception." Together, these movements could bring about "historic" results, not just for science and philosophy, but all of life: *"The Scientific World-Conception serves life,"* they proclaimed, *"and life receives it"* (1929/1973, 317, 318).

Neurath, an economist and socialist reformer, especially championed the unification of the sciences. As tools to improve the quality of life, they needed to be connectible and unified so that they might be deployed simultaneously and usefully (see Neurath 1931a/ 1983, 3–54; 1932a/1983, 59; 1936a/1983, 132–3). To help facilitate this connectibility, Neurath promoted a "physicalist," empirical language of science which consisted of ordinary language from which metaphysical and unscientific terms had been removed. Neurath's infamous crusade against metaphysics (especially his Index of Prohibited Words), his faith in the future of unified science, and even his expertise in the ISOTYPE system for museums and public exhibitions – all these projects dovetailed in his work on behalf of the Unity of Science Movement.[3]

Beginning in roughly 1935, the Movement's headquarters were Chicago and The Hague. Morris and Carnap taught at the University of Chicago, and the University of Chicago Press published the new *Encyclopedia*.[4] Though his colleagues wished otherwise, Neurath remained living in The Hague, where he arrived in 1934 after fleeing Vienna. There he established an Institute for the Unity of Science and, for his ISOTYPE work, an International Foundation for Visual Education.

The Movement also had healthy roots in New York City, whose intellectual culture welcomed logical empiricism and Neurath's Movement as two halves of a politically important intellectual project. In their eyes, Neurath's new *Encyclopedia* would be something like a more scientific, less literary counterpart to their journal *Partisan Review* (PR). Both groups prized internationalism and scientific socialism, and they both believed that their writings and publications would help promote and realize these goals.[5]

The philosophers among the New Yorkers – including John Dewey, Sidney Hook, Ernest Nagel, Horace Kallen, and Abraham Edel – were first to greet logical empiricism and the Movement.

---

[3] For more on Neurath's Index of Prohibited Words, see Reisch (1997); for more on ISOTYPE see Neurath (1973, 214–48), Galison (1990), Reisch (1994).

[4] For more information about the *Encyclopedia*, see Reisch (1995).

[5] On the New York intellectuals and *Partisan Review*, see Cooney (1986), Jacoby (1987).

Ernest Nagel hosted Neurath when he arrived in the autumn of 1936 and ushered him into the city's politicized philosophical scene. After one Saturday-evening social gathering – most likely a reception for Neurath – Neurath asked Nagel to provide an inventory of those who had attended. Nagel replied with thumbnail sketches of Hook, Meyer Schapiro, and Edel ("The above three men are particularly good friends of mine") as well as J. V. McGill, Y. Krikorian, Daniel Bronstein, Albert Hoftstadter, William Gruen, Phillip Wiener, Herbert Schneider, John Herman Randall, Jr., Horace Friess, and John Allen Irving. Except for William Malisoff, whom, Nagel acknowledged, Neurath already knew, Nagel described their academic specialties, their degrees of "sympathy with a thorough-going empiricism," and the extent and prestige of their publications. He also explicitly addressed their politics and ethnic backgrounds: Hook and Schapiro were "Marxist"; Randall and Friess were both "liberal with socialist leanings"; Allen had "materialist leanings" and "recently has been flirting with communism." Schneider had "some sympathy with some of the practical achievements of Italian fascism." Most "were Jewish and I think without exception have left sympathies in politics" (Nagel to Neurath, October 13, 1936, ONNH).

Nagel specified their political orientations because he knew that Neurath was always scouting for intellectual and scientific talent to join the Unity of Science Movement. It was neither a secret nor a scandal in this milieu that one reason to unify the sciences was to cultivate them and selectively hone their strengths as tools for social and economic planning. Few at this gathering would have conceived of logical empiricism as a strictly technical, apolitical discipline. J.V.McGill, for example, had just helped establish the new Marxist journal *Science & Society* to which several figures in the Unity of Science Movement would later contribute.[6] In its first issue McGill wrote "An Evaluation of Logical Empiricism" (1936), in which he urged logical empiricists to adopt a metaphysics that was friendly to dialectical materialism. Their disdain of

---

[6] For example, in *Science & Society*'s early issues Abraham Edel and Ernest Nagel contributed (mainly) book reviews. Schlick's student Albert Blumberg, whose philosophical career was interrupted by a nearly two-decade career in communist party politics, also helped found this journal.

metaphysics, McGill believed, would potentially hold back the coming revolution. Two years before, William Malisoff founded *Philosophy of Science* in which, until his death in 1947, he editorialized aggressively about science as a servant of "the people" (Malisoff 1946).

Neurath was warmly welcomed into this politicized philosophical scene. He enlisted Malisoff to publish articles and book reviews related to the Movement. He convinced John Dewey to overcome his reservations about logical empiricist dismissals of metaphysics and write for the forthcoming *Encyclopedia* (which he did, twice). And Neurath became fast friends with Horace Kallen and Sidney Hook. Hook offered to help translate and publish some of his writings and attempted (with Nagel) to find Neurath a position at the New School for Social Research. Later, when Neurath and his new wife Marie Neurath were interned as prisoners of war in England after fleeing Holland, most of these friends and colleagues sent Neurath money to help him reestablish his home and base of operations (Nagel to Neurath, April 20, 1938, ONNH; Neurath to Hook, September 14, 1941, ONNH). One short letter to Neurath from Hook ends with an apology: "Please do not judge the warmth of my affection by the length of this letter. We talk about you here in New York often and regard you as one very close to us indeed" (Hook to Neurath, June 27, 1939, ONNH). This "we" probably extended beyond the New York philosophers into the larger circle of New York intellectuals. That same year, for example, Neurath exchanged letters with novelist James T. Farrell, who had asked Neurath about the fashionable theory that Nietzsche had paved the way for the rise of Nazism (Farrell to Neurath, April 16, 1939; Neurath to Farrell, July 5, 1939, ONNH).

Though they were based in Chicago, Morris and Carnap were also well connected to New York. Before and during the war, Morris corresponded with Dewey and met often with Kallen, Hook, and Nagel. Carnap corresponded professionally with Dewey (though they never came to agreement over the cognitive status of ethical propositions) and became friends with Hook and Schapiro.[7] When Carnap taught at Harvard in the summer of 1936, one of his students

---

[7] These relationships are mentioned in Nagel to Neurath, October 13, 1936, ONNH; Morris to Neurath, March 3, 1940, January 24, 1940, and January 31, 1943, ONNH.

was William Gruen, a young professor of philosophy at City College who met Neurath at the reception. Neurath did not need to recruit Gruen because Carnap had already converted him. Nagel noted in his inventory that Gruen "regards himself as a logical positivist."

INSTITUTIONAL CONNECTIONS: NEW YORK AND CHICAGO

In 1939 Gruen wrote a substantial piece in PR titled "What Is Logical Empiricism?" (1939). He answered that logical empiricism was an important tool for cultural and social criticism and explained that Neurath's new *Encyclopedia* was "a cooperative work which promises to be one of the most important events in modern intellectual history." This was because "the philosophy of *unified science* has special bearing on social problems": "It widens the domain of scientific method to embrace all intellectual and practical enterprise. And in its anti-metaphysical methodology it constitutes a challenge not merely to traditional, speculative philosophy, but to every form of transcendentalism in the social sciences" (Gruen 1939, 65). In Gruen's eyes, the new program was just what the New York socialists needed. Because "the need for social action demands that social science be unencumbered by doctrines which have no active, operative significance" (77), Gruen argued, "logical positivism offers an effective critical instrument" (65). It could help clean Marxism's stables of the metaphysical elements lurking within dialectical materialism, and it could sharpen tools of literary criticism. If Marxists brushed up on their physicalism, and art critics were better acquainted with logical reducibility of statements to observables, he explained, then logical empiricism's "full advantages" could find "realization in the field of esthetics, ethics, and political thought" (77).

Another article in PR praised the Unity of Science Movement while surveying the general semantics movement of the 1930s. Authors Albert Wohlstetter and Morton White criticized S. I. Hayakawa, Alfred Korzybski, and other popularizers as mere "amateurs in semantics." "Serious exponents of the study of meaning," they noted, "are concentrated for the most part in the Unity of Science Movement" (1939, 51, 52). Carnap, Tarski, Lukasiewicz, Philipp Frank, and Joseph Woodger were the real "friends of semantics," while the pretenders "have not advanced social science one whit by their inept exploitation of the theory of meaning" (1939, 57).

Logical empiricism and the Unity of Science Movement debuted in the pages of PR as, more or less, two aspects of one program that was to be admired, emulated, and utilized for advancing criticism and social science. In turn, several of the New York philosophers besides Dewey accepted Neurath's invitations to write monographs for the new *Encyclopedia*. Dewey explained that, besides the technicalities involved, unity of science was "a social problem" (1938). Nagel wrote on probability, Edel wrote on ethics, and Schapiro was on board to write a monograph about art and literary criticism (though it was never completed) (Dewey 1938; 1939; Nagel 1939; Edel 1961).

COMMON ENEMIES

Though Morris made the University of Chicago a center of the Unity of Science Movement, it was also the home of a counter-movement led by Mortimer Adler and the university's president, Robert Maynard Hutchins. Hutchins and Adler had a quite different vision of education and civilization in the modern world than the logical empiricists and the New Yorkers. For them, science was an utterly objective and valueless enterprise. Were science and scientific thinking to be a basis for modern life, they feared, civilization would descend into barbaric nihilism. Culture required instead a framework of metaphysical, super-scientific insights which Adler claimed to have found in Thomas's *Summa*. Allying themselves with Catholic philosophers and theologians (much to the puzzlement of Chicago's philosophy department, considering that Adler was Jewish), the two crusaded for neo-Thomism in higher and adult education.[8] Not surprisingly, Morris's overtures to Hutchins on behalf of the Unity of Science Movement and the new *Encyclopedia* never went far (Reisch 2005).

Between the neo-Thomists, on the one hand, and the New Yorkers and the logical empiricists, on the other, distrust and dislike

---

[8] For Hutchins's proposals for integrating Thomism into American culture and education, see Hutchins (1936).

smoldered until 1940. Then it exploded, twice. In March, Bertrand Russell lost his job at the City College of New York before he had even entered a classroom. Lawsuits were filed, and a devoutly Catholic judge, offended by some of Russell's published comments about sexuality, ruled that Russell's appointment was invalid and "an insult to the people of the City of New York" (quoted in Dewey and Kallen 1941, 225).

The New York philosophers were enraged, but they could not save Russell's position. Dewey and Kallen assembled and edited a book, *The Bertrand Russell Case* (Dewey and Kallen 1941), in which Hook's growing anti-Stalinist militancy was given pride of place in the book's closing chapter. Under the title "The General Pattern," Hook insisted that the Russell case was only one instance of a larger creep of authoritarianism and totalitarianism in America, "particularly with reference to education" (Hook 1941, 188). Secularism and naturalism were under siege, Hook announced, and the "spearpoint" of the attack was "the Catholic Church." Adler and Hutchins were helping to conduct "a widespread and subtle campaign" to "persuade the American people that the basic values and attitudes of our democratic way of life may not be able to withstand the attacks of totalitarianism, from without and within, unless they are fortified by supernatural sanctions" (Hook 1941, 197, 198). The unity of science thesis, as well as logical empiricist critiques of metaphysics and apriorism, were made-to-order for this and subsequent attacks that Hook launched against the neo-Thomists.[9]

The second explosion occurred in September when Adler addressed the many intellectuals who had gathered at the first Conference on Science, Philosophy and Religion in Their Relation to the Democratic Way of Life, a New York–based series of conferences in which Morris and Frank participated during the 1940s.[10] With Europe mired in war, Adler read a paper titled "God and the Professors" in which he earnestly claimed that civilization's ills were caused by university professors who failed to heed his and Hutchins's proposed educational reforms. Forget Hitler, Adler

---

[9] Hook examines the disunified architecture of knowledge upheld by Hutchins and Adler in Hook (1941, 204–5).

[10] See, e.g., Morris (1942a). For a general account of these conferences and further information about Philipp Frank's involvement, see Beuttler (1997).

argued, "the most serious threat to democracy is the positivism of its professors, which dominates every aspect of modern education and is the central corruption of modern culture. Democracy has much more to fear from the mentality of its teachers than from the nihilism of Hitler" (1941, 128). From the vantage of Manhattan, Morris and Carnap were stationed on the front lines of this battle. Hook warned Morris that his job was probably in danger. After all, Adler urged that "until the professors and their culture are liquidated" (1941, 134), there can be no hope for modern culture. "The implications of that speech are unmistakable," Hook wrote as he urged Morris "to take the offensive. Now is the psychological time for it" (Hook to Morris, December 19, 1940, CMP). But Morris did not heed Hook's battle call. As we shall see, Morris often shied away from heated intellectual and political confrontation.

Hook wrote his own response to Adler (Hook 1940) and in 1943 organized an elaborate counterattack in PR – a symposium titled "The New Failure of Nerve." It featured articles by Hook, Dewey, and Nagel in support of Hook's thesis that Adler and other Thomist critics of philosophical naturalism, science, and scientific philosophy were simply running away from the real cultural challenges created by the rise of science (Hook 1943).[11] Dewey's article, "Anti-Naturalism in Extremis," supported Hook's thesis and criticized the antinaturalists for losing faith in "human capacities" and peddling "escapism and humanistic defeatism" (Dewey 1943, 33, 39). Nagel appealed to the unity of science thesis to dismiss the various dualisms (material, immaterial; qualitative, quantitative) propping up neo-Thomism. He also discussed different kinds of "reductionism" to argue that they were not, as neo-Thomists charged, so mischievous or threatening to civilization. Nagel then explained why science and a scientific philosophical orientation were the true friends of social and cultural progress:

It is not wisdom but a mark of immaturity to recommend that we simply examine our hearts if we wish to discover the good life; for it is just because men rely so completely and unreflectively on their intuitive insights and passionate impulses that needless sufferings and conflicts occur among

[11] To specify the *new* failure of nerve, Hook borrowed Gilbert Murray's thesis that the ancients living prior to the Christian era had run from the intellectual and civic responsibilities bequeathed them by Hellenism.

them. The point is clear: claims as to what is required by wisdom need to be adjudicated if such claims are to be warranted; and accordingly, objective methods must be instituted, on the basis of which the conditions, the consequences, and the mutual compatibility of different courses of action may be established. But if such methods are introduced, we leave the miasmal swamps of supra-scientific wisdom, and are brought back again to the firm soil of scientific knowledge. (Nagel 1943, 54)

With their shared respect for logical empiricism and the Unity of Science Movement in the background, Morris, Carnap, Neurath, and most of the New York intellectuals would have heartily endorsed Nagel's elegant defense of scientism and social and economic planning.

MCCARTHYISM AND THE DECLINE OF COMMUNISM IN AMERICA

The leftist, progressive milieu that received logical empiricism and the Unity of Science Movement in the 1930s did not last long. Stalin's machinations against Trotsky and other revolutionaries, suspicions about the reported success of Stalin's agrarian reforms, and, finally, revelations in August 1939 about the Nazi-Soviet nonaggression pact led many intellectuals to swing toward the right. Political confusions and uncertainties were manifest in the theme of "disillusionment" that dominated titles in intellectual magazines and journals. As PR announced in 1947, "the Left has fallen into a state of intellectual disorientation and political impotence."[12] While some became agnostic, others moved to the far right, their former ardor for Marxism and proletarian revolution finding new outlet in anti-Stalinist liberalism and libertarianism.[13] By the late 1940s, the cold war between the United States and the Soviet Union had begun, and there was increasingly little room in professional philosophy of science for the Unity of Science Movement or any program that was not essentially technical and apolitical.

One reason for this depoliticization was anticommunist attacks against universities and intellectuals. Though the era was named for

---

[12] This unsigned introduction appears with Hook (1947).
[13] Worthwhile surveys of intellectuals during the cold war include Jacoby (1987) and Saunders (1999).

Joseph McCarthy, the anticommunist senator from Wisconsin, the FBI's J. Edgar Hoover and his library of files on suspected individuals and organizations were the real engine of the cold war's red scare. For several reasons, college professors were easy targets for Hoover and other anticommunists. Since many had been leftist and politically active in the 1930s, they had things to hide in the 1950s. Anticommunists also took an active interest in intellectuals because of the widespread view that Moscow sought to invade America not only militarily but ideologically. Seminar rooms and lecture halls were feared to be natural settings in which the future leaders of America could be indoctrinated with communism. In addition, for those intellectuals who were accused of being communists or teaching subversive subjects in their classes, neither erudition nor analytical rigor provided effective defense against the charges of politicians, civic leaders, or veterans groups that often led or sponsored campus investigations. The result was a "climate of fear" that dominated most campuses and made many intellectuals nervous and cautious.[14]

Principles of academic freedom, in addition, provided little protection for academics who were members of the Communist Party. For most Americans came to believe with University of Washington President Raymond Allen that such membership was no mere political orientation. It was, rather, a mental or psychological sickness marked by intellectual dependence on authoritarian dogma.[15] Though "honest, nonconformist thought" was to be prized and "honest liberals and indigenous radicals ... certainly perform an essential function in the American University," Allen rationalized, membership in the Party was out of bounds. It prevented any teacher from being "a free seeker after the truth" (Allen 1949, section II). Even one-time socialist leader Norman Thomas agreed: "The right of the communist to teach should be denied because

---

[14] The phrase "climate of fear" was commonly used by (so-called) anti-anticommunists who were critical of McCarthy, the FBI, and legislation empowering campus investigations (such as the Internal Security Act of 1950). University of Chicago President Robert M. Hutchins wrote a popular article in *Look* magazine titled "Are Our Teachers Afraid to Teach?" (Hutchins 1954).

[15] The stereotype of communists as beholden to a foreign power in their thoughts had a popular psychological counterpart called "neurotic susceptibility" as described, e.g., in Herberg (1954, 13).

he has given away his freedom in the quest for truth" (quoted in Klingaman 1996, 365). The popular conservative author William F. Buckley insinuated that the ideological and intellectual perversity of communists and those who would defend them was yet more sordid. He called them "academic freedomites" (Buckley 1951, 149).

Against this intimidating rhetorical backdrop, many campuses required faculty to sign patriotic loyalty oaths in the early 1950s. Investigations took place, among others, at the University of Washington, Harvard, The City College of New York, University of Buffalo, Wesleyan, University of Minnesota, University of Arkansas, University of Michigan, University of Chicago, University of California, Reed College, Temple University, Ohio State, and Rutgers.[16] The result was depoliticization of most campuses. According to Schrecker, "Political reticence ... blanketed the nation's colleges and universities. Marxism and its practitioners were marginalized, if not completely banished from the academy. Open criticism of the political status quo disappeared. ... Teachers ... played it ... safe, pruning their syllabi and avoiding controversial topics" (Schrecker 1986, 339). The American academy was no refuge from the ideological pressures and fashions of the cold war. "The academy did not fight McCarthyism," Schrecker concluded from her study. "It contributed to it." By the late 1950s, "all was quiet on the academic front" (Schrecker 1986, 340).

THE UNITY MOVEMENT AFTER THE WAR

In mid-1939 the Unity of Science Movement seemed to be a great success in America. Roughly half of the first 20 *Encyclopedia* monographs had appeared and were selling more briskly than expected. Neurath, Morris, and Carnap also formulated plans for additional volumes – a new unit comprising 100 monographs (in 10 volumes) of mainly descriptive studies of the actual relations among the sciences. (Neurath envisioned yet another 100 monographs treating education, medicine, law, and engineering, as

---

[16] The groups most often targeted included physicists, English professors, and economists. Once the sizes of departments are normalized, however, as John McCumber tallies the numbers in Schrecker's research and AAUP bulletins, it was philosophers who were most likely to fall "afoul of right-wing vigilantes" (McCumber 2001, 26).

well as a "visual thesaurus" utilizing ISOTYPE images.) With the *Encyclopedia* underway, the rescued *Erkenntnis* now under the title *The Journal of Unified Science*, and plans for the new book series *The Library of Unified Science* moving forward, the Movement was growing as successfully as anyone had hoped (Reisch 1995, 23–7; Morris 1960). Soon, in September, another Congress for the Unity of Science would convene at Harvard University.

The congress at Harvard foreshadowed the Movement's impending demise. When participants gathered to hear broadcast news about Hitler's invasion of Poland, they observed the beginning of a war that would slow their collaboration almost to a halt. And when they heard the philosopher Horace Kallen during the formal sessions argue that the values and methods behind "unity of science" were dangerously "totalitarian" (Kallen 1940), they saw that some of the anticommunist, antitotalitarian arguments and values that would propel much cold war scholarship could be directed against the Movement and its leaders. As we shall see below, these arguments and the values they drew on would encumber the Movement and prevent it from regaining the momentum it would lose to the war and Neurath's death in late 1945.

Shocked and saddened by Neurath's death, Morris, Carnap, and now Philipp Frank, one of Neurath's oldest and dearest friends, attempted to lead the Movement into the postwar world. Morris and Frank, who was then teaching physics and philosophy at Harvard, reestablished Neurath's Institute for the Unity of Science in Boston. The new Institute, they hoped, would decentralize leadership and avoid excessive reliance on any one individual, as was the case with Neurath (University of Chicago Press memorandum, September 13, 1946, UCPP, Box 346, Folder 4). With Rockefeller Foundation funding and with Frank as its president, the Institute was reborn in 1947 within the American Academy of Arts and Sciences. Its main tasks were to promote unified science and the *Encyclopedia*, sponsor research in sociology of science – a topic that Frank especially championed – and resume the international congresses that connected the Movement with scientists and the educated public.

Frank successfully organized some conferences and publications, but the Institute did not thrive (see *Proceedings of the American Academy of Arts and Sciences*, vol. 80, nos. 1–4 and Frank 1956).

There were problems with Frank's leadership, and the Institute lost its funding after only six years (Reisch 1995, 33–4). Nor did Frank receive as much support as he would have liked from his logical empiricist colleagues. He sometimes begged Morris, Nagel, and others to send him popular or semipopular essays for Institute-sponsored publications. At the same time, Herbert Feigl, Egon Brunswik, and Hans Reichenbach were eager to organize private, professional conferences outside of the Institute and its mandate. These emphasized the technical, formal problems that came to dominate philosophy of science in the 1950 and later years (Reisch 2005). Feigl also founded his own counterpart to the Institute, the Minnesota Center for the Philosophy of Science.

For several reasons, the profession loosened its ties to Frank's Institute in the 1950s and assumed an apolitical profile in the intellectual and academic landscape.[17] Besides the positive rewards of academic professionalism at a time when most universities were growing, flush with students and government cash, the Movement's postwar leaders – Carnap, Morris, and Frank – vividly experienced the anticommunist "climate of fear." They experienced institutional pressures of academic life, personal pressures from colleagues and federal investigators, and winds of intellectual fashion that explicitly opposed the Unity of Science Movement's collectivist and socialist orientation.

COLD WAR PRESSURES: CARNAP

In the early 1950s, Carnap turned down UCLA's Flint Visiting Professorship and two speaking invitations at Berkeley to protest the state's loyalty-oath requirement and the dismissal of faculty who had refused to sign. Carnap wrote to Berkeley's President Robert Sproul that his decisions in each case were "expressions of solidarity with the dismissed colleagues, and of protest against the violation of the principle that scholarship, teaching ability, and integrity of character should be the only criteria for judging a man's fitness for an academic position" (Carnap to Robert Gordon Sproul, October 22, 1950, ASP

---

[17] The Institute was inactive during the 1960s and legally dissolved in 1971; its assets taken over by the Philosophy of Science Association (Reisch 2005).

RC 085-29-11).[18] It is uncharacteristic of Carnap to use vague notions like "integrity of character." Yet such slogans eased relations between administrations and faculty at the time. When Carnap wrote to Berkeley's chair in philosophy, William Dennes, the notion was explicitly absent: "I am opposed in principle to the idea that *any but academic considerations* should qualify a man as fit or unfit for teaching." Still, Carnap admitted that he too would have bended to the pressures of the situation: "If I held a post at the University of California, I presume I would have signed the statement under protest in order to protect my livelihood" (Carnap to Dennes, October 12, 1950, ASP RC 085-29-02; emphasis added in first quote).

Three years later, in 1954, Carnap accepted an offer from UCLA to succeed Hans Reichenbach, who had died the previous year. Carnap was still nervous about the situation. Reichenbach, also a native German, did not have an easy time in California. During the war he and his family were classified as enemy aliens and subject to strict curfews and travel restrictions (Reichenbach to Morris, May 24, 1942, CMP). Now, Carnap wrote to his colleagues, he was "taking the plunge" and accepting UCLA's offer: "The political situation there does not look too good and inspires little confidence. On the other hand, my appointment presumably has not met any opposition on that score" (Carnap to "friends," March 6, 1954, CMP).

In fact, Carnap's personal political situation was not very good, for he was being investigated by the FBI, who took much interest in Carnap's sponsorship of various causes and organizations, most of which were promoted in the pages of the communist newspaper *The Daily Worker*.[19] Typically, Carnap sponsored humanitarian causes (such as clemency for Julius and Ethel Rosenberg, who were executed for espionage in 1953) and internationalist causes (such as U.S. recognition of the People's Republic of China).

The FBI believed that Carnap's public sponsorship of these and other causes made him worthy of investigation as a potential subversive, one of the many college professors often rumored to be importing communism into the United States. They interviewed

---

[18] This and other documents in the Carnap Collection quoted by permission of the University of Pittsburgh. All rights reserved.

[19] Carnap's FBI file was obtained by the author through a Freedom of Information Act request.

Carnap's friends and colleagues in Princeton and Chicago and asked whether anything about "the subject" suggested "communist activity." On the one hand, they learned that Carnap was a famous, dedicated, and stereotypical intellectual ("highly impractical, eccentric, and very engrossed in his subject") who often worked in bed because of his chronic back pain. No informants reported seeing or hearing "anything indicating that subject was a Communist sympathizer of any kind." One who claimed to have known Carnap first in Prague in the early 1930s said "the subject is interested '99% in scholastic matters and has little or no interest in politics of any kind.'" Given the many causes that Carnap supported in the pages of *The Daily Worker*, however, that statement was hyperbolic, if not false, and may have aroused their curiosity further.

Whether or not Carnap knew he was being investigated (almost surely his friends would have told him), his case illustrates how the FBI helped maintain the climate of fear that paralyzed academic leftism. Through this and other investigations, they vividly warned the intellectuals and citizens they interviewed that even if they were not communists they ought to avoid activities or projects that might seem "pink" or sympathetic to communism. For they too might become the subject of one of Hoover's investigations.

COLD WAR PRESSURES: MORRIS

There is no evidence that the FBI investigated Morris, but he feared that they might. In 1953, a former student, one Harold Josif, became embroiled in controversy while working for the American Foreign Service. In his defense, it appears, Josif asked Morris to supply an affidavit. Morris wrote an earnest letter on Josif's behalf, praising him as intelligent, capable, and a most patriotic, noncommunistic American: "There was never in his thoughts or attitudes the slightest trace of anything that could be called pro-Communist in any degree. Indeed his personality as I know it seems diametrically opposed to the Communist totalitarian mentality." Then, in the margin of this one page letter, Morris testified to his own political rectitude: "Perhaps it may be relevant to state that I have opposed the totalitarian attitude in my book *Paths of Life*. ... My last work, *The Open Self*, is a defense of American democracy against the forces that threaten it from within and without" (Morris to "Whom It May Concern," May 6,

1953, CMP). Though the title of Morris's *The Open Self* (1948) was born of the cold war's popular dichotomy between open and closed (Soviet) societies, neither this book nor Morris's *Paths of Life* (1942) would have impressed an anticommunist such as Hoover or McCarthy as a defense of American democracy.

Morris defended himself against possible anticommunist scrutiny for at least two reasons. One was his history. He visited the Soviet Union in the 1930s and China in the late 1940s (on the eve of revolution), while his bibliography and professional memberships proclaimed his enduring interests in humanism and worldwide cultural unification.[20] At a time when McCarthy could proclaim that Johns Hopkins sinologist Owen Lattimore was "the top Russian espionage agent" (quoted in Klingaman 1996, 193) in the country and partly responsible for the rise of communist China, Morris could plausibly have supposed that anticommunists would target him.

Second, Morris was by temperament politically cautious. In 1955 he protested Illinois's loyalty oaths by refusing a visiting position offered to him by the University of Illinois's Institute of Communications Research. As Carnap had protested the oaths in California, Morris decided in advance that he would decline the offer if Illinois's Governor Stratton signed the oath requirement into law. While awaiting Stratton's decision, Morris's friend and colleague Charles Osgood at the Institute encouraged him to take a public, aggressive stand:

I would sign the appointment papers [thus accepting the position] and then, if you wish to go through as you told the Governor, I would later refuse to sign the special Loyalty Oath – this would automatically fire you! But ... I would make sure that the Illinois newspapers are notified in advance of your plans and that you make a public statement. ... [T]he whole point, as I see it, is to impress on the public mind the distinction between disloyalty and unwillingness to be pushed into essentially unconstitutional behavior by politicians. (Osgood to Morris, July 11, 1955, CMP)

But Morris was not so confrontational: "If I am not a state employee [,] I see no moral obligation to become one just in order to provoke trouble." Besides, he told Osgood, "it would be at least something of

---

[20] Morris contributed extensively to the journal *East-West* (often as a referee) and belonged to the American Humanist Association.

a protest not to come to the University under the present circumstances." This something-of-a-protest would be (and was) imperceptible to "the public mind" that Osgood urged Morris to help educate. Morris knew it. "I hope you don't feel that I am letting you down," he apologized (Morris to Osgood, July 14, 1955, CMP).

COLD WAR PRESSURES: FRANK

Carnap's investigation by the FBI was triggered by its investigation of Philipp Frank. That investigation had been sparked by a rumor landing on FBI Director J. Edgar Hoover's desk reporting that Frank, some 10 years before taking his position at Harvard, "came to the United States for the purpose of organizing high level Communist Party activities" (Hoover to Pentagon, August 13, 1952).[21] The rumor turned out to be false, the investigation revealed, because Frank had not in fact been in America during those years. But it was not preposterous from an anticommunist point of view. In 1947, for instance, Hoover warned of communist attempts to "infiltrate the so-called intellectual and creative fields" (Klingaman 1996, 419). A year before, President Truman's Executive Order 9835 specified that "reasonable grounds exist for belief that [a] person ... is disloyal to the Government of the United States" if they belong to any "organization, association, movement, group or combination of persons, designated by the Attorney General as totalitarian, fascist, communist, or subversive" (Klingaman 1996, 416). At the time of his investigation, Frank was the head of an institute whose very name promoted a goal – unity of science – that was seen as increasingly pink and subversive.

UNIFIED SCIENCE AND TOTALITARIANISM

As the influential New York intellectuals variously turned away from Marxism, Soviet socialism, and Stalin in the late 1930s and early 1940s, some became suspicious of the values and methods they saw – or believed they saw – embedded in the Unity of Science Movement. None was more aggressive or persistent than Horace

---

[21] Frank's FBI file was obtained by the author under a Freedom of Information Act request.

Kallen, the student of William James and cofounder of the New School for Social Research. After first making his charges at the Fifth International Congress for the Unity of Science at Harvard (Kallen 1940), Kallen aired them again in 1946 in a long, six-article exchange in *Philosophy and Phenomenological Research* with Neurath and, briefly, Morris (Kallen 1946; 1946a; 1946b; 1946c; Morris 1946; Neurath 1946; 1946a). Kallen claimed that the very ideas of "unity" and "unified science" were politically and culturally totalitarian:

In despotic countries ... not only are the lives and labors of the people "unified," their thoughts boilerplated; also the arts and sciences are "unified" to the respective orthodoxies of the fascist, nazi, communist and clericalist dogmas. What does not conform to those imperialist pretensions cannot be truth, must be willful error, must be heresy which betrays the unity of the faith and deserves, therefore, the bitterest punishment and ultimately the most painful death a totalitarian imagination can devise. (1940, 82)

Just as a healthy society would wither under totalitarian despotism, so the sciences would atrophy under the iron-fisted program that Kallen took unified science to be.

Unfortunately, Kallen ignored Neurath's many disclaimers – beginning at least with the Vienna Circle's Manifesto – urging that the Movement's efforts to unify the sciences were to be democratic. They were not an attempt to impose on science some philosophical or political plan (much less, one designed by an individual or a cabal). Neurath organized the International Congresses, for example, not to give marching orders, but rather to facilitate and regularize debate about how bridges among the sciences might be built. "Our program is the following," he once wrote: "no system from above, but systematization from below" (Neurath 1936b/1983, 153). Like the sailors in Neurath's famous boat (Cartwright et al., 89–166), scientists would chart a direction freely and without the benefit of metaphysical foundations or some (allegedly) superscientific theory of science. That is why, he wrote in the *Encyclopedia*, "the whole business will go on in a way we cannot even anticipate today" (Neurath 1944, 47).

Kallen overlooked the collective and democratic epistemology at the core of Neurath's program because he was more interested in antitotalitarian politics. Thus Kallen demanded (without detecting the obvious irony) that the Movement adopt some conception of "unity of science" that conformed to his preferred pluralistic and libertarian doctrines:

[P]erhaps the sciences are in their essence centrifugal, and that their unity is but the consequence of pressure from without, not of impulsion from within.... Perhaps [unity of science] means and need mean no more than the mutual guarantee of its liberty by each science to each, ... [or] union of the sciences seeking each to preserve and to enhance its individuality and freedom.... "Unity" would mean liberation and exaltation of diversities. (1940, 83)

Kallen's attack was relentless and often hyperbolic. On one occasion he depicted Neurath as a hapless apologist for Lysenkoism: "Might it not, then, be better, in the manner of the realistic Soviets, to nationalize scientific inquiry altogether and make of all scientific inquiry a handmaiden to the wants and works of the State?" (Kallen 1946a, 517). In the end, Neurath was reduced to utter disbelief that his friend construed even basic parts of logical empiricism (such as Neurath's proposal for a physicalistic language of science) as so politically mischievous: "That this [language] is full of totalitarian danger can surely not be inferred, as Horace thinks, from the working of my papers" (Neurath 1946a, 528).

While Kallen rejected the Unity of Science Movement from the libertarian right, unified science – albeit it a variety closely connected to dialectical materialism – continued to be embraced by the intellectual communist left. In 1950, for example, the British communist philosopher Maurice Cornforth reminded his readers that unity of science was an important piece of communism's postwar agenda. In his book *In Defense of Philosophy*, Cornforth reissued Lenin's complaint that logical empiricists were insufficiently materialist to assist the coming revolution. The idea of unifying the sciences, however, remained a glittering, admirable goal.[22] "The real unity of science" could be achieved, he wrote, "by the organized pressing forward of research in all fields of science in accordance with a single plan – directed towards a single practical

---

[22] Unity and interrelation were commonly viewed as watchwords of dialectical materialists. For example, Sidney Hook once complained that "ideas in any field are for them weapons since, according to the philosophy of dialectical materialism, all fields are interrelated" (1950, 17).

goal, the enlargement of knowledge in the service of the people"
(Cornforth 1950, 156). Nagel reviewed Cornforth's book and took
exception to nearly all of it. "But," Nagel emphasized, "there is one
feature of the book which is perhaps more important than its general
philosophic incompetence – namely, the explicit assumption that
science flourishes best under regimentation. Mr. Cornforth ...
believes that just as capitalist production must inevitably be
replaced by socialist production, so bourgeois science must be succeeded by a planned, unified science." "If Mr. Cornforth has his
way," Nagel reasoned, "the conditions under which modern science
can contribute to human welfare and human dignity may disappear
from the face of the earth" (Nagel 1952, 650). In at least one,
important sense, Kallen had won his debate with Neurath. With the
cold war and anticommunist investigations in the universities in
full swing, one of the profession's most able and influential leaders
took it to be almost self-evident that unified science was a kind of
authoritarian "regimentation" that would oppose both scientific
and cultural progress.[23]

PRESSURES INSIDE THE PROFESSION: FRANK ATTACKED

The dubious political reputation that unified science gained in the
1950s helps explain a curious review of Frank's book *Philosophy
of Science* (Frank 1957). It appeared in *Philosophy of Science*, the
journal of the Philosophy of Science Association. Frank was president
of the Association for several years after the death in 1947 of Malisoff,
its founder. But Frank's standing and reputation did not save him
from being portrayed as a confused philosopher who had converted to
neo-Thomist authoritarianism. So argued one Charles Kegley, a
minor figure among philosophers of science, who reviewed Frank's
book in 1959.[24] Kegley's claim that Frank indulged in Thomism is so
incorrect that it reads less like a mistaken interpretation of his

---

[23] These commonplaces about freedom and organization in scientific practice were
also driven by parallel debates concerning postwar science, including the Lysenko
controversy in the Soviet Union and, in the United States, civilian versus military
control of atomic energy and the initial organization of the National Science
Foundation.

[24] Kegley later became a prominent theologian.

writing than a willful effort to discredit Frank personally and politically. Echoing the widespread view that communists were emotionally off-balance, Kegley wrote that when Frank's colleagues peruse his new book they "are likely to raise their eyebrows in surprise at a number of points," for Frank has "much to say about science, but says it in a somewhat special way and, as I wish to point out, with rather astonishing assumptions" (1959, 35). This "somewhat special" aspect to Frank's recent thinking is this alleged conversion to Thomist fundamentalism: "Is philosophy necessarily concerned with first principles? Something has evidently developed in Professor Frank's thinking in recent years which enamours him with this notion" (1959, 37–8). The result of this alleged conversion, Kegley gasped, "is disturbing to say the least" (1959, 38).

If Kegley intentionally red-baited Frank, he did so because Frank's book charted a course for the profession that continued to embrace Neurath's unity of science program and emphasize sociological and "extra-scientific" aspects of science (Frank 1957, 354–60). Since science needed to be free of all political and social encumbrances, Kegley seemed to reason, philosophy of science required leaders who exalted freedom, not first principles or neo-Thomist dogma. Echoing both Kallen's charge that totalitarianism lurked within the unity of science program and the popular stereotype of intellectually straitjacketed communists secretly beholden to an alien power, Kegley insisted that Frank was neither sufficiently free nor freedom-loving to lead the profession:

Any author who presents a philosophy of science which is beholden to Aquinas and the Thomistic system ought to scrutinize his task and its implications and to state his position forthrightly.... Furthermore, in an age which suffers from censorship and thought-control by secular and religious authorities, the cause of free inquiry is hardly aided by reverence for an age which, after all, burned Giordano Bruno and forced Galileo to recant. Surely our comprehension of the spirit of philosophy and of science, and the strengthening of that spirit throughout the world today, lies in other directions. (1959, 39)

Though Frank was defended a year later in a short article by James F. Rutherford (1960), there is little indication that Frank or his projects were embraced by the profession after the Institute declined in the 1950s. The Philosophy of Science Association was reorganized in 1958, without Frank's leadership, and he published little afterwards (see Ducasse 1959 and Reisch 2005). Kegley's attack, appearing one year later, thus announced and confirmed the profession's drift away from the Unity of Science Movement. "The spirit of philosophy and of science," as Kegley put it, lay "in other directions." Frank died in 1966.

PRESSURES INSIDE THE PROFESSION: CARNAP ATTACKED

While Rudolf Carnap was arguably philosophy's leading logical empiricist, Sidney Hook became without doubt its leading anticommunist. The two locked horns in 1949 when Hook learned that Carnap was a public signatory for the Cultural and Scientific Congress for World Peace (known as the Waldorf Conference after the New York City hotel where it was held). Hook would not stand for it and sat down at his typewriter: "If you actually have enrolled yourself as a sponsor, I am confident that you are unaware of the real auspices of the Conference. It is being run by people whose first act, if they came to power, would be to liquidate you and people like you." Hook was extremely agitated as he looked forward to the public demonstrations he planned to hold at the event: "This business is no ordinary thing, as you will learn by developments in the next few days. Anybody who is still a sponsor by the time the party-line begins to sound off at the Conference, will be marked for life as a captive or fellow traveler of the Communist Party" (Hook to Carnap, March 29, 1949. ASP 088-38-10).

Carnap wrote "?!" in the margin next to Hook's use of "liquidate" – the same inflammatory and threatening verb Adler had used some 10 years before to attack positivist philosophers. Carnap had good reason to be both alarmed and puzzled. This business was indeed extraordinary. The main wave of anticommunist investigations in universities was just beginning, and Hook publicly supported the view that communists should not be permitted to teach (Hook 1950; 1953; 1953a). Though Hook did not believe Carnap was a communist, he believed Carnap was acting like one in a highly visible way.[25] He

---

[25] The FBI would later agree with Hook. Carnap's sponsorship of the Waldorf Conference is noted in Carnap's FBI file.

did not need to explain that this could jeopardize Carnap's career. Nor was Hook being hyperbolic when he implied that this business was potentially a matter of life and death. Japanese Americans were detained in concentration camps in California during the war, and, as Carnap surely knew, Reichenbach and his family lived under curfew in Los Angeles during the early 1940s. Were a third world war to erupt between the Soviets and the Americans, and were Carnap perceived widely as a communist, then more than his career could be at risk. Hook had a point.

Though Hook does not refer to the Unity of Science Movement, his attack nonetheless helps explain the Movement's fate. Hook could not abide even the appearance of communist sympathy among intellectuals because he firmly believed that Western intellectual and cultural life was immediately threatened by the creep of Soviet communism and authoritarianism. Though Hook did not attack the Unity of Science Movement on these grounds, his good friend Horace Kallen did. Whatever form it might take – political, philosophical, or scientific – Hook and Kallen were determined to purge from intellectual and cultural life anything they took to be sympathetic with totalitarianism or Soviet communism.

In the end, Carnap stood his ground. He gave his name to support the Congress's pacifist ideals, and he would not withdraw that support. Nor would he capitulate to "anticommunist hysteria," to the "grossly exaggerated ... picture of the 'serious threat to democracy' by communism in America as it is drawn by the press ... and by the State Department"; or to the "cold-war politics of our government" which treats all opportunities for rational conversation among political adversaries as heated confrontations. Yes, Carnap admitted, given the "fear and intimidation operating in this country to an extent unprecedented so far," it "might be 'wise' for the moment" to withdraw his name. But "in view of the great aim of preserving the peace" he would not do so, and he did not (Carnap to Hook, March 24, 1949, ASP RC 088-38-13). (For more on the Hook-Carnap exchange, see Reisch 2005.)

HAYEK VERSUS COLLECTIVISM

These federal, institutional, and personal pressures against the continuation of the Unity of Science Movement were strengthened by parallel trends in scholarship that made the Unity of Science Movement of the 1950s seem anachronistic and bound to fail. One of the most powerful trends was the rise of libertarian individualism over and against "collectivism" in social and economic thought.[26] Though Kallen's arguments against Neurath reflected this trend, its most popular source was Friedrich Hayek's *The Road to Serfdom*.

Published in 1944, Hayek's *Serfdom* worked against the Unity of Science Movement in multiple ways. First, Hayek helped eliminate the socialist middle ground within the dichotomy of capitalism and totalitarianism that came to dominate cold war thinking. Socialism was not an alternative to totalitarianism (or "serfdom"), Hayek argued, because as a matter of historical fact socialism paved the way for it: "the rise of fascism and nazism was not a reaction against the socialist trends of the preceding period but a necessary outcome of those tendencies" (1944, 3–4). With all socialist middles excluded, it would only become easier to suppose (as Kallen did) that since the Unity of Science Movement was not a study in pluralism and libertarianism, it must therefore be totalitarian and authoritarian.

Hayek also attacked the Movement at its methodological core: planning. Attempts to coordinate people in the interests of a global, coherent plan – economic, social, military – will be crippled by dissatisfaction that naturally invites dictatorship: "dictatorship is the most effective instrument of coercion and the enforcement of ideals and, as such, essential if central planning on a large scale is to be possible" (1944, 70). However simple, Hayek's argument was persuasive. *Serfdom* flew off bookshelves and was serialized in the popular magazine *Reader's Digest*.

Despite Hayek's attack on planning and his dislike of "positivism" in science and philosophy, there were some remarkable alignments between Hayek and Neurath.[27] Both championed an Epicurean utilitarianism that took individual happiness as a basic value; both criticized naive scientism holding that science supplies a

---

[26] Other issues and trends for which there is no room here include a postwar revival of anti-intellectualism and an ongoing critique of scientism holding that science and scientific philosophy are powerless to understand political and historical forces. See Reisch (2005).

[27] Useful essays on relations among Hayek, Popper, and Neurath include Uebel (2000a) and Cat (1995).

complete and true world-picture; and both opposed fascism and found it lurking in unsuspected places. While Hayek was writing *Serfdom*, for example, Neurath argued that Plato's writings were dangerously totalitarian (Neurath 1945; Neurath and Lauwerys 1945). Neurath reviewed *Serfdom* and began his review on just this common point: "Let us be grateful to authors who show up concealed Fascism." But Neurath's agreement with Hayek stopped there: "we cannot go all the way with Hayek in his relegation of all planning to this category [of fascism]." Neurath saw no foundation for Hayek's a priori rejection of the possibility that collective interests might prevail over individual interests; that societies, nations, or – in the case of the Unity of Science Movement – scientists might succeed in "planning as a co-operative effort, based on compromise." Neurath held to the possibility that "world planning based on co-operation would perhaps give rise to a world-wide feeling of responsibility for other people's happiness" (Neurath 1945a/2004, 546, 547).

Yet Hayek and the many intellectuals who moved from the left to the right during and after the war no longer shared Neurath's enduring faith in collectivism. Were logical empiricism and its Unity of Science Movement to engage scientists, architects, educators, and others around the globe, success would require an international climate of cooperation and trust. But the climate of the cold war was very different, dominated by themes such as anticommunism and anticollectivism, the precariousness of freedom and the near-inevitability of despotism or dictatorship. These themes appear equally in well-known landmarks such as Hayek's *Serfdom* or Popper's *The Open Society and Its Enemies* (1952) and in the publications and private correspondence of logical empiricists and their cold war critics. They also appear in popular culture of the 1950s. The magazine *House Beautiful*, for example, editorialized against modern architecture and design (with which the Vienna Circle allied itself in its manifesto; see Neurath, Carnap, and Hahn 1929). This esthetic vanguard of the 1920s and '30s was actually politically subversive, warned the magazine's editor in 1953. Modern design and Mies van der Rohe's counterintuitive slogan "Less is more" were really efforts to assist an impending communist takeover by manipulating the American mind and eroding common sense (Gordon 1953).

TO THE ICY SLOPES

While Frank and Carnap were investigated by the FBI, and Morris feared that he might be, Neurath – even though he died shortly before the cold war – continued to cast a long, pink shadow over the Movement. Since Neurath was known (as *Time* magazine put it) for his "strong socialist leanings in politics" (Time 1939), Neurath's widow Marie Neurath believed in the 1950s that it might be difficult or impossible to publish Neurath's writings in America. Surprisingly, that is what Neurath's former critic Horace Kallen wished to do. He corresponded with Marie about this possibility and asked Morris for his advice about Neurath's widow's concerns. Morris only confirmed her fears: "I share Marie's sense of caution. I have met people who think Otto, and indeed the whole unified science program, is communistic" (Morris to Kallen, October 8, 1957, Kallen papers, AJA).

Why would Kallen wish to publish Neurath's writings after so aggressively attacking them years before? He wanted to honor Neurath's character and humanistic goals, he explained, because "Otto was so much more than *a mere logical empiricist*": "He had an enormous amount of compassion, a deep feeling for people as people, and an eagerness to serve their liberation and enrichment through the philosophic and sociological arts" (Kallen to Morris, May 7, 1957, CMP; emphasis added). Kallen's memories of Neurath's humanitarianism were sweetened by the profession's transformation. The intellectual work of a logical empiricist, Kallen knew, was now disengaged from social, economic, educational, or humanitarian problems. A new mode and attitude in philosophy of science – technical, professional, and apolitical – had become dominant.

The transformation was fairly sudden. In 1955, two years before this conversation between Kallen and Morris, Frank's Institute became moribund for lack of funds. In 1959, as Frank's professional decline was sealed by Kegley's attack, a new image of logical empiricism began to appear. In a full-page advertisement in *Science* (vol. 129, May 8, 1959), a stylized photo-portrait of Hans Reichenbach floated above a quote from his writings and the corporate byline of the RAND Corporation, the first government-sponsored "think tank" to enlist intellectual talent for military research.

The advertisement invited mathematicians, logicians, and analysts of all kinds to seek employment working on projects related to national security.

If logical empiricists were now being courted by the military and the political right, the profession officially disclaimed any substantive political orientation. That same year, 1959, Herbert Feigl, whose Minnesota Center for the Philosophy of Science had by then eclipsed Frank's Institute, announced that science and philosophy of science were value-free: "Science can never, by its very nature, provide a reason for our fundamental obligations or for the supreme goals of life," he explained in the volume *Current Issues in the Philosophy of Science*. Perhaps nodding to the profession's socially engaged past, Feigl defended this circumstance as proper and logically inevitable. Criticizing "the scientific enterprise" or "a genuinely scientific outlook in philosophy" for "these limitations ... would be like reproaching a weaving loom for its incapacity to produce music" (Feigl 1959, 16).

As Kallen praised Neurath in his letter to Morris, he had in mind this disjunct between philosophical theory and technique, on the one hand, and their application in civic, cultural, and political life, on the other. Having complained in the 1940s that logical empiricism had the wrong political edge; he was now dismayed that philosophy of science had *no* political edge. That is another reason why he wished to promote Neurath's writings. "Such a book," he told Morris, "could save logical empiricism, etc. etc. from the barrenness into which it seems to me to have fallen" (Kallen to Morris, May 7, 1957, CMP).

Kallen was not the only critic of this "barrenness." *The Structure of Scientific Revolutions* would appear in 1962 and begin persuading a generation of philosophers of science that any valuable "image" of science must seriously address the historical and sociological processes that connect scientific theory to the world in which it is practiced and sustained. Because of this need for "caution" that Morris voiced, however, Neurath's writings, his distinctively social and historical approach to understanding and promoting science, and the once-popular Movement that he founded to promote this approach remained obscure for at least another decade. The first volume of Neurath's translated writings appeared in 1973, appropriately titled *Empiricism and Sociology* (1973).[28]

[28] This work was supported by a grant from the National Science Foundation (SES-0002222). For critical comments and conversations about this essay and its subject matter I would like to thank Friedrich Stadler, Elisabeth Nemeth, Thomas Uebel, Alan Richardson, Don Howard, Gary Hardcastle, Warren Schmaus, Michael Davis, Jack Snapper, Bob Ladenson, Vivien Weil, Fred Beuttler, Abraham Edel, Seth Sharpless, Nathan Hauser, and Robert Cohen. For assisting my research in their collections and permission to publish quotations, I also thank those curating the following archival collections: The Horace Kallen Papers at the Jacob Rader Marcus Center of the American Jewish Archives, Cincinnati Campus (AJA); The Rudolf Carnap Papers at the Archives of Scientific Philosophy, University of Pittsburgh (ASP); The Charles Morris Papers at the Peirce Edition Project at IUPUI (CMP); The Otto Neurath Nachlass at Rijksarchief in Noord-Holland, Haarlem, The Netherlands (ONNH); The University of Chicago Press Papers at the Department of Special Collections, Regenstein Library, University of Chicago (UCPP).

Part Two: Logical Empiricism: Issues in General Philosophy of Science

4 Coordination, Constitution, and Convention

The Evolution of the A Priori in Logical Empiricism

A standard picture of the conception of a priori knowledge developed within the logical empiricist tradition runs as follows. This conception arose primarily in the context of the philosophy of mathematics – where, in particular, it was intended to provide an alternative to the Kantian theory of synthetic a priori knowledge that would be both acceptable from an empiricist point of view and more adequate to mathematical practice than the simple-minded empiricism associated with John Stuart Mill. Here the logical empiricists found an answer in the logicist philosophy of mathematics of Gottlob Frege and Bertrand Russell, according to which mathematics is reducible to logic (the new mathematical logic developed by Frege and Russell) and is therefore analytic a priori, not synthetic a priori. There is thus no need of the Kantian faculty of pure intuition, and, at the same time, we can still (thanks to the richness and complexity of Frege's and Russell's new logic) do justice to both the a priority and the complexity of our actual mathematical knowledge. The heart of the logical empiricists' answer to Kant, therefore, is that his main example of synthetic a priori knowledge, pure mathematics, is not synthetic after all. All that we ultimately need to explain the possibility of pure a priori knowledge in the exact sciences is the analytic a priori.

This picture, as I have said, is geared primarily to the philosophy of mathematics. But it can be easily extended to the philosophy of empirical knowledge as well. Just as Frege's and Russell's logicism, on this standard picture, provided an acceptable alternative (to Kant's) in the philosophy of pure mathematics, Rudolf Carnap's *Der logische Aufbau der Welt* (1928) provided a parallel alternative explanation of the possibility of empirical knowledge. In particular, whereas Frege and Russell explain the possibility of mathematical knowledge by reducing it to a more certain basis in logic, Carnap's *Aufbau* explains the possibility of empirical knowledge in general (including highly theoretical knowledge in mathematical physics) by reducing it to a more certain basis in immediate sensory experience. Moreover, just as Frege's and Russell's logicist reduction is essentially mediated by logical definitions of the fundamental concepts of mathematics, Carnap's parallel phenomenalist reduction is mediated by definitions, in the language of *Principia Mathematica*, of all empirical concepts (including highly theoretical concepts) in terms of a primitive basis in subjective sensory experience. These definitions, in both cases, are of course themselves analytic, and so the concept of analytic a priori knowledge suffices (contra Kant) to provide a full explanation of the possibility of our knowledge in both cases. Neither mathematical knowledge nor empirical knowledge requires the Kantian synthetic a priori, and so radical empiricism triumphs in both cases – once, that is, that the new mathematical logic due to Frege and Russell is itself already in place.

As is now well known, however, this standard picture is much too crude.[1] My aim here is to further contribute to a more sophisticated understanding by exploring the evolution of the logical empiricists' attempts to revise and reconfigure the Kantian conception of the a priori from Moritz Schlick's early epistemological thought to Carnap's mature philosophy of formal languages or linguistic frameworks first articulated in his *Logical Syntax of Language* (1934). In the earlier period, as we shall see, philosophical attention was focused on problems in the foundations of geometry and physics associated with Einstein's general theory of relativity, and issues in the foundations of logic and mathematics played a decidedly secondary role. Moreover, these problems in the foundations of geometry and physics were intimately intertwined with issues in the philosophy (and psychology) of sense perception and thus with more general issues in the epistemology of empirical knowledge. Finally, whereas Carnap's *Aufbau* does represent perhaps the most

---

[1] This kind of conception is presented, most famously, in Quine (1951), (1969), where it is used as a jumping-off point for Quine's own radically holistic epistemology. For a typical version of the resulting standard picture of logical empiricism see Giere (1988, 22–8).

important stage of the developments I here aim to describe, it was only after the *Aufbau*, in the period culminating in the publication of *Logical Syntax of Language*, that problems in the foundations of logic and mathematics took center stage. The logical empiricists' evolving perspective on the nature and character of a priori knowledge in the exact sciences therefore began with problems in the *empirical* sciences (physical geometry and mathematical physics) and only then turned to the issues in the foundations of logic and mathematics that the more standard picture takes as its starting point.

The developments I aim to describe of course trace their origin to the original Kantian conception of a priori knowledge, and this conception, in turn, is best approached, in the present context, against the background of a new problem of coordinating abstract mathematical structures with concrete objects of sensory experience characteristic of modern mathematical physics. Thus, in the premodern, Aristotelian-Scholastic natural philosophy that preceded modern physics, the mathematical structures used to represent the natural world and our concrete sensory experience of this world fit together smoothly and unproblematically. The earth assumes its natural place at the center of a finite Euclidean sphere representing the whole of physical space; the heavenly bodies execute perfectly uniform circular motions with respect to this center; and the four natural elements (earth, water, air, and fire) assume natural places concentrically arranged around this center, such that they then move in Euclidean straight lines back to their natural places when violently removed therefrom. In modern mathematical physics, by contrast, this entire hierarchical arrangement is destroyed. Physical space is now represented by the totality of three-dimensional Euclidean extension, infinite in all directions, wherein there are no privileged positions and therefore no natural places. On the contrary, there are now an infinite number of possible relative spaces (reference frames), each centered on an arbitrarily chosen reference body: the earth, the sun, and so on. None of these relative spaces has so far been privileged, and there is therefore a deep ambiguity at the heart of the modern conception of space and of motion – the problem, that is, of absolute versus relative motion. Finally, whereas the representation of time, in the premodern universe, is similarly unproblematic and unambiguous, being measured by the natural state of uniform circular motion of the heavenly bodies (more precisely, the outermost sphere of the fixed stars), the natural state of uniform motion, in the modern universe, is rectilinear inertial motion – a state of motion that is never actually observed and that, in addition, also inherits the deep ambiguity afflicting the representation of space: relative to *which* of the infinite number of possible relative spaces does an inertially moving object move uniformly and rectilinearly?

In modern mathematical physics, therefore, neither space nor time nor motion has a natural and unambiguous relation to our concrete sensory experience. Yet, if mathematical physics is to be possible as a genuine empirical science, some such relation must, nonetheless, be necessarily in place. Kant's solution to this problem, in the briefest possible terms, runs as follows.[2] Our concrete sensory experience is itself framed and thereby made possible by a pure mathematical structure: the pure intuition of space providing an infinite three-dimensional Euclidean "container" as the pure form of our (outer) sensible intuition. We know a priori, therefore, that all sensory experience must exactly conform to the laws of Euclidean geometry, which thereby acquires a necessary applicability to all objects of our experience. This move leaves the problem of absolute space and absolute motion still unsettled, however, and so our philosophical bridge between mathematical physics and sensory experience requires a second step – by which a second pure a priori faculty, the intellectual faculty of understanding, is applied to ("schematized" in terms of) the pure forms of sensible intuition (including time as the form of inner intuition). This procedure results, via an instantiation or realization of the pure relational categories of substance, causality, and community, in (Kant's version of) Newton's three laws of motion: the conservation of mass, the law of inertia, and the equality of action and reaction. These laws, in turn, define a privileged class of relative spaces or reference frames, the inertial reference frames (as we would now put it), wherein the law of inertia then holds. They also define an actual empirical procedure for approximating such a reference frame in our sensory experience, the procedure of *Principia* Book III, whereby

---

[2] For further discussion of Kant's philosophy of (Newtonian) mathematical physics see Friedman (1992).

Newton determines the center of mass of the solar system as a very good approximation to such a frame. In this way, our modern mathematical representations of space, time, and motion acquire a definite relation to sensory experience after all, but only by a rather circuitous procedure essentially mediated, in Kant's eyes, by synthetic a priori principles originating in the necessary structure of our human cognitive faculties. These principles are a priori, for Kant, precisely because it is only on their basis that precise scientific experience – genuine empirical knowledge – is first possible.[3]

With Albert Einstein's formulation of the general theory of relativity in 1916, however, our problem takes a radically new turn. For this theory not only declares the principles Kant originally took to be synthetic a priori (Euclidean geometry and the Newtonian laws of motion) to be no longer universally valid; it also creates a further, and even more radical, difficulty in coordinating the mathematical structures used theoretically to describe the physical world to our concrete sensory experience. Where Newtonian physics employs an infinite three-dimensional Euclidean space as its most fundamental mathematical representation, the general theory of relativity employs a four-dimensional (semi-) Riemannian space-time manifold of variable curvature. And, whereas infinite three-dimensional Euclidean space can be plausibly taken, as it was for Kant, as a pure form of our sensible intuition, which is naturally and essentially connected with our sensory perceptual experience, the space-time structure employed in general relativity is an entirely nonintuitive, entirely abstract mathematical structure. Indeed, it is for precisely this reason that both Einstein and the logical empiricists saw an intimate connection between the new space-time structures employed in the general theory of relativity and the new view of pure mathematical geometry associated with David Hilbert, according to which pure geometry is an entirely formal or abstract axiomatic system having no intrinsic relation whatsoever to either space perception or any other kind of sensory experience.[4]

---

[3] For discussion of the relationship between "scientific" and "ordinary" experience in Kant see Friedman (2002a).

[4] Einstein himself makes this connection in his celebrated paper "Geometry and Experience" (1921). For discussion see Friedman (2002).

Moritz Schlick, in his *Space and Time in Contemporary Physics* (1917) and *General Theory of Knowledge* (1918), was the first thinker within the logical empiricist tradition to address these problems.[5] Schlick begins by generalizing Hilbert's conception of the abstract formal concepts of pure geometry – that they are "implicitly defined" by the formal axioms governing them entirely independently of their intuitive or other extra-axiomatic content – to all of the concepts of empirical science. In this way, in particular, Schlick enforces a very general distinction between perfectly precise and definite abstract concepts (*Begriffe*), all of which are taken to be implicitly defined purely formally à la Hilbert, and relatively crude and indefinite sensory images (*Vorstellungen*), which can never have precisely defined meanings. Schlick is thereby able to enforce a parallel general distinction between knowledge (*Erkennen*) and acquaintance (*Kennen*), where the latter involves immediate sensory givenness, but the former requires merely a successful designation of reality, in Schlick's terminology, by abstract concepts. In this way, our characteristically abstract mathematical theories of contemporary physics (especially Einstein's general theory of relativity, of course) can thereby count as successful examples of empirical knowledge (indeed, as paradigmatic of successful empirical knowledge) in spite of – and even because of – their highly nonintuitive character.

As Schlick is well aware, however, a difficult problem lurks precisely here. Since the concepts of contemporary mathematical physics are thus entirely formal and abstract, and are characterized, in particular, solely by implicit definitions having no connection whatsoever with space-perception or any other kind of sensory experience, how is it possible for them to acquire the necessary relation of designation (*Bezeichnung*) or coordination (*Zuordnung*) to empirical reality in the first place? Schlick here proceeds by what he calls the method of coincidences – which is modeled, appropriately, by the use of space-time coordinates in the general theory of relativity. Suppose, for example, that I want to coordinate a particular abstract geometry with physical reality. I have no immediate acquaintance, according to Schlick, with objective

---

[5] For more detailed discussion see Friedman (1997). Compare also Friedman (1999, ch. I, postscript).

physical space but only with the subjective psychological spaces characteristic of my various sensory fields – visual, tactile, and so on. It may happen, however, that I notice singularities or coincidences in a number of sensory fields (the coincidence of the point of my pencil with my finger tip in visual space, for example, or a parallel coincidence in tactile space when I feel the point of the pencil pressed against my finger), and it may further happen that such singularities or coincidences in a number of sensory fields themselves coincide in time, such that one occurs only when the other does (as in the visual and tactile coincidences of finger and pencil point just mentioned). To represent such relationships between different psychological spaces I may then embed them systematically in a single abstract conceptual space, whereby different singularities or coincidences in different sensory spaces are all mapped onto or coordinated with the same quadruple of real numbers representing the space-time coordinates of an objective physical event. In this way, objective physical space first arises as what we might call a conceptual projection of the various intuitive or psychological spaces; and what Schlick calls concrete or ostensive definitions, picking out immediately given objects in one or another sensory field, are thereby embedded within a system of implicit definitions.

Hans Reichenbach, in his *Theory of Relativity and A Priori Knowledge* (1920), takes a less psychological but more Kantian approach to the same problem. In a crucial chapter entitled "Knowledge as Coordination" Reichenbach also begins from the Hilbertian conception of the role of implicit definitions in pure mathematics. In applied mathematics or mathematical physics, however, we are faced, in addition, with the problem of coordinating such an abstract formal system with physical reality. This type of coordination differs from more familiar coordinations (such as purely mathematical mappings, for example), in that only one side of the coordination – the mathematical formulas making up the system of implicit definitions in question – is actually given to us, whereas the other side, physical reality, is in no way given independently but rather must first be defined by the very procedure of coordination itself. Here Reichenbach, like Schlick, appeals to the use of spatiotemporal coordinates in physics, but, unlike Schlick, he also appeals to a distinguished class of physical principles – which Reichenbach calls coordinating principles or axioms of coordination – whose role is precisely to ensure that the coordination we are in the process of setting up is, in an appropriate sense, uniquely defined. Thus in Newtonian physics, for example, the coordinating principles are again the Newtonian laws of motion (recall the Kantian view of these principles), which uniquely define, in the appropriate sense, the class of Newtonian inertial frames of reference or coordinate systems. In the special theory of relativity, however, the relevant principles are the modified Einsteinian laws of motion, which uniquely define, in the same sense, the class of Lorentzian inertial frames or coordinate systems. In general relativity, finally, the relevant principles serve to pick out the much wider class of coordinates compatible with the variably curved yet infinitesimally Lorentzian (that is, semi-Riemannian) manifold underlying all general relativistic space-time structures.

Reichenbach distinguishes, on this basis, between two meanings of the a priori originally combined in Kant: necessary and unrevisable, fixed for all time, on the one hand, and "constitutive of the concept of the object," on the other (see Reichenbach 1920, 46/1965, 48).[6] Coordinating principles cannot be a priori in the first sense, of course, because we have just seen that they change from theory to theory as our scientific knowledge expands and develops. Nevertheless, they are still a priori in the second sense, Reichenbach contends, for unless they are antecedently in place our mathematical theories have no empirical content – no coordination with physical reality – at all. Indeed, physical reality is first defined or constituted by these principles, insofar as axioms of coordination introduce an element of invariance (and thus objectivity) into our description of nature (under Galilean transformations, Lorentz transformations, and so on). Therefore, although coordinating principles or axioms of coordination certainly change with time, and under pressure of empirical findings, they are still to be sharply distinguished from what Reichenbach calls axioms of connection – from ordinary empirical laws such as the law of universal gravitation, in the context of Newtonian physics, or Maxwell's

---

[6] For further discussion see Friedman (1999, ch. 3). Here and in what follows I give page numbers for the German original followed by those of the English translation (except where the paragraph references remain the same). All translations are my own.

equations for the electromagnetic field, in the context of special relativity.

Reichenbach (1920, 110/1965, 116) criticizes Schlick's *General Theory of Knowledge* for objecting to "the correct part of Kant's theory, namely, the constitutive significance of coordinating principles," and this sparked a correspondence between the two in the fall of 1920.[7] Schlick explains that he entirely accepts the distinction between constitutive principles and ordinary empirical laws. Indeed, it is only because he finds this distinction so obvious that he may have neglected sufficiently to emphasize its importance in his earlier work. Nevertheless, it is inappropriate, Schlick argues, to characterize such constitutive principles as examples of a priori knowledge in the sense of Kant. We should rather characterize them as conventions in the sense of Henri Poincaré – judgments that are neither true nor false but are simply laid down as stipulations. Reichenbach replies that Schlick's argument simply amounts to a terminological recommendation, and he holds, accordingly, that they now appear to be in complete agreement on all essential points. Nevertheless, Reichenbach accepts Schlick's terminological recommendation in his work on the foundations of geometry and relativity from this time forward, when he now consistently uses the terminology of convention and eschews all further defense of the Kantian idea of a priori constitutive principles (see Reichenbach 1922; 1924; 1928).[8]

This exchange with Reichenbach also left an indelible impression on Schlick. In particular, in the second (1925) edition of *General Theory of Knowledge* Schlick added an entirely new section entitled "Definitions, Conventions, and Empirical Judgements."[9] Whereas the first edition had recognized only two types of definitions, axiomatic or implicit and concrete or ostensive, the second edition makes a threefold distinction between implicit definitions (which

---

[7] For a useful discussion of this exchange see Coffa (1991, 201–4), and compare also Friedman (1999).

[8] Reichenbach came to have qualms about Poincaré's conventionalism as well, since it increasingly appeared to him to neglect the properly empirical element in physical geometry. But this aspect of Reichenbach's mature view lies outside the scope of the present discussion.

[9] This is § 11 of the second edition. For further discussions (and references) concerning the material in this paragraph and the next see Friedman (2002).

make no reference to empirical reality at all), concrete or ostensive definitions (which directly coordinate a concept with an intuitively presented object of acquaintance), and what he now calls conventions – which, as Poincaré has shown, are crucial for an understanding of how we achieve a coordination between concepts and empirical reality in the mathematical exact sciences. Schlick illustrates the point with the example of time measurement. We might begin, for example, by stipulating that the times during which the earth rotates once around its axis are equal (sidereal day). This, Schlick explains, is "at bottom a concrete definition, because the stipulation refers to a concrete process [taking place] in a single heavenly body given only once." We find, however, that it is simpler and more convenient to allow corrections to this stipulation (arising from tidal friction, for example) based on "the greatest possible simplicity of the laws of nature" – that is, the "fundamental equations of physics" such as the laws of motion – and it is here, and only here, that we find conventions properly speaking. Thus conventions in the present sense are not concrete coordinations to particular physical processes (as in what we now call operational definitions, for example), but rather fundamental principles of mathematical physics providing general prescriptions for establishing and then correcting such concrete coordinations. The laws of motion, for example, supply such principles for the measurement of time, just as the laws of geometry do for the measurement of space.

The principles Schlick now characterizes as conventions, therefore, are just what Reichenbach (1920) had called coordinating principles or axioms of coordination. The one point Schlick adds to Reichenbach's earlier work is the idea, due to Poincaré, that it is only simplicity, in the end, that determines our otherwise arbitrary choice of such principles. In the case of time measurement, for example, we may choose to define the equality of times by some other stipulation – by using the heartbeat of the Dalai Lama, say, rather than the laws of motion applied to celestial bodies. Such a stipulation would in no way be false, for it is only on the basis of some or another such convention that the notions of temporal equality and uniformity can be empirically well defined in the first place. But such a nonstandard stipulation would introduce intolerable complications into our overall system of mathematical physics, and this is why we prefer the stipulation based on the laws of motion. Similarly, as Schlick argues in the fourth (1922) edition of *Space and Time in Contemporary Physics*, we are free to retain Euclidean geometry in the context of the general theory of relativity if we wish, but this, too, would introduce intolerable complications into our physics. We therefore prefer the standard convention for coordinating general relativity with physical reality given by Einstein's principle of equivalence, which asserts, as Schlick understands it, that the laws of special relativity must be valid in infinitesimally small regions. And this then implies that we use an infinitesimally Lorentzian or semi-Riemannian manifold of variable curvature to represent physical space-time rather than a Euclidean structure. It is not that Euclidean geometry is false; it is simply less simple and therefore less convenient.

During the same time that Schlick and Reichenbach were corresponding – and, as a result, revising their earlier ideas – about coordinating principles, constitutive principles, and conventions, Carnap was completing his first published work, his doctoral dissertation *Der Raum*, defended in 1921 and published in 1922. Here Carnap develops his own neo-Kantian solution to the problem of coordination based on a threefold distinction between *formal, physical*, and *intuitive* space.[10] The first two have essentially the same meanings they had in Schlick and Reichenbach, but intuitive space is a pure form of sensible intuition in the sense of Kant; it does not, however, have the full metrical structure of Euclidean space but merely the topological structure of *infinitesimally* Euclidean space – the structure common to all Riemannian manifolds, whether of constant or variable curvature. The key point is that, since all objects of physics are "contained" in our spatial pure form of sensible intuition, the mathematical structures of formal space apply to the objects of physical experience through the mediation of intuitive space. Unlike in Kant, however, the structure provided by intuitive space is merely topological, whereas mathematical physics of course requires a full metrical structure. Here Carnap appeals to the conventionalist account of metrical structure in general relativity earlier articulated by Schlick; and so Carnap distinguishes, accordingly, between two different levels of "experience-constituting" form.

---

[10] For futher discussion (and references) concerning the material in this paragraph see Friedman (1999, ch. 2).

Topological form is necessary or unique, and it is a priori given by the pure form of our sensible intuition, whereas metrical form is not necessary but "optional" (*Wahlfrei*), and it can be given only by a convention or stipulation in the sense previously defended by Schlick and Poincaré.[11]

In the years immediately following the publication of *Der Raum*, Carnap abandoned his commitment to the synthetic a priori and therefore his commitment to an a priori intuitive space functioning as a pure form of sensible intuition. Nevertheless, the distinction between two levels of experience-constituting form – topological or necessary form and metrical or optional form – continued to shape his conception of how the abstract structures of mathematical physics relate to the concrete contents of sensory experience. And Carnap made essential use of precisely this distinction in seeking a new kind of accommodation between empiricist and Kantian strands of thought. In particular, in "Dreidimensionalität des Raumes und Kausalität" (Three-Dimensionality of Space and Causality, 1924) Carnap distinguishes between the primary world of subjective immediate sense experience and the secondary world of three-dimensional, causally ordered physical objects. The primary world is the product of a "necessary formation" yielding a particular (topological) spatio-temporal ordering of the originally given data of sense (one temporal dimension and two spatial dimensions), and no experience is possible at all without this primary ordering. The secondary world, by contrast, is the product of an "optional forma-tion" – involving a large variety of possible alternatives – yielding the full four-dimensional causal structure described in physics; and so it depends, as before, on a conventional stipulation in the sense of Schlick. Thus empiricism or "positivism" is correct in stressing the fundamental importance of the primary world, and in emphasizing that the world described by mathematical physics has no uniquely necessary structure. But Kantianism and neo-Kantianism are equally correct in stressing the constitutive or "object-generating" function of the secondary world and, in particular, the necessity for

---

[11] Physical geometry remains just as empirical as any other part of physical theory, however, for the requisite convention must depend, in the end, on the overall simplicity of our total system of geometry plus physics – precisely the criterion earlier invoked by Schlick in this same context.

some or another such causal structure (with one temporal and *three* spatial dimensions) for finding univocal lawlikeness in the objects of experience.[12]

We know that *Der logische Aufbau der Welt* was written largely in the years 1922–5, during the very period, as we have seen, that Reichenbach, Schlick, and Carnap himself were struggling with issues about coordination, constitution, and convention initially arising in the context of Einstein's general theory of relativity. Indeed, Carnap and Reichenbach had struck up a correspondence during these years, based on their common interest in "methodological problems created by Einstein's theory of relativity," and, after the two had met one another at a conference they coorganized in Erlangen in 1923, Reichenbach put Carnap in contact with Schlick (see Carnap 1963, 14, 16, 20). As a result, Schlick invited Carnap to lecture in Vienna in 1925, where he presented lectures to Schlick's Philosophical Circle based on the *Aufbau* project – then entitled *Entwurf einer Konstitutionstheorie der Erkenntnisgegenstände* (Outline of a Constitutional Theory of the Objects of Experience). Carnap returned to the University of Vienna in 1926 as Schlick's assistant, with his *Entwurf* serving as his *Habilitation*, and what we now know as the Vienna Circle was born. The assimilation of Carnap's *Aufbau* project was one of the first orders of business.

As recent scholarship has made abundantly clear, the standard picture of the *Aufbau* as primarily a contribution to radical empiricist or phenomenalist foundationalism is at the very least grossly exaggerated (see, e.g., Haack 1977; Sauer 1985; 1987; Richardson 1990; 1992; 1998; Friedman 1999, Part Two). I now want to argue that it is much better understood in the context of the issues we have just been discussing – the problem of forging a new kind of relation between abstract mathematical structures and concrete

---

[12] See Carnap (1924, 108–9): "The neo-Kantian philosophy is not acquainted with the primary world, since their conception that the forms of experience [of the secondary world] are necessary and unique prevents them from recognizing the distinction between the primary and the secondary world. Their true achievement, namely, the demonstration of the object-generating function of thought, remains untouched, however, and underlies our conception of the secondary world as well. The positivist philosophy, on the other hand, recognizes only the primary world; the secondary world is only an optional reorganization of the former, effected on grounds of economy." (Here Carnap clearly has *Machian* "positivism" in mind.)

sensory experience in the wake of Einstein's general relativity theory, which provided, as we have seen, its immediate background. In this context, I believe, the *Aufbau* is best understood, in fact, as a further articulation and generalization of the program begun in Carnap (1924) – a program aiming, in particular, to exhibit the complementary strengths of both "positivism" and more Kantian approaches to epistemology.[13]

Thus, we again begin with the primary world of subjective immediate sensory experience, now called the realm of the auto-psychological, and our initial aim is to characterize the topological formal structure distinctive of this realm. Under the influence of Gestalt psychology, Carnap views the given stream of experience in an originally holistic fashion, not yet differentiated into individual sensations. Our task, accordingly, is to explain how such individual sensory elements (the basic elements) are then differentiated, on the basis of an originally holistic basic relation of remembrance-of-part-similarity (compare note 13). This task is solved by the method of quasi analysis, the main result of which is that we are finally able to distinguish one sensory field from another (visual, tactile, auditory, and so on) on the basis of their purely formal properties. Using the topological definition of dimension number recently contributed by Karl Menger, for example, we can say that the visual field is the unique sense modality having exactly five dimensions – two of spatial position and three of color quality. This characterization uniquely picks out the visual field from all other sense modalities by what Carnap calls a purely structural definite description making no reference whatsoever to intuitively felt sensory qualities.

---

[13] See again the passage quoted in note 12. An analogous well-known "conciliatory" passage occurs in the *Aufbau* itself. See Carnap (1928, § 75): "The merit of having discovered the necessary basis of the constitutional system thereby belongs to two entirely different, and often mutually hostile, philosophical tendencies. *Positivism* has stressed that the sole *material* for cognition lies in the undigested [*unverarbeitet*] experiential *given*; here is to be sought the *basic elements* of the constitutional system. *Transcendental idealism*, however, especially the neo-Kantian tendency (Rickert, Cassirer, Bauch), has rightly emphasized that these elements do not suffice; *order-posits* must be added, our 'basic relations.'" For further discussion see Haack (1977), Sauer (1985), (1987), Richardson (1990), (1992), (1998), Friedman (1999, Part Two).

The use of such purely structural definite descriptions – free of all ostensive reference to essentially private features of experience – is, according to Carnap, characteristic of modern mathematical physics, which, more than any other discipline, has thus implemented a necessary "desubjectivization" of experience.[14] Therefore, if we can characterize even the realm of subjective sensory experience in this way, we will have taken an essential first step in explaining how modern abstract mathematics can apply to concrete experience. To complete the explanation, however, it is necessary to consider what Carnap had earlier called the secondary world – now called the realm of the physical. Our initial move is to set up a correspondence or coordination between color points in the visual field and colored surfaces of ordinary perceptual objects by projecting the former onto abstract points in four-dimensional real number space subject to a number of constraints (continuity, connectedness, and so on), yielding what Carnap calls the perceptual world. We then construct the true physical world, the world of physics, by the "physico-qualitative coordination" (*physikalisch-qualitativ Zuordnung*) – which, for example, projects colored points on physical surfaces, in accordance with current electrodynamic theory, onto mathematical micro-physical features of such surfaces responsible for scattering light of corresponding frequencies. It is only at this stage, that of abstract mathematical physics, that what Carnap calls a univocal consistent intersubjectivization of experience is possible.[15]

Carnap's procedure is reminiscent of Schlick's in *General Theory of Knowledge*, but there are also some very important differences between the two. In the first place, whereas abstract mathematical structure, for Schlick, is given by Hilbertian implicit definitions, the purely structural definite descriptions employed by Carnap are explicit definitions: they aim to pick out a definite object in the

---

[14] See Carnap (1928, § 16), which takes precisely the conceptual apparatus of general relativity ("four-dimensional tensor or vector fields," "the network of world-lines with the relations of coincidence and proper time") as paradigmatic of this "desubjectivization."

[15] For this claim, in the context of the constitution of the world of physics by the "physico-qualitative coordination," see Carnap (1928, § 136). What Carnap appears to have in mind here is an argument analogous to Carnap (1924), according to which only the fully quantitative world of physics yields a spatio-temporal structure exhibiting univocal lawlikeness (see the paragraph to which note 12 above is appended) – indeed, Carnap (1928, § 136) refers to Carnap (1924).

domain of the constitutional system by specifying it as the *unique* such object satisfying purely formal conditions.[16] The visual field, for example, is the one and only sense modality having exactly five dimensions. The perceptual world is the one and only coordination of color points in the visual field to abstract quadruples in four-dimensional real number space satisfying Carnap's constraints. Finally, in the case of the physical world, the formal principles used to enforce a parallel condition of uniqueness are just the coordinating principles, constitutive principles, or conventions that had been earlier discussed in the context of the general theory of relativity.

This becomes clear when Carnap introduces the physico-qualitative coordination and the world of physics in section 136 of the *Aufbau*, which refers to his earlier discussions of this problem in both Carnap (1924) and "Über die Aufgabe der Physik" (On the Task of Physics, 1923) (compare note 15). The aim of this last paper, in particular, is to generalize the account of physical coordinating principles – viewed as conventions in the sense of Schlick and Poincaré – originally presented in the chapter on physical space in *Der Raum*, so that such principles quite generally are chosen by conventional stipulation from a number of alternatives, on the basis, once again, of overall simplicity. Accordingly, Carnap (1923, 97) characterizes such principles as follows: "[They are] *synthetic a priori propositions*, however, not exactly in the Kantian transcendental-critical sense. For this would mean that they express necessary conditions of the objects of experience, themselves conditioned by the forms of intuition and of thought. But then there could only be *one* possible form for the content of [a system of physics]. In reality, however, its construction is left in many ways to our choice."[17]

---

[16] Carnap (1928, § 15) makes this point very clearly while referring to Schlick, Hilbert, and Carnap (1927).

[17] Carnap (1923, 90) begins as follows: "After a long time during which the question of the sources of physical cognition has been violently contested, it may perhaps already be said today that pure empiricism has lost its dominance. That the construction of physics cannot be based on experimental results alone, but must also apply non-empirical principles has indeed been already been proclaimed for a long time by philosophers." Such "non-empirical principles," as the context makes clear, are precisely what Poincaré (and Hugo Dingler) had called conventions. Thus Carnap here has in mind an accommodation between

In the *Aufbau*, however, Carnap decisively rejects all suggestions of the synthetic a priori. For the relevant coordinating principles for mathematical physics now function as just the conditions that ensure uniqueness in the purely structural definite description by which the world of physics is first introduced by definition. So Carnap can now assert, more generally, that there are two and only two cognitive sources at work in the constitution of our scientific knowledge – objects are uniquely picked out from all other objects by definition (*explicit* definition) and then further investigated and characterized by experience: "According to the conception of constitutional theory there are no other components in cognition than these two – the conventional and the empirical – and thus no synthetic a priori [components]" (see Carnap 1928, § 179).[18] Precisely because Carnap has here converted Schlick's implicit definitions into explicit definitions, he is now able to give very clear and specific meaning to the idea that the relevant coordinating principles or conventions are nonempirical as well as nonsynthetic.

This leads to an even deeper point of difference. Schlick's formulation of the problem of coordination is sharply and explicitly dualistic. On the one side are the abstract, entirely nonintuitive conceptual structures given by a formal system of implicit definitions; on the other are the concrete, entirely nonconceptual sensory representations with which we are immediately acquainted. By replacing implicit definitions with purely structural definite descriptions Carnap has finally transcended this dualistic problematic as well. For, as Carnap himself points out in the course of distinguishing his method from Schlick's, structural definite descriptions achieve uniqueness only by making essential reference to an empirical, extralogical domain (see again Carnap 1928, § 15).[19] In the present case our empirical domain is given as the set of elementary experiences on which the basic relation is defined. The visual field is the unique five-dimensional sense class constructible

"positivism" and "neo-Kantianism" analogous to that envisioned in Carnap (1924).

[18] This same section also contains Carnap's explicit attempt conclusively to differentiate himself from the Marburg School of neo-Kantianism. For further discussion see Friedman (1999, ch. 6, postscript).

[19] In this same section Carnap refers also to Reichenbach's (1920) conception of "knowledge as coordination."

from these elementary experiences; the perceptual world is the unique assignment of colors to space-time points (satisfying Carnap's constraints) constructible in this same domain; and so on. In sharp contrast to a system of implicit definitions, then, a constitutional system in Carnap's sense is already attached to the empirical world from the very beginning, and there can be no problem at all of coordinating purely abstract conceptual structures to entirely non-conceptual intuitive sensory content. The earlier problem of coordination addressed by Schlick's method of coincidences (and by Reichenbach's conception of "knowledge as coordination") is instead entirely absorbed within the constitutional system itself, as we construct a purely structural coordination or mapping between one part of the system (the autopsychological realm) and another part of the very same system (the physical realm).

Carnap has thereby transformed an initially epistemological problem into a purely logical project. The problem of coordinating conceptual structure and sensory experience in general is solved simply by including what we would now call a nonlogical primitive term at the basis of our constitutional system, and the more specific problem of coordinating the abstract structures of modern mathematical physics with concrete empirical reality is solved by constructing a logical coordination or mapping between the autopsychological and physical realms. As I have suggested, however, none of these logical devices are motivated by the concerns with epistemic certainty typical of empiricist foundationalism, nor is Carnap here particularly concerned with the problems in the foundations of mathematics addressed by traditional logicism.[20] Carnap turns to these problems in earnest only after the completion of the *Aufbau*, and this work is carried out during a period (the late 1920s and early '30s) when logicism in the traditional Frege-Russell sense is generally acknowledged to have failed. Carnap's response to this situation – the classical foundational debate between logicism, formalism, and intuitionism – is his *Logical Syntax of Language*

---

[20] Carnap (1928, § 107) simply assumes, with reference to *Principia Mathematica*, that all of mathematics can unproblematically be reduced to logic. Carnap's relatively sophisticated understanding of the type theory of *Principia Mathematica* does play an essential role in his epistemological project, however, for we can turn implicit definitions into explicit definitions, in general, only by a device equivalent to quantification over sets or classes.

(1934), which attempts to forge a kind of synthesis of all three positions that diffuses or dissolves this debate by revealing the various correct elements in all three positions.[21]

Carnap's idea, more specifically, is to reinterpret each of the three positions in question as *proposals* to formulate the total language of science in one or another way – using one or another set of formal rules as providing the underlying logic of this language. Intuitionism is the proposal to use only the weaker rules of the intuitionistic logical calculus (in which the law of excluded middle is no longer universally valid) as our underlying logic. Formalism is the proposal to use the stronger rules of classical logic, but only if an appropriate consistency proof in the meta-language is possible – a proof that proceeds by representing both classical logic and mathematics as axiomatized within a single formal system. Logicism, finally, is the proposal to use both classical logic and mathematics in a formulation that makes it clear that logical and mathematical rules are of the same kind – that they are, in an appropriate sense, analytic. Logicism also emphasizes, at the same time, that the application of mathematics in empirical science is central, so that, in particular, we focus our attention on an axiomatization of total science – formal as well as empirical – in which the analytic sentences are clearly demarcated from the synthetic or empirical sentences (see especially Carnap 1934, §§ 16, 17, 78, 84).

Each of these proposals has something important to be said for it. Intuitionism is correct that it is perfectly possible to formulate alternatives to the familiar classical rules – which intrinsically, as it were, have just as much claim to logical "correctness." Indeed, using such weaker logical rules is certainly safer if one is particularly concerned to avoid the possibility of contradiction in the system of mathematics. Moreover, formalism is also correct, in Carnap's view, to have similarly emphasized the importance of the question of consistency, and to have pointed out, in addition, that this question can fruitfully be addressed by the program of meta-mathematics.

---

[21] Carnap's evolving responses to the "foundations crisis" of the late 1920s include Carnap (1930), (1931). For further discussion see Friedman (1999, ch. 9, § II). See also Goldfarb (1996). In this connection, in particular, it is important to note that Carnap was the only thinker in the logical empiricist tradition to articulate a developed response to either the foundations crisis of the late 1920s or Gödel's incompleteness results, which, in a sense, marked the end of this period.

Unfortunately, as Gödel's results seem conclusively to have shown, a consistency proof of the required kind appears to be impossible. Overall, then, Carnap prefers the logicist proposal. We formulate both classical logic and mathematics within a single system of total science – leaving aside, for the moment, the question of consistency – because this provides us with the simplest and most convenient version of the mathematics needed for empirical science. In addition, even through we can no longer hope to reduce classical mathematics to logic à la Frege and Russell,[22] we can still preserve the insights of classical logicism that logical and mathematical sentences, unlike empirical and physical sentences, are analytic – entirely dependent on the meanings of their logical (as opposed to nonlogical or descriptive) terms.[23]

Carnap's (dis-)solution of the classical debate in the foundations of mathematics can therefore be seen as a generalization, of sorts, of the relativized and/or conventional conception of the a priori found in the earlier work of Schlick, Reichenbach, and Carnap himself. Just as, in this earlier work, there is no fixed a priori framework of physical theory (that is, no fixed set of coordinating principles), now, in *Logical Syntax*, there is no fixed a priori framework – no uniquely "correct" set of formal rules – definitive of logic and mathematics. Just as (at least after Reichenbach is converted to Poincaré's terminology by Schlick) the a priori framework of physics is the product, in the end, of a conventional or pragmatic choice based on the overall simplicity and tractability of our total physical theory, now the a priori framework definitive of logic and mathematics themselves is similarly the product of a conventional or pragmatic choice based on the very same considerations.[24]

---

[22] Classical mathematics, for Carnap, is now formulated by taking all mathematical terms as primitive and all problematic set-theoretical principles as axiomatic – including the axiom of infinity and the axiom of choice. For further discussion of Carnap's philosophy of mathematics see Friedman (1999, Part Three), Goldfarb and Ricketts (1992).

[23] For the crucial distinction between logical and descriptive terms, and the resulting distinction between analytic sentences (L-rules) and synthetic sentences (P-rules), see Carnap (1934, §§ 50, 51). For further discussion see again Friedman (1999, Part Three).

[24] For further discussion of the relationship between Reichenbach (1920) and Carnap (1934) see Friedman (1999, ch. 3).

Nevertheless, by the time Carnap is immersed in the program of *Logical Syntax* almost all traces of the epistemological problem that had motivated this earlier work – the problem of establishing a coordination between abstract logical and mathematical structure and concrete sensory experience – have disappeared. To be sure, there is one place where Carnap touches on, as an example, the earlier problems concerning physical geometry that had so exercised Schlick, Reichenbach, and the Carnap of *Der Raum*; but this same section makes it perfectly clear that all of these earlier problems are now entirely subordinated to the new, purely logical problem of establishing a sharp formal distinction between logical expressions, on the one side, and nonlogical or descriptive expression, on the other.[25] And the entire point of this distinction, of course, is to make possible a similarly formal distinction between analytic and synthetic sentences in the following section (see note 23). It is by no means surprising, then, that Carnap, during the same period, makes a point of explicitly renouncing all ambitions to address epistemological problems in the earlier sense at all – including the epistemological problems addressed in the *Aufbau*. Epistemology, in all of its traditional guises (even in the purified and attenuated form it took in the *Aufbau*), is now to be replaced by the entirely new discipline of *Wissenschaftslogik* (the logic of science) – the program of formulating and logically investigating a variety of forms for the total language of science, so that educated pragmatic decisions among them may then be made.[26]

It is in the context of this program, of course, that Carnap first places the concept of analytic truth at the very center of his philosophy, to undergird a sharp distinction, in particular, between the logical investigation of possible language forms or linguistic frameworks, on the one side, and empirical investigation of the natural world within one or another such framework, on the other. And it is at precisely this point, accordingly, that Quine's opposition to the concept of analyticity acquires its force – as an opposition, in particular, to Carnap's attenuated version of classical logicism. For

[25] See Carnap (1934, § 50), which illustrates the distinction between logical and descriptive terms by contrasting the metric in a space of constant curvature with the variably curved space-time structure of general relativity. For further discussion see Friedman (1999, chs. 3, 4).

[26] See Carnap (1936); for further discussion, see Richardson (1996).

Carnap can defend this view, as we have seen, only by operating with a very strong version of higher-order logic, where, in addition, all the problematic set-theoretical principles that had been explicitly flagged as such within the traditional debate (such as the axiom of infinity and the axiom of choice) are simply taken as axiomatic (see note 22). Quine now suggests, against this background, that logic should rather be identified with first-order logic, and, once we make this move, it follows that classical mathematics, with its very strong existential commitments, is not part of logic after all. It should rather be viewed as formulated within the now entirely autonomous mathematical discipline of axiomatic set theory, where, in partic- ular, its existential commitments stand out clearly and explicitly from the first-order logical background via quantified first-order logical variables. Moreover, and this is perhaps the most important point, Carnap appears to have no ready resources for easily blocking this move. Carnap himself has argued that our choice of logic is made on purely pragmatic grounds, and Quine can now suggest, quite plausibly, that precisely such grounds actually favor first-order logic – on the basis of such factors as its simplicity, economy, the availability of a complete proof procedure, and so on. In this way, Quine can construct a kind of reductio, as it were, of Carnap's pragmatic version of logicism: we decide on first-order logic on broadly pragmatic grounds, and, once we do so, Carnap's attenuated defense of the analyticity of classical mathematics therefore fails.

The route from here to Quine's own form of radical epistemolog- ical holism is now quite short. The very strong existential com- mitments of classical mathematics have been encapsulated within the bound first-order variables of axiomatic set theory – an autono- mous mathematical discipline going far beyond the first-order logi- cal background of the language in which it is formulated. How, then, are these strong existential commitments to be justified? Based on ontological and epistemological scruples deriving from an under- lying philosophical outlook sympathetic to traditional nominalism and empiricism, Quine had first hoped entirely to avoid such com- mitments on the basis of a program of "constructive nominalism." Once he acknowledges that this program cannot succeed, however, his characteristic form of radical epistemological holism then pre- sents itself as an attractive empiricist alternative. For we can now view our total system of natural science as a conjunction of set theory with various scientific theories standardly so called – a conjunction which is tested as a whole by the deduction (in first-order logic) of various empirical consequences within this total system. The existential commitments of set theory are thus empirically justified to the same extent, and in the same way, as are our "posits" of any other theoretical entities in natural science.[27]

Here we encounter a very important point of difference between Carnap's empiricism and Quine's. Carnap's conception is quite distinct from traditional empiricism, in that sense experience, for Carnap, has significance for science only if it is already framed and structured within the abstract forms supplied by logic and mathematics, so that undigested or immediate sense experience, by contrast, is merely private and subjective, with no objective scientific meaning at all. Thus experience, for Carnap, has fundamentally the same meaning it had in Kant, and it is for this reason, in the Preface to the second edition of the *Aufbau*, that Carnap describes his view (clearly echoing Kant) as "a synthesis of traditional empiricism with traditional rationalism."[28] Quine's view, by contrast, is much closer to traditional empiricism, in that he takes more ordinary sense experience – in a relatively undigested and not yet mathematically structured form – as the fundamental paradigm for all other types of knowledge. The problem is always to see how other types of knowledge, especially abstract mathematical knowledge, can be justified or explained in terms of this particular paradigm, and it is

---

[27] This general line of thought, taking its starting point from the acknowledged failure of Goodman and Quine (1947), is initiated in Quine (1948) and continues to play a central role throughout his philosophical career: see, e.g., Quine (1955, § VI), (1960, § 55).

[28] For the full passage see Carnap (1961, x/1967, vi): "This common thesis [of empiricism and rationalism] is often formulated in the following simplified version: the senses supply the material of knowledge, reason works up [*verarbeitet*] this material into an ordered system of knowledge. The task therefore consists in arriving at a synthesis of traditional empiricism with traditional rationalism. Earlier empiricism correctly emphasized the contribution of the senses, but it did not recognize the significance and peculiarity of logical-mathematical formation. Rationalism, to be sure, grasped this significance, but it believed that reason could not only supply form, but it could also create new content from itself ('a priori')." Compare notes 3, 12, 13, and 17, together with the paragraphs to which they are appended, for the evolving relationship between Carnap's characteristic conception of (scientific) experience and Kantian and neo-Kantian conceptions.

this problem, as we have seen, that ultimately issues in Quine's radical epistemological holism.

As soon as we grasp this distinction, however, it is clear that Quine's version of empiricism is in no way compulsory. Indeed, from the point of view of modern mathematical natural science, I believe, it is simply perverse to maintain ontological and epistemological scruples concerning our mathematical knowledge on the basis of a prior commitment to traditional empiricism – to take more ordinary sense experience as epistemically paradigmatic and mathematical knowledge, by contrast, as philosophically problematic. This becomes especially clear in the development of Einstein's general theory of relativity, for this theory is only possible in the first place against the background of a particularly abstract form of modern mathematics having no intrinsic connection with spatial perception or any other kind of "ordinary" sense experience. It was for precisely this reason, as we have seen, that this theory, in particular, led to both a rejection of Kant's original doctrine of synthetic a priori principles and a new, relativized conception of such principles arising from the problem of coordinating modern abstract mathematics with concrete sensory experience. And it was for precisely this reason, as we have also seen, that Einstein's theory did not result, for the logical empiricists, in a revived version of traditional empiricism, but rather in a transformation – and relativization – of a more Kantian approach to epistemology.

It is true that a rejection of the synthetic a priori was definitive of what these philosophers meant by their empiricism. In particular, Kant's original conception of synthetic a priori knowledge was now clearly unacceptable from the point of view of the most recent scientific developments – both within pure mathematics and logic and within mathematical natural science. Modern mathematics can no longer be viewed as rooted in our spatio-temporal intuition or any other kind of sensory experience, but rather concerns abstract formal structures having no intrinsic or immediate empirical interpretation at all. Moreover, in the most recent developments in mathematical physics, principles Kant paradigmatically took to be synthetic a priori (Euclidean geometry and the Newtonian laws of motion) are now quite explicitly overthrown. In response to the first set of developments (especially developments in modern mathematical logic) the logical empiricists opted, on the whole, for some or another version of traditional logicism, culminating in the attenuated form of this doctrine articulated in Carnap's *Logical Syntax*. In response to the second set of developments, however, the logical empiricists created a dynamical or relativized version of the Kantian a priori: a conception of mathematical natural science as framed by coordinating principles, constitutive principles, or conventions, on the basis of which alone empirical natural science in the proper sense of the word is then possible.

The moral of Quine's work, from this point of view, is that we can no longer maintain both parts of this logical empiricist response to the demise of Kant's synthetic a priori. We can no longer maintain, in particular, that modern mathematics is continuous with logic in the traditional logicist sense of being analytic. But we need not be forced, at the same time, into the Quinean position of radical epistemological holism in which there is nothing left of the a priori at all; for, as I have suggested, this further step is based on an initial – and quite independent – commitment to a rather naïve form of traditional empiricism, which, as we have also seen, is quite disconnected from the important advances in modern *empirical* natural science the logical empiricists took as their model.[29] What we are now in a position to see, finally, is that this disconnect between problems in the foundations of pure mathematics and problems in the foundations of mathematical physics was prefigured in the development of logical empiricism itself. It was prefigured, in particular, when Carnap, in the early 1930s, explicitly turned away from the problems in the philosophy of empirical knowledge that had originally motivated his philosophical project and applied

---

[29] For my own attempt to defend a version of the logical empiricist conception of relativized a priori principles against Quinean holism see Friedman (2001). On this conception we view mathematical physics as consisting of three asymmetrical functioning parts: a theory of abstract mathematical structures belonging to pure mathematics (Riemannian manifolds, for example), properly empirical laws formulated using the resources of such structures (such as Einstein's field equations of gravitation), and coordinating principles (such as Einstein's principle of equivalence) giving a physical or empirical interpretation to some particular mathematical concept (coordinating the mathematical notion of geodesic, for example, to the trajectories of freely falling bodies affected only by gravitation). We make no attempt, however, to defend any version of logicism – even Carnap's attenuated version – but simply take modern mathematics at face value. In this way, in particular, we avoid the Carnap-Quine problematic of analytic truth.

himself, almost exclusively, to problems in the foundation of logic and mathematics arising from the "foundations crisis" of the late 1920s.[30] That we are no longer in a position to provide a general philosophical account of the a priori in both pure mathematics and mathematical physics (as both Kant himself had done and the logical empiricists aimed to do) is perhaps the most important outcome of the developments we have examined here.

[30] See notes 21, 21, 22, and 26, together with the paragraphs to which they are appended.

5 Confirmation, Probability, and Logical Empiricism

THE HYPOTHETICO-DEDUCTIVE METHOD

Confirmation and probability are the objects of much attention on the part of logical empiricists. In the first place, confirmation is connected with the ideal represented by the hypothetico-deductive (H-D) method, reflecting the idea that scientific knowledge results from the interplay of laws, advanced by way of hypotheses, and singular statements regarding observational findings. Only well-established scientific laws allow for the application of the H-D method and can provide a sound basis for prediction and explanation. Most logical empiricists regard confirmation as the natural candidate for establishing scientific laws. Another candidate is corroboration, embraced by Popper *contra* logical empiricism.

A lucid description of the interplay between laws and observational statements, which is at the core of the H-D method, is to be found in the following passage by Hans Hahn, anticipating the notion of corroboration:

laws of nature are *hypotheses* which we state tentatively; but in stating such laws of nature we implicitly state many other propositions ... as long as these implicitly stated propositions ... are confirmed by observation, the laws of nature are corroborated and we continue to hold on to them; but if these implicitly asserted propositions are not confirmed by observation, the laws of nature are not corroborated and we go on to replace them by others. (Hahn 1933a/1987, 38)

This process rests on the predictive character of scientific laws, for "so long as the predictions that flow from a scientific proposition come true, or at least come true in an overwhelming majority of cases, the proposition is corroborated" (1933a/1987, 43).

Logical empiricists' concern with confirmation imprints the debate on cognitive significance. Once the problems raised by general sentences (including or not theoretical terms) and predictive statements showed the inadequacy of the verification principle, and a more liberalized version of empiricism came into play,[1] it led immediately to confirmation and probability. As a matter of fact, Carnap first mentioned the notion of "degree of confirmation" – the key concept of his logical interpretation of probability – towards the end of "Testability and Meaning" (1936–7), after having proposed a revision of verificationism, by means of the theory of partial definitions. In a similar vein, around the same years Reichenbach developed a probabilistic theory of cognitive significance in an attempt to go beyond verifiability (see Reichenbach 1936).

There is a whole array of positions characterizing the attitude taken by logical empiricists towards confirmation and probability. While both Carnap and Reichenbach saw confirmation and probability intertwined, other authors, including Richard von Mises and Friedrich Waismann, addressed probability quite apart from confirmation. Conversely, Carl Gustav Hempel devoted strenuous efforts to the clarification of a "qualitative" notion of confirmation that he did not regard as strictly linked to probability. Probability was for Hempel somewhat of a side interest that he took up when writing his dissertation under Reichenbach but did not cultivate much in his later writings.[2]

To be sure, probability was for logical empiricists an object of interest of its own, independently of confirmation, as an ingredient of contemporary science. Their concern for probability is testified by the presence of a session on probability at the conference on the "Epistemology of the Exact Sciences" held in Prague in 1929, whose proceedings were printed in the first issue of *Erkenntnis*. This publication, which includes contributions by Hans Reichenbach, Richard von Mises, Paul Hertz, Friedrich Waismann, and Herbert Feigl, addresses probability in connection with the crisis undergone

---

[1] The story of this debate has been told among others by Hempel and Joergensen. See Hempel's "Empiricist Criteria of Cognitive Significance", in (1965, pp. 101–9) and Joergensen (1951).

[2] Hempel wrote only a couple of articles on probability, which are now published in English in Hempel (2000). In these writings he put forward a finitistic variant of Reichenbach's frequentism.

by causality and determinism after the developments of science at the beginning of the twentieth century.

Confirmation can be quantitative or qualitative, depending whether it does or does not admit of degrees. Qualitative confirmation conveys the idea that a general hypothesis is confirmed by observational evidence, in case the latter is in accordance with positive instances of the hypothesis in question. Among those who concentrated on qualitative confirmation, one should mention in the first place Hempel, whose work will be surveyed in Section 2. Quantitative confirmation is expressed in terms of probability values. A sophisticated attempt to develop a logic of quantitative confirmation was made by Carnap, who embedded it in the framework of logical probability. A quantitative notion of confirmation was also worked out by Reichenbach within his frequency theory of probability. The ideas of these authors will be recollected in Section 3.

CONFIRMATION

In his *Studies in the Logic of Confirmation*, Hempel makes an attempt "to give precise definitions of the two nonquantitative relational concepts of confirmation and disconfirmation", through the formulation of some "general objective criteria" (1945, 6). To fulfill this task, he starts by setting the principle that a general hypothesis is confirmed by its positive instances and invalidated by its negative instances, a principle that he calls "Nicod's criterion". Given a hypothesis expressed by a conditional sentence of universal form, the criterion says that such a hypothesis is confirmed by a positive instance, that is, by the observation of an object which satisfies both the antecedent and the consequent of the conditional, whereas it is disconfirmed by a negative instance, that is, by an object which satisfies its antecedent but not its consequent. To this criterion, meant to reflect our intuitive idea of confirmation, Hempel adds an "equivalence condition", saying that if a sentence, expressing a piece of evidence, confirms or disconfirms a hypothesis expressed in a given way, it must be counted as confirming or disconfirming every equivalent formulation of the same hypothesis.

Although intuitive and apparently plausible, these two principles lead immediately to paradoxical results, such as the following. Take the hypothesis (1) "all ravens are black". This is equivalent to (2) "all non-black things are non-ravens" and to (3) "any particular thing is not a raven and/or is black". By Nicod's criterion a sentence stating that an object is not black and not a raven confirms (2), while a sentence stating that an object is not a raven and/or is black confirms (3), but by the equivalence condition these sentences confirm also (1). The unpleasant consequence is that the hypothesis "all ravens are black" is confirmed not only by black ravens, as our intuition would suggest, but also by any object which is not a raven, like a white shoe, or is black, like a lump of coal.

A way out of this paradox was proposed in the forties by Janina Hosiasson-Lindenbaum (Hosiasson-Lindenbaum 1940), building on an idea taken up in subsequent literature by various authors, especially of Bayesian inspiration. It points to a possible way of differentiating between instances of the paradoxical and nonparadoxical kind, on the basis of the fact that a nonparadoxical instance of a hypothesis increases its prior probability to a greater degree than a paradoxical instance. However, a solution of this kind, which is not meant to rule out the paradoxical results, but rather to suggest a way of handling them, falls out of the realm of the qualitative approach embraced by Hempel and calls for a quantitative notion of confirmation.

In an attempt to cope with such difficulties, Hempel added to Nicod's criterion and the equivalence condition some further conditions of adequacy for confirmation. These include the following: "entailment condition" (E): If A entails B, then A confirms B; "converse entailment" (CE): If A entails B, then B confirms A; "special consequence" (SC): If A confirms B, and B entails C, then A confirms C. Notice that, although it cannot be expected that the notion of confirmation satisfies the general version of transitivity – "If A confirms B, and B confirms C, then A confirms C" – a weak transitivity principle is expressed by (SC). Unfortunately, the apparently plausible conditions (CE) and (SC), taken together, lead to a paradox known as the "transitivity paradox". The following example illustrates. Let A be the statement "This apple is green", B a statement expressing the Newtonian theory, and C the conjunction A & B. Then it follows from (CE) that A confirms C. Since C entails B, there immediately follows, by virtue of (SC), that A confirms B. This means that (CE) and (SC) together imply that the statement "This apple is green" confirms the Newtonian theory.

More generally, it follows from (CE) and (SC) that any proposition confirms any proposition. The paradoxical nature of this conclusion consists in the fact that it trivializes confirmation, by contradicting what Mary Hesse calls "the tacit condition that confirmation must be a selective relation" among propositions (1974, 142).

According to Carnap, a main problem of Hempel's approach is that of conflating two concepts of confirmation: one absolute and one relative, which is based on relevance. On the contrary, Carnap distinguishes between confirmation in the absolute sense $p\ (h,\ e)$, defined with reference to the "total" available evidence, and "relevance confirmation" $C\ (h,\ d)\ =\ p\ (h,\ d)\ -\ p\ (h)$, defined as a probability function of two probabilities, namely, the initial probability $p\ (h)$ and the final probability $p\ (h,\ d)$ obtained by updating $p\ (h)$ on the basis of an additional piece of experimental information d. Carnap regards relevance confirmation as the genuine sense in which a hypothesis can be said to be confirmed by the given evidence and calls it "positive relevance" (Carnap 1950a, Introduction and § 86; see also Salmon 1975 on this point). He shows that Hempel's conditions become inadequate if positive relevance is assumed, and concludes that "the task of finding an adequate *explicatum* for the classificatory concept of confirmation defined in ... non-quantitative terms is certainly an interesting problem; but it is chiefly of importance for those who do not believe that an adequate *explicatum* for the quantitative confirmation can be found" (ibid., 467). Carnap's inductive logic is meant to fulfil this task. Hempel himself, in cooperation with Paul Oppenheim and Olaf Helmer, made an attempt at defining a quantitative notion of confirmation, known as H_2O theory, from the initials of its proponents.[3]

Hempel's notion of confirmation is undermined by a further problem, known as "Goodman's paradox". In a number of writings of the late forties and early fifties, culminating with the book *Fact, Fiction, and Forecast*, Nelson Goodman showed that certain hypotheses are not confirmed at all by their positive instances, as

[3] See Hempel and Oppenheim (1945). A parallel article is Helmer and Oppenheim (1945), which appears in the volume of *Philosophy of Science* that also contains Carnap's "On Inductive Logic" (pp. 72–97). Some interesting remarks on the genesis of the H_2O theory of confirmation, which cannot be recollected in detail, are to be found in Rescher (1997).

required by Nicod's criterion. His argument goes as follows: suppose that all emeralds examined before a certain time *t* were green. Up to that time, experimental evidence supports the hypothesis that all emeralds are green, which is confirmed by all sentences stating that emeralds *a*, *b*, *c*, and so forth have been observed to be green. Goodman then introduces the predicate "grue", which has the peculiarity of applying to all things examined before a certain time *t* just in case they are green, but to other things just in case they are blue. What happens before *t* is that, for each sentence stating that a certain emerald is green, there obtains another sentence stating that the same emerald is grue. Such sentences will count as confirming the generalization that all emeralds are grue, which is again well supported by observational evidence. This paradoxical result obviously threatens the predictive character of laws, because before *t* the prediction that all emeralds to be examined after *t* are green, and the prediction that they are grue, are equally admissible and well supported by observation, but if an emerald observed after time *t* is grue, it is blue, not green. "Thus although we are well aware which of the two incompatible predictions is genuinely confirmed, they are equally well confirmed according to our present definition. ... We are left once again with the intolerable result that anything confirms anything" (Goodman 1955, 74–5).

Goodman's problem calls attention to the difference between lawlike hypotheses and accidental generalizations. Predicates like "grue" are not "projectible", in the sense that they do not allow one to pass from observed to unobserved cases, and should not appear in the formulation of lawlike hypotheses. However, discriminating between lawlike and accidental generalizations has proved a far from easy task, as testified by the ongoing debate on this issue (see Stalker 1994 in this connection). Goodman's way out of this paradox appeals to the notion of "entrenchment", based on the "record of past projections" of predicates (94). But this is a pragmatical notion, whose acceptance forces one to abandon the syntactical approach to confirmation – a conclusion that was later accepted also by Hempel.

The search for a solution of the problems raised by qualitative confirmation has eventually taken the path of quantitative confirmation. The main trend in this connection is represented by Bayesianism, whose basic idea – namely, that an initial evaluation of probability is updated in the light of new information, to result in a final probability evaluation – offers a natural way of dealing with confirmation in a probabilistic fashion. As argued in the next section, both Carnap and Reichenbach, albeit supporters of different interpretations of probability, endorsed Bayesian method.

The inductivist approach embraced by the majority of logical empiricists was strongly criticized by their contemporary Karl Popper, upholder of a version of the H-D method based on an uncompromising form of deductivism. According to Popper, scientific knowledge is not attained by induction, and it makes no sense to talk about the verification, or even the confirmation, of general hypotheses. On the contrary, scientific knowledge is acquired by means of a procedure that is modeled upon the kind of inference known as *modus tollens*. A hypothesis, usually in the form of an implication, is asserted by way of a conjecture, and some means of refuting it through a comparison with experimental evidence is sought. In case observational data disprove one of the consequences of such a hypothesis, it is falsified. According to Popper, a decisive merit of falsification amounts to its being a conclusive method. In fact, one negative instance is enough to refute the initial hypothesis, whereas verification is a never ending procedure, because it would require an infinity of positive instances to verify inductively a general hypothesis.

Popper's falsificationist methodology by "conjectures and refutations" embodies a notion of corroboration, defined in terms of resistance to severe tests. Degree of corroboration is not a probability, but it is a function of probabilities that can vary between -1 and $+1$ (see Popper 1934). As a matter of fact, the probabilities that enter in the determination of the degree of corroboration are the same employed by Bayesian method, namely, the probabilities of a certain hypothesis and a given evidence, and the likelihood of the evidence relative to the hypothesis in question. In view of this, a number of authors have compared Popper's corroboration method with Bayesian confirmation, in spite of Popper's fierce opposition to Bayesianism. (On this point see Gillies 1998, Festa 1999, and Kuipers 2000.)

PROBABILITY

The logical empiricists' debate on the nature of probability shows two major trends, namely, the frequency interpretation embraced by the Berlin group, and the logical interpretation, more popular in the Viennese milieu, which was fully developed by Carnap in his American years.

The idea that probability is strictly connected to frequencies traces back to the origin of the notion of probability in the seventeenth century, but was developed into a full-blown interpretation of probability in the nineteenth century by Robert Leslie Ellis and John Venn. A decisive contribution to this interpretation was given by Richard von Mises and Hans Reichenbach. Starting in the second decade of the last century, von Mises worked out a view of probability as relative frequency, meant to apply to the phenomena described by the natural sciences, and in particular by statistical mechanics. The fundamental notion, within von Mises's perspective, is that of "collective", defined on the basis of two fundamental conditions: firstly, the relative values of its attributes must possess limiting values; secondly, these limiting values must remain the same in all partial sequences which may be selected from the original sequence in an arbitrary fashion (in other words, the sequence has the property of randomness). Collectives are infinite random sequences, characterized by attributes whose frequencies tend to a limit. The principles of the probability calculus are defined in terms of collectives, on the basis of four operations – selection, mixing, partition, and combination – that specify four different ways in which new collectives can be derived from others. According to von Mises, one can meaningfully speak of probability only with reference to a well-specified collective. In other words, single-case probability attributions are meaningless. This opens a major problem that Reichenbach tried to overcome.

Von Mises's theory is the expression of a radical empiricism, combined with an operationalist approach. While giving a way of measuring probabilities on the basis of frequencies, von Mises wants to reduce probability to an observable and measurable quantity. However, the operationalist character of von Mises's theory is undermined by the adoption of infinite sequences, a condition weakened by Reichenbach, in an attempt to gain wider applicability to frequentism. Von Mises sticks to the idea that a mathematically accurate probability theory requires infinite random sequences, and believes that probability as an idealized limit can be compared to other limiting notions, such as velocity or density (see von Mises 1939, ch. 14).

Other problems arise in connection with von Mises's definition of randomness, which does not support a demonstration that there are random sequences, except for the trivial case of sequences whose attributes have probability 0 or 1. Various authors, including Alonzo Church and Abraham Wald, have tried to improve von Mises's definition to cope with this difficulty. However, a satisfactory definition of an absolute notion of randomness has not been produced. The topic has provoked a vast debate, whose main tendency, shared among others by Andrej N. Kolmogorov and Per Martin-Löf, is that of grounding randomness on the notion of complexity.

Von Mises's main concern was to work out a conception of probability suited for application to science. (See the last chapter of von Mises 1928, dedicated to "Statistical Problems in Physics".) He mentions the kinetic theory of gases, Brownian motion, radio-activity, and Planck's theory of blackbody radiation, as typical fields that can be treated probabilistically, and argues that the phenomena dealt with by such theories can be reduced to "chance mechanisms" having the features of collectives. Moreover, von Mises believed that frequentism could be extended to all branches of science, including quantum mechanics, which he welcomed as the expression of an indeterministic attitude that he embraced with enthusiasm. It is questionable whether frequentism is applicable to quantum mechanics, where single-case probability attributions are made, but quite apart from this problem, which remains open, frequentism, also thanks to von Mises's work, enjoyed great popularity among physicists.

Von Mises does not devote much effort to methodological questions, including induction and confirmation. He essentially describes the interplay between theory and experience along the lines of the H-D method. The role ascribed to induction reflects the basic presuppositions of his frequentism: in general, the first step is to make the hypothesis that a repeatable event (a "mass phenomenon") displays stability of relative frequencies and randomness, then its consequences are tested against experience. Von Mises does not go into the details of how this is done; he simply says that "the notion of the infinite collective can be applied to finite sequences of observations in a way which is not logically definable, but is nevertheless sufficiently exact in practice" (1928, 85).

A more careful attitude towards epistemological problems, including confirmation and the justification of induction, was taken by Hans Reichenbach,[4] who started working on the frequentist notion of probability around 1915, in connection with the interpretation of scientific theories. In the thirties, he further developed his views on probability and induction, in an attempt to answer the problem of cognitive significance. In this regard, Reichenbach urged the need to go beyond verifiability, and stressed the link between the significance of scientific statements and their predictive character, taken as a condition of their testability. He regarded his own theory of probability as a "theory of propositions about the future" (1936, 159), including a probabilistic theory of meaning, in which "the two truth-values, true and false, are replaced by a continuous scale of probability" (ibid., 154). Reichenbach's attitude towards the foundations of scientific knowledge is deeply probabilistic: he maintained that a reconstruction of science in tune with scientific practice should be grounded on probability, not truth. Such a probabilistic attitude goes hand in hand with an equally deep confidence in the logical approach adopted by logical empiricism, which made him develop his theory of probability as a form of "probability logic".

For Reichenbach degrees of probability can never be ascertained *a priori*, but only *a posteriori*, and the method by which degrees of probability are obtained is "induction by enumeration."

This is based on counting the relative frequency [of a certain attribute] in an initial section of the sequence, and consists in the inference that the relative frequency observed will persist approximately for the rest of the sequence; or, in other words, that the observed value represents, within certain limits of exactness, the value of the limit for the whole sequence. (1935/1971, 351)

This procedure is reflected by the "rule of induction": if an initial section of n elements of a sequence x_i is given, resulting in the frequency fn, we posit that the frequency fi $(i > n)$ will approach a limit p within $fn \pm \delta$ when the sequence is continued. As suggested by Reichenbach's formulation of the rule of induction, a probability attribution is a "posit", namely, "a statement with which we deal as true, although the truth value is unknown" (ibid., 373).

---

[4] For an overview of Reichenbach's philosophy see Salmon (1979).

The notion of "posit" occupies a central role within Reichenbach's frequentism, where it bridges the probability of a sequence and the probability of the single case. The idea is that a posit regarding a single occurrence of an event receives a weight from the probabilities attached to the reference class to which the event in question has been assigned, which should be "the narrowest class for which reliable statistics can be compiled". In this way Reichenbach tries to cope with the problem of the single case opened by von Mises's frequentism. With respect to von Mises's theory, Reichenbach also relaxes the randomness requirement, by admitting sequences which are "pseudo-random", or sequences which are random relative to a limited domain of place selections. Though it goes to Reichenbach's merit to make an attempt at solving the problem of the single case, his proposal is beset with difficulties. A major problem concerns the individuation of the proper reference class to which single events should be assigned.

Posits differ depending on whether they are made in a situation of "primitive" or "advanced" knowledge. A state characterized by knowledge of probabilities is "advanced", while a state where this kind of knowledge is lacking is called "primitive". In a state of primitive knowledge the rule of induction represents the only way of fixing probability values, while in a state of advanced knowledge the calculus of probabilities applies. The problem of confirmation arises within advanced knowledge, and its solution is entrusted to Bayesian method. Reichenbach embraces an objective form of Bayesianism, according to which the probability of hypotheses is obtained by Bayes's rule, combined with a frequentist determination of prior probabilities.

Posits made in a state of advanced knowledge have a definite weight and are called "appraised". They conform to the principle of the greatest number of successes, which makes them the best posits that can be made. Posits whose weight is unknown are called "anticipative" or "blind". Although the weight of a blind posit is unknown, its value can be corrected. Scientific method is a self-correcting procedure, which starts with blind posits and goes on to formulate appraised posits that become part of a complex system, in a continuous interplay between experience and prediction, as suggested by the title of one of Reichenbach's major works: *Experience and Prediction* (1938). While the soundness of this system is largely guaranteed by logic, induction is its only nonanalytical assumption. It becomes therefore vital to give an argument for the justification of induction.

Reichenbach's argument for the justification of induction is pragmatic in character and is based on the approximate character of blind posits: we know that by making and correcting such posits we will eventually reach success, in case the considered sequence has a limit. Since blind posits rest on the rule of induction, Reichenbach's argument applies to the latter, and says that "the rule of induction is justified as an instrument of positing because it is a method of which we know that if it is possible to make statements about the future we shall find them by means of this method" (1935/1971, 475). In other words, starting from the idea that induction cannot be logically justified, Reichenbach "vindicates" it on pragmatic grounds, on the basis of the consideration that it is a necessary condition for making good predictions. A number of authors, including Ian Hacking and Wesley Salmon,[5] have tried to supply Reichenbach's argument – which justifies a whole class of asymptotic rules – with further conditions, devised to restrict its applicability to the rule of induction. In spite of their efforts, the problem remains open.

The justification of induction adopted by Reichenbach is in tune with Herbert Feigl's approach to the problem. Feigl, who coined the term "vindication", made a distinction between two kinds of justification procedures, one in terms of "validation" and one in terms of means with respect to ends (see Feigl 1950). Whenever we have an inductive argument ascribing a certain degree of probability to a hypothesis, we first apply the validation procedure. This allows us to justify the given argument, by virtue of the available evidence supporting the conclusion and of the rule which led to determine that particular probability value. Validation of an inductive rule requires an appeal to more general standards, which serve as fundamental justifying principles. A similar method is commonly used in deductive logic, where, to justify a theorem, we go backwards in the deductive chain until we get to the axioms. This kind of process must inescapably stop once the basic standards are reached, since it

---

[5] For a survey of the literature on the topic, including an interesting proposal, see Salmon (1991).

is no longer possible to appeal to more fundamental principles. To justify the basic principles, we must seek the second kind of justification, namely, vindication. This appeals to pragmatic considerations, like the evaluation of whether the means employed are suitable to the achievement of some desired end. Given that the task of induction is that of widening our knowledge by formulating successful predictions, Feigl proposes to regard an inductive method as vindicated, if it can be shown that it enables us to formulate correct predictions about future events.

Reichenbach's frequentism is more flexible than von Mises's, because it allows for single-case probabilities, develops a theory of induction, and contains an argument for its justification. A further difference amounts to the fact that the logical approach adopted by Reichenbach is absent from von Mises's perspective, which is instead oriented towards operationalism. Reichenbach was concerned that his theory might be conflated with that of von Mises, or seen as a development of it. In a letter of 1949 to Bertrand Russell, he writes that his own theory is "more comprehensive" than that of von Mises, "since it is not restricted to random sequences", and further observes that "Mises does not connect his theory with the logical symbolism. And Mises has never had a theory of induction or of application of his theory to physical reality" (Reichenbach 1978, vol. II, 410).

Reichenbach's frequentist epistemology was criticized by Ernest Nagel, whose monograph, *Principles of the Theory of Probability*, appeared in 1939 as part of the *International Encyclopedia of Unified Science*. Nagel objects to Reichenbach's notion of weight that the weight of a proposition is not easier to establish than its truth, and disagrees with him on the idea that frequentism can support a satisfactory notion of confirmation of general hypotheses (see Nagel 1939a on Nagel's criticism of Reichenbach). Influenced by the doctrine of "leading principles" formulated by Charles Sanders Peirce, Nagel embraces a "truth-frequency" theory of probability, according to which probability refers to an inference from one set of propositions to another, and denotes the relative frequency of the effectiveness of such an inference. On this view, probability is a theoretical notion, and probability statements are tested by comparing their consequences with observed frequencies. This brings Nagel's interpretation of probability close to the "propensity theory" that was anticipated by Peirce and later resumed by Popper, who applied it to the interpretation of quantum mechanical probabilities.

Unlike Reichenbach and von Mises, Nagel maintains that probabilities are not obtained only by the observation of sequences, but can also be deduced from established theories. He embraces a form of pragmatism according to which "the term 'probability' is not a univocal term, for it has different meanings in different contexts" (1936, 26). The unifying character of the different uses of probability made in different contexts is given by the fact that it represents a measure of the success of a certain type of inference. But to what kinds of propositions such an inference applies is determined in ways that vary according to the context in which they occur. Similar considerations hold for confirmation, which is one of the contexts to which probability applies. Nagel is convinced that his truth-functional frequentist view can be successfully applied to confirmation, and raises various objections against Carnap's theory of confirmation (see Nagel's article in Schilpp 1963, together with Carnap's "Replies").

The main supporters of the logical interpretation of probability within logical empiricism are Friedrich Waismann and Rudolf Carnap. In addition, logicism has attracted the attention of a number of authors, including the economist John Maynard Keynes and Ludwig Wittgenstein, who deals with it in his *Tractatus Logico-Philosophicus*. Waismann appeals to Wittgenstein's position, with the intent of proceeding one step further in the same direction. Probability is taken to be a logical relation between statements, "a relation which could be called the degree of 'logical proximity' of two statements" (1930, 9). To introduce probability, Waismann starts from a parallel with deductive logic. When the scope of a proposition includes that of another, we say that the second follows from the first, or that there is a relation of entailment between them. This kind of relation can be generalized to the case in which the scope of one proposition partially overlaps with that of another. Probability as a logical relation between propositions applies to this case.

Waismann proceeds to define a measure of the magnitude of a scope, by fixing three conditions: (1) such a measure has to be a real, nonnegative number, (2) a contradiction has measure 0, (3) given two incompatible statements, the measure of their disjunction is given by the sum of their measures. Statements to which these conditions are applicable are called "measurable". Probability applies to measurable statements and is defined as follows: given two statements p and q, the probability assigned to the statement q by the statement p is "the magnitude of the common scope of p and q in proportion to the magnitude of the scope of q" (ibid., 11). The author points out that "what is probable is not the proposition, but our knowledge of the truth of a proposition", adding that "this view has nothing to do with subjectivity; for what it brings out is the logical relations between propositions, and no one will want to call these subjective" (ibid., 12). A similar attitude was taken by Carnap, who retained an objective view of probability, while embracing the logical interpretation. Waismann stresses that, in addition to a logical aspect, probability has an empirical side, having to do with frequency, though probability is "*more* than a mere record of frequency" (ibid., 20). The conclusion reached by the author is that "only by taking both elements into account can we reach a satisfactory elucidation" (ibid., 21).

Carnap's treatment starts precisely where Waismann's stops, with the admission of two concepts of probability. Carnap calls them "probability$_1$", or logical probability, and "probability$_2$", or empirical probability, taken in the frequentist sense, and claims that they are both important and useful. Probability$_1$ expresses the "degree of confirmation" attributed by a given body of evidence to a certain hypothesis. A statement of this kind is analytical and can be established by logical analysis alone. A statement of probability$_2$ is empirical and is based upon the observation of facts. Carnap's interest in the notion of quantitative confirmation was triggered by the problem of cognitive significance, and the work he devoted to this notion in the thirties and forties can be regarded as a continuation of his work in semantics. Degree of confirmation is introduced as a semantical notion, by definition time-independent, exactly as the notion of truth. Sentences expressing degrees of confirmation are analytic, and their logic, namely, inductive logic, is an extension of deductive logic.

Being logical and analytical, probability$_1$ can be unknown only in the sense that for various reasons, such as lack of information, we cannot calculate its value. On the contrary, probability$_2$ is taken to represent a physical magnitude, whose value is in general unknown. Making use of relative frequencies one can estimate probability$_2$, but such estimates are expressed in terms of probability$_1$. Carnap's interpretation of probability$_2$ is akin to Reichenbach's. Carnap thought that probability$_2$ had already been sufficiently developed by others, including Reichenbach, and concentrated on probability$_1$. The latter is assigned a twofold role: on the one hand, it is a method of confirmation; on the other, it is a method of estimating probability$_2$, or the corresponding relative frequencies. The logic of probability$_1$, or inductive logic, is developed in Carnap's major works of the fifties: *Logical Foundations of Probability* (1950a) and *The Continuum of Inductive Methods* (1952). The logic of degree of confirmation is developed as an axiomatic system, formalized within a first-order predicate calculus with identity, which applies to measures of confirmation defined on the semantic content of statements. Carnap shows that there is a complete correspondence between the two meanings of probability$_1$. In other words, a one-to-one correspondence between confirmation functions and estimate functions is established, and it is shown that these form a continuum.

In the sixties the interpretation of logical probability in terms of "degree of inductive support", adopted by Carnap in his early writings and retained in the first edition of *Logical Foundations of Probability* (1950a), was abandoned. Starting with the preface to the second edition (1962), logical probability, when does not represent an estimate of relative frequency, is interpreted as a fair betting quotient. Contextually, Carnap's late writings incorporate a justification of inductive logic in terms of coherence, taken as the fair betting quotient to be attached to bets on a hypothesis h, given a body of evidence e. The adoption of coherence in this connection was suggested to Carnap by Abner Shimony, in an attempt to cope with a problem raised by John Kemeny in connection with the justification of the basic principles of probability$_1$ (see Shimony 1992 on this point). From then on, Carnap regarded inductive logic not only as "the logical theory of all inductive reasoning", but also as "a rational reconstruction of the thoughts and decisions of an investigator" (Carnap 1950a, XV).

Such a turn towards decision theory fostered the opinion that in his late writings Carnap came closer to subjectivism. As a matter of fact, Carnap sometimes referred to his own position as "subjectivist", but a truly subjectivist point of view, like that upheld by Frank Plumpton Ramsey and Bruno de Finetti, seems irreconcilable with Carnap's logicism. The divergence lies in the fact that subjectivism takes a descriptive approach and is concerned with the actual beliefs of agents, while Carnap's logicism takes a normative approach and is concerned with *rational* credibility functions. The stress on rationality, which is a common trait of the views on probability put forward by logical empiricists regardless of the interpretation of probability adopted, is absent from the writings of subjectivists, who deny that there is only one correct probability assignment to be made on the basis of the available evidence. (On this point see Galavotti 2003, which contains a comparative discussion of the philosophy of probability of Reichenbach, Carnap, and de Finetti; see also Galavotti 2005.)

In his late writings, Carnap weakened his logicism in various ways. For one thing, he abandoned the conviction, upheld in the fifties, that there is an "ideal system" of inductive logic; in addition, he assigned a certain role to pragmatic considerations, in connection with the choice of credibility functions. (See Carnap's letter to Kuhn quoted in Reisch 1991 and the reply to Burks in Carnap 1963a.) But it should be added that Carnap never ceased to stress the rationality of inductive methods, as opposed to their successfulness. As a matter of fact, in the sixties Carnap banished the notion of successfulness from his own approach to inductive logic, and abandoned Reichenbach's pragmatic justification of induction, endorsed in his early writings (see Carnap 1945 and 1945a), in favor of a justification based on the notion of "inductive intuition" (see Carnap 1968 and 1963a). Carnap's pragmatist turn regarding the choice of inductive methods is therefore counterbalanced by his departure from a pragmatic approach to the justification of induction, and by the increasingly aprioristic character ascribed to rationality. This is reflected by the claim, contained in his "Replies" in Schilpp's volume, that "questions of rationality are purely a priori" (1963a, 981) and by his aversion to "the widespread view that the rationality of an inductive method depends upon factual knowledge, say, its success in the past". Such an attitude marks a sharp difference between Carnap's logicism and subjectivism.[6]

---

[6] The difference between logicism and subjectivism is clearly seen by Schramm (1993). However, Schramm seems to believe that in his late writings Carnap adhered to subjectivism.

Unlike subjectivists, who deal with "credence", taken as the agent's belief at specified times, Carnap grounds inductive reasoning on "credibility", taken as the initial credence of a hypothetical human being before experiencing empirical data. Such a credence is modified by conditionalization in the light of experiential data, along the lines suggested by the conditions of rationality imposed on inductive functions by inductive logic. This process is performed in a way similar to Bayesian conditioning. (See Good 1965 on the relationship between Carnapian and Bayesian conditioning.)

Carnap's view of inductive reasoning as compounded by a logical element, fixed *a priori*, and an empirical element, represented by factual information taken as certain, has been considered an oversimplification by Richard Jeffrey (1965 and 1992), who heralded a flexible version of Bayesianism which accommodates interval-valued degrees of belief, higher-order probabilities, and uncertain evidence, and regards standards of rationality as cultural artifacts, rather than aprioristic canons. As to the interpretation of probability, Jeffrey shares the subjectivism of Ramsey and de Finetti, and takes probability as the degree of belief in the occurrence of an event entertained by a person in a state of uncertainty. Jeffrey's attitude is not isolated: despite Carnap's efforts, Bayesian method is usually associated with subjectivism, rather than logicism.

BACK TO CONFIRMATION AND THE HYPOTHETICO- DEDUCTIVE METHOD

Carnap's confirmation functions have the drawback of assigning null posterior probability to universal generalizations on the basis of any body of evidence whatsoever, for the simple reason that general hypotheses can only have null prior probability. The problem of assigning a nonzero probability to universal hypotheses affects all Bayesian confirmation measures and is a major point of disagreement between Popper and the upholders of Bayesianism. Carnap's reaction to this problem was to emphasize instance confirmation (see Carnap 1950a, 2nd ed., 571–4).

A related solution is suggested by the consideration that, although general sentences have 0 probability, the same does not hold for their instances. If $p(h) > 0$, $p(h|e) > p(h)$ if and only if $p(e|h) > p(e)$, but if $p(h) = 0$, also $p(h|e) - p(h) = 0$. However, $p(e|h) > p(e)$

also when $p(h) = 0$. Therefore, confirmation functions depending on $p(e|h)$ and $p(e)$ can discriminate between hypothesis having probability o. This consideration inspired a number of measures of confirmation. Work in this connection has been done by John Kemeny and Paul Oppenheim (1952) and more recently Theo Kuipers (2000), Ilkka Niiniluoto (1987), and Roberto Festa (1999). Stressing the already mentioned analogy between Bayesian measures of confirmation and Popperian measures of corroboration, these authors have proposed "mixed" methods, inspired by a pluralistic attitude. (A survey of such methods is to be found in Niiniluoto 1998.) Other authors, including Jaakko Hintikka (1966) and Sandy Zabell (1997), made an attempt at modifying Carnap's systems, to assign positive probability values to universal hypotheses. (A good survey of Hintikka's contribution is to be found in Kuipers 1997.) The main trend in this debate seems to endorse an eclectic attitude, allowing for various confirmation measures, each of which is endowed with a peculiar methodological significance.

The paradoxes of confirmation found in the Bayesian framework various solutions, often inspired by old ideas. For instance, Janina Hosiasson-Lindenbaum's intuition that the hypothesis that all ravens are black is confirmed to a greater degree by nonparadoxical evidence than by paradoxical evidence has been developed along Bayesian lines by Patrick Suppes (1966) and John Irving Good (1983). Similarly, Goodman's notion of "entrenchment" has been redefined in Bayesian terms by a number of authors. (See Stalker 1994, particularly the articles by Elliott Sober, Brian Skyrms, and Patrick Suppes.)

Investigations into the nature of confirmation, and especially the debate between Bayesians and upholders of various kinds of non-Bayesian approaches – such as Popper's falsificationism and Glymour's (1980) bootstrapping theory of confirmation – paved the way to the conviction that the hypothetico-deductive method codified by logical empiricists is an oversimplification, and that scientific method is far more complex than depicted by the H-D approach. This conviction is at the core of an increasingly pluralistic and pragmatical attitude, imprinting the present-day literature on the topic.

6 The Structure of Scientific Theories in Logical Empiricism

THE THEORY QUESTION

A central question of philosophy of science, arguably the most central one, is "What is the structure of scientific theories?" Some contemporary philosophies of science have challenged the centrality of this "theory question" (henceforth T-question), arguing that it is more important to get an adequate understanding of the practice of scientific inquiry. Yet the logical empiricists placed great emphasis on theory: "Theories ... are the keys to the scientific understanding of empirical phenomena: to claim that a given kind of phenomenon is scientifically understood is tantamount to saying that science can offer a satisfactory theoretical account of it" (Hempel 2001 (1970), 218). Hence, investigating the structure of these "keys" ought to be a central task for philosophy of science. As has been often observed, the basic problem of logical empiricism was how to be a good empiricist and at the same time "logical." Or, to cast it in a more historico-philosophical setting, the problem was how the empiricist legacy of philosopher-scientists such as Ernst Mach and Pierre Duhem could be combined with the exigencies of modern logic and mathematics. As will be shown, this problem is intimately related to the problem of answering the T-question in an acceptable empiricist way.

The importance the logical empiricists attributed to the T-question does not mean that they always formulated it explicitly. Often they addressed it by asking questions about the nature of scientific knowledge, or they embedded it in more general problems such as "What is the structure of empirical science?" or "What is the structure of the language of empirical science?" Another, more empiricist way of dealing with the T-question was to investigate the structure of what may be called the empirical evidence of empirical theories. This was done in the so-called protocol sentence debate of the Vienna Circle that took place in the early thirties of the last century (see Uebel 1992). In their mature accounts, however, the logical empiricists intended to answer the T-question quite explicitly (e.g., Carnap 1966 or Hempel 2001).

In the philosophy of science of the twentieth century one may distinguish three different kinds of answers to the T-question: according to the *syntactic* view a theory essentially has the structure of an axiomatized system of sentences. This has been challenged by the *semantic* view that conceptualizes a theory as a collection of nonlinguistic models, mathematical ones or of other types. Both accounts are opposed by the view that a theory is a more or less amorphous entity consisting of sentences, models, problems, standards, skills, practices, etc. Not having a better word, we may call this a *pragmatic view.* Usually, logical empiricism is identified with a strictly syntactic view. As we shall see, this claim is in need of qualification.

The T-question has a bearing on all central philosophical topics logical empiricism struggled with, in particular, the analytic/ synthetic distinction, the difference between mathematical and empirical theories, problems of verification and meaningfulness, description and explanation, and questions concerning the realist or instrumentalist character of scientific knowledge. It goes without saying that we cannot deal with all these topics in detail. Rather, we will concentrate on problems of meaningfulness of scientific terms, and how the difference between mathematical and empirical theories is to be conceptualized. With respect to the T-question, Carnap was the most influential figure among the logical empiricists. Often, his answer has been identified with *the* logical empiricists answer in general. This is misleading. The accounts of Reichenbach,[1] Neurath, Hempel, or Feigl, to name but a few, cannot be considered as inessential variations of Carnap's. Moreover, Carnap's thought underwent important changes during the almost 40 years when he was dealing with the problem. Hence, *the* answer of the logical empiricists to the T-question does not exist. Rather, we

---

[1] The variant represented by the work of Reichenbach will not be dealt with here since his work features prominently in the discussion of the logical empiricist philosophy of physics in Chapter 8.

find a family of more or less closely related accounts covering a much larger spectrum than is usually acknowledged by the post-empiricist critics of logical empiricism. As will be treated in some detail, logical empiricism not only comprised strictly syntactic approaches to the T-question, but also semantic and pragmatic ones that took into account historical and sociological aspects of scientific theorizing.

The outline of this chapter is as follows: In Section II we recall the essential components that determined the logical empiricists' answers to the T-question: on the one hand, the problem of taking into account the conventional, logical, and mathematical aspects of our theories, and, on the other hand, to do justice to the empirical character of our knowledge. As will be shown, a particularly important role for the emergence of a genuine logical empiricist account of scientific theories was played by the axiomatization of mathematical theories whose main exponent was Hilbert (see Hilbert 1899; 1901; 1916). As is shown in Section III, Carnap's early answers to the T-question may be described as a stepwise emancipation from the dominating pattern of axiomatization of mathematical theories. Neurath's maverick "encyclopedic" approach is treated in Section IV. His account reveals that logical empiricism was in no way restricted to a strictly syntactic approach. In Section V we discuss several stations of Carnap's thinking culminating in his *The Methodological Character of Theoretical Concepts* (1956). Section VI deals with the solution of the problem of theoretical terms proposed by Ramsey already in 1929 and reinvented by Carnap in the late fifties. In Section VII some of the later logical empiricist approaches (in particular Hempel's and Nagel's) are considered. They may be characterized by the fact that they took into account pragmatic and historical considerations. This feature is usually attributed to the postempiricist approaches only. In Section VIII we close with some observations on the relation between logical empiricists and postempiricist answers to the T-question.

AXIOMATIZATIONS AND CONVENTIONS

Any answer to the T-question is marked by the specific scientific and philosophical context in which it is located. In the case of logical empiricism, this truism leads into a thicket formed by the interpretations, adaptations, and sometimes even plain misunderstandings of the doctrines of the philosophers and scientists that influenced the logico-empiricist approach. Let us concentrate on two figures who represented complementary currents in the debate dealing with the T-question, David Hilbert and Duhem. Hilbert is the exponent of the axiomatic approach that had provided a widely accepted answer to the T-question for mathematical theories, while Duhem is the scientist-philosopher who insisted that the structure of empirical theories is essentially different from that of the mathematical or formal theories, acknowledging at the same time the importance and even indispensability of mathematics for empirical science. Hence, "Hilbert" and "Duhem" should not be considered simply as components to be combined in one way or another; rather, they act as forces pulling in opposite directions.

Hilbert's axiomatization of mathematical theories, in particular geometry, provided a fairly satisfying answer of the T-question for mathematical theories. Mathematical theories are to be conceived as relational systems whose entities are defined by implicit definitions that may be considered as axioms in disguise. As an early logical empiricist witness for Hilbert's influence one may mention Schlick's *General Theory of Knowledge*, where geometric concepts are regarded as entities "whose only being consists in being bearers of the relations laid down by the system of axioms" (Schlick 1918, § 7/ 1985, 34).[2] The challenge for an empiricist philosophy science was to adapt Hilbert's answer to the case of empirical theories. Hilbert himself had put this problem on the agenda: in his epoch-making lecture delivered at the International Congress of Mathematicians at Paris in 1900 he had stated his "Sixth Problem" in the following way: "The investigations on the foundations of geometry suggest the problem: to treat in the same manner, by means of axioms, those physical sciences in which mathematics play an important part; in the first rank are the theory of probabilities and mechanics" (Hilbert 1901, 14).

It seems that Hilbert considered the axiomatization of physical theories perhaps "more complex" than that of geometry, but not in principle different. His approach tended to blur the difference between mathematics and the empirical sciences. Indeed, Hilbert

---

[2] This is almost exactly the definition of theoretical terms given by Hintikka (1998).

maintained that given what he had determined as the fundamental equations of his *Grundlagen der Physik:* "the possibility is approaching that in principle physics becomes a science of the kind of geometry: certainly the most magnificent glory of the axiomatic method which here, as we see, put the most powerful instruments of calculus, i.e., the calculus of variations and invariant theory, to its service" (Hilbert 1916/2001, 407). Most physicists and philosophers did not share Hilbert's enthusiastic expectations. Although virtually all logical empiricists agreed on the importance of Hilbert's work in the axiomatization of mathematics, they remained skeptical with respect to the axiomatization program as formulated in the *Sixth Problem*. The basic reason for their reluctance probably was that they considered it as a metaphysically charged program threatening to deprive the natural sciences of their empirical foundations. An important ally in the logical empiricists' struggle against the empiristically unacceptable metaphysical tendencies in Hilbert's axiomatization program was conventionalism as presented in the works of French scientist-philosophers such as Duhem, Henri Poincaré, Abel Rey, and others.[3] Duhem was a vigorous defender of the empirical character of empirical theories. He subscribed to a strictly antimetaphysical conception of science free of those Kantian ingredients that could have disturbed the logical empiricists, whereas Poincaré's philosophy of science had somewhat heterodox Kantian features.

Accepting that a purely mathematical axiomatization was not a fully satisfying answer to the T-question for empirical theories, the logical empiricists began to develop other models of the structure of empirical theories designed to incorporate an axiomatic mathematical system as only one component of the more complex conceptual apparatus of an empirical theory. Thereby they came to describe pictorially the structure of an empirical theory as a "free-floating" system of concepts which mutually determine their respective meanings somehow anchored in reality. This geometric metaphor can be traced back to Schlick (1918) but can be found in the works of

---

[3] In the following I concentrate on Duhem not only for reasons of space but also because Duhem's radical conventionalism is the version of conventionalism that is most congenial to Logical Empiricism. This is not to deny the important role Poincaré played for many Logical Empiricists.

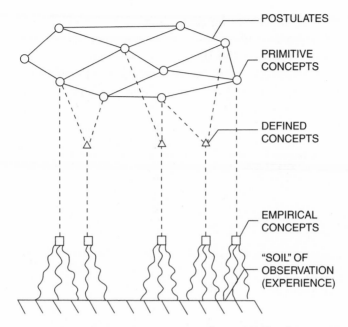

POSTULATES

PRIMITIVE
CONCEPTS

DEFINED
CONCEPTS

EMPIRICAL
CONCEPTS

"SOIL" OF
OBSERVATION
(EXPERIENCE)

FIGURE 6.1.   A logical empiricist picture of a scientific theory. Reprinted
with permission from Feigl, Herbert. "The Orthodox View of Theories:
Remarks in Defense as Well as Criticism." In Michael Radner and Stephen
Winokur (eds.), *Theories of Physics and Psychology*, Vol. 4, Minnesota
Studies in the Philosophy of Science. Minneapolis, MN: University of
Minnesota Press, 1970, p. 6.

various authors, for example, Carnap (1939, 1966), Hempel (1952),
or Feigl (1970). Its content may be illustrated by the well-known
diagram shown in Figure 6.1

A pictorial diagram such as this one can be interpreted in many
ways. The logical empiricists, in rough terms, interpreted it in
terms of a two-language model of empirical theories: the structure
of an empirical theory T is described by the structure of the language L in which T is formulated. L has two essentially different
components, to wit, a vocabulary LO used for the description of
the lower empirical level, and a vocabulary LT dealing with the
formulation of concepts and postulates of the upper theoretical
level. Moreover, there was assumed to be some sort of translation
manual which allowed (at least partially) one to interpret the
statements of the upper theoretical level in terms of the empirical

level with the help of correspondence rules or bridge laws. In this way, there was a kind of "upward seepage" of meaning from the observational terms to the theoretical concepts (see Feigl 1970, 7). As will be discussed in more detail below, the alleged "seepage" of meaning pointed toward a crucial problem of the logical empiricists' account of empirical theories, to wit, how the "free-floating" theoretical concepts obtained at least some kind of empirical meaning whereby they could be distinguished from meaningless metaphysical terms.

The above diagram is to serve only as a rough map; even the "received view" attributed to the logical empiricists in the fifties and sixties is more complicated (see Suppe 1989). Nevertheless, the pictorial description provided by this diagram may serve as a first orientation of the core problem that the logical empiricists from Schlick onwards were struggling with, namely, philosophically to understand how empirical science succeeds in bringing together two different components, the theoretical and the empirical. The problematic relation of these two components is already dealt with in Duhem's *The Aim and Structure of Scientific Theory* (1906). According to him, a physical theory "is a system of mathematical propositions, deduced from a small number of principles, which aim to represent as simply, as completely, and as exactly as possible a set of experimental laws" (Duhem 1906, 19). The main aim of such a representation is "intellectual economy" in the sense of Ernst Mach, not a true description of how the world "really looks." To achieve this kind of economic representation, a physical theory has to deal with two different kinds of facts: on the one hand, one has the symbolic (or theoretical) facts expressed in the language of pure mathematics, and on the other hand, the experimental (or practical) facts described in ordinary language. One of Duhem's most original theses maintained that there is no direct translation between the two areas. Rather, there is a many-many correspondence: to every symbolic fact there corresponds an infinity of experimental facts and vice versa. It is up to the scientist to interpret these correlations in an adequate manner (Duhem 1906, ch. 8). Duhem's distinction of symbolic and experimental facts was not immediately acceptable to logical empiricists. They could not settle the empirical character of empirical theories simply by ontological stipulations; rather, they had to rely on the structure of the language(s) of empirical sciences.

Thus, the common format of all logico-empiricist answers of the T-question is that they attempt to explicate the specific structural features of the languages of empirical sciences which render them empirical sciences.

EARLY ANSWERS

Maintaining a difference between the empirical and the purely mathematical, and, at the same time, giving a plausible answer to the problem of how science succeeds to "[master] reality through ... systems of hypotheses and axioms" (Neurath, Carnap, and Hahn 1929/1973, 311) was a problem that concerned not only the logical empiricists. The neo-Kantians of the Marburg school, the most important rival of logical empiricism in the 1920s, were at pains to explain the differences between mathematical and empirical sciences in a way that did not to blur the distinction between both domains in an untenable way. Although logical empiricists and neo-Kantians started from a similar base, in the end they came to different conclusions. Nevertheless, in the twenties neo-Kantians' and logical empiricists' answers to the T-question had much in common. In *Substance and Function* Cassirer proposed the following differentiation between mathematical and empirical concepts:

In contrast to the mathematical concept, however, in empirical science the characteristic difference emerges that the construction which within mathematics arrives at a fixed end, remains in principle *incompleteable* within experience. But no matter how many "strata" of relations we may superimpose on each other, and however close we may come to all particular circumstances of the real process, nevertheless there is always the possibility that some co-operative factor in the total result has not been calculated and will only be discovered with the further progress of experimental analysis. (Cassirer 1910, 337/1953, 254)

According to Cassirer, the difference between mathematical and empirical concepts resided in the fact that the latter are open ("incompleteable"), whereas the former are closed: the implicit definition of a point in Euclidean geometry fixes the meaning of this concept once and for all. Cassirer claimed that the key concepts of empirical science had a "serial form" (*Reihenform*) in that their meaning was not fixed once and for all by a single theoretical framework; rather, it emerged in a series of theoretical stages in the ongoing evolution of scientific knowledge.[4] His thesis resembled the guiding idea that would be of utmost importance also for the logical empiricists' approach to the T-question, namely, that the theoretical concepts of empirical theories are somehow "open" concepts, lacking full meaning and being only partially determined by any given conceptual framework. In contrast to Cassirer, however, the logical empiricists were not content to express this idea only in a vague and metaphorical way.

When Carnap started investigating the T-question in the late twenties, he began in a rather ingenuous manner emphasizing the close resemblance between mathematical and empirical concepts. According to him, both were closed, that is, fully determined within one system. The most naive answer to the T-question Carnap ever gave may be found in his *Abriss der Logistik* (Carnap 1929). It closely followed the lines of the axiomatic approach outlined by Hilbert in *Foundations of Geometry* (Hilbert 1899). As a dedicated follower of Whitehead and Russell's *Principia Mathematica*, Carnap considered the "theory of relations" as the most important part of logic, and the axiomatization of scientific theories as the most important application of the theory of relations. It is "expedient for the presentation of conceptual systems and theories ... of the most different realms: geometry, physics, epistemology, theory of kinship, analysis of language etc. Thereby, the definitions and deductions in these areas get a precision that can hardly be obtained otherwise which does not hinder, but rather facilitates the practical work" (Carnap 1929, 2). One should note that here Carnap did not make a difference between mathematical and empirical theories. Both can be axiomatized in the same way as had been suggested already Hilbert almost 30 years earlier.

It was in the conceptual practices of mathematics and empirical science that a difference emerged eventually. Although in *Abriss* such a difference was still lacking, already here Carnap pointed out

---

[4] This claim may be traced back to the core thesis of the Marburg neo-Kantian school, according to which the "fact of science is a fact of becoming" (Natorp 1910, 14).

that the explication of the structure of empirical theories is ultimately a practically motivated endeavor:

The [*Abriss*] ... does not intend to present a theory, rather it aims to teach a practice. ... The result of a logicist treatment of a domain is first an analysis of its concepts and assertions, and then a synthesis in two forms: the concepts of the domain are defined step by step from some appropriate basic concepts and thereby ordered in form of a conceptual genealogy ("constitutional system"); the assertions are deduced step by step from appropriately chosen basic assertions ("axioms") and thereby ordered in a genealogy of assertions ("deductive system"). (Carnap 1929, iii)

At the time, axiomatizing was for Carnap "simply to order the sentences on the one hand, and the concept of some non-logical domain according to their logical dependencies" (Carnap 1929, iii). Although axiomatization may be regarded as a fruitful heuristic for the logical analysis of scientific theories, it did not answer the epistemological and ontological problems concerning empirical knowledge. In particular, it did not express any difference between the empirical and the mathematical. But, obviously, there *is* a difference between mathematical and empirical theories. Not *all* concepts of empirical theories can be defined by implicit definitions. There is more in empirical theories than implicitly defined mathematical structures. The problem is to find out what it is, and how it affects the structure of empirical theories.

What renders empirical theories empirical may best be studied by investigating their empirical bases. At least this was the way the logical empiricists tackled this problem in the so-called protocol sentence debate.[5] Often logical empiricism has been blamed for having naively accepted the "myth of the given" according to which there is an unproblematic stratum of empirical knowledge on which the more lofty stages of theoretical knowledge can be built.[6] A closer inspection of protocol sentence debate reveals that this is an oversimplification. Although sometimes the empirical base was indeed called "the given," the logical empiricists did not consider "the given" as something unproblematic. The problem of the given rather was the question of the proper form and structure of the statements

---

[5] For a detailed presentation of the various stages of this debate see Uebel (1992).
[6] The diagram of Section II may convey such an idea.

that deliver empirical evidence. Interpreted in this manner, the protocol sentence debate was one episode in the logical empiricists' ongoing struggle to come to terms with the T-question by concentrating on the component of empirical theories complementary to the one that "Hilbertian" answers of the T-question emphasize, the "free-floating" theoretical concepts.

Of course, neither the empirical base nor the theoretical structure can be studied in isolation. A balanced account has to investigate both components. Hence, from the mid-1930s onwards, Carnap and other logical empiricists described empirical theories by two complementary types of concepts. Their characterization varied: sometimes they were called "primitive" versus "introduced" (Carnap 1936/37), then "elementary" versus "abstract" (Carnap 1939) or "observational" and "theoretical" concepts (Carnap 1956). The varying interpretations of the two kinds of concepts show that what is most important is their complementarity. Their duality aims to account for the specific practice of empirical theories, which comprises activities as testing, confirming, or (conditional) falsifying that have no (direct) analogues in the formal sciences. Logical empiricist answers to the T-question are best described as attempts to characterize the linguistic practices of empirical theories that distinguish them from mathematics and other formal sciences. Carnap's proposals maintain that empirical theories are characterized by "open" concepts. In the first approximation, this openness can be considered as a partial underdetermination that may be reduced in the ongoing development of science. This does not, however, make the open character of scientific theories disappear, since new underdetermined "theoretical" concepts may be introduced. In *Testability and Meaning* Carnap intended to capture the distinct conceptual practice of the empirical sciences under the rubric of confirmation and testing. The point was to explicate the open character of dispositional terms of empirical theories. Dispositional terms being forerunners of the later theoretical concepts, it is therefore of secondary importance whether Carnap gave a satisfactory account of dispositional terms or not. Rather, his account is remarkable for being his first attempt to distinguish between formal and empirical theories in terms of the different kinds of concepts they use.

NEURATH'S ENCYCLOPEDISM

More than any other logical empiricist, Neurath was convinced that an adequate answer of the T-question for empirical theories could not consist in modifications of the answer Hilbert had given for mathematical theories. Although he did not deprecate the role of logic and mathematics for empirical science, Neurath always insisted that empirical theories were of a quite different sort from mathematical and other formal theories. For him, formalization and mathematization were useful tools but with a limited scope of application. He was one of the few logical empiricists who did not take it for granted that scientific theories should be thought of as formal axiomatic systems endowed with some sort of empirical interpretation. Instead, he aimed at an explication of those characteristics of scientific theories that do *not* fit the neat and clean systems that preoccupied his colleagues. Calling his account "encyclopedism," he stressed the contrast between "encyclopedia" and "system," the latter being an axiomatized system of propositions in Hilbert's sense. Hence, the central task of Neurath's encyclopedism was to answer the question "What is the structure of an encyclopedia of unified science?" According to him, the attempt to answer this question by invoking some sort of "deductive system" was to commit the sin of metaphysical "pseudorationalism" overstating the possibilities of human rationality.

The basis of Neurath's encyclopedism was a robust physicalism according to which all intellectually respectable concepts can be defined ultimately in terms of physicalist concepts and/or the concepts of logic and mathematics. It is important to note that physicalistic concepts are not to be identified with concepts of physics. Rather, Neurath placed the everyday language of spatio-temporally located things and processes in the center. This physicalist everyday language had to be cleansed of metaphysical phrases and possibly be enriched by scientific concepts. Hence, the Neurathian physicalist language as the language of unified science is a mixed language. Moreover, this "universal jargon" unavoidably contains precise *and* vague terms. On the one hand, one has the physicalist base language with its unclear and ambiguous common day concepts, called by Neurath *Ballungen* ("congestions"); on the other hand, there is the "highly scientific language" with its neat "formulas." For him, the common language with its *Ballungen* is an indispensable part of empirical science that can never be eliminated in favor of a clean and fully analyzed language:

If we want to embrace the entire unified science of our age, we must combine terms of ordinary and advanced scientific languages, since in practice, the terms of both languages overlap. There are certain terms that are used only in ordinary language, others that occur only in scientific language, and finally terms that appear in both. In a scientific treatise that touches upon the whole range of unified science, therefore, only a "jargon" that contains terms of both languages will do. Neurath (1932–3/1983, 92)

A difficult problem faced by Neurath's account is how the interactions of the precise and imprecise elements are to be conceptualized. This problem corresponds to that in the standard account of how the *correspondence rules* or *bridge laws* are to be conceptualized. Neurath did not say very much on this topic; he insisted, however, on the general thesis that an empiricist could never accept an answer to the T-question that ignored the part of the *Ballungen* and solely dealt with that of "formulas." This means that an empiricist answer to the T-question cannot be content with an answer that takes into account only Hilbertian aspects of empirical theories.

Neurath's model of scientific knowledge may be characterized as pragmatic in the sense that it conceived an empirical theory as an inhomogenous entity that comprises components that fall under different syntactical, semantic, and pragmatic categories. In his criticism of Popper's falsificationalism, he described his conception of empirical knowledge as follows:

We start from masses of sentences whose connection is only partly systematic, which we discern only in part. Theories and single communications are placed side by side. While the scholar is working with the help of part of these masses of statements, supplementary additions are made by others, which he is prepared to accept in principle without being quite certain what the logical consequences of this decision might be. The statements from the stock with one really works use many vague terms, so that "systems" can be always be separated only as abstractions. The statements are linked to each other sometimes more closely, sometimes more loosely. The interlocked whole is not transparent, while systematic deductions are attempted at certain places. ... one could say that we ... start from *model-encyclopedias;* this would express from the outset that systems of clean statements are not put forward as the basis of our considerations. (1935/1983, 122)

Summarizing, we may say that in Neurath's encyclopedism the T-question appears in the form "What is the structure of a 'model-encyclopedia'?" Neurath's answer to this question is largely negative: encyclopedias do *not* have the structure of axiomatized systems, deductive derivations do *not* play an all-embracing role, etc. Rather, encyclopedias exhibit the local, limited, and often ambiguous character of human knowledge. Although Neurath concentrates on encyclopedias instead of theories, his encyclopedism nevertheless exhibits an analogy to the orthodox two-language account with his stress on the complementarity of exact mathematical or logical formulas and imprecise *Ballungen.* Hence, with respect to its underlying structure Neurath's special brand of logical empiricism may not be so special after all.

ON THE ROAD TOWARDS A THEORY OF THEORETICAL CONCEPTS

In "Testability and Meaning" Carnap treated the T-question from a decidedly dynamic point of view: the main problem of philosophically understanding empirical science was to understand how *new* terms may be introduced into the scientific discourse and how they become endowed with meaning. There were essentially two methods to achieve this. The first we already know from the mathematical and other formal sciences, the method of explicit definition. This method also is applied in the empirical sciences, but the characteristic method of these sciences is another one, namely, the method of reduction.

Let us consider the following simplified example.[7] Suppose a scientist wishes to introduce a new predicate Q, for instance, "spin," "helicity," or whatever.[8] He may do this by an explicit definition,

---

[7] The account of reduction pairs Carnap proposes in "Testability" is actually more sophisticated than the one sketched here. For our purposes, however, the technical details are irrelevant.

[8] As a concrete special example for the method of introducing new terms by reduction, Carnap discussed dispositional terms such as "visible," "fragile," or

but often, he will be able to determine the meaning of Q only partially. For certain empirical circumstances Q1 he possesses experimental methods that allow him to claim that Q obtains, and given other empirical circumstances P1 that Q does not obtain. In still other circumstances he simply does not know whether Q obtains or not. Formally, this may be expressed by a "reduction pair" (Q1, P1) of sentences:

$$Q1 \rightarrow Q \text{ and } P1 \rightarrow \text{not } Q.$$

Carnap's procedure can be rendered more perspicuous by assuming that we have an interpretation of the predicates involved. Then predicates P, Q ... are represented by their extensions, that is, the sets of objects to which they apply, and a reduction pair (Q1, P1) may be considered as an approximation of the extension of Q "from below" and "from above" by the inclusions $Q1 \subseteq Q \subseteq P1$, $CP1$ being the set theoretical complement of the extension of P1.

The reduction pair (Q1, P1) partially determines the predicate Q in that it asserts that the extension of Q contains that of Q1 and is disjoint from P1. This is only a partial determination that may be further improved by further reduction pairs (Q2, P2), (Q3, P3), etc. The introduction of new terms by the method of reduction pairs has the advantage that it renders the development of scientific theories more continuous. If one always fixed the meaning of a new predicate Q by relying on the experimental methods just available, one would have to revoke the definition of Q at every new stage of the development of science. Relying on the methods of reduction pairs allows for a more flexible attitude with respect to meaning variance; we need not rescind the determinations laid down in the previous stage but can simply supplement them. Carnap's introduction of new terms by reduction pairs instead of explicit definitions may be considered as a first attempt to take into account the open character of the theoretical concepts. We are thus led to an important

---

"soluble," arguing that the reductive introduction of these concepts cannot be replaced by explicit definitions. As Hempel remarked, reduction pairs do not solve the problem of dispositional terms, which requires a conception of lawlike sentences not provided in "Testability"; see Hempel (1963, 689). Thus one may consider as the most interesting feature of Carnap's account not the treatment of dispositional terms, but rather the advent of what soon was to become the problem of theoretical terms.

distinction between the terms of the language for science: primitive terms with fully determined meaning on the one hand, and terms introduced by reduction pairs, whose meaning was only partially defined by the primitive terms, on the other hand. In *Testability and Meaning* Carnap is not very explicit about the epistemological and methodological relevance of this distinction, but later it will occupy center stage.

From about 1935 Carnap was a firm adherent of Tarskian semantics. Hence it was only natural for him to apply the apparatus of semantics to the task of answering the T-question. For this purpose Tarskian semantics had to be modified to cope with the distinction between elementary (observable) and abstract (theoretical) terms. One may say that Carnap struggled with this problem until the early 1960s, when he thought he finally had found a solution in terms of the Ramsey sentence of a theory (see Carnap 1966, ch. 24). The first step in this direction was to note that we need not give a semantical interpretation for every term, since the physical terms form a system and are interconnected (1939, 204). That is to say, a physically interpreted calculus inherits the holistic character of the system of implicit mathematical definitions. Although already in 1939 one can find a two-language account in Carnap's work, its full-fledged, classical version only appears in "The Methodological Character of Theoretical Concepts" (1956). There the discussion was explicitly couched in the framework of a Tarskian semantics, and problems of partial *interpretation*s of theoretical terms came to the forefront. Moreover, the discussion of their meaningfulness is explicitly relativized to specific theories: a theoretical term may be meaningful with respect to one theory but not meaningful with respect to another (1956, 48, 50).[9] Carnap no longer dealt with the general problematic of the structure of scientific language but concentrates on the T-problem quite explicitly. The principal thesis of the open character of theoretical concepts is maintained and strengthened. Instead of explaining conceptual openness in terms of (multiple) reduction sentences, Carnap now argued that this feature is more adequately represented by the so called C-rules (correspondence rules) that connect the terms of the theoretical vocabulary

[9] This may be a result of the constant criticism of Hempel, who emphasized time and again the necessity to relativize the considerations to specific theories.

with those of the observational vocabulary. The particular form chosen for the C-rules is not essential; Carnap requires only that these rules connect sentences of the observational language LO with certain sentences of the theoretical language LT, "for instance, by making a derivation in the one or the other direction possible. These rules are similar to the 'correlative definitions' of Reichenbach and the operational definitions of Bridgman but may be more general" (Carnap 1956, 48).

We have reached what may be considered as the "received view's" answer to the T-question. If τ is an empirical theory, the vocabulary of τ is divided into the theoretical vocabulary LT and an observational vocabulary LO. Assuming finite axiomatizability, the axioms of τ can be expressed as a conjunction of purely theoretical postulates T and (mixed) correspondence postulates C. Thus a theory τ may be written as

$$T\&C = (\ldots t_1, \ldots, t_k, \ldots) \& (\ldots o_1, \ldots, o_j; \ldots t_1, \ldots, t_k, \ldots)$$

where the first conjunct represents the theoretical postulates T of τ, and the second (mixed) conjunct represents the correspondence postulates C. Against a common interpretation of the received view it must be stressed that the underlying distinction between observational and theoretical concepts was viewed as a pragmatic issue that might have various solutions. As Carnap himself put it: "The line separating observable from nonobservable is highly arbitrary" (1966, 227). The important point was that in the practice of science such a cut was always made to take into account the open character of at least some of the theory's concepts.

Returning to the problem of meaning, and ignoring the technicalities, the criterion of meaningfulness states that a theoretical term t is meaningful relative to T & C if there is a sentence S(t) and a purely observational sentence S(o) such that S(t) & T & C is not logically false and implies S(o). In the simplest case, a meaningful term already occurs in a correspondence rule, but there may be meaningful terms related to the observational level in a more indirect way. Since Carnap had become extremely liberal with respect to the correspondence rules, this meaning criterion is very weak. Nevertheless, it is not vacuous, since it can spot at least some meaningless "metaphysical" terms. Equally important, obviously meaningful terms came out as meaningful. Nevertheless, the criterion did not meet unanimous approval as "the" solution of the meaning problem. Critics spotted various technical difficulties: for instance, the meaningfulness of terms could be altered by innocent, purely linguistic manipulations or insignificant alterations of the theory (Kaplan 1975; Rozeboom 1960). As Kaplan put it: "It appears to be extremely difficult to toe that fine line between the electron and the absolute" (1975, 88). In sum, growing insight into the intricacies of scientific concept formation led the logical empiricists to the conclusion that a fully adequate answer to the T-question was much more difficult than they had thought when they started the endeavor of clarifying the structure of empirical theories with some sort of Hilbert-style axiomatization. It became doubtful if such an answer could ever be found in the realm of purely formal considerations, and it was this doubt that paved the way towards an account that overcame the limitations of a purely syntactic approach.[10]

RAMSEY'S APPROACH

By the measure of the standard histories according to which logical empiricism was discarded in the late sixties/early seventies, the Ramsey approach may be considered as logical empiricism's last stand on the T-question. This assessment is problematic for at least two reasons: first, because that particular answer to the T-question was formulated by Ramsey himself already in 1929,[11] and second, because long after the "death" of logical empiricism, the Ramsey approach to the T-question continues to find prominent advocates (e.g., Papineau 1996; Hintikka 1998) who can hardly be characterized as orthodox logical empiricists.

The Ramsey approach attempts to explicate the meaningfulness of theoretical terms in a semantical framework that strictly distinguishes

---

[10] A skeptical conclusion of this kind was drawn by Feigl, who declared that the ultimate reason why entities like "entelechies," "souls," and "spirits" are excluded from the realm of respectable scientific entities in contrast to legitimate ones such as atom, magnetic, or field is that the former "do not add anything to the explanatory power of the extant empirical laws and theories" (1950, 218–19).

[11] As Psillos has documented (2000), in the late fifties Carnap literally reinvented Ramsey's approach without realizing it; it was Hempel who enlightened him about this.

between analytic and synthetic truth. Carnap wanted to maintain the important insight that theoretical concepts are open concepts in the sense that they lack a complete interpretation. The content of theoretical terms is too rich to be exhausted by observational consequences. On the other hand, Carnap wanted to draw a sharp line between analytic and synthetic sentences that would enable him to distinguish clearly between pure mathematics and physics that contains mathematics only in applied form. Such a distinction can be drawn given fully interpreted observational statements and meaning postulates (Carnap 1966, ch. 27), but a real difficulty arises for the case of theoretical concepts whose meaning is only partially determined. The problem is to render the openness of theoretical concepts compatible with a strict analytic/synthetic distinction. Here, Ramsey's answer to the T-question comes to the rescue. Slightly modifying the account of the theory structure sketched in the previous section let us characterize an empirical theory as a complex conjunction T & C $(t_1, \ldots, t_n, o_1, \ldots, o_m)$ of theoretical and correspondence postulates. With respect to meaningfulness of T & C, problems are caused by its theoretical terms. Ramsey proposed to solve these problems by simply eliminating all theoretical terms, replacing the sentence T & C $(t_1, \ldots, t_n, o_1, \ldots, o_m)$ by the theory's Ramsey sentence R_T & C defined as

$$R_T \ \& \ C := \exists x_1 \ldots \exists x_n \ T \ \& \ C \ (x_1, \ldots, x_n, o_1, \ldots, o_m).$$

As is easily proved, the Ramsey sentence R_T & C is true if and only if the complex sentence T & C is true. However, in R_T & C the theoretical terms have disappeared, at least from the surface. In their place are variables. The variable x_i does not refer to any particular class, and the Ramsey sentence asserts only that there are at least some classes that satisfy certain conditions. We no longer need to care about the meaning of the theoretical terms, or so it seems. This has led some philosophers to the conclusion that the Ramsey sentence is an expedient tool to eliminate the bothersome theoretical terms. Actually, things are more complicated: if we consider "being a value of a bound variable" as a necessary and sufficient condition for existence, then the Ramsey sentence R_T & C is clearly an existential claim for the theoretical terms it allegedly eliminates. There is an ongoing debate on the question whether the Ramsey approach is to be interpreted as a realist, an instrumentalist, or a neutral stance towards the existential status of the entities the theoretical terms refer to. It seems Carnap preferred the last interpretation, but he can hardly be said to have maintained a clear and unambiguous position (see Psillos 1999, ch. 3).

The second problem the Ramsey approach was to solve was explication of the analyticity of the theoretical language LT. Given a theory $T \& C$ and its Ramsey sentence $R_T \& C$, we may form the conjunction $R_T \& C \ \& \ (R_T \& C \rightarrow T \& C)$, sometimes called the "Carnap sentence" of the theory (see Lewis 1970). As is easily seen, the Carnap sentence has no factual content. Carnap took it as a sort of generalized meaning postulate of the theory that was to be considered as the analytical part of the theory. On the other hand, the Ramsey sentence may be considered as the synthetic part of the theory since it exactly implies its observational consequences (Hempel 1958, 80). The theory and its Ramsey sentence are functionally equivalent. Even if one were to accept the Ramsey sentence as a solution of Carnap's problem of neatly separating the analytical and the synthetic parts of empirical theories, the discussion about the ontological implications of the Ramsey account of empirical theories still continues. Since the advent of the model-theoretic account of theories the discussion has gained a new impetus, as many of its supporters claim that it represents clear progress over the syntactical account of logical empiricism. We cannot go into the details here, but Hempel was certainly right that Ramsey sentences do not provide a satisfactory way of avoiding theoretical concepts. This has been confirmed by most recent authors on the problem. Moreover, there may be nonformal, pragmatic reasons why theoretical concepts cannot be eliminated.

PRAGMATIC, REALIST, AND INSTRUMENTALIST INTERPRETATIONS

Not all logical empiricists followed Carnap into the logical thicket of possible interpretations of the Ramsey sentence. Some pursued more down-to-earth issues concerning the T-question aiming at what may be called a pragmatic elucidation of the structure of empirical theories that reflected more clearly the essential features of the practice of empirical science. In this group one finds authors such as the later C. G. Hempel, Ernest Nagel, Herbert Feigl, and

Philipp Frank. The general tenor of their contributions is that formal and logical means for modeling the structure of empirical theories are important but should not be overestimated. According to them, informal, in particular historical and pragmatic, considerations played an indispensable role for understanding the structure of empirical theories. Sharing more or less the same basic model, they differed considerably in the details of how they understood the structure of empirical theories. These interpretative differences concerned in particular the assessment of pragmatic, realist, or instrumentalist features of scientific theorizing.

Hempel's general contribution to logical empiricism may be seen in his insistence that logical empiricist philosophy of science must not lose sight of "real" science in favor of what may be called "philosopher's" science. Hempel explicitly criticized the so-called received view that most philosophers and scientists took as the official doctrine of logical empiricism: "I think that it is misleading to view the internal principles of a theory as an uninterpreted calculus and the theoretical terms accordingly as variables, as markers of empty shells into which the juice of empirical content is pumped through the pipelines called correspondence rules" (2001 (1969), 61). To improve this less than optimal state of affairs Hempel reinterpreted the standard conception. Instead of conceptualizing a theory as an abstract calculus C and a set R of rules of correspondence, he conceived a it as composed of a class of "internal principles" I and a class "bridge principles" B. Superficially, the component I corresponds to the uninterpreted calculus, and B to the rules of correspondence. This formal similarity, Hempel is at pains to point out, is misleading. There is a profound difference between the received view and his (I, B)-proposal. The distinction between I and B is not made in terms of the "theoretical" versus the "observational." Rather, the cut is made between the "antecedently known" and the "new theoretical" vocabulary. This cut is relative to the theory in question and largely a matter of pragmatic convenience. This implies, in particular, that "the elements of the pretheoretical vocabulary need not, and indeed should not, generally be conceived as observational terms ... : in many cases the antecedently known vocabulary will contain terms originally introduced by an earlier theory" (Hempel 1969/2001, 52).

Thus, although Hempel's internal principles will typically use a theoretical vocabulary, they cannot be viewed as a totally uninterpreted calculus. An analogous difference exists between the rules of correspondence and Hempel's bridge principles: according to the standard account the correspondence rules assign empirical meaning to the expressions of the calculus, and hence they look like metalinguistic principles which render certain sentences true by terminological convention (Hempel 2001 [1970], 229). For Hempel, this does not correspond to the actual practice of science. Although some scientific statements may be initially introduced by "operational definitions," they usually change their status in response to new empirical findings and theoretical developments and become subject to revision in response to further empirical findings and theoretical developments. Hempel is well aware of the consequences of these moves away from the standard conception: "In fact, it should be explicitly acknowledged now that no precise criterion has been provided for distinguishing internal principles from bridge principles. In particular, the dividing line cannot be characterized syntactically ... for ... both internal principles and bridge principles contain theoretical as well as antecedently available terms" (Hempel 1970/2001, 231). Hence there is no hope to find means by which the "new" theoretical terms are bestowed with meaning by some kind of transfer of meaning from the old "antecedently understood" terms to the new "theoretical" ones through explicit or implicit definitions: "We come to understand new terms, we learn how to use them properly, in many ways besides definition: from instances of their use in particular contexts, from paraphrases that can make no claim to being definitions, and so forth" (1970/2001, 233). This pragmatic description of how we come to terms with new concepts is rather close to Kuhn's approach according to which the usage of a new paradigm is learned by example and apprenticeship rather than by explicit definitions. Theoretical concepts, just like the concept of living organism, are "open-ended" (1970/2001, 233).

Hempel was not the only logical empiricist who felt misgivings with the "standard conception," in particular with its "uninterpreted calculus." Nagel also made proposals to improve the received account. In *The Structure of Science* (Nagel 1961) he attempted to enhance the standard account in two ways. First, he proposed to introduce a third component for the description of the theory's structure that should provide "an interpretation or a model for the abstract calculus, which supplies some flesh for the skeletal structure in terms of more or less familiar conceptual or visualizable materials" (Nagel 1961, 90). His main example of such a "model" was Bohr's planetary model of the atom. It should be noted, however, that Nagel's "model" did not just serve as heurististic means for visualization; rather, the statements induced by the model had a systematic function much like the formulas of the calculus. Through such a model the theoretical concepts of the theory received a fuller interpretation. Sticking to a specific model, Nagel admitted, runs the risk that features of the model may mislead us concerning the actual content of the theory. Actually, the theory may have many distinct models. If one likes, one may consider Nagel's proposal to introduce a model as a major component of a theory's structure, as a forerunner of the so-called semantic view of theories that was to flourish long after the dismissal of logical empiricism.[12]

Nagel's second amendment of the traditional answer of the T-question was his insight that scientific knowledge does not have (at least not up to now) the form of one great unified theory. Rather, it presents itself as a complex network of interrelated theories. Consequently, a natural widening of the T-question is to study the structure of this network constituted by theories and various "intertheoretic" relations. Nagel concentrated on intertheoretic relations that provided reductions of theories (Nagel 1961, ch. 11). According to him reduction is an essentially deductive relation: a primary theory T is reducible to a secondary theory T* if it is possible (1) to provide a common language for the theories T and T* ("condition of connectability"), and (2) to derive T from T* ("condition of derivability"). As the paradigmatic example for such a reduction Nagel considered the relation between thermodynamics and statistical mechanics. Later, "postpositivist" accounts of reduction relations blamed Nagel's proposal for being "too

---

[12] Indeed, the semantic view characterizes a theory "as comprising two elements: (1) a population of models, and (2) various hypotheses linking those models with systems in the real world" (Giere 1988, 85). This two ingredients are then related to each other by "relations of similarity" in a way that structurally resembles the base diagram of the Logical Empiricists (Giere 1988, 83).

deductive" to serve as a realistic account of actual science, but the emphasis Nagel put on deduction does not mean that he restricted the philosophical analysis of reduction solely to its logico-deductive aspects. If a reduction in his sense is intended to be more than just a logical exercise, the primary (reducing) science has to be "supported by empirical evidence possessing some degree of probative force" (Nagel 1961, 358). This means that history of science has a bearing on the topic of reducibility: "the question whether a given science is reducible to another cannot in the abstract be usefully raised without reference to some particular stage of development of the two disciplines. The question of reducibility can be profitably discussed only if they are made definite by specifying the established content at a given date of the sciences under consideration" (Nagel 1961, 361–2). Nagel's account was intended to elucidate the global logical structure of scientific knowledge without losing sight of its historical context.

Not all logical empiricists showed a pronounced preference for matters logical with respect to the T-question. Feigl's importance resides less in his contributions to the task of elucidating the formal structure of theories and more in the particular interpretation of the formal apparatus he proposed.[13] He was the logical empiricist most eager to reconcile logical empiricism with some sort of realism. In the 1950s he touted himself as an "empirical realist" (1950, 221). He explicitly rejected the standard account according to which the postulates concerning the theoretical terms had a purely instrumentalist reading. According to him, "The system of statements and concepts that constitutes our scientific knowledge is best understood as a network that connects the directly confirmable with the indirectly confirmable" (ibid., 217). He admitted, of course, that theoretical entities may be unobservable but he insisted that they are "indirectly confirmable." This may be considered as a realist variation of the standard theme to elucidate the relation between the two basic components of scientific knowledge. But Feigl also emphasized the following point (1970, 13): "It should be stressed,

---

[13] Feigl once went so far to trace back the essentials of the Logical Empiricist account of empirical theories to an early (pre-Vienna) paper of Carnap that may well be classified as belonging to his neo-Kantian period (cf. Carnap 1923; Feigl 1970, 3). This stance betrays, to put it mildly, that Feigl did not pay too much attention to the amendments that had taken place since then.

and not merely bashfully admitted, that the rational reconstruction of theories is a highly artificial hindsight operation which has little to do with the work of the creative scientist." In an analogous way as in science, in philosophy of science as well idealizations and simplifications are indispensable. What philosophy of science is after is not to give us empirical theories as they "really are," but models of those theories that may help us to understand the structure and the aims of scientific knowledge.

Feigl's subscription to a realist version of empiricism should not be taken as evidence for a predominance of realist currents in the logical empiricism of the fifties and sixties of the last century. Quite the contrary is true. For instance, the physicist Frank, who had been Einstein's successor at the German University in Prague, stuck to a pragmatic instrumentalism. Having started his philosophical career as a radical conventionalist and instrumentalist inspired by Poincaré and Duhem, later he submerged his conventionalism and adopted an attitude according to which logical empiricism might be understood as a logically refined version of pragmatism:

In contrast to the method of pragmatism, however, they [the logical empiricists] not only tried to characterize the system of science in a general and somewhat indefinite way by saying that the system is an instrument to be invented and constructed in order to find one's way among experiences, but also – and instead – they investigated the structure and the construction of this instrument. The investigation took place through an analysis of the method by which physics orders experiences through a mathematical system of formulas. (Frank 1949, 105)

In a similar fashion to Carnap in *Abriss*, Frank claimed that the clarification of the internal structure of empirical theories is preeminently guided by practical interests. In contrast to Carnap, however, Frank never engaged in serious work on the formal structure of empirical theories. Instead, he took the logical empiricist model to be valid at least in broad outline and developed an instrumentalist-pragmatic interpretation of it. He considered the "new" logic of Whitehead and Russell as a useful tool to "improve the ideas of Mach and James to a really scientific world conception" (Frank 1949, 105). Hence, the relation between the formal-constructive efforts to answer the T-question by Carnap and those working in a similar style and authors such as Feigl and Frank, who were more engaged in formulating epistemological interpretations, can be characterized as a sort of division of labor: the first concentrated on the more formal aspects leaving space for pragmatic considerations provided by the work of the latter. Although the two accounts are not always easily reconciled, it is remarkable that all considered themselves as working on a common project, namely, of elucidating how we "master reality through systems of hypotheses and axioms," as it was once put in the manifesto.

For reasons of space, we cannot deal with authors like Henry Margenau (1950), or Norman R. Campbell (1953), who developed quite similar accounts of empirical theories, although strictly speaking they cannot be characterized as logical empiricists. Nevertheless, it should have become clear that speaking of *the* logical empiricist view of theories is seriously misleading in so far as such an expression suggests that there was a unique logical empiricist answer to the T-question.

THE DISMISSAL OF LOGICAL EMPIRICISM

Postpositivist philosophers of science such as Feyerabend, Putnam, and others dismissed the logical empiricist answers to the T-questions as totally misleading and wrong-headed from the outset. To bring home their point they found two rhetorical maneuvers extremely useful. First, the plurality of logical empiricist answers to the T-question was reduced to what the postpositivists ominously dubbed the "received" or the "orthodox view." Moreover, the fact that logical empiricism had taken into consideration many pragmatic and historical aspects of scientific theorizing was systematically ignored. A striking evidence for this attitude was the utter neglect of Neurath's encyclopedism by virtually all of the postpositivist critics. Second, the logical empiricists' claims were stated in an overly strong fashion, not considering them as proposals or as models for the elucidation of the structure of empirical theories, but as "dogmas."[14] Thereby, an allegedly unbridgeable gap between the

---

[14] The tendency to portray Logical Empiricism as an obsolete doctrine centering around certain "dogmas" started with Quine's "Two Dogmas" of 1951. It reached its late and somewhat ridiculous culmination in the early eighties when allegedly "six or seven dogmas of Logical Empiricism" were discovered.

logical empiricist account and its modern ("enlightened") successors was constructed that played down as far as possible many of the existing similarities. Actually, many of the themes of postpositivist philosophy of science are extensions and variations of ideas found already discussed in the logical empiricism, whose variety and intellectual flexibility tends to be grossly underestimated. For instance, the distinction between observational and theoretical terms was never thought to be one that could be drawn in a clear-cut manner once and for all. Logical empiricism was much more liberal and pragmatic than many of its heirs believe. Even many of the seemingly radically novel arguments against a too rigid conception of the structure of empirical theories can already be found in Neurath.

With hindsight, then, the dismissal of logical empiricism as hopelessly obsolete was somewhat hasty, brought about more by interest-guided reconstructions than by solid new arguments. In particular, the complacent attitude of many postpositivist thinkers that postpositivist philosophy of science has moved far ahead of its empiricist ancestors is in need of qualification, to say the least. Carnap, Neurath, Feigl, and others were well aware of the fact that philosophy of science is engaged in making models of scientific theories. Its task is not to explicate what scientific theories "really are." Rather, the models of scientific theories it offers us are more or less adequate, depending on the purposes they are made for. Moreover, since there is no reason to expect that scientific theories of all times and types will always have the same structure, the T-question is unlikely to receive just one answer. Nevertheless, it seems equally unlikely that answers that completely ignore the proposals of logical empiricism will be good ones.

Part Three: Logical Empiricism and the Philosophy of the Special Sciences

7 The Turning Point and the Revolution

Philosophy of Mathematics in Logical Empiricism from *Tractatus* to *Logical Syntax*

I am convinced that we now find ourselves at an altogether decisive turning point in philosophy. And that we are objectively justified in considering that an end has come to the fruitless conflict of systems.

Bertrand Russell and Gottlob Frege have opened up important stretches in the last decades, but Ludwig Wittgenstein (in his *Tractatus-Logico-Philosophicus*, 1922) is the first to have pushed forward to the decisive turning point.

Moritz Schlick, 1930[1]

Its philosophy of logic and mathematics was what most characteristically distinguished logical empiricism from previous forms of empiricism or positivism. This is the aspect that gave it the name *logical* empiricism, and gave it the hope of succeeding where the nineteenth-century attempts at a scientific empiricism by such figures as Comte, Mill, and Mach had failed. The inability of these thinkers to supply a plausible account of mathematics had undermined the claim of empiricism to be the philosophical approach most adequate to modern science. It was generally agreed that Mill's empiricist account of arithmetic had not succeeded. He had portrayed the truths of arithmetic as empirical generalizations,

---

[1] From "Die Wende der Philosophie" (The Turning Point in Philosophy), which opened the first issue of *Erkenntnis* (1930, 5, 6/1979, vol. 2, 155). We have provided our own translations of the German texts; for ease of reference, the place of the relevant passage in the available translation is indicated following the orginal reference.

obtained inductively from repeated experience of counting. Mach had offered a similar account of geometrical proof. Common to these nineteenth-century empiricist approaches to mathematics had been their *psychologism*, their classification of mathematical truth as a kind of empirical truth about mental processes.

From a present-day vantage point, Frege's critique of Mill and of psychologism more generally looks devastating. It is hard for us to imagine how, after that, empiricist accounts of mathematics could still have been taken seriously. But what was still missing was a *positive* account of mathematics to replace the empiricist one. The positive accounts of mathematics offered by Frege and then, more notoriously, by Russell, had not seemed persuasive to empiricists. Nineteenth-century mathematicians had persuasively reduced analysis to the arithmetic of the natural numbers, while Frege and Russell had reduced arithmetic to logic, and gone a long way towards showing that there are no specifically mathematical concepts or entities that are not already present in our most basic tools of thought. But for scientific empiricists, this had only pushed the problem of the status of mathematics *down* a level; it now became a problem of the status of *logic*. And on that score, neither Frege nor Russell had been helpful. They had taken opposite approaches to this problem, both still remaining within the Kantian framework. Frege had extended to arithmetic the *analytic* status of logic. Geometry remained synthetic, in his view, but he had nothing useful to say about the nature of analytic, logical truth itself, or the resulting difference between arithmetic and geometry. Russell, on the other hand, accepting Kant's view of mathematics as *synthetic a priori*, took its reduction to logic as extending that status downwards to the laws of logic themselves. This was even harder for empiricists to swallow.

Moritz Schlick, for one, did not accept it, before he came to Vienna in 1922. He adhered, rather, to a psychologistic view along the lines of Mill or Mach. Unlike Kant, he thought the truths of arithmetic to be *analytic*.[2] And analytic sentences, he writes in one

---

[2] He had apparently not heard of Frege at this point; in any case, Frege's logicism (unlike Russell's) still left geometry aside as a special case. For Frege, geometry retained its Kantian status of synthetic a priori, which would have been unsatisfactory to Schlick, who accepted Helmholtz's view that the question whether physical space is Euclidean or non-Euclidean was an empirical one.

of his early papers, are *verified* by the immediate *perception* (in inner sense) that the subject and predicate (or the expressions on both sides of an equality) have the same meaning (Schlick 1910, 441–3/1979 vol. 1, 76–9). Schlick specifically rejects Russell's view (which he called the "independence theory of truth") that analytic sentences, including those of mathematics, are true *independently* of such mental verification:

An act of judgement and the logical sentence [expressing it] are not completely separate things; above all, the logical sentence – including its truth – is nowhere to be found independently of the act of judgement. Indeed it is contained in that act and arises from it by abstraction. The logical is contained in the real act of judgement not because of a fortuitous accident by which a truth happens to be manifested [in judgement] that also maintains some separate existence. The case is rather as follows: the logical meaning has its location only *in* the psychic experience and in no way exists outside it. The two are just plain impossible to separate; the judgement as a logical figure,... with its timeless character, comes into being simply by abstracting everything individual and temporal from the real act of judgement.... When we subtract everything that is a psychological product from our representation [*Vorstellung*] of the number 2, *nothing* is left. (Schlick 1910, 404–5/1979 vol. 1, 54–5)

There could hardly be a more uncompromising statement of psychologism; the number two is *entirely* accounted for as a "psychological product". When we take that away, "*nothing* is left". Schlick's view changed significantly in the decade or so before he came to Vienna. Under the influence of Hilbert, he came to accept that axiomatically ("implicitly") defined concepts (with no psychological roots at all) play a central role in theoretical science. But he was never able to relate these axiomatic concepts convincingly to empirical concepts, and made no progress beyond Mill or Mach on the critical problem of specifying the *status* of mathematics in a way that was compatible with scientific empiricism.

Against this background it is easier to appreciate what a revelation Wittgenstein's *Tractatus* was for the Vienna Circle. It solved what had been, in their eyes, the fundamental problem of empiricism. For them, this was the "turning point in philosophy", and during the 1920s their philosophy of mathematics was rooted in that of the *Tractatus*. We describe this view in Section I. But in fact the Circle was aware from the start that this view required some drastic surgery to be useful for their purposes, and they discussed these problems, which are the subject of Section II, very openly. The logical empiricists were unable to move beyond their original framework in any fundamental way, though, until 1931, when Carnap showed the way with his new ideas that were eventually formulated as the "syntax" program in 1932–4. This transition came in two steps, which we describe in Sections III and IV. These post-1931 developments were presented in a rather technical form, however, and were published just at the time that the European logical empiricists were scattered to the winds by the Nazis. So the "syntax" idea and its successors did not achieve the widespread notoriety of the earlier, Wittgensteinian approach and was often misunderstood. It was, we conclude by emphasizing (against still widespread prejudice to the contrary), a fundamental break with that earlier view.[3]

THE *TRACTATUS* CONCEPTION AS TURNING POINT

The nineteenth-century empiricists had rejected Kant's account of mathematics as synthetic a priori, for it implied that some non-trivial knowledge is not empirical. A consistent empiricism, they agreed, required the reduction of all genuine knowledge to observable facts. Kant had thought that mathematics is an exception to this. He had not really given any persuasive arguments for this view, but had essentially taken it for granted as evident. He was one of the first to notice, though, that classical Aristotelian syllogistic logic

---

[3] A full history of logical empiricist philosophy of mathematics would have to describe many byways we have to omit here. We focus largely on the Wittgensteinian "turning point" that inspired the Vienna Circle's early doctrine, and then Carnap's efforts first to work *within* that framework, later to overcome it. Our reason for this focus is that Carnap's development was what led to the "revolution" we describe in parts III and IV, which is widely regarded as the most innovative development within logical empiricist philosophy of mathematics. More foundationally oriented readers will prefer more of an emphasis on Felix Kaufmann's phenomenologically oriented intuitionism, Hans Hahn's logicism, Schlick's notion of implicit definition, and Karl Menger's attempts to mediate between Brouwer and the logicist ideas prevalent in the Circle. Gödel, who does play a role in our story, may well have been influenced by some of these currents in the later formulation of his philosophical ideas. We omit them only in the interest of telling a coherent story in a limited space.

could not account for all the reasoning processes in mathematics, which must therefore, he thought, be synthetic. By this he meant that the sentences of arithmetic and geometry predicate more of their subjects than could be found in the subjects themselves; $5 + 7 = 12$, he claimed, was to assert something about 5 and 7 that we could not know just by considering these two individual items in isolation. Lest one be tempted to judge Kant's philosophy by this apparently rather feeble example, he is on much stronger ground in geometry, where it really seems almost miraculous that we should be able to extract something as unobvious as the Pythagorean theorem from the apparently obvious axioms. There must, therefore, he thought, be something in the axioms that, while obvious to us intuitively, actually goes beyond anything directly observable; the axioms, he said, are built into our perceptual system. It is impossible for us to doubt them. And the *reasoning process* of mathematics, he thought, must go beyond mere logic. Our intellects are evidently capable of a kind of *synthesis* that goes beyond what the trivial mechanical procedures of mere logic (by which he meant Aristotelian logic) can achieve on their own.

Nineteenth-century empiricists had a twofold task, then, in responding to Kant's philosophy of mathematics. First, they had to show that all the *axioms* were empirical. And, second, they had to show that all mathematical *reasoning processes* were not dependent on the human mind (i.e., that they were just as mechanical as traditional Aristotelian logic). The first of these tasks they felt had essentially been achieved by the 1870s, mainly in the work of the German physicist and physiologist Hermann von Helmholtz. The second task was a little more complicated. Certainly Frege had taken the first step in 1879, when he envisaged (and began to spell out) a purely formal or mechanical system of logic that, unlike Aristotelian logic, was fully capable of accounting exhaustively for every step in all the reasoning processes of both arithmetic and geometry (the *axioms* of geometry, for Frege, remained synthetic a priori). But mathematics was developing very rapidly during this period. By the beginning of the twentieth century Georg Cantor's set-theoretic apparatus for infinite numbers had become well established and raised serious questions for logicism. Ernst Zermelo had responded, on behalf of the Hilbert school, with an axiomatization of set theory, which eventuated in a clear distinction, unavailable to Frege, between logic and set theory. Russell, on the other hand, had responded with his theory of types, which still made the reduction of mathematics to logic possible, at the cost of a very small number of axioms of uncertain status.[4] Russell himself, followed by certain well-known set theorists such as Fraenkel (and by the young Carnap), had argued that these axioms could (or should) be regarded as "logical", thus rescuing his reduction of mathematics to logic, as sketched in his *Principles of Mathematics* (1902) and partly carried out in his and Whitehead's *Principia Mathematica* (1910–12).

This was the situation when the *Tractatus* was published in 1922. Wittgenstein rejected Russell's arguments for the logical status of the questionable axioms, but accepted both Frege's conception of logic as a purely syntactic, mechanical system *and* Frege's account of mathematical reasoning as purely logical. Far more important to the Vienna Circle than these particular arguments, though, was Wittgenstein's response to Frege's and Russell's "universalist" conception of logic. Though Frege and Russell had, as we saw, taken opposite philosophical approaches to the assimilation of mathematics to logic (Frege making arithmetic analytic, while Russell at least initially made logic synthetic), they shared with Aristotle, Kant, and many other philosophers the view that the laws of logic (whatever their status, analytic or synthetic) were laws of *everything*; they governed all being – physical, mental, and otherwise. They were, according to Russell, like the laws of physics, only more general. So even if the logicist reduction of all mathematics to logic could be made to work, the *status* of this logic-and-mathematics was not really compatible, before Wittgenstein, with an empiricist view.

Wittgenstein himself was not an empiricist, but his account of logic broke with Frege's and Russell's universalism and put forward a radically different conception of the nature of logic. Logical laws were not about anything extralinguistic, in this conception. They were not laws of everything, pertaining to a universe of objects and expressed transparently in language along with other sorts of facts. Instead, language itself was regarded as a *medium*, as not part of the world but as representing the world to us. Though imperfect, it was

---

[4] Such as the axioms of infinity, choice, and reducibility.

still, as in Frege and Russell, a universal medium. It represented the world to us, Wittgenstein thought, by means of logical pictures that were somehow isomorphic to facts in the world. Complex facts were represented by compound sentences (pictures) constructed from sentences representing simple facts by the logical truth functions ("and", "or", "not", "if-then"), which are completely determined by their truth tables. Language was governed by a system of rules, then, connected to the world by this picture theory of meaning.[5] The truths of logic were a by-product of this representational function of language. They ceased to be part of what language describes, and became instead an artifact of the representational capacity of language. As such, logical truths became tautological and empty, despite still being universal (see the exposition in Ricketts 1996, 59–64). Hans Hahn, like the rest of the Vienna Circle, thought this idea of critical importance:

If one wants to regard logic – as this has in fact been done – as the study of the most general qualities of objects, as the study of objects in general [*überhaupt*], then empiricism would in fact be confronted here with an impassable hurdle. In reality, though, logic says nothing whatever about objects. Logic is not something that is to be found in the world. Logic only arises, rather, when – by means of a symbolism – we *speak about the world*. ... The sentences of logic say nothing about the world. (Hahn 1929, 56/1980, 39–40)

This was Schlick's "turning point", which so impressed and inspired the Vienna Circle. Apart from Russell himself, they were the first careful readers of the *Tractatus*. Schlick was called to the chair in the philosophy of the inductive sciences at the University of Vienna in 1922, the same year as the *Tractatus* first appeared in book form. Soon after his arrival, the first of several close, line-by-line readings of the text in the Schlick circle's weekly meetings began. By 1926, when Carnap moved to Vienna, Schlick and his assistants Feigl and Waismann were meeting personally with Wittgenstein and reporting on these conversations to the full Circle. Soon after

---

[5] The degree to which each component of this view represents Wittgenstein's own, as opposed to one he puts forward in the early parts of the *Tractatus* only dialectically, so that we can better appreciate its self-undermining character in the later parts, is controversial; see Ricketts (1996, esp. 88–94). Our discussion of the Vienna Circle's ideas is independent of this question.

Carnap's arrival another line-by-line reading of the *Tractatus* began, in the Circle, and eventually Carnap also joined the personal meetings with Wittgenstein – until Wittgenstein excluded him in 1929. But from about that time until Wittgenstein's departure for Cambridge, Waismann took careful notes of the conversations so as to report the master's words back to the Circle more accurately. (This later became a book: Waismann [1967].)

This fascination with the *Tractatus* derives from the Circle's perception that Wittgenstein had finally solved the age-old Platonic problem of the cognitive status of logic (and thus, in their minds, mathematics), making it safe for empiricism. "It really does seem on first sight as if the very existence of mathematics must mean the failure of pure empiricism – as if we had in mathematics a knowledge about the world that doesn't come from experience, as if we had a priori knowledge", Hans Hahn had said. "And this evident difficulty for empiricism is so plain, so brutal, that anyone who wants to hold a consistent empiricism has to face this difficulty" (Hahn 1929, 55–6/1980, 39–40). Wittgenstein had solved this problem, in the Circle's view. "Wittgenstein's book exerted a strong influence upon our Circle", Carnap later said. "We learned much by our discussions of the book, and accepted many views as far as we could assimilate them to our basic conceptions" (Carnap 1963, 24). "The thinking of our Circle was strongly influenced by Wittgenstein's ideas, first because of our common reading of the *Tractatus* and later by virtue of Waismann's systematic exposition of certain conceptions of Wittgenstein's on the basis of his talks with him" (Carnap 1963, 28). Carnap specifically included himself in these statements: "For me personally, Wittgenstein was perhaps the philosopher who, besides Russssell and Frege, had the greatest influence on my thinking" (Carnap 1963, 25).

It is generally now taken for granted by many Wittgenstein scholars that, despite this very thorough involvement with the text of the *Tractatus* and with Wittgenstein personally, the Circle fundamentally misunderstood some of Wittgenstein's intentions. But it should be kept in mind that their priority was to *apply* Wittgenstein's ideas to their overriding project of a consistent empiricism that could account for mathematics and mathematical science, not to remain faithful to Wittgenstein's own intentions.

PROBLEMS WITH THE *TRACTATUS* CONCEPTION

The Vienna Circle's Wittgensteinian solution to the old problems carried a high price tag. Linguistic representation was limited to truth-functions of "atomic sentences", which the Vienna Circle (and Wittgenstein as well, at least at certain points during the late 1920s and early 1930s)[6] thought of as simplest observation statements, along the lines of Mach's "elements" (or the "elementary experiences" of Carnap's *Aufbau*). This created two headaches for the Vienna Circle. First, not even a fragment of actually existing science could be expressed as finitary truth functions of simple observation statements. Indeed, it seemed that most theoretical science could not be expressed, or had no meaning, within the *Tractatus* framework.[7] The second problem was perhaps not Wittgenstein's own, but was suggested by Wittgenstein's emphasis on the impossibility of representing the representation relation itself in language. This conception seemed to exclude the possibility of meta-linguistic discourse. This problem was much discussed in the Vienna Circle in 1930–1. Gödel, for instance, is recorded as asking on one occasion "how the discussion of logical questions could be justified, as it involves the utterance not of any meaningful sentences but only of elucidations [*Erläuterungen*]. This raises the question how admissable elucidations are to be demarcated from metaphysical pseudo-sentences" (ASP/RC 081-07-11, reprinted in Stadler 1997, 288/ 2001, 254). Hardly a sentence in the *Tractatus* itself (or any of the Vienna Circle publications) could reasonably be construed as a truth function of atomic sentences. And Wittgenstein himself had made this self-undermining conclusion explicit in the final sentences of his book.

These consequences of the *Tractatus* were unacceptable to the Vienna Circle because they conflicted with their central project of rational reconstruction. If much of existing theoretical science fails to qualify as meaningful, and discourse about language is excluded in any case, then it becomes impossible even to compare different

---

[6] In a conversation of 1930–1, for instance, he says that "object" in the *Tractatus* is "used for such things as a colour, a point in visual space, etc" (Lee 1980, 120).

[7] If a scientific theory is a truth function of observation sentences, then it *can* only be a statement about a finite number of instances, not a universal law. This was why the picture theory, combined with the Circle's empiricism, made theoretical science as ordinarily conceived impossible.

expressions regarding their precision or their usefulness for some practical purpose. It becomes impossible to say, for instance, that a rationally reconstructed concept is *more precise*, or *more useful*, than the concept to be reconstructed. This obstructs the Vienna Circle's practical critique of metaphysics and unclear thinking, and undermines its entire Enlightenment project. It was imperative, therefore, to address these two problems.

Though the Circle discussed these problems in Wittgensteinian terms, they approached them with their own agendas firmly in mind. The constitution system of Carnap's *Aufbau*, in particular, had left a good deal of unfinished business. It had been criticized (by Reichenbach and Eino Kaila)[8] for failing to accommodate certain modes of inference required in actual science, such as empirical induction, probability, and statistical inference.

An even more serious problem was raised by axiomatic systems. The explicit definitions in which Carnap had (nominally, at least) constructed the whole of knowledge in the *Aufbau* could not accommodate "implicit definitions" of concepts in axiomatic systems. Schlick, influenced by Hilbert, had made such implicit definitions central to his treatise *General Theory of Knowledge* (1918; 2nd ed. 1925). He had contrasted them with ordinary ostensive or "concrete" definitions based on psychological abstraction, which he portrayed as the traditional form of concept formation in science. Only with the recent domination of mathematical physics (especially in the theory of relativity), he said, had axiomatic systems come to dominate the exact sciences. The problem, though, was that while concretely defined concepts had a clearly identifiable empirical content, implicitly defined concepts did not:

an implicit definition has nothing in common with reality, no connection with it; implicit definition rejects such connection purposely, and in principle; it sticks to the realm of concepts. A system of truths created with the aid of implicit definition rests nowhere on the foundation of reality, but rather floats freely. . . . In general, we deal with the abstract only to apply it to the concrete. But – and this is the point to which our investigation returns

---

[8] Kaila's (1930) critique was the first book-length assessment of the Vienna Circle; it focused its criticisms almost exclusively on Carnap's *Aufbau*. It frequently invokes Reichenbach (1929), which argues (pp. 26ff./1978, vol. 2, 141ff.) in favor of realism and against positivism, though not explicitly against Carnap.

again and again – the moment a conceptual relation is applied to a concrete example, exact rigor is no longer guaranteed. Given real objects, how can we ever know with absolute certainty whether they stand in precisely those relations to each other which are fixed in the postulates by means of which we can define our concepts? (Schlick 1918/1925, 55/1985, 37–8)

Einstein, who during the early 1920s frequently conversed with Schlick about this very issue, had famously declared that "Insofar as the sentences of mathematics refer to reality, they are not certain, and insofar as they are certain they do not refer to reality" (Einstein 1921a, 3). In the same vein, Schlick said that although implicit definition is a means to making concepts absolutely precise, this has required "a radical separation of the concept from intuition, of thought from reality. We relate the two spheres to each other, certainly, but they appear in no way connected; the bridges between them are demolished" (Schlick 1918/1925, 56/1985, 38).

Given their adherence to Wittgenstein's framework, however, the Vienna Circle could not be satisfied with this. It was imperative to bring axiomatic, implicitly defined concepts within the ambit of explicit definitions and truth-functional combinations of atomic sentences. Carnap sat down to address this problem soon after he arrived in Vienna, and from 1927 to 1930 spent most of his time on a large-scale project to reconcile axiomatic definitions with logicism and transform implicit into explicit definitions, or, as he said, to transform "improper concepts" into "proper concepts" (so called because they were explicitly constructed, with fixed meanings to which, e.g., the law of excluded middle applied).[9] The result was a large, unfinished manuscript entitled *Investigations in General Axiomatics*. In the framework set forth in this treatise, axiomatic systems are not regarded as purely syntactic, in the way Hilbert and Schlick had described them, but are given a fixed range of interpretations within a basic system, a *Grunddisziplin*, as Carnap called it, of arithmetic and set theory. This made it possible to regard axiomatic systems as having content, as long as it could be shown that the sentences of the *Grunddisziplin* itself had definite meanings. So

[9] This is discussed in Carnap (1927), which also makes very explicit the connection of the *Axiomatics* project with the *Aufbau* and the Wittgensteinian conception of meaning.

every theorem of an axiomatic system has a definite meaning, since it is interpreted in the *Grunddisziplin*.

Within this framework, Carnap set out to explore the relations among the various properties of axiom systems, especially the relation among the different definitions of "completeness" of an axiom system current at the time. His main result, and the central theorem of the first part of the *Axiomatics* manuscript, proves that an axiom system is categorical if and only if it is complete (in modern terms). This theorem, Carnap hoped, could help to sort useful axiom systems determining "proper concepts" from defective ones – those to which, for example, the law of excluded middle then failed to apply. Thus, in particular, axiomatic arithmetic was inferred to be complete, as the Peano axioms were known to be categorical.[10]

Within his *Axiomatics* manuscript, though, there is no attempt to explain how the *Grunddisziplin* acquires its fixed interpretation. This task Carnap attempted in a loose sketch he wrote down in Davos in April 1929, when he was attending the "Europäische Hochschultage" where Heidegger and Cassirer debated the legacy of Kant.[11] The sketch was headed, ambitiously, "New Foundation for Logic" (*Neue Grundlegung der Logik*). Its main idea is to erect a Hilbertian axiomatic superstructure on a Wittgensteinian basis. The atomic sentences are pictures of elementary facts, as in the *Tractatus*. But other signs, not given a definite meaning in advance, may also be added and treated just like atomic sentences, as may "inference rules" governing the transformation of given sentence forms into other sentence forms. All sentences containing the meaningless signs still have a definite meaning, Carnap argues, as they confine the total space of possibilities to certain rows of the truth-table of a complete truth-functional state-description of the world (of the kind envisaged by Wittgenstein). The only requirement

---

[10] This project is discussed in our (2001, 145–72), where we also give a more detailed account of the importance of this theorem for Carnap's *Aufbau* project as well as the Vienna Circle's entire philosophy of logic and mathematics. Carnap's proof of it is actually correct, in his own terms, despite appearances, but fails to capture what he intended, as we discuss in detail in that paper, and as Carnap himself realized in 1930, even before Gödel's incompleteness results later that year.

[11] On the whole background to this meeting, and its wider significance, see Friedman (2000a).

of a "logic" so constructed – evidently intended as a preliminary sketch for building a *Grunddisziplin*[12] – is that it not allow inference to any atomic sentence that is not already among the premises. Axiom systems may then be framed within such a "logic", and all theorems resulting from them can likewise be assigned a definite meaning because they constrain the truth-table of the complete state-description of the world.[13] This is the case even if they contain signs for infinite sets. These, Carnap says, are licensed within his system, though not purely "formalistically" as in Hilbert; they have a definite meaning, even if not a complete one:

If now, to introduce the infinite, one "adjoins ideal propositions" (Hilbert), i.e. writes down formulas that have no contentful meaning, but permit us to derive the mathematics of the infinite, then we have once again been able to determine the meaning of the signs introduced as meaningless ones, by investigating for which logical constants the formulas would become tautologies. (UCLA/RC1029/Box 4/CM13, 62)

Unlike Hilbert, Carnap admits no purely formal, uninterpreted signs. Despite this, he calls his idea "radical formalism" because it allows not only logical inferences, but any sort of scientific inference – including, relevantly, inductive inference in empirical science or statistical inference – to be employed as part of a "system of logic" in this way. All these inferences are now at the same level. In a talk at Reichenbach's seminar in late 1929, Carnap said that all such inferences could be assimilated to truth-functional inference like that described by Wittgenstein. We can regard any mode of inference, whether in mathematics or in empirical science, he said, formalistically, as a rule for transforming sentences of a certain specified form into sentences of a different form. We can even take

---

[12] Though there is no explicit provision for the quantifiers, Carnap may have intended to develop them axiomatically, as Hilbert and Ackermann (1928, 22–3 and 53–4) had for both the propositional and the predicate calculus. The terminology of the "New Foundation" coincides with Hilbert and Ackermann, where the quantifiers are introduced by "formal axioms", which are distinguished from the "inhaltliche" (material, contentful) rules of inference – the term also used by Carnap.

[13] This idea, too, seems to have been suggested by the *Tractatus*, which says "The truth or falsehood of every single sentence changes something in the general construction of the world. And the range [*Spielraum*] that is left its construction by the totality of atomic sentences is precisely that which the most general sentences delimit" (5.5262).

axiomatic systems of infinitary mathematics and theoretical physics in this way. (Carnap's shorthand notes for this talk are preserved in UCLA/RC1029/Box 4/folder CM13, item 3.) In a lecture in Warsaw of December 1930 he said, along these same lines, that there is only one rule of inference in science: We can transform a sentence however we like, but the conclusion is to have no more content than the premises; it is to constrain the range of possibly true atomic sentences no less than the premises;that is, no new atomic sentences are recognized as true. All laws of logic, as well as all rules of inference in science, he maintains, follow from this principle (ASP/RC 110–07–35, 2).

Though this idea is not thought through, and is in many ways incomplete, it indicates how Carnap was attempting to extend a truth-functional Wittgensteinian language to one usable for mathematics and science, though the kind of solution Carnap was considering saw for mathematics very much the role that Wittgenstein had envisaged for it in the *Tractatus:* "The sentence of mathematics expresses no thought. In life it is never the mathematical sentence we need. We use the mathematical sentence *only* to derive sentences that do not belong to mathematics from other sentences that also do not belong to mathematics" (Wittgenstein 1922, 6.21–6.211). In the course of 1930, however, this somewhat shaky "New Foundation for Logic" collapsed. Three developments contributed to undermine it. First, Carnap's central theorem of the *Axiomatics* fell victim to Gödel's first incompleteness theorem. As Gödel indicated in the discussion following the famous symposium on the philosophy of mathematics in Königsberg in September 1930 (at which Carnap had been the spokesperson for logicism, Heyting for intuitionism, and von Neumann for formalism), there could be true arithmetic sentences that were not provable:

One can even (given the consistency of classical mathematics) give examples of sentences (of the kind stated by *Goldbach* or *Fermat*) that are correct in their content, but not provable in the formal system of classical mathematics. By adding the negation of such a sentence to the axioms of classical mathematics, one obtains a consistent system in which a sentence whose content is false is provable. (Hahn et al. 1931, 148/1984, 128)

Second, the incompleness result had an even more fundamentally devastating effect on logicism itself, which the Vienna Circle had relied on to guarantee the tautological (and thus empty) character of mathematics and indeed of all logical reasoning. The Circle had needed this to undermine the metaphysical idea that conclusions about the real world could be reached by reasoning alone, without factual knowledge (Carnap 1930a, 25/1959, 145). But now it turned out that there could be sentences of arithmetic that, despite the logicist explicit definition of the numbers, were not decidable after all.

Third and finally, the apparent incompatibility of meta-linguistic discourse with Wittgenstein's framework was, as we saw, a fundamental barrier to the Vienna Circle's larger goals, and they sought to overcome it. The new work in mathematical logic, especially by Hilbert, Gödel, and Tarski, made essential use of the distinction between a language and its meta-language. This work appeared to be rigorous, indeed, more rigorous than older logical work like Russell's. It thus seemed to represent a clear counterexample to what the Vienna Circle read into Wittgenstein's final sentences. Still, there was the difficulty that "elucidations", meta-linguistic sentences of the kind Wittgenstein and the Vienna Circle themselves had used in their writings, seemed impossible to put *either* in the form of truth functions of atomic sentences *or* in the mathematical form that Gödel and Tarski were using. Thus by the end of 1930, the basis for the Vienna Circle's entire philosophical edifice was crumbling.

THE REVOLUTION, STEP I: SYNTAX

On January 21, 1931, Carnap came down with a fever. That and the problems described in the previous section kept him awake the following night. But as he tossed and turned, the solution to all his problems came to him in a flash. Or so he says in his autobiography:

After thinking about these problems for several years, the whole theory of language structure and its possible applications in philosophy came to me like a vision during a sleepless night in January 1931, when I was ill. On the following day, still in bed with a fever, I wrote down my ideas on forty-four pages under the title "Attempt at a Metalogic". These shorthand notes were the first version of my book *Logical Syntax of Language*. (Carnap 1963, 53)

These shorthand notes present a radically different perspective from the Wittgensteinian one of the "New Foundation" two years previously.[14] Carnap has here adopted the fully formal, "meta-logical" viewpoint of Gödel and Tarski, according to which the logical language is a system of uninterpreted marks rather than meaningful signs. In the perspective of the "New Foundation", the atomic sentences had been pictures of atomic facts, which had given them their meaning. In the "Attempt at a Metalogic", an atomic sentence is a finite sequence of superscript dots, followed by the letter "f" with a finite sequence of subscript dots, followed by a left parenthesis, followed by the letter "a" with a finite sequence of subscript dots, followed by a right parenthesis, e.g.:

$$^{.....}f \ldots (a \ldots)$$

An atomic sentence, then, was just a finite string meeting certain conditions and consisting of instances of finitely many basic marks (*Zeichen*). In the "New Foundation", a sentence had been a tautology because of what it says, or not, about the world. In the "Attempt at a Metalogic", being a tautology is a property of a string of marks that is defined entirely in terms of its outer form – the type and order of the marks occurring in it. No use is made of the "meaning", "designation", etc., of the marks in defining the central notions of truth-value assignment, consequence, tautology, and the like. Carnap even mentions that the undefined notion "true" might be better to avoid entirely.[15]

From the viewpoint of modern logic, this idea may not seem particularly momentous. Even at the time, it represented no technical innovation; Hilbert and others had been writing on formalism in connection with axiomatics for decades, and the methods of Gödel and Tarski were essentially that. But though Carnap's first attempt to formulate his "meta-logic" was in terms of a particular formal system, his aim was not merely the mathematical study of a given formal logical system. His new idea was precisely to *apply* the insights of Hilbert, Gödel, and Tarski to the entirety of human

---

[14] These notes are preserved in Carnap's papers at the Young Research Library, UCLA, and we discuss them in more detail in our forthcoming paper "Carnap's Dream: Wittgenstein, Gödel, and *Logical Syntax*".

[15] In the margin of p. 3 of the manuscript, Carnap has scrawled, "Regarding the undefined concept '*true*'. It is completely different from the other concepts of metalogic. Perhaps avoidable? [Perhaps] just define which atomic sentences are the "basis" of a sentence, and how. (?)"

knowledge. As we saw above, he had previously accepted Wittgenstein's basic account of the logical language framework in which all science was to be expressed, as the basis for the project of rational reconstruction. In that context the "meta-logical" perspective of regarding language purely as a system of rules, without reference to anything outside itself, was indeed a revolutionary idea.

Before Wittgenstein, language had been regarded as an essentially transparent medium for the expression of thought. The laws of logic were considered by Frege and Russell to be laws of thought, judgment, or perhaps nature – but certainly not of language. Wittgenstein had recognized that they were laws of language. He had been the first to consider the entirety of language as nothing but a system of rules. But he had arrived at this idea via a theory of representation that forced language to consist always and everywhere in a *particular system* of rules, arising necessarily from the representational function of language – the picture theory. The possibility of representation determined a particular form of linguistic intuition, so to speak. This elementary logic built into our form of representation was, like a Kantian form of intuition, an inescapable straight-jacket. The very nature of language, in Wittgenstein's view (at least as seen by the Vienna Circle), prevented us from stepping outside it. One could call this quasi-Kantian view "Wittgenstein's prison".

Under the suggestive influence of Hilbert's formalist approach and the technical work of Gödel and Tarski, Carnap was able to escape from Wittgenstein's prison by taking Wittgenstein's own idea of language as governed by a system of rules one step further. Carnap distinguished the representational or meaning function of language from its purely combinatorial one, and now took the *latter*, rather than the former, as his starting point. The meta-logical methods developed in pursuit of the very mathematical results (such as the incompleteness theorem) that had led to the disintegration of his Wittgenstein-based position in the "New Foundation", it turned out, also showed a way of breaking out of Wittgenstein's prison, and making the structure of language itself the object of logical study.

As opposed to the confinement of all possible knowledge within the absolute constraints imposed by a (naturally or metaphysically) fixed structure of our means of expression, the new recognition that linguistic structure could itself be investigated opened up a whole new method for the unification and clarification of knowledge. Thus Carnap retained Wittgenstein's idea of language as a system of rules, but threw off the shackles of Wittgenstein's prison in favor of the logicians' meta-logical perspective. He comprehensively and definitively turned his back on the picture theory of the *Tractatus* – and thus also on its foundationalism. Meaning was no longer built up from some basic (naturally occurring or metaphysically unavoidable) components, but was now determined entirely by rules. Rules can be determined by humans. The upshot of Carnap's dream, then, was a liberation from the manacles of a fixed structure imposed on the human mind by natural or metaphysical factors beyond human control. If Wittgenstein's insight into the formal nature of logical truth had been the turning point in philosophy, then January 1931 was the revolution it ushered in, where the Vienna Circle's voluntarism[16] could finally find its proper scope and expression. With respect to Wittgenstein's prison, this change was literally an overnight transformation from slave to master.

But there were still many obstacles to be overcome in working out the new idea. Carnap began, in the "Attempt at a Metalogic", with the notion that by keeping the logical object language free of assumptions, there would be a distinguished meta-language in which arithmetic could be read off from the dot sequences of the object language.[17] Thus the numbers are not defined as higher-order concepts in the Frege-Russell logicist style, but "purely as figures" (*rein figurell*), on the basis of the dot sequences attached to the symbols. Arithmetical properties and statements then belong to the meta-language. Thus, for example, the commutativity of addition $n + m = m + n$ was supposed to follow from the fact that n-many dots written to the left of m-many dots gives the same series of dots as writing them to the right of m-many dots. The question of the need for mathematical induction *in the meta-language* is considered, but dismissed with some optimism.

If arithmetic was to be formulated in the meta-language of logic, then mathematical analysis was to be formulated in its

---

[16] Jeffrey (1995) discusses Carnap's voluntarism in particular; for the Vienna Circle more widely (esp. the so-called left Vienna Circle), see Uebel (2004).

[17] An addition of February 7, 1931, to the manuscript says, "the syntax of the rows of dots is arithmetic" (p. 1).

meta-meta-language. For real numbers are properties or series of natural numbers, and properties of them and statements about them properly belong one level up. Carnap may have been guided, in this idea, by Russell's suggestion, in his introduction to the *Tractatus*, that one could perhaps break out of Wittgenstein's prison by using a scheme involving a hierarchy of languages:

> These difficulties suggest to my mind some such possibility as this: that every language has, as Mr. Wittgenstein says, a structure concerning which, *in the language*, nothing can be said, but that there may be another language dealing with the structure of the first language, and having itself a new structure, and that to this hierarchy of languages there may be no limit. (Introduction to Wittgenstein's *Tractatus*, 23)

Having now found the mechanism for such a scheme in the form of "meta-logic", applying it to achieve a hierarchy consisting of language, meta-language, meta-meta-language, and so on[18] must have indeed seemed rather compelling, at first sight.

THE REVOLUTION, STEP 2: TOLERANCE

Carnap soon realized that the restricted system of the "Attempt at a Metalogic" would not permit him to express certain essential meta-logical concepts, such as *provability*. The combinatorial theory required for their formulation was every bit as complicated as arithmetic itself. Thus in the late spring of 1931, Carnap decided to move to a conventional axiomatic arithmetic in the *object* language, so that the axiomatized arithmetic could then be used to express the meta-language, using Gödel's method of arithmetization. In a series of talks Carnap gave to the Vienna Circle in June and July of 1931 about the syntax idea, he explains the difference this makes to his system quite vividly: "The difference between arithmetic metalogic and the metalogic portrayed previously is this: arithmetic metalogic

---

[18] The "Attempt" ends with a summary in four points: "(1) The particular *natural numbers* occur as signs of *the language itself*. (2) The so-called '*properties of natural numbers*' are not proper properties, but syntactic (Wittgenstein: internal) ones, so are to be expressed in the *metalanguage*. (3) A particular *real number* is a property or sequence of natural numbers, so is also to be expressed in the *metalanguage*. (4) The *properties of real numbers* are not real properties, but syntactic properties (with respect to the syntax of the metalanguage), and thus *to be expressed in the meta-metalanguage*" (p. 44).

treats not the empirically available, but all possible configurations. Our previous metalogic is the descriptive theory of certain given configurations, it is the geography of language forms, while the arithmetized metalogic is the geometry of language forms" (ASP/RC 081–07–18; reprinted in Stadler 1997, 325/2001, 290). This move had the further advantage of collapsing the entire hierarchy of languages and meta-languages into itself, at least in principle, by iterating Gödel's method of arithmetizing the meta-language in the object language. Thus it appeared (for a time at least) that one could now get by with only a single language after all.

However well this seemed to work, there was a price to be paid for it. For the very thing that had made the "meta-logical" solution possible – that is, the precise definablity of the central meta-logical notions and their expressibility in the object language – was also responsible for the essential incompleteness of the logical treatment of mathematics. The identification of the logical with the formal seemed to restrict its scope to only what can be expressed with very limited means. If, however, there were no intrinsic constraints on the sorts of formal properties of formulas that could be considered, then perhaps there could be a formal criterion for mathematical truth *different* from mere provability. Since Gödel had shown that provability was insufficient – there were "true" arithmetical statements not derivable from the axioms – the identification of such a criterion was essential. Carnap seems to have developed such a criterion sometime in the latter part of 1931, in the form of the notion of *analyticity*. This was to be a stronger sort of logical truth than provability in a formal system, but was still to be determined strictly in terms of the formal character of the symbols.

Analyticity was apparently to take the place of provability as the generalized notion of tautology or logical truth. To understand how this was intended, consider the analogy of a chess game. Think of the starting position of the pieces as the axioms, the permitted moves as the rules of inference, and a sequence of moves ending in checkmate as a proof of a theorem. But now observe that there are configurations of pieces on the board that constitute checkmate, but cannot be reached from the starting position by any sequence of permitted rules. Such a configuration represents an analytic sentence that has no proof. In this way, the definition of analytic sentence can be phrased entirely formally, in accordance with all the same rules of inference, and yet still be wider than provability. Thus the absolute, Wittgensteinian conception of tautology could be saved, and indeed finally extended beyond propositional logic in accordance with the Vienna Circle's original ambitions.

Such a notion of analyticity was apparently defined in the first draft of the *Logical Syntax*, entitled *Metalogik*. From the evidence available it is clear that the definition was defective. Gödel objected to it, pointing out that it will be *impossible* to give a correct definition of it in *any* meta-language that can be faithfully represented in the object language, for instance, by arithmetization. This fact has since become known as Tarski's theorem on the indefinability of truth. Thus it turns out that Carnap's single-language approach will not work after all.

Carnap did eventually, with Gödel's help, work out a new definition of "analytic", but this definition, which had previously been so crucial, was not even deemed important enough to include in the first edition of *Logical Syntax of Language*; it was omitted "for reasons of space" (Carnap 1934, vii; for the subsequent career of the analyticity concept in Carnap's thought, see our 2007). The problem with it was that the notion of analyticity it defined was not absolute, but rather in a certain sense, conventional. It gave a notion of "analytic in *L*", but only with respect to *another* language *L'*, used for the interpretation of *L*. There might be a natural or conventional choice for *L'* – type theory of the next higher type, or axiomatic set theory – but it could hardly be claimed that any particular such choice is the *correct* notion of analytic for a given language. This *language relativity* of the central notions of meta-logic turned out to be more important to Carnap than the particular meta-logical definitions themselves.

In his first publication after this exchange, we find that a new tone has suddenly entered Carnap's writing, one that was much closer in spirit to the scientific temperament of the Vienna Circle than the absolute and somewhat oracular style of Wittgenstein: "In my view the issue here is not between two conceptions that contradict each other, but rather between *two methods for constructing the language of science, which are both possible and justified*" (Carnap 1932a, 215/ 1987, 457). The context for this first appearance of a new kind of pluralism is the epistemological question about the form of the observation language (or "protocol language") in science. Carnap is very explicit about his change of position:

Not only the question whether the protocol sentences are inside or outside the syntax language, but also the further question regarding their precise specification, is to be answered, it seems to me, not by an assertion, but by a stipulation [Festseztung]. Though I earlier left this question open ... I now think that the different answers are not contradictory. They are to be taken as proposals for stipulations [Vorschläge zu Festsetzungen]; the task is to investigate these different possible stipulations as to their consequences and assess their usefulness. (Carnap 1932a, 216/ 1987, 48)

In *Logical Syntax of Language*, a year or two later, Carnap formulated this new attitude as a "principle of tolerance", and announced it with some excitement in the book's preface:

The range of possible language forms, and thus of different possible logical systems is ... incomparably larger than the very narrow range in which modern logical investigations have so far operated. Up to now there have only been occasional small departures from the language form given by *Russell*, which has already become classical. ... The reason for not daring to depart further from this classical form would appear to lie in the widespread view that such departures must be "justified", i.e. it must be shown that the new language form is "correct", that it represents the "true logic". It is one of the main tasks of this book to eliminate this view as well as the pseudoproblems and pointless squabbles arising from it. (Carnap 1934, iv-v/ 1937, xiv-xv)

The first attempts to escape from the "classical" forms – which themselves went back only one or two generations! – were certainly daring, he says. "But they were hobbled by a striving for 'correctness'". He concludes with the famous words: "But now this barrier is overcome: before us lies the open sea of free possibilities" (Carnap 1934, vi/ 1937, xv).

The principle is stated, in the text of the *Logical Syntax* itself, in the context not of epistemology, as in its first application, but of philosophies of mathematics, particularly intuitionism. It is expressed as the exhortation to state meta-theoretic (or, as he now calls them, logic-of-science [wissenschaftslogische]) proposals in precise terms, as explicit rules or definitions, within the formation or transformation rules of a precisely defined language or calculus:

> Once it is understood that all pro- and anti-intuitionist considerations are concerned with the form of a calculus, the question will no longer be asked in the form "What *is* the case?" but rather "How do we *want* to set this up in the language being constructed?" ... And with that, the dogmatic frame of mind that often makes the discussion unfruitful is banished. (Carnap 1934, 42/1937, 46–7)

This "dogmatic frame of mind" results, in Carnap's view, from the reliance on inherently vague philosophical "considerations" (*Erörterungen*) rather than on precise statements of definitions and rules. He indicates how he has tried, in Language I of the *Syntax*, to capture the philosophical concerns (expressed in various gradations of finitism or constructivism) voiced by Brouwer, Kaufmann, Wittgenstein, and others. But, he points out, there is no way of telling whether he has expressed *precisely* what they have in mind, as they have not expressed their views as proposed precise definitions and rules, but only in terms of vague *Erörterungen* that leave many specific questions open, when one gets down to the brass tacks of constructing an actual language (Carnap 1934, 44/1937, 49). Or they impose restrictions and requirements that appear to be normative.

Carnap's most general statement of the principle of tolerance, therefore, addresses these tendencies directly, contrasting them with his own program of precise and explicit rules:

> Our attitude to demands of this kind may be stated generally by the *principle of tolerance: we do not want to impose restrictions but to state conventions.* ... *In logic there are no morals.* Everyone can construct his logic, i.e. his language form, however he wants. If we wants to discuss it with us, though, he will have to make precise how we wants to set things up. He has to give syntactic rules rather than philosophical considerations. (Carnap 1934, 44–5/1937, 51–2)

Only by *replacing* the vague concept with a precise equivalent can the practical merits or drawbacks of a proposal be judged, for some defined purpose. And under the new regime of pluralism, where there can be no criterion of inherent "correctness", practical usefulness is the only criterion left for deciding whether a proposal should be pursued or left aside. The principle of tolerance fits well, then, into the project of "rational reconstruction" pursued by the earlier Vienna Circle, and sets the stage for the successor project of "explication", which Carnap would not formulate explicitly until after 1945.[19] And he is careful to apply the insistence on precision to his own work as well. Attention and criticism should be focused, he repeatedly insists, not on the "inexact" informal reflections in the text, but on the precise definitions given in terms of the proposed calculi.

AFTER *LOGICAL SYNTAX*

In Sections I and II we discussed a position – the "turning point" initiated by the *Tractatus* – that was shared by most members of the Vienna Circle and by other logical empiricists, such as there were, until about 1930. In Sections III and IV, on the other hand, we focused more narrowly on Carnap and Gödel, leaving other developments aside. There are good reasons for this. After 1931 Carnap was no longer in Vienna; he had taken up a chair at the German University in Prague. The Nazi takeover in Germany of January 1933 not only sent all the German outposts of logical empiricism into exile or under cover, but made it evident that those remaining in Austria and elsewhere in Europe were under threat. Hans Hahn, Carnap's main interlocutor in Vienna on questions of logic and mathematics (apart from Gödel), died that same year, and soon after that Schlick was assassinated by a deranged student. In other words, Carnap's new doctrine simply did not have *time* to become the object of general discussion within the Vienna Circle. Neurath was its only whole-hearted adherent, and he emphasized mainly epistemological aspects of the idea that were somewhat misunderstood by Schlick and others.[20]

Also, Neurath resisted Carnap's move to semantics the year after the *Logical Syntax* was published. This move of Carnap's has often been misunderstood as a fundamental break. In fact, as most scholars now agree (Creath 1990; Ricketts 1994 and 1996a; Awodey and Carus 2005), the shift to semantics does not represent a

---

[19] The classical exposition of this project is in Carnap (1950a, ch. 1); for further discussion, see Stein (1992), Awodey and Carus (2004), and Carus (2004, § II).

[20] Including Russell, who said that according to this "attempt to make the linguistic world self-sufficient", "empirical truth can be determined by the police" (Russell 1940, 147–8). Carus (1999) discusses these misunderstandings; Neurath's position is explained in detail in Uebel (1992).

fundamental discontinuity in Carnap's thought. As we saw above, the original syntax idea represented, above all, a rejection of *meaning* in Wittgenstein's sense. Meaning, in this "absolutist" view, as Carnap later called it, retained a certain arbitrariness or obscurity. Certain sentences that seemed obviously "meaningful" (e.g. Newton's laws) failed to meet Wittgenstein's criteria. And what authority did those criteria claim? Only that of philosophical arguments, not that of precisely specified concepts embedded in a language framework defined by explicit rules. Before January 1931, Carnap and the Vienna Circle had been "in the grip of a picture", the picture of language deriving its meaning by truth-functional concatenation of atomic sentences representing atomic facts. But then Carnap discovered that he could retain Wittgenstein's basic insight without this picture, by extending a Hilbertian or Tarskian formalist view from logic and mathematics to the whole of knowledge.

It seemed entirely reasonable, at that point, to conclude that it was the Wittgensteinian theory of "meaning" that had blocked the way to this outcome. The response, accordingly, was a complete proscription of meaning: *nothing* extralinguistic could constrain the acceptability of a precise meta-language for the logic of science. The shift away from the Wittgensteinian view had meant a corresponding shift from trying to *incorporate* "philosophical" (*wissenschaftslogische*, "elucidatory") discourse into the language of science itself to the construction of a precise *meta*-language for the language of science.[21] This was a drastic change of perspective. The criterion of empiricism, for instance, now had to be reformulated as a constraint on the scientific object language – that is, as a set of formation and transformation rules in the meta-language, an *internal* constraint, from "above" – rather than a requirement of *meaning* – that is, in terms of conditions for verification, an *external* constraint, from "below" (Ricketts 1994). The

---

[21] In the Vienna Circle, he says, "the philosophical problems in which we were interested ended up with problems of the logical analysis of language," and since "in our view the issue in philosophical problems concerned the language, not the world", the Circle thought that "these problems should be formulated not in the object language but in the metalanguage". It was therefore "the *chief motivation* for my development of the syntactical method," to develop a "suitable metalanguage" that would "essentially contribute toward greater clarity in the formulation of philosophical problems and greater fruitfulness in their discussions" (Carnap 1963, 55, our emphasis).

critique of metaphysics, above all, was similarly reexpressed, as a proscription of meaning in the meta-language.[22]

But the new syntactic view led Carnap, as we saw, directly to the principle of tolerance. The syntactic view required a definition of what it means to "follow from the rules", and Gödel had shown that the traditional, intuitive definition – provability – did not suffice. A separate and richer meta-language was required for this definition, and there is no reason to single out any particular such meta-language as "correct". But the principle of tolerance and its new pluralism no longer supported the proscription of meaning, at least as made precise in Tarski's new semantic theory. Under the new pluralism, the criteria for considering a concept or language are simply (1) specifiability by explicit rules and (2) practical usefulness. Under (1), the semantic definitions of "designation" and "truth" qualify; whether they qualify under (2) cannot be decided until various possible semantic languages have been tried out and applied to the problems we want to solve.[23] The proposal in *Meaning and Necessity* to employ these definitions in the "method of extension and intension" (Carnap 1946) can be regarded as

---

[22] As made explicit in the famous paper Carnap (1932), mainly known for its advocacy of physicalism. This epistemological aspect is certainly present there. But the new syntactical doctrine, in fact, *motivates* the paper's physicalistic conclusions. After an introductory discussion about the idea that all objects and facts are of a single kind, we are told that these expressions are a concession to the customary "material" (*inhaltliche*) way of speaking. The "correct" way, Carnap says, speaks of words rather than "objects" and sentences rather than "facts", for a philosophical investigation is an analysis of *language*. In a footnote he indicates that a comprehensive, strictly formal theory of language forms, which he calls "metalogic", will soon be forthcoming, and will justify the "thesis of metalogic" here invoked, that "meaningful" (*sinnvolle*) philosophical sentences are the metalogical ones, i.e., those that speak only of the form of language. This represents a radically different basis for the critique of metaphysics from the one Carnap had previously adopted from Wittgenstein, whereby meaningful sentences were those that derived their meaning from atomic sentences by truth-functional combinations. Atomic sentences, as pictures of atomic facts, no longer play any role in distinguishing meaningful from meaningless sentences.

[23] Carnap never claimed to have arrived at the definitive semantics; he presented his formulation as a first attempt, to get things started and as a basis for discussion: "I believe ... semantics will be of great importance for the so-called theory of knowledge and the methodology of mathematics and empirical science. However, the form in which semantics is constructed in this book need not necessarily be the most appropriate for this purpose. This form is only a first attempt; its particular features ... may possibly undergo fundamental changes in their further development" (Carnap 1942, xii).

an *explication* of – a replacement for – the previously vague, somewhat obscure and arbitrary, conception of "meaning".

Carnap's rejection of meaning foundationalism in January 1931 had been all of a piece. Seen from our present perspective, though, this original syntax view can be regarded, retrospectively, as having been composed of a number of different elements that would later turn out to be separable: (a) the requirement that a language be entirely specified by explicit rules, (b) distinction between a language (a calculus, a purely syntactic symbol system) and its possible interpretations, and (c) the prohibition of interpretation or meaning in the elucidatory (*wissenschaftslogische*) meta-language.

Tolerance depends on (a) and (b), which survive unscathed and undiminished into Carnap's semantic period. (So it is rather misleading to call them "syntactic"; Carnap's original term "meta-logical" might be more appropriate.) What does not survive is (c), the overreaction against Wittgensteinian "meaning" that accompanied the original insight. In distinguishing between a language and its interpretation, Carnap's first (and, as we saw, understandable) response was to reject that imprecise notion of meaning entirely. But this restriction was loosened when he saw that interpretation could be specified by explicit rules (governing satisfaction, designation, and truth), in accordance with component (a) of the original syntax idea.

This new position, which remained Carnap's for the rest of his career, has been subjected to many assaults since it was articulated in the 1930s. The most notorious assailant was Quine, whose famous 1951 paper "Two Dogmas of Empiricism" essentially portrayed Carnap's later position as a kind of relapse into the presyntactic, Wittgensteinian "verification theory of meaning" that Carnap had overcome in January 1931 (Quine 1951/1953, 41). In *Word and Object* (Quine 1960), Quine opened a different front, shifting attention from the Vienna Circle's preoccupation with syntax and semantics to what Carnap, by then, would have called the *pragmatic* (and partly *empirical*) question how a language can in practice convey content. Most analytic philosophers have followed Quine in these respects, though this consensus has gradually begun to fray a little.[24]

---

[24] Serious dissent began with Stein (1992) and Isaacson (1992), while Richard Creath's introduction to his (1990a) provided a more balanced view than had previously been available. See also Bird (1995) and Carus (2004).

The posthumous publication of Gödel's critique of Carnap (Gödel 1995) has recently called forth another stream of papers, reappraising Carnap's philosophy of mathematics and that of logical empiricism more generally.[25]

Despite all these discussions, however, logical empiricism is still largely identified with the 1920s view discussed in Sections I and II. This is the view portrayed in A. J. Ayer's *Language, Truth, and Logic*, for instance, which is still regarded even by many reputable philosophers as a definitive and exemplary statement of "logical positivism" or "logical empiricism".[26] We hope to have shown, here, that this is a gross distortion. While this view was certainly the Vienna Circle's starting point, they were aware of its fundamental defects from the beginning and worked steadily to overcome them. What is more, they *did* overcome them. In 1931 Carnap developed a *new* platform on which many of the previous logical empiricist positions could – in somewhat revised form – rest, and this new position *rejected* the previous one. The significance of the new meta-logical or syntactic viewpoint, Eino Kaila agreed after discussion with Carnap in the summer of 1931, lay precisely in its "elimination of verification by comparison with facts" (*Ausschaltung der Verifikation durch Vergleich mit Sachverhalten*) (ASP/RC, diary entry of June 26, 1931). The significance of the new position, in other words, lay in its rejection of the previous, foundational one. The fact that this position appeared too late to be discussed while the Vienna Circle could still be considered a going concern was a quirk of fate. Seventy years later, we should stop holding the starting point of logical empiricism against it, and should look not where it came from but where it was headed.

[25] Much of this attention has focussed on Gödel's view that Carnap's overall framework, based on the principle of tolerance, is self-undermining (e.g., Friedman 1999, ch. 9; Potter 2000, ch. 11). Gödel's argument is accepted to varying degrees; most commentators, like Goldfarb and Ricketts (1992), have held that Carnap's view can be upheld only in a weakened or diluted (and rather empty) form. We respond to these arguments, identifying an error in Gödel's argument, in Awodey and Carus (2003), on behalf of Carnap's position in *Logical Syntax*, and in Awodey and Carus (2004) on behalf of Carnap's later position.

[26] It is so regarded, for instance, with almost no reference to any actual members of the Vienna Circle, in the recent two-volume history of analytic philosophy by Scott Soames (2003, chs. 12–13).

8 Logical Empiricism and the Philosophy of Physics

INTRODUCTION

Moritz Schlick, Hans Reichenbach, Rudolf Carnap, Philipp Frank, Herbert Feigl, and Carl Hempel all studied physics at university. Relativity theory and quantum theory, the two revolutionary developments of twentieth-century physics, happily coincided with the rise and consolidation of logical empiricism. Yet the designation "philosophy of physics" was little used by the logical empiricists themselves, while, with notable exceptions, they produced little of what is currently understood under that head, viz., detailed investigations into particular aspects or interpretations of physical theories. Certainly, there are important works of Reichenbach's, a few of Schlick's, mostly from his pre-Vienna days, and one or two others, recognizably belonging to philosophy of physics. Nonetheless, it is something of an anachronism to speak of logical empiricism's "philosophy of physics".

One reason is that logical empiricist orthodoxy allotted but a narrow window to the legitimate practice of "scientific philosophy". Carnap's 1934 declaration that *"we pursue Logical Analysis but no Philosophy"* is perhaps characteristic (Carnap 1934a, 28, emphasis in original). Frank, a working physicist, warned that philosophical deliberation continually posed the threat of becoming an "opium for science" (Frank 1932, viii/1998, 11),[1] and that the very meaning of the term "philosophy of natural science" was to be sharply demarcated from all manner of "school philosophy". Rightly understood, it applied either

---

[1] Where possible, the translations are mine but reference to an existing translation is made for purposes of comparison.

to "the exact working out of the (observational) meaning of scientific symbols" or else to "a part of a sociology of science", investigating "determinate observable processes arising in the connections between natural scientific theories and other expressions of human activity" (Frank 1932a, 156). Some years later, however, he acknowledged the "quite natural" tendency of some scientists, even those "very competent in their fields", to "succumb to the temptation to make statements on ontology". Such lapses were "very natural" but it must not be forgotten, Frank insisted, that "ontology is nothing but the use of ordinary language in a domain where it loses its meaning" (Frank 1946, 482). It is small wonder that Henry Margenau, when addressing the annual meeting of the American Physical Society in December 1941 in its first ever symposium on "The Philosophy of Physics", chose the deliberately provocative topic "Metaphysical Elements in Physics". Lamenting the phobia surrounding the term "metaphysics", the philosophically engaged Yale physicist observed: "Our time appears to be distinguished by its *taboos*, among which there is to be found the broad convention that the word *metaphysics* must never be used be used in polite scientific society" (Margenau 1941, 176). The present generation of philosophers of physics is no longer so afflicted; to the contrary, some conceive their research as the pursuit of metaphysics through physics (see, e.g., Redhead 1994). Whatever one's views on the viability of metaphysics, it is difficult not to recognize the relaxation of this taboo as a genuinely liberating advance.

On account of his nonpositivist leanings, Reichenbach's conception of philosophy of natural science was considerably more ecumenical. While denominated a method for the "logical analysis" of scientific theories, it closely engaged with salient technical and interpretive questions of modern physical theories, issues still resonating with contemporary philosophers of physics. Accordingly, this overview of logical empiricism and philosophy of physics is largely directed to Reichenbach's expansive discussions of relativity theory, quantum theory, and thermodynamics, and to related topics of causality, determinism, and the direction of time.

THE THEORY OF RELATIVITY

Logical empiricism was conceived under the guiding star of Einstein's two theories of relativity. Schlick's early monograph *Space and Time in Contemporary Physics*, appearing in 1917 initially in the pages of the scientific weekly *Die Naturwissenschaften*, was the first notable attempt at a philosophical elucidation of the general theory of relativity. Distinguished by the clarity of its largely nontechnical exposition, it also received Einstein's enthusiastic praise for its philosophical conclusions, favoring a conventionalism *à la* Poincaré over both neo-Kantianism and Machian positivism. Hans Reichenbach was one of five intrepid attendees of Einstein's first seminar on the theory of general relativity given at Berlin University in the tumultuous winter of 1918–19; his detailed notebooks survive. That theory is the subject of Reichenbach's first book (1920), dedicated to Einstein, as well as of his next two books (1924, 1928) and numerous papers in the 1920s. The transformation of the concept of space by the general theory of relativity is the topic of Rudolf Carnap's Ph.D. dissertation at Jena in 1921. More than mere lay expositions of the theory, all of these works were principally concerned to show how the philosophy of natural science should be necessarily transformed in its wake, by rebutting or correcting neo-Kantian and Machian perspectives on general methodological and epistemological questions of science. In this regard, Einstein's 1905 analysis of the conventionality of simultaneity in the theory of special relativity was paradigmatic, prompting Reichenbach's own method of analyzing physical theories into "subjective" (definitional, conventional) and "objective" (empirical) components. But Reichenbach also addressed questions concerning the meaning or significance of the fundamental principles of general relativity, together with issues of causality and determinism, conventionalism, and the causal theory of time.

The Principles of General Relativity and General Covariance

The very name of Einstein's theory of gravitation designated a philosophical ambition rather than a physical achievement. Einstein promoted his theory as a Machian-inspired generalization of the earlier "restricted" or "special" principle of relativity that had eliminated physical reference to "absolute time" by postulating that the (nongravitational) laws of physics remain the same in all inertial reference frames. In the same way, he urged, a "general theory of relativity" should "relativize inertia", eliminating any reference to "absolute" space-time background, including the global inertial frames of the special theory. By its very name, the general theory of relativity seemingly countenanced only motions and positions conceived as relations among physical objects. Absent any privileged reference frames, the theory required that all physical laws be expressed in generally covariant equations, having the same form in all systems of coordinates. Indeed, Einstein used the terms "principle of general relativity" and "principle of general covariance" virtually synonymously, whereas they are now regarded as quite distinct. In any case, such declarations set off a debate over the meaning of relativity, invariance, and covariance principles that still shows no sign of abating (Norton 1993).

It is then easy to understand that misconceptions about the relativity of all motions afflict the writings of Schlick (1917a; 1922), Reichenbach (1924), and Frank (1917). The most careful discussion, of Schlick's, maintained that whereas Mach had affirmed the relativity of motions for merely epistemological reasons, Einstein's theory actually establishes complete relativity on the basis of a principle of equivalence resting on the empirically attested identity of inertial and gravitational mass (Schlick 1922/1979, vol. 1, 236–7). In fact, from the latter identity follows only the so-called weak principle of equivalence, that all bodies, regardless of mass or internal structure, fall in a gravitational field with the same acceleration. Beyond this, Einstein added the hypothesis that an observer would not be able to distinguish between phenomena in a frame S_1, at rest in a homogeneous gravitational field that imparts an acceleration $-\alpha$ in the x direction to all objects, and those in a frame S_2 with constant acceleration α in the x direction. This "Einstein principle of equivalence", however, pertains only to isolated small regions where there is an *ideally homogeneous* gravitational field (a situation rarely, if at all, found in nature). Moreover, it obviously extends the principle of relativity only to uniformly accelerated motions. Yet, as was quite common at the time, both Schlick and Reichenbach, in a mistaken effort to extend relativity to all motions, recast the Einstein principle of equivalence into a general "infinitesimal principle of equivalence". Alleged to be applicable also to infinitesimal regions of *nonhomogeneous* gravitational fields wherein space- and time-variation of gravity can be ignored,[2] this principle is really a second-order idealization and is plagued with conceptual and technical difficulties (for discussion, see Norton 1985). Einstein's own efforts to implement a complete relativization of inertia à la Mach led him by 1917 into the thickets of relativistic cosmology, and there the problem has largely remained (Einstein 1917). (For a recent survey of some of the issues involved, see Barbour and Pfister 1995.)

As regards general covariance, E. Kretschmann notably pointed out in 1917 that the principle, understood "passively" as complete coordinate generality in the formulation of a physical theory, has no particular physical content, and nothing *per se* to do with a principle of relativity. On the other hand, the theory of general relativity does not succeed in accomplishing a complete relativization of inertia.[3] While admitting the correctness of Kretschmann's observation, Einstein nonetheless continued to regard the principle of general covariance as a fertile "heuristic" guiding his three-decade-long search for a unified theory of fields. Understood "actively", in terms of the "diffeomorphism invariance" of dynamical laws, it is the postulate that there is no such thing as "empty space". This is essentially a demand that physical interactions should be formulated as "background independent", a highly substantive constraint on physical theory.

Of contemporary interest is a little-known attempt by Schlick (1920) to endow the principle of general covariance with physical significance. Now, Einstein's reasons for investing the requirement of general covariance with a substantive, not a merely formal, content stemmed from a conviction that "empty space" – the bare manifold with its topological structure – could not be a physical object. Rather, the manifold becomes physical space-time only in the presence of one or another "individuating field", paradigmatically, the metrical field of gravitation. Because many of the relevant details are to be found only in Einstein's private correspondence, these reasons remained obscure until revealed by recent historical investigations into the

---

[2] Schlick (1922, 69–70/1979, vol. 1, 247); Reichenbach (1920, 27/1965, 28–9). Reichenbach (1922/1978, vol. 2, 38, n. 20) admits the 1920 discussion is "not quite correct", referring to Reichenbach (1921). However, the claim there (380) that locally, gravitational fields can always be "transformed away" is also false.

[3] One reason has to do with its so-called initial value problem. A brief but good discussion is in Earman (1989, 104ff.).

so-called Hole Argument (*Lochbetrachtung*) (see Stachel 1989, 1993, and Norton 1984; the term "individuating field" is Stachel's). Independently, Schlick argued that the principle of causality – in the form stipulated by Maxwell – required the condition of general covariance ("independence of the laws of physics from absolute coordinate systems"). Maxwell had argued that the very possibility of causal laws presupposed that *like* occurrences can be identified. This condition can be satisfied only if causal differences between two bodies do not depend upon their particular location in space and time, "but only on differences in the nature, configuration, or motion of the two bodies concerned" (Maxwell 1876, 13). Thus two like bodies at different locations, or different times in the "same" location, *can* fall under a common causal law *only if space and time do not explicitly enter into the differential equations of physics*. Transposing the language of Maxwell's argument to "events" in space-time, Schlick maintained that the principle of causality, affirming a contiguous propagation of cause from point-event to point-event, presupposed "a principle of separation" (*ein Prinzip der Trennung*), that "like things" can exist apart from one another without in any way being materially influenced by such separation (Schlick 1920, 467). Without the validity of such a principle, the possibility of causal laws applying to like but not identical occurrences, disappears. In that case, Schlick further reasoned, the only explanation of observed regularities would lie in the fantastic, but logically possible, hypothesis of individual causality.

Schlick's argument, seeking the physical significance of general covariance in a further elucidation and extension of the principle of causality, resurfaced over a decade later as a "principle of separation" underlying Einstein's criticism of the quantum theory.[4] In the celebrated 1935 EPR (Einstein, Podolsky, and Rosen) paper, separability (an isolation condition generally termed "locality" in the contemporary literature) appears in the misleading guise of a condition for the attribution of "physical reality" to distinct quantum systems. Yet it has been shown that the not-quite-successfully-stated intent of Einstein in this paper was to pose to quantum theory a dilemma

---

[4] For further discussion, see Ryckman (2005). It is known that Einstein and Schlick were in close contact in 1920; see Howard (1984). Fine (1996, 36) notes Einstein's use of the term *Trennungsprinzip* in a letter to Schrödinger of June 19, 1935.

between causality (action-by-contact) and completeness: Either quantum theory violates causality, holding that real states of spatially separated objects are not independent of each other. Or, quantum theory is not complete; the ψ (state) function for the combined system provides only an incomplete description, contrary to the claim of standard quantum mechanics (see Fine 1996, ch. 3). In 1964 Bell demonstrated that Einstein's separability requirement gives rise to an inequality violated by statistical correlations predicted by quantum mechanics between parts of such "entangled" systems; subsequently, the predicted correlations have been observed (discussed further below) (Bell 1964; Aspect et al. 1982).

Conventionality of Simultaneity

Einstein's first paper on relativity in 1905 argued that a physically meaningful notion of the simultaneity of two events E_1 and E_2, occurring at arbitrarily distant spatial locations, cannot be simply assumed but required a physical means of comparison. His proposal was to synchronize clocks at different locations by light signaling. Suppose at location A, a light ray is emitted at time t_1 (event E_A) toward another distant location B, so that it arrives at B (event E_B) and is immediately reflected back to A, arriving at time t_2 (event E_C). Then Einstein stated that clocks at A and B could be synchronized by *stipulating* that the event E_D at A, occurring at time $(t_1 + t_2)/2$ (as measured at A), is *simultaneous* with E_B. This is equivalent to a stipulation that the travel times of the light ray in each direction are the same (a vacuum is supposed between A and B). An assumption is also made that light is the fastest possible means of signaling between A and B. In lieu of any physical method to measure the one-way velocity of a light ray, this amounts to a definition (of *standard synchrony*). Emphasizing that such a definition is by no means necessary, Reichenbach (and following him Adolf Grünbaum) regarded Einstein's definition as a *convention* rather than a fact about the physical universe. *On the basis of the empirical facts known at* A, Reichenbach argued, one can affirm only that the event E_D at A, regarded as simultaneous with E_B at B, in fact may occur anywhere in the interval $t_2 - t_1$ between events E_C and E_A: logically, any event occurring within this interval might be chosen. More precisely, the convention concerns the arbitrary choice of a number ε $(0 < \varepsilon < 1)$ such that E_D simultaneous with E_B is posited to occur at time $t_3 = t_1 + \varepsilon (t_2 - t_1)$ (Bell 1964; Aspect et al. 1982). Einstein's choice of $\varepsilon = \frac{1}{2}$ corresponds to standard synchrony, but in principle any other permitted value of ε would serve equally well.

The conclusion has been resisted on a number of grounds: physical, mathematical, and methodological. Unfortunately, all attempts – which continue to be made – to demonstrate that the one-way velocity of light *can* be measured without tacit reliance upon equivalent conventions must be accounted as failures. Another kind of argument against the conventionality thesis is based on the theorem of David Malament (1977), stating that the standard simultaneity choice $\varepsilon = \frac{1}{2}$ is the only nontrivial simultaneity relation definable in terms of the relation of (symmetric) causal connectibility in Minkowski space-time. Recent attention has focused on a number of assumptions on which Malament's theorem depends, with the result that the issue is today widely regarded as unsettled (for a survey of recent discussions, see Janis 2002).

Metric Conventionalism

A cornerstone of Reichenbach's "logical analysis" of general relativity is "the relativity of geometry", the thesis that an arbitrary geometry may be ascribed to space-time (holding constant the usual underlying topology) if the laws of physics are correspondingly modified. It provides the canonical illustration of Reichenbach's methodological claim that conventional or definitional elements, in the form of "coordinative definitions" associating mathematical concepts with "elements of physical reality", are a necessary condition of empirical cognition in science. At the same time, however, the thesis is embedded in an audacious program of *epistemological reductionism* regarding space-time structures, first fully articulated in his "constructive axiomatization" of the theory of relativity (1924). Metrical properties of space-time are deemed less fundamental than "topological" ones, whilst the latter are derived from the temporal order of events. But time order in turn is reduced to that of causal order, and so the whole edifice of structures of space-time is regarded epistemologically derivative, resting upon ultimately basic empirical facts about causal order and a prohibition against action-at-a-distance. The end point is "the causal theory of time", a type of relational theory of time presupposing the validity of the causal principle of action-by-contact (*Nahewirkungsprinzip*). We shall need to discuss these different stages of the argument for metrical conventionalism separately.

The argument is best understood through its origins in Reichenbach's first monograph on relativity (1920), written from a neo-Kantian perspective. His principal innovation was to modify the Kantian conception of *synthetic a priori* principles, rejecting the sense of "valid for all time" while retaining that of "constitutive of the object (of knowledge)". As has been recently discussed, this led to the conception of a theory-specific "relativised *a priori*", according to which any fundamental physical theory presupposes the validity of systems of, usually quite general, theory-specific principles (Friedman 1999; Ryckman 2002). In linking purely formal mathematical notions with objects of perception, such "coordinating principles" are indispensable for defining, and so "constituting", the "objects of knowledge" within the theory. Furthermore, the epistemological significance of relativity theory is to have shown, contrary to Kant, that such systems may contain mutually inconsistent principles, and so require emendation. The "relativization" of *synthetic a priori* principles is then a direct epistemological result of the theory of relativity. There is also a transformation in the method of philosophical investigation of science. In place of Kant's "analysis of Reason", "the method of analysis of science" (*der wissenschaftsanalytische Methode*) is proposed as "the only way that affords us an understanding of the contribution of our reason to knowledge" (Reichenbach 1920, 71/1965, 74). Relativity theory is deemed a shining exemplar of this method, for it has shown that the metric of space-time describes an "objective property" of the world, once the subjective freedom to make arbitrary coordinate transformations (the coordinating principle of general covariance) is recognized.[5] The thesis of metrical conventionalism had yet to appear.

But soon it did. Still in 1920, Schlick objected, both publicly and in private correspondence with Reichenbach, that "principles of

---

[5] "The theory of relativity teaches that the metric is subjective only insofar as it is dependent upon the arbitrariness of the choice of coordinates, and that independently of these it describes an objective property of reality" (1920, 86–7/1965, 90).

coordination" were precisely statements of the kind Poincaré had termed "conventions" (Coffa 1991, 201ff.). Moreover, Einstein, in a much-discussed lecture of January 1921 entitled "Geometry and Experience", argued that the question concerning the nature of space-time geometry becomes an empirical question only if certain *pro tem* stipulations regarding the "practically rigid body" of measurement are made.[6] By 1922, the essential pieces of Reichenbach's "mature" conventionalist view were in place (Reichenbach 1922a, an article translated into French by L. Bloch); the canonical exposition is in section (entitled "The Relativity of Geometry") of *Die Philosophie der Raum-Zeit-Lehre* (completed in 1926, published in 1928). Following the broad argument of Einstein's essay, Reichenbach maintained that questions concerning the empirical determination of the metric of space-time must face the fact that only the whole theoretical edifice comprising geometry and physics admits of observational test. Unlike Einstein, however, Reichenbach's "method of analysis of science" is concerned with the epistemological problem of factoring this totality into its conventional or definitional, and empirical components.

This is done as follows. Empirical determination of the space-time metric presupposes a choice of "metrical indicators" made by laying down a "coordinative *definition*", for example, that the metrical notion of a "length" is coordinated with some fiduciary physical object. A standard choice coordinates units of "length" with marks on "infinitesimal measuring rods" supposed rigid (Einstein's "practically rigid bodies"). This, however, is only a convention, and other physical objects or processes might be chosen. (In Schlick's fanciful example, the Dalai Lama's pulse could be chosen as the physical process defining units of time [1925, 66/1985, 72].) Of course, the chosen metrical indicators must be corrected for certain distorting effects (temperature, magnetism, etc.) due to the presence of physical forces, termed "differential forces", indicating that they affect various materials differently. However, Reichenbach argued, the choice of a rigid rod as standard of length is tantamount to the claim that there are no nondifferential – "universal" – distorting forces that affect all bodies in the same way and cannot be screened off. In the absence of

---

[6] *"Pro tem"* in view of Einstein's (1921) recognition of the inadmissibility of the concept of "actual rigid bodies"; see Ryckman (2005, chs. 3 and 4).

"universal forces" the coordinative definition regarding rigid rods can be implemented and the nature of the space-time metric empirically determined, for example, finding that paths of light rays passing close to the surface of the sun are not Euclidean straight lines. Thus, the theory of general relativity, on adoption of the coordinative definition of rigid rods and perfect clocks ("universal forces = o"), affirms that the geometry of space-time in this region is of a non-Euclidean kind. The point, however, is that this conclusion rests on a convention governing measuring rods. One could, alternately, maintain that the geometry of space-time was Euclidean by adopting a different coordinative definition, for example, holding that measuring units expanded or contracted depending on their position in space-time, on the supposition of "universal forces". Then, consistent with all empirical phenomena, one could find that Euclidean geometry is compatible with Einstein's theory. Then whether general relativity affirms a Euclidean or a non-Euclidean metric for the solar gravitational field rests upon a conventional choice regarding the existence of "universal forces". Either hypothesis may be adopted since they are empirically equivalent descriptions; their joint possibility is referred to as "the relativity of geometry". Just as the choice of "standard synchrony" of clocks ($\varepsilon = \frac{1}{2}$) is simpler but "logically arbitrary", Reichenbach recommends the "descriptively simpler" alternative in which "universal forces" do not exist. To be sure, "descriptive simplicity has nothing to do with truth", that is, has no bearing on the question of whether space-time actually has a non-Euclidean structure (Reichenbach 1928, 47/1958, 35).

It is rather difficult to understand the significance that has been accorded this argument. Carnap, in his "Introductory Remarks" to the posthumous English translation of this work, singled it out on account of its "great interest for the methodology of physics" (Reichenbach [1958], vii; dated July 1956). Reichenbach himself deemed "the philosophical achievement of the theory of relativity" to lie in the methodological distinction between conventional and factual claims regarding space-time geometry (Reichenbach 1928, 24/1958, 15, translation modified), and he boasted of his "philosophical theory of relativity" as an incontrovertible "philosophical result": "*the philosophical theory of relativity, i.e., the discovery of the definitional character of the metric in all its details, holds independently of experience ... a philosophical result not subject to* the criticism of the individual sciences" (Reichenbach 1958, 177). Yet the result is neither unchallenged by science nor an untrammeled consequence of Einstein's theory of gravitation. Consider, first of all, the shadowy status accorded to "universal forces". A sympathetic reading may suggest that the notion served usefully in mediating between a traditional *a priori* commitment to Euclidean geometry and the view of modern geometrodynamics, where gravitational force is "geometrised away" (see Dieks 1987). For, as Reichenbach explicitly acknowledged, gravitation is itself a "universal force", coupling to all bodies and affecting them in the same manner (Reichenbach 1928, 294–6/1958, 256–8). Hence the choice recommended by descriptive simplicity is merely a stipulation that metrical appliances, regarded as "infinitesimal", be considered as if at rest in an inertial (i.e., nongravitational) system (see, e.g., Reichenbach 1924, 115–16/1969, 147). Accordingly, Reichenbach's conventionalist choice is equivalent to the assumption that measurements take place in regions considered small Minkowski space-times (arenas of gravitation-free physics). By the same token, however, consistency required an admission that "the transition from the special theory to the general one represents merely a renunciation of metrical characteristics" (Reichenbach 1924, 155/1969, 195) or, even more pointedly, that "all the metrical properties of the space-time continuum are destroyed by gravitational fields" where only "topological properties" remain (Reichenbach 1928, 308/1958, 268–9). To be sure, these conclusions are supposed to be rendered more palatable in connection with the epistemological reduction of space-time structures to the causal theory of time (see below).

In retrospect, Reichenbach's treatment of space-time measurement is plainly inappropriate, revealing the same fallacious tendency manifested by appeal to the "infinitesimal principle of equivalence" noted above, *viz.*, that the generically curved space-times of general relativity can be considered as pieced together from little bits of flat Minskowski space-times. Mathematically inconsistencies aside, the analysis affords only a metaphorical physical meaning to the central theoretical concept of general relativity, the metric tensor $g_{\mu\nu}$ of (variable) gravitational fields, or the series of curvature tensors derived from its uniquely associated affine connection. Since the components of such sectional curvatures at a point of space-time are physically manifested and can be measured, for instance, as the tidal forces of gravity, they can hardly be accounted as due to the presence of conventionally adopted "universal forces". In addition, the concept of an "infinitesimal rigid rod" in general relativity cannot really be other than the *interim* stopgap Einstein recognized it to be. For it cannot actually be "rigid" due to these tidal forces; in fact, the concept of a "rigid body" is already forbidden in special relativity as allowing instantaneous causal actions. Such a rod must indeed be "infinitesimal", that is, sufficiently short so as to not be stressed by gradients of the gravitational field; just how short depending on strength of local curvatures and on measurement error (Torretti 1983, 239). But even so it can hardly serve as a defined *general* standard for metrical notions. In fact, as Weyl had already emphasized, precisely which physical objects or structures are most suitable as space-time metrical indicators should be decided on the basis of gravitational theory itself. From this enlightened perspective, measuring rods and clocks are objects that are far too complicated and so inappropriate. Following Weyl's lead, current relativity theorists regard the metric of space-time as in principle constructable from light rays and parameterized affine trajectories (corresponding to small "clocks") (see the readable discussion in Geroch 1978). In this way, Reichenbach's emphasis on conventional stipulation in determining metrical relations in general relativity can be avoided (see Weyl 1921, 285–6/1953, 313–14; for a recent treatment, see Ehlers, Pirani, and Schild 1972).

"Topological" Conventionalism

Already in 1921, Reichenbach conceived that the order of time as well as the four-dimensional structure of space-time could be objectively characterized through the structure of the causal relation alone (Kamlah 1989, 453). In his 1928 work, he sought to show that "the system of relations of causal order, independent of any metric, is the most general type of physical geometry", in fact, the culmination of empiricist analysis of the concepts of space and time prompted by the theory of relativity (Reichenbach 1928, 307/1958, 268). This is taken to mean that statements about "topological" properties of space-time, regarding the order of coincidences of point-events (i.e., all intersections of world lines) in nonvanishing finite ("cut out") regions, "are the most secure expressions we can make about the order of space and time" (Reichenbach 1928, 324/1958, 283). To be sure, Reichenbach here used the term "topological" in a deviant sense, having nothing to do with the characteristic notions of topology, of neighborhood, convergence, or continuity. Rather it refers to the "objective" system of coincidences, not at all dependent on an observer, therefore "independent of all arbitrariness" and an "ultimate fact of nature". Even so, the formulation is misleading for "topological facts" become so only after legislation of a coordinative definition. Just as empirical determinations of metrical properties of space-time depend upon prior coordinative definitions about the behavior of rods and clocks, so empirical determination of the "topological properties" of space and time require a prior stipulation of the validity of the principle of causality: "Topology is an empirical matter as soon as we introduce the requirement that no causal relations must be violated" (Reichenbach 1928, 98/1958, 80, original emphasis).

While it is allowed that whether there are causal anomalies can be decided by "normal inductive methods", at the same time, causal structure is an *a priori* schema of order in the universe: "Time, and through it, causality supplies the measure and order of space: not time order alone, but the combined space-time order reveals itself as the ordering schema governing causal chains, as the expression of the causal structure of the universe" (Reichenbach 1928, 307/ 1958, 268, translation modified).

Reichenbach considered the "topological properties of time" separately from those of spatial topology. Indeed, the latter rest on the former pursuant to a further reduction of temporal relations to causal ones in the "causal theory of time". The empiricist task is to identify causal processes as physically manifesting, and so defining, the respective "topological properties". For time, the order properties of *earlier, later,* and *temporally indeterminate* are considered such properties that are preserved even in the most general gravitational fields where metrical properties had been "destroyed" (Reichenbach 1928, 308/1958, 268-9). These properties are coordinated to the behavior of "first signals" (light rays), and so the "topological problem of time measurement" rests upon a stipulation that no causal process propagates with a velocity exceeding that of light. Spatially, the causal principle affirms that causal effects cannot reach more distant points of space without having first to pass through those that are closer; the validity of this principle appears to rest upon both empirical and, it seems, *a priori* grounds (Reichenbach 1928, 314–15/1958, 275). In any case, the concepts of neighborhood and spatial order are defined by reference to the validity of the principle of action-by-contact (*Nahewirkungs-prinzip*), "the most fundamental principle of spatial order": "the neighborhood relations of space are to be chosen in such a way that the principle of action by contact is satisfied" (Reichenbach 1928, 315/1958, 275). This suggests that change of spatial topology generally leads to causal anomaly. For, having *"assume(d) a topology of space which leads to normal causal laws"* (Reichenbach 1928, 98/1958, 80, original emphasis), dimensional change may well result in causal anomaly. Prohibition against "causal anomalies", violation of the principle of contiguous action, is a cornerstone of Reichenbach's analysis of space-time structure in the 1920s.[7] As will be seen, it is also central to his analysis of quantum mechanics two decades later; in the interim, the status of the principle underwent a radical change.

The Causal Theory of Time

Philosophical attempts to show that temporal ordering relations may be reduced to (or analyzed in terms of) physically primitive but specifically nontemporal relations long antedate the theory of relativity, going back at least to Leibniz (see, e.g., Mehlberg 1936). Nonetheless, relativity theory provided a new impetus for these efforts, and Reichenbach was among the first to propose that relativity theory naturally led to a causal definition of time wherein temporal relations are reduced to causal relations.[8] Initially the

---

[7] In his 1915 Ph.D. dissertation on the concept of probability (see Reichenbach 1916/1917), Reichenbach regarded the principle of causality neither as logically necessary nor empirically verifiable but a necessary precondition for scientific knowledge, and in that sense *a priori*. The *Nahewirkungsprinzip* is a synthetic *a priori* "principle of coordination" (*Zuordnungsprinzip*) in his neo-Kantian book on relativity theory (1920).

[8] Reichenbach was apparently unaware of the similar proposals of A. Robb in Cambridge going back to 1914. Winnie (1977) presents Robb's approach, with a proof of the central result, that *"the causal structure of Minkowski space-time contains within itself the entire geometry (topological and metrical structure) of Minkowski space-time"*.

temporal ordering of events imposed by a fundamental causal relation was taken to distinguish the direction of time supposedly characterized by irreversible processes. Within a few years, that claim is modified by an admission that the theory of relativity did not require a direction of time, but is based solely on the assumption of an ordered time; consequently he treated the problem of the direction of time separately (Reichenbach 1924, 21–2/1969, 29; cf. 1956, 42).[9]

Reichenbach's causal theory of time appeared initially in section 6 ("Axioms of Time Order") of his "constructive axiomatization" (1924). Consistent with the goal of an "epistemologically rigorous" axiomatization of relativity theory, the time order of events is defined on the basis of their observable characteristics rather than on a subjective phenomenalistic "direct perception" of this order. An event E_2 is defined to be *later than* another event E_1 occurring at the same spatial point P if and only if there is a physically possible causal chain $s_1, s_2, \ldots s_k$ wherein E_1 coincides with s_1 and E_2 coincides with s_k. and each S_i is the cause of S_{i+1} (Van Fraassen 1970, 173). "Physical possibility" requires that causal processes propagate at less than the velocity of light. While enabling individual identity over time (*genidentity*), the definition prohibits closed timelike curves (Reichenbach 1924, 22/1969, 29; 1928, 165/1958, 142). But the definition also unnecessarily limits the generality of analysis, for it presupposes the space-time concept of *coincidence of events*, normally considered part of the fundamental ontology of relativity theory (Earman 1972, 78–9; Van Fraassen 1970, 173). More worrying is that the definition assumes that the structure of causation involves an asymmetrical relation distinguishing cause and effect, whereas a rather straightforward objection is that *cause* is distinguished from *effect* precisely by temporal order. In response, Reichenbach further elaborated the "method of the mark", employed, virtually without comment, in 1924, to distinguish cause from effect and so justify a primitive asymmetrical causal relation: "If E_1 is the cause of E_2, then a small variation (a mark) in E_1 is associated with a small variation in E_2,

---

[9] There are space-time models satisfying the field equations of general relativity that do not admit a globally consistent time directionality (*are not temporally orientable*); such space-times may admit intuitively pathological features. A well-known example, due to Gödel (1949), violates Reichenbach's prohibition against closed timelike curves and so arguably permits "time travel". For discussion, see Earman, (1995, ch. 6).

whereas small variations in E_2 are not associated with variations in E_1" (Reichenbach 1929, 53/1978, vol. 2, 185–6).

It is generally conceded that the "mark method" still tacitly presupposes temporal concepts. In particular, a mark must be *irreversible* since if E_2 did not bear the relevant mark, it could not be causally connected with E_1. But the notion of irreversibility appears inextricably connected with the notions of temporal order supposed eliminated (Grünbaum 1973, 182ff.). Perhaps sensitive to these difficulties, Reichenbach, and later advocates of the causal theory of time, subsequently explored a weaker program whereby temporal order is analyzed only up to a specification of "the direction of time". This takes the form of defining a ternary relation of "betweenness" whereby E_3 is temporally between E_1 and E_2 if and only if either E_1 is prior to E_3 and E_3 to E_2 or the reverse (E_2 to E_3 and E_3 to E_1). Accordingly, the relation of "betweenness", jointly with that of "is simultaneous with", suffices to temporally order events, and so supply an asymmetrical causal relation, but does not distinguish a unique direction of time. In a posthumously published work, Reichenbach proposed two different programs for a physically definition of "betweenness" and so the causal asymmetry of temporal order: the first in terms of the reversible processes of classical mechanics, the second in terms of probability relations. Neither of these survives general objections raised against the causal theory of time (see Earman 1972).

THE DIRECTION OF TIME AND THERMODYNAMICS

"The problem of the direction of time" emerged in the last quarter of the nineteenth century with the kinetic theory of gases, arising in the conflict between the time-reversal invariance of the laws of classical mechanics and the Second Law of Thermodynamics, taken as affirming that the entropy – the measure of disorder – in the universe never decreases. Beginning in the 1870s, the Austrian physicist Boltzmann argued, not without controversy, that the irreversible direction of entropy of a macrosystem is consistent with the statistical behavior of enormous numbers of microprocesses (e.g., collisions of gas molecules), each governed by the time-reversible processes of classical mechanics. That is, the Second Law is a statistical law: it is only extremely improbable that the entropy of a complex physical system could ever decrease, so that a more ordered (less-probable) state would follow a less-ordered (more probable) state. Hence the direction of physical processes, and so the direction of time, is explained as a statistical trend from less probable to more probable configurations of molecules: positive time is defined as the direction in which the overwhelming number of thermodynamical processes occur. However, as Boltzmann's Viennese colleague Loschmidt objected, given the time-reversal invariance of the underlying dynamical laws, for every microstate a that evolves from lower to higher state b of entropy, there must be a microstate b', with entropy equal to b, which evolves to another state a', whose entropy is equal to that of a. The "reversibility objection" was never satisfactorily answered (Reichenbach 1956, 116–17). (A classic discussion, also a source for Reichenbach, is Ehrenfest 1911; see also Sklar 1993.) Even as Reichenbach viewed Boltzmann's statistical definition of time direction as his "great contribution to physics and to philosophy" (Reichenbach 1956, 134), he nonetheless sought an empiricist clarification of Boltzmann's argument that would be an adequate response to the reversibility objection. The price to be paid is that "we cannot speak of a direction for time as a whole; only certain sections of time have directions, and these directions are not the same" (Reichenbach 1956, 127).

The idea is to consider just the statistics of macroscopic physical systems; only such systems can provide an observational basis for the definition of time direction. Begin by taking into account a section of the entropy curve of the universe having a long upgrade (showing increase of entropy). Consistent with the frequentist interpretation of probability he advocated, Reichenbach introduced "the hypothesis of the branch structure", regarded as empirically attested, that a very large number of macroscopic systems can be statistically treated as separate, having "branched off" from the comprehensive system that is the rest of the universe (Reichenbach 1956, 135ff.).[10] A simple illustration of a branch system is that of a footprint on a beach (a highly ordered state of grains of sand,

---

[10] The branch structure hypothesis rests on five assumptions, each considered to be an empirical hypothesis that has been "convincingly verified". For discussion of these assumptions, see Sklar (1993, 318ff.).

presumably traceable to a past interaction before branching) which gradually erodes and disappears through the action of weather or tides. To be sure, any *given* branch system may display an apparent anti–Second Law fluctuation, for example, a "footprint" might be created by wind or waves, without intervention of a human foot. Still, Reichenbach argued, if one averages over an ensemble of branch systems (such as the beach at a crowded resort), such anomalous behaviors become statistically insignificant amidst the entropy-increasing processes in the vast majority of branch systems.

The definition of temporal direction as entropic increase thus considers the statistics of thermodynamic processes in a large number ("ensemble") of macroscopic systems that can be treated as effectively isolated. Because of their indefinite isolation, branch systems may be found that are initially in lower entropy states than their surrounding environments, yet observation will almost always show that their evolution is toward higher and higher relative states of entropy. Then it is an "empirical hypothesis" that there is a parallelism of entropic increase in the branch systems and in the universe as a whole. Accordingly, the humanly known direction of temporal order ("positive time") is *defined* in terms of the direction of "most" (nearly all) thermodynamic processes in the branch systems along that section, if such direction exists (Reichenbach 1956, 127). For it is "only this reflection of the general trend in many individual manifestations" that "is visible to us and appears to us as the direction of time" (Reichenbach 1956, 131). But "we cannot speak of a direction for time as a whole", and so the notions of *past* and *future* are relativized to a "particular section of the entropy curve of the universe" with its attendant branch systems that alone are observable.

Recent scrutiny of Reichenbach's argument notes that it "contain(s) the most thorough discussion in the literature of the attempt to derive Second Law behavior from the cosmological entropic asymmetry" (Sklar 1993, 320). However, Sklar pinpoints a fundamental difficulty, namely, that its key hypothesis, the "principle of parallelism of entropy increase", is not derivable, as is claimed, from empirically verified hypotheses. Rather it arises from an "apparently innocuous posit" concerning how the states of the branch system are arranged, *viz.*, in the *same* time order (Sklar 1993, 324). Once again it has been demonstrated how difficult it is to eliminate certain temporal notions without tacitly presupposing others. A more wide-ranging critique of Reichenbach's empiricist analysis of temporal anisotropy targets the "dogma", held also by others, that "considerations about irreversibility and entropy are absolutely crucial to every aspect of the problem" (Earman 1974, 15). In particular, a "thicket of problems" emerges once the "problem of the direction of time" is set within the framework of relativistic space-time theories, where, as Earman has shown, the Reichenbach definition of a "branch system" is inherently ambiguous. Moreover, since temporal orientation is a possible global space-time property, a discrepancy in assigning time direction may well arise with the result of a nonrelativistic method, such as Reichenbach's, of determining time direction through entropic increase. (J. J. Halliwell et al. [1994] is a recent survey of physical approaches to temporal asymmetry.)

CAUSALITY AND DETERMINISM

The status of the so-called law of causality and that of related issues of determinism and indeterminism were matters of some delicacy for logical empiricism, as is reflected in considerable internal controversy and disagreement. Emancipation from "metaphysics", "rationalism", and all forms of "school philosophy" meant that formulations such as "state A_0 is always followed by states A_1, A_2" (Frank 1932, 231) or "everything in the world takes place according to law" (Schlick 1931/1979, vol. 2, 177) had to be treated with some circumspection. Frank, for example, observed that the classical (unresticted) formulation of the validity of the causal principle, as Laplacean determinism, held, if at all, only for simple systems of point masses and not for more complicated systems such as are considered in, for example, hydrodynamics. In any case, it is to be rejected for the presupposition of a superhuman intelligence (Frank 1932, 36/1998, 51). For the logical empiricists, statement of the causal principle, if meaningful, could be regarded only a tautology or as a prediction of actual sense experiences. Yet neither option was really adequate. If tautologous, what could be made of the dramatic transformation in quantum mechanics, pointed to by the quantum physicists themselves, in the standing of the causal principle? If a statement about sense experiences, the principle appears to be false. Neither deflationary option appears consistent with broad avowals of the principle's significance made by logical empiricists themselves, that "the causal principle is a *conditio sine qua non* for knowledge of nature" or that "our whole science, even our whole practical life, is apparently based on the continual application of the law of causality" (Schlick 1920/1979, vol. 1, 309); Frank 1932/1998, 238). In the end, the problematic status of the causal principle was largely cloaked under the ostensibly less metaphysical topics of explanation and inductive confirmation.

The tensions are readily evident in Schlick's several discussions of the problem. Before coming to Vienna in 1922, in his influential *Allgemeine Erkenntnislehre* (1918) Schlick maintained, on largely Humean grounds, that the supposition of "strict causality" – same cause, same effect – admits not a theoretical, but only a practical, justification. Nature never returns the same cause twice; a cause is "strictly speaking, infinitely complicated", and so the most that can be affirmed is that similar effects follow similar causes, which often does not hold. Nonetheless, strict validity of the causal principle is a *postulate* for science; without it, the pursuit of knowledge of nature would be senseless (Schlick 1918, 340/1985, 395). Science, however, deals only with facts, not demands or wishes, and so acceptance of this postulate, without the least possibility of being able to demonstrate it, is a practical act, rooted ultimately in a biological drive for knowledge. On the other hand, in his 1920 essay on the causal principle (discussed earlier in this chapter), Schlick argued that the causal principle has an unobjectionable and empirically tested form in exact science. On the *assumption* of no action-at-a-distance, Schlick posed what is essentially the "initial value problem" for a field theory like general relativity: Given fixed initial and boundary conditions for a specified spatial region, the time evolution of that data surface is univocally determined by the partial differential equations of the field laws. However, confirmation of these differential laws can only be indirect, since integral laws alone are empirically attested, but these are compatible with a wide set of differential microlaws. Here a choice is called for on grounds of simplicity. In 1931 Schlick returned to the problem, attempting to face the implications for the causal principle – now glossed as "all events are in principle predictable" – occasioned by the new quantum theory. Heavily freighted at this time with the influence of Wittgenstein, Schlick regarded the causal principle as not at all an empirical principle that may be confirmed or refuted, but a regulative maxim for forming statements. Like all directives, or rules, it is "neither true or false, but good or bad, useful or idle", and the lesson of the quantum theory is that "this principle is *bad*, useless or idle, and incapable of fulfillment" (Schlick 1931/ 1979, vol. 2, 196).

For Reichenbach, the issues of causality and determinism in physics are fundamentally bound up with core problems of a probabilist and empiricist epistemology and theory of meaning. His initial view, articulated in his Ph.D. thesis of 1915, was unabashedly Kantian: the principle of causality is synthetic *a priori*: neither logically necessary nor empirically verifiable but a necessary condition for scientific knowledge. As seen above, his empiricist doctrine of space and time culminates in a reductive analysis resting on the supposition of the validity of the principle of action-by-contact. As "he weaned himself only gradually from Kantian conceptions" (Maria Reichenbach in Reichenbach [1965], xvii), he came subsequently to regard the causal principle, as in his book on quantum mechanics (see section 4), as a high-level convention, or "extension rule", that may or may not be admissible for physical descriptions. At the end of his life, the causal principle is viewed as an empirical claim that has been falsified according to Feynman's formulation of quantum electrodynamics, wherein a positron is interpreted as an electron going "backwards in time" (Reichenbach 1956, 268–9).[11]

Despite these changes in view, in the early 1920s Reichenbach gave the first of many attempts to reformulate the principle in purely probabilistic and empirical terms. Already in 1923, in a paper unpublished until 1932, but read and commented upon by Schrödinger in 1924, Reichenbach claimed that both causal laws and statistical laws are "special forms of a more general assertion dealing with the existence of probability laws in the physical world". For this reason, the problem of quanta should "not be handicapped by a faith in the necessary existence of causality" (Reichenbach 1932/ 1978, vol. 2, 370). A 1925 paper proved especially influential for Reichenbach's later work, with the modified claim that a

---

[11] As Kamlah (1991) points out, Reichenbach regarded Feynman diagrams in rather too literal a fashion.

quantitative description of all natural phenomena is possible without the hypothesis of "strict causality". On the other hand, classical determinism (strict causality) is held to be an unphysical idealization or fiction on the grounds that one can never write down a function ("limit function") that completely describes the state of the world at an instant t of time (Reichenbach 1925).[12] Meanwhile, Reichenbach attempted to formulate an empirically meaningful principle of determinism; it appears in section 20 of an article for the *Handbuch der Physik*, published in 1929 but written in the mid-1920s. Clearly distinguishing between causality and determinism, he held that causality is an implication $A \mapsto B$, an asymmetrical relation between A and B. Determinism is an extrapolation beyond this, the claim that given an instantaneous state of the world, it is possible to calculate univocally both the past and future. It is a "risky consequence" drawn when insufficient attention is paid to "the probability character of knowledge". In such form, it is useless to physics. Thus a "modest reformulation" based on the method of approximation used elsewhere in science is proposed: *"through more exact knowledge of the effective parameters, the probability of the prediction can be increased arbitrarily close to probability 1"* (Reichenbach 1929/1978, 195, emphasis in original). In a subsequent section (entitled "The Epistemological Situation in Quantum Mechanics") of the same article, certainly written after the appearance of Heisenberg's paper (1927, see below) on the uncertainty relations, the "modest reformulation" of section 20 has been revised: *"the probability in the calculation of events cannot be made to approach arbitrarily close to 1 but is instead restricted to a limit below 1"*. Here the said limit is a monotonic function of quantum numbers discernibly differing from 1 only for elementary events. The governing idea, merely broached there, is an attempt to describe atomic events in the context of "the macroscopic *concept of space*" by reconceptualizing the "idea of a *regular determinacy* of events." Recast in this probabilistic form, Reichenbach asserted that the thesis of determinism became meaningful for physics, that is,

[12] The nonphysical character of such a limit function was pointed out by Schrödinger (letter to Reichenbach of January 25, 1924, as translated in Reichenbach [1978b], 328–32). Schrödinger was critical of Reichenbach's 1923 stipulation that "a complete governing sequence of functions" converged – regarded as a necessary condition for a complete description of the world at time t.

empirically testable (Reichenbach 1929/1978, 217, emphases in original).

These suggestions, under the title "Continuous Probability Sequences", are developed to some extent in a technical paper, appearing in 1929 in the *Zeitschrift für Physik*, at the time the leading journal for quantum physics (Reichenbach 1929a; a synopsis appears in § 45 of Reichenbach 1935 or § 46 of Reichenbach 1949). The basic idea is that of random processes in continuous time. But how are we to imagine such a continuously acting chance? Reichenbach adopted the observable zigzag path of particles in Brownian motion (e.g., motes of dust in the afternoon sunlight streaming through a window) as the prototype of every causal chain (Reichenbach 1935, 253). Now there are two common ways of understanding such seemingly random behavior. Either the motion is deterministic, in which case continuous time is presupposed, and only an "infinity of influences" is held responsible for the observed course of phenomena proceeding *as if* acting by chance. Or the process is viewed as fundamentally stochastic, which, at least for a probability frequentist like Reichenbach, implies the discreteness of time (since frequencies apply only to discrete events). However, the exhaustiveness of the disjunction is rejected in Reichenbach's proposal to construct a continuous time probabilistic conception. His intent is to interpret continuous lines of causal connection ("causal chains") as probability sequences ("probability chains") in which later elements are only probabilistically determined by preceding ones. Determinism, however, holds infinitesimally: the consequences ensuing from every point-event are determined with certainly (with probability 1) for infinitesimal increments of time. With finite time increments between point-events, the probability decreases continuously. Such a world, according to Reichenbach, "possesses *causal connection* only in the small, while in the large it possesses *probability connection*" (Reichenbach 1929a, 307).

Reichenbach's research program of the early 1930s sought to embrace both classical and quantum physics within this probabilistic conception of causal connection as a convergent process. In predicting, at time t_1 the state of some course of events at the later time t_2 with the probability $1-\delta$ (for $\delta \ll 1$), one can at t_1 specify the future with a certain exactness E. But for this same value of E, another time t_3 can be chosen for which the probability of prediction becomes arbitrarily small (less than any given small value ε). In this way, Reichenbach initially sought to interpret the Heisenberg uncertainty ("indeterminacy") principle as affirming that not only every causal chain, but also the limit to which the chains approach with increasing accuracy of observation, has the character of a continuous probability sequence (Reichenbach 1935, 253; cf. 1949, 250). In the context of quantum mechanics, this becomes a program to find a probability density function $d(q, p)$ introduced for each combination of conjugate variables (such as position and momentum). The program is explicitly rejected by Reichenbach in section 26 in his 1944 book on quantum mechanics (see below). But for a number of years in the 1930s, he maintained that his epistemological critique of the principle of causality had prefigured the new quantum mechanics, and that the Heisenberg principle was an "exact instance" of his generalization of the principle of causality as a continuous "probability chain".[13]

QUANTUM MECHANICS

The development of logical empiricism was well underway when the new quantum mechanics arrived in 1925–6, and positivist currents among certain quantum physicists were broadly welcomed.[14] Schlick appropriated pronouncements of Heisenberg and others in a publicized defense of positivism against the realist metaphysics of his teacher Planck (Schlick 1932). In another paper of 1931, he cited the alleged overthrow of causality in quantum mechanics as further evidence for the logical empiricist tenet that there are no necessary principles of empirical knowledge (Schlick 1931). But only Philipp Frank and Hans Reichenbach wrote at all extensively on quantum theory. An adherent of a neo-Machian

---

[13] Reichenbach (1930b, 181): "the Heisenberg indeterminacy principle of quantum mechanics" presents "an exact instance" (genau der Fall) of Reichenbach's probabilistic generalization of the idea of causality. In the English translation (1978, vol. 2, 338), this is translated as "an exact analogue".

[14] In particular, Heisenberg's insistence (1927) that the new theory (his matrix mechanics) pertained only to observable quantities. However, Reichenbach initially demurred from Bohr's viewpoint that one could not have, jointly, a space-time and a causal description of quantum phenomena, a postulate of the doctrine of complementarity. See Reichenbach (1991).

positivism, the bulk of Frank's considerable writing on quantum theory was devoted to exposing various ideological appropriations or confusions, the "misinterpretations" of "idealistic", "spiritualistic", or "materialistic" philosophies (Frank 1936/1949, 160). On the other hand, despite distrust of all "philosophical interpretations" of physical theories, Frank supported the Copenhagen line on quantum theory, and indeed attempted to induce Bohr "to join the camp of outspoken positivists" (Beller 1999, 176). In Frank's assessment, the core claim of the Copenhagen thesis of "complementarity", rightly understood, was not a "philosophical interpretation" at all but rather a linguistic prophylactic regarding meaningful statements whose careful use might be recommended even to prominent physicists. For this reason, Frank regarded the Copenhagen interpretation as "fully compatible with logical empiricism", presumably seeing no need for further improvement on that score. Reichenbach alone treated the foundations of quantum mechanics in something like the present sense of the term, but the full treatment did not appear until 1944 in a book whose central claim is that any causal interpretation of quantum mechanics leads to causal anomalies. But this signaled that the guiding idea of "probability chains" (chains of statistical causation) and indeed the main objective of Reichenbach's endeavors in philosophy of physics since 1926, the assimilation of quantum theory into the framework of his more general probabilistic account of causality, had come to grief. In place of a causal interpretation, Reichenbach proposed a "restricted interpretation", according to which certain quantum mechanical statements are considered meaningful, but possessing "indeterminate" truth value, an explicit alternative to the "restricted" interpretation of Copenhagen.

Philosophical analysis of quantum mechanics is needed, Reichenbach wrote in the "Preface", because the physical interpretation of the theory had shown that "something had been achieved in this new theory ... contrary to traditional concepts of knowledge and reality", but not in fact what this something is. Stipulating that "the philosophy of physics should be as neat and clear as physics itself", Reichenbach promised a philosophical illumination of the transformation in the concept of physical knowledge. Such treatment must be "free of metaphysics" but also unconstrained by "the operational form of empiricism" that resists treating quantum mechanical statements as pertaining to "an atomic world as real as the ordinary physical world".[15] The transformation in traditional concepts of knowledge concerned the relation between "phenomena" and what are termed "interphenomena", a distinction more or less parallelling the standard distinction between observed and unobserved entities or states and similarly a matter of degree. "Phenomena" are not to be understood as "observable in the strict epistemological sense" but rather are atomic occurrences readily inferred – and so "directly verified"– by macroscopic events such as clicks in a Geiger counter, marks on photographic film, or tracks in a Wilson cloud chamber (Reichenbach 1944, 21). As the name suggests, "interphenomena" are inferred occurrences; having a much less direct relation to observation, they are interpolated (as "hidden variables") between phenomena (e.g., assigning a particle an exact trajectory in the double slit experiment) in order to furnish a causal description of quantum mechanical experiments consistent with their observable statistical relations. The sense of "normal causality" in play holds that effects propagate continuously through space but also posits probability relations between cause and effect, in accordance with Reichenbach's notion of "probability chains".

Now, according to Reichenbach's conventionalist "theory of equivalent descriptions", there is always a *class* of *admissible* (and so *empirically equivalent*) descriptions encompassing the unobserved objects and events underlying a theory's observational content. Since such theoretical constructions do not augment the observational content, any one of them can serve as well as any other and can be considered "true", despite wide differences regarding unobserved objects (Reichenbach 1944, 19). In classical physics, the admissible descriptions always include a "normal system" satisfying two conditions. The first states that the laws of nature are the same whether or not objects are observed. This is really an assertion that the principle of action-by-contact ("which the whole of macroscopic physics has shown to be an intrinsic component of the principle of causality"; Reichenbach 1946, 239–47, 239) is valid

---

[15] In this regard, there is a fundamental disagreement with Frank, for whom both wave or particle interpretations "lead us into 'deep water', however, if we take them too seriously, which means if we regard them as statements about reality" (1957, 244).

also for unobserved objects. The second condition requires that the states of objects do not depend upon being observed. Since each member of the class of admissible descriptions by definition furnishes a complete description of all observations, the usual choice of the "normal system" as the one "true description" is merely a matter of "descriptive simplicity". In quantum physics the situation is somewhat more delicate. There, Reichenbach argued, the second condition does not obtain. The reason is the unbreachable limit to the precision of simultaneous measurement of certain observables as stated in Heisenberg's (1927) uncertainly principle ("Principle of Indeterminacy").[16] Recall that Heisenberg showed that, for any wave function $\Psi(x, t)$ describing the motion of a quantum particle, the accuracy with which the, for example, x coordinate of the particle's position and, simultaneously, the particle's linear momentum p_x (in the x direction) can be measured is bounded by an inequality,

$$\triangle x \cdot \triangle p_x \geq \frac{1}{2} \hbar,$$

where $\triangle x$ is the root mean square deviation (the "uncertainty" in knowledge) of x, $\triangle p_x$ is the similar "uncertainty" of p_x, and $\hbar$ is Planck's original constant h divided by $2\pi = 1.055 \times 10^{-27}$ erg-sec. On account of this definite limit to what can be known about such complementary ("noncommuting") observables as x and p_x at the same time t, Reichenbach affirmed that a "normal system of description" for quantum mechanics cannot satisfy condition 2.

What about condition 1? For a chosen experiment, it is possible to construct an "exhaustive" or complete description of quantum microphysical interphenomena satisfying normal causality, yet only in a very *attenuated* sense. This is shown, for example, by the dual wave and particle accounts of the familiar interference and two-slit experiments. While either the wave or the particle interpretation by itself gives rise to a "causal anomaly", it is possible to "transform away" the anomaly by changing to the other description but only in the context of a *given* experiment (Reichenbach 1944, § 7).[17] In fact,

[16] An "observable" is any physical quantity that is, in principle, measurable.

[17] In the wave interpretation, a causal anomaly arises in interference experiments in which a wave front extended over a large region is instantaneously "swallowed" by a pointlike registration on a detection screen. In the particle interpretation of

however, a particle interpretation alone or a wave interpretation alone is possible only in limiting cases, and in general both are necessary. Hence, Reichenbach advanced the larger claim that there cannot be an exhaustive interpretation of all quantum mechanical interphenomena in every possible experiment that is free of anomalies and consistent with the observed statistical results of quantum measurements. Such an interpretation would be a causal characterization of all unobserved parameters and functional relations that, if known, would enable the simultaneous assignment of definite values to all quantum mechanical observables (i.e., both commuting and noncommuting) in all physical states of the system (Reichenbach 1944, 33, 139). In this way determinate values would be assigned to all observables even when the system is *not* in an eigenstate for a given observable.[18] An exhaustive interpretation would thus *complete* the assignments of definite values to all observables, filling in the gaps left by ordinary quantum theory, but on pain of violating the requirements of normal causality, *viz.*, the principle of action-by-contact that underpins macrophysics and is known to hold for observables. In § 26 of his book, Reichenbach offered a proof that such causal chains, regarded as a special case of probability chains, cannot provide such exhaustive causal supplementation of quantum mechanics. Since Reichenbach regarded his notion of probability chains as expositing the only legitimate understanding of physical causality, this result, "the Principle of Anomaly in Quantum Mechanics", is a second principle that, he claimed, must augment the Heisenberg uncertainty principle "if a complete account of the status of causality within a

the two-slit experiment, the probability of a particle going through one slit and registering on a detection screen at a point *P* depends upon whether the other slit is open or not, a kind of "action at a distance".

[18] In the usual Hilbert space formalism of quantum mechanics due to von Neumann (1932), observables are represented by linear operators on the ("Hilbert") vector space associated with the quantum system, each particular state of the system being represented as a particular vector (or "ray") in Hilbert space. The operators and vectors (physical states) are connected by a familiar rule known as the "eigenvalue-eigenstate link" (*eigen* is German for "proper"). This affirms that an observable has a determinate value for a given state if and only if measurement of the observable is certain to lead to that value, its so-called eigenvalue. In this special case, the state is said to be an eigenstate of that observable. In the general case, one cannot speak of an observable having a value for a particular state, but only of its having an average value for that state.

quantum-mechanical physics is to be given" (Reichenbach 1948, 340–1). Just as the Heisenberg principle has ruled out normal causality for observables on account of the violation of condition 2, so the Principle of Anomaly is taken to show that normal causality cannot be restored at the level of unobservables, violating condition 1.

Then follows the thesis for which Reichenbach's book is best known: a three-valued semantics for quantum mechanical statements (Reichenbach 1944, §§ 29–30; see also the discussion in Jammer 1974, 364–73). A "restrictive interpretation", as opposed to an "exhaustive" one, contains descriptions only of phenomena, not of interphenomena. Such interpretations constrain the meaning or warranted assertability of quantum mechanical statements in various ways. In the "Bohr-Heisenberg" (i.e., Copenhagen) restrictive interpretation, statements attributing definite values to noncommuting observables, viz., assigning precise values at the same instant to quantities such as position and linear momentum, are regarded as meaningless. Reichenbach was dissatisfied with this restrictive rule for two reasons. One is that the Copenhagen prohibition has a metalinguistic formulation, deeming "meaningless" certain apparently well-formed statements in the object language of quantum mechanics. The other reflects Reichenbach's opposition to pure positivism: the Copenhagen proscription is deemed unreasonable because physics cannot get by without any description of interphenomena. An alternative, but preferable, restrictive interpretation is that the semantics of quantum mechanical assertions be evaluated according to a three-valued logic (Reichenbach 1944, 43, 144ff.). This allows statements attributing exact values to noncommuting quantities to be considered meaningful but assigns them a middle truth value "indeterminate", that is, as neither "true" nor "false".[19]

---

[19] Reichenbach's recommendation of a truth-functional three-valued logic as the adequate semantics for quantum mechanical statements must be distinguished from other programs, both earlier and later, for a "quantum logic". These nonstandard logics, arising in the Hilbert space formalism, consider quantum mechanical statements as algebraic structures for which the distributive laws (for conjunction and disjunction) do not hold. It must also be noted that Bohr, Born, and Pauli saw Reichenbach's recommendation either as equivalent to the Copenhagen interpretation, or as imposing an unnecessary burden. See Bohr (1948, 317); Born (1949, 107–8); and Pauli (1947, 177–8).

Following this overview, it is possible to look a bit more closely at several salient issues raised by the book and in several related papers that subsequently appeared. Two fundamental changes in outlook are in evidence. The first concerns the meaning of the Heisenberg uncertainty relations. As he had *not* done previously, Reichenbach now viewed the "Principle of Indeterminacy" as "a revision of the statement of causality". While continuing, as before, to assimilate the Heisenberg relations to the growing trend of statistical laws in physics, a trend anticipated in his empiricist critique of causality in 1925, by 1944 these relations are seen as introducing a novel, hitherto unanticipated, modification of the causal principle (Reichenbach 1944, 3). Recall that according to Reichenbach's probabilistic conception of causality, perfect knowledge of all causally relevant variables of a physical system is regarded an unphysical idealization, and so strict causality might be upheld only for a microstate infinitesimally close in time to an original state. But the Heisenberg principle's "specific version of the criticism of causality" showed that this probabilistic reformulation of causality still contained the unwarranted assumption that simultaneous measurement to arbitrary accuracy of the values of all observables is possible. As seen, this is because, for noncommuting observables, these values *cannot in principle be precisely known* (i.e., known to a precision less than the order of magnitude of Planck's constant). In consequence, strict causality, in the empiricist sense of precise prediction, does not even obtain infinitesimally: there also can be but statistical laws for observed values for physical states separated by infinitesimal time increments.

The second major innovation, the *Principle of Anomaly*, comes in the train of the first. Despite its various (and perhaps inequivalent formulations) formulations, the gist of it is that a consistent and complete causal supplementation of quantum mechanical phenomena will always violate "normal causality".[20] As noted above, statements about causal anomalies can be avoided in *restrictive* interpretations, those refraining from making true or false assertions regarding unobserved values of observables. While such assertions cannot be verified to be true on account of the Heisenberg

---

[20] A slightly different formulation is that "The class of descriptions of interphenomena contains no normal system" (Reichenbach 1944, 33).

uncertainty relations, Reichenbach suggested that they can be nonetheless introduced as *conventions* or *definitions*, hence as meaningful statements, in *exhaustive* physical descriptions. That such descriptions lead to violations of "normal causality" is not in itself sufficient reason to dismiss them from the class of admissible descriptions for quantum systems. This means, however, that normal causality, the principle of action-by-contact, has become a *convention* or *definition* governing certain physical descriptions and not others, and not, as hitherto regarded, a core constitutive principle of physical theories. The question now is merely whether such a convention governing quantum descriptions can be "carried through", for this "depends on the structure of the physical world". Reichenbach thought he had a proof that this is not the case, and that "causal anomalies are ... inherent in the nature of the physical world", the ontological significance of the Principle of Anomaly. Of course, "restrictive interpretations", refraining altogether from statements about interphenomena, "do not establish a normal causality either". As there is no interpretation of quantum mechanics – neither "exhaustive" nor "restrictive" – containing a "normal system", the conclusion is drawn that all inductive indication points to the fact that the relations among observables of quantum mechanics do not admit of causal supplementation (Reichenbach 1944, 44, 129). Hence, contrary to the "Copenhagen" line of Bohr and Heisenberg, assertions concerning causal supplementation *can* be included in meaningful quantum mechanical discourse because they are claims that are quite likely to be *false*.

Reichenbach's conclusion of the likely impossibility of a causal interpretation of quantum mechanics is undoubtedly a *volte face* but is considerably ambitious in its own terms, and worth being put in context. Since 1932 a proof of John von Neumann's had been widely understood to have shown the impossibility of causal "hidden variable" theories of quantum mechanics (von Neumann 1932/1955, 209–11, 305–28). Given this pedigree, there arose "the dogma that there could exist no causal version of quantum mechanics that was observationally equivalent to standard quantum mechanics" (Cushing 1994, 144). Max Born's assessment in 1949 is perhaps representative: von Neumann had shown that "no concealed parameters can be introduced with the help of which the indeterministic description could be transformed into a deterministic one" (Born 1949, 109). Though not the first to do so, Reichenbach recognized, though he didn't closely diagnose (first done in 1966 by J. Bell), a contentious assumption of the von Neumann proof: that "for all kinds of statistical assemblages the laws of quantum mechanics, expressed in terms of ψ-functions, are valid." That is, the von Neumann proof excluded from consideration "physical systems for which the statistical relations controlling their parameters are not expressible in terms of ψ-functions". But then, "if the indeterminism of quantum mechanics is questioned, this assumption will be equally questioned" (Reichenbach 1944, 14, and fn. 3).[21] Cognizant of this restrictive assumption in von Neumann's proof, Reichenbach boldly sought, through his Principle of Anomaly, to conclusively demonstrate the impossibility of an exhaustive causal interpretation of quantum mechanics. His "proof", employing the notion of a "chain structure" developed in his book on probability (1935), attempts to show that there is no way of inserting causal chains (special cases of "probability chains") behind the observed statistical relations of quantum mechanics (Reichenbach 1944, 122–9).[22] The Principle of Anomaly may be then regarded as "the ultimately decisive argument against all claims of causality in the physical world ... mak(ing) impossible any exhaustive description of unobservables in the sense assumed for classical physics" (Reichenbach 1946, 243).

Does the Principle of Anomaly in fact "exclude the introduction of causality, in any sense, into the world of quantum mechanical objects" (Reichenbach 1944, 117)? With a bit of reconstruction, Roger Jones gave, some years ago, a precise statement of the mathematical content of the Principle of Anomaly (Jones 1979). He showed that the necessary condition for the existence of an exhaustive interpretation in Reichenbach's sense is

[21] More precisely, von Neumann's assumption is that the rule holding that the linear combination of any two Hermitian operators represents an observable, while the linear combination of expectation values is the expectation value of the combination, which is true of quantum mechanics, is also true for all states (including the "dispersion free" states postulated by "hidden variables"); see Bell (1966).

[22] The proof takes the form of showing that there is no relative probability function for determining the value of a measured parameter u, given simultaneous and exact values of two noncommuting observables (such as position and linear momentum).

the existence of a joint probability distribution of all physical quantities in all states of a quantum system. Arguing that the Principle of Anomaly is the first of a series of "no joint distribution theorems", Jones then proved a theorem, regarded as equivalent to the Principle of Anomaly, affirming that there is no joint probability distribution for noncommuting quantities that is both consistent with the probabilities assigned by quantum mechanics to observables and free of causal anomalies. But then, as Jones himself noted, Reichenbach's conception of a complete, that is, exhaustive, description is quite strong, raising the question of whether the requirement of the necessary joint probability distributions is a reasonable one. As Arthur Fine has argued, the very existence of such joint distributions follows from the usual definition of the relevant quantities as random variables, thus raising the question of whether quantum mechanical quantities are legitimately so treated.[23] If they are, then by definition they will have a joint distribution. In that case, an exhaustive description in Reichenbach's forbidden sense appears to be a species of a wider genus of a "reductive realism" that in fact was famously demonstrated by Bell (1964) to be inconsistent with the predictions of standard quantum theory. This would seem to be something of a vindication of Reichenbach.

On the otherhand, in the "pilot wave theory" of De Broglie and Bohm, parameters are introduced into nonrelativistic wave mechanics that transform it into a causal and strictly deterministic theory. This is an exhaustive interpretation that, contrary to the claims of both von Neumann and Reichenbach, is completely empirically equivalent to standard quantum mechanics, so far as is known[24]. Is it then a counterexample to the Principle of

---

[23] Fine (1982) argues that common to hidden variable theories (and manifest in the Bell inequalities) is the provision of joint distributions for noncommuting observables, probability distributions rejected in quantum mechanics as not well defined. See Shimony (1984) for criticism of Fine's claim.

[24] See Bell (1982). In the De Broglie–Bohm theory there are two evolution equations, the Schrödinger equation for ψ (t) and a first-order evolution equation for the positions (configuration) of particles. According to Goldstein (1998, 40): "This deterministic theory of particles in motion completely accounts for all the phenomena of non-relativistic quantum mechanics, from interference effects to spectral lines, to spin."

Anomaly?[25] The De Broglie–Bohm theory is an explicitly nonlocal theory. But whether it contains overt "causal anomalies" in Reichenbach's sense is debatable (given the vagueness of criteria for a "causal anomaly"), for its nonlocality is benign and cannot be employed to violate relativistic constraints on supraluminal signaling.

[25] Reichenbach (1944, 32), thought that the theory in De Broglie's formulation was such a counterexample. For the contributions of Bohm to the theory, see Cushing (1994).

9 Logical Empiricism and the Philosophy of Psychology

Logical empiricism, as is well known, was deeply intertwined with both physics and logic. Rudolf Carnap, Philipp Frank, Hans Hahn, Hans Reichenbach, Moritz Schlick, Friedrich Waismann, and, later, Herbert Feigl and Carl Hempel all pursued research programs inspired particularly by the achievement of relativistic physics and informed, to quite various degrees, by such accomplishments in logic as Gottlob Frege's account of mathematical knowledge, David Hilbert's program of axiomatization and implicit definition, Ludwig Wittgenstein's *Tractatus*, Bertrand Russell's theory of types, Kurt Gödel's incompleteness results, and Alfred Tarski's theory of truth. Quite often these thinkers were not merely inspired by the profound achievements of relativity and mathematical logic, but (as in the case of Schlick and Reichenbach especially) developed, as their own central philosophical projects, accounts of the validity and objectivity they took to be embodied in these advances in the natural and formal sciences. Thus to a considerable extent the history of logical empiricism reflects, and even parallels, the history of physics and logic in the late nineteenth and early twentieth centuries.[1]

Yet a review of logical empiricists' writings reveals an affinity toward and a growing interest in behaviorism, neobehaviorism, Gestalt, and psychophysics – varieties of experimental psychology that flourished in the 1920s and 1930s. The affinity is reflected in

---

[1] See, e.g., Schlick (1917), Reichenbach (1920), and Frank's retrospective (1949), as well as the commentaries in Friedman (1999), Ryckman (2003, this volume) and Richardson (1998). Not all the logical empiricists came to their work from physics or logic. Otto Neurath's extensive background in economics and sociology (see Cartwright et al. 1996), for example, was integrated with the pursuit of antimetaphysics and a philosophical *neue Sachlichkeit* for which he is now well known.

part in the occasional use of particular results or concepts from one or another of these forms of experimental psychology. In section 67 of his *Logischer Aufbau der Welt*, for instance, Carnap appeals to Gestalt psychology to justify his choice of unitary, holistic elementary experiences over sensory atoms as the domain of the autopsychological constitution system. More significantly, in section 122 he acknowledges that developments in psychology may well require revisions to that constitution system. More often the affinity surfaces in more diffuse ways, for example, in claims to the effect that experimental psychology (behaviorism especially) displays an intellectual attitude in step with logical empiricism. Thus, to take one example, we find in the *Wissenschaftliche Weltauffassung: Der Wiener Kreis* (The Scientific World Conception: The Vienna Circle), the Vienna Circle's 1929 "manifesto" authored (though not signed) by Hahn, Neurath, and Carnap, the assertion that "the attempt of behaviorist psychology to grasp the psychic through the behavior of bodies, which is at a level accessible to perception, is, in its principled attitude, close to the scientific world conception" (Carnap et al. 1929/1983, 315). Such similarity of attitude was later cited by Herbert Feigl, one of the Circle's youngest members, as a central reason why he and other logical empiricists were subject to such a "friendly reception" from American experimental psychologists upon their emigration to the United States, and, further, why logical empiricism enjoyed such "remarkable success" there (Feigl 1969, 660, 662, 667).

But logical empiricism's attention to experimental psychology was driven not just by the utility of its results or the similarity of its attitudes, but also (perhaps, indeed, more) by the perceived need to clarify its concepts. The *Wissenschaftliche Weltauffassung*'s overture to behaviorism, for example, follows on the heels of this rather cautious assessment of scientific psychology as a whole:

The linguistic forms which we still use in psychology today have their origin in certain ancient metaphysical notions of the soul. The formation of concepts in psychology is made difficult by these defects of language: metaphysical burdens and logical incongruities. Moreover there are certain factual difficulties. The result is that hitherto most of the concepts used in psychology are inadequately defined; of some, it is not known whether they have meaning or only simulate meaning through usage. So, in this field nearly everything in the way of epistemological analysis still remains to be done; of course, analysis here is more difficult than in physics. (Carnap et al. 1929/1983, 315)

This call for definition and epistemological analysis in psychology is, as it were, the flip side of the sympathetic overtures logical empiricism made toward experimental psychology. But rather than coming across as a critical challenge or, worse, an invitation to a turf battle, this call actually articulated a sentiment shared widely among logical empiricists and experimental psychologists. Consequently, a considerable amount of energy in the 1930s was directed toward precisely this project of defining and analyzing psychological concepts. After embracing the physicalist language in the early 1930s, for example, Carnap turned his attention to the manner in which psychology could be cast in physical language, lecturing on that topic in 1930 and in 1932 publishing "Psychologie in physikalischer Sprache" (Psychology in Physicalist Language) in *Erkenntnis*. The efforts to render psychology in physicalist terms continued. In 1933 Otto Neurath published the monograph *Einheitswissenschaft und Psychologie* (*Unified Science and Psychology*). In 1935 a symposium devoted to "psychology and the natural sciences" appeared in *Revue de Synthèse*; to this Schlick contributed an article titled "De la Relation entre les Notions Psychologiques et les Notions Physiques (On the Relation between Psychological and Physical Concepts) Carnap contributed "Les Concepts Psychologiques et les Concepts Physiques sont-ils foncièrement différent?" (Are Psychological Concepts and Physical Concepts Fundamentally Different?)" and Hempel an essay titled "Analyse Logique de la Psychologie" (The Logical Analysis of Psychology). Finally, the journal *Philosophy of Science*, established in 1934, published at least 10 full-length articles (out of approximately 100) addressing psychology in its first four years, among them Herbert Feigl's "Logical Analysis of the Psychophysical Problem: A Contribution of the New Positivism," Charles Hartshorne's "The Parallel Development of Method in Physics and Psychology," "The Relation of the Attributes of Sensation to the Dimensions of the Stimulus" by E. G. Boring, "Psychology as a Science of Objective Relations" by Egon Brunswik, and E. C. Tolman's "Psychology versus Immediate Experience." These articles appeared among several other discussion notes and reviews concerning psychology; there is comparable attention paid to physics, but to no other sciences, including sociology, chemistry, or biology.[2]

Here two clarificatory points concerning logical empiricism's interest in psychology are called for, to avoid the impression that logical empiricism was party to approaches within the philosophy of psychology that it in fact vigorously rejected. In a preliminary fashion, it must be emphasized that logical empiricism was interested only in *experimental* psychology, or, to put the same point another way, its interest in psychology extended only so far as psychology was, or could be fashioned as, a natural science. What, precisely, constituted a natural science was subject to increasing dispute among the logical empiricists, but suffice it to say the logical empiricists were not inclined toward anything resembling clinical psychology *as such*, that is, toward anything that presented itself as primarily a tool for securing mental health or, more broadly, toward attaining a kind of understanding or knowledge not provided by science. When their attention did turn toward topics outside the traditional fold of experimental psychology, as, for example, when Carnap mentioned his interest in extrasensory perception, or when any number of other logical empiricists referenced Freudian psychology, these topics were typically approached as potential domains of experimental knowledge, to be assimilated into traditional experimental psychology (see Carnap 1963, 26). Thus, for example, the *Wissenschaftliche Weltauffassung* suggests Freudian psychoanalytic theory as a promising resource for explaining the "wrong path of metaphysics" (307), and Carnap (1963, 58) recounts the efforts of Neurath and others in late 1932 to cast Freudian psychoanalytic theory in physical terms (see also Feigl 1969, 632).

The logical empiricists' insistence that psychology be approached as a natural science, subject to the general principles of logic, should squelch any impression that the use of psychological concepts by the logical empiricists inclined them toward *psychologism*, that is, the view that logical entities like propositions, sentences, meanings, or the like were ultimately psychological entities, or further that logical laws can be explained by reference to psychological laws.

---

[2] Sociology did receive extended treatments from both Otto Neurath (see, e.g., his 1931c and 1973) and Edgar Zilsel (1941).

Followers, as they were, of Frege and Wittgenstein (whose *Tractatus* insisted unequivocally that "psychology is no more closely related to philosophy than any other natural science" [4.1121]), the logical empiricists had no sympathy for psychologism. Carnap's *Logische Syntax der Sprache*, for example, echoes Wittgenstein's injunction against confusing psychology and philosophy: "in ... philosophy the psychological questions must first of all be eliminated; these belong to psychology, which is one of the empirical sciences, and are to be handled by it with the aid of its empirical methods" (Carnap 1934/1937, 278).

Given logical empiricism's considerable interest in experimental psychology, even amidst its rather intense attention to relativistic physics and modern logic, the question arises of why experimental psychology merited such interest. In seeking an answer here, it is, I believe, important not to discount the very real momentum the movement's adherents felt, combined with the sense, as we saw above in the *Wissenschaftliche Weltauffassung*'s comment, that in psychology "nearly everything in the way of epistemological analysis still remains to be done." It is inviting to impose a Kuhnian framework on this historical moment, seeing in the logical empiricists' analysis of concepts of physics a paradigm of philosophical achievement and in the working out of similar analyses in psychology the puzzle-solving of normal science, a project which, as Kuhn emphasized, is at the time inviting, even exciting. Such excitement was no doubt in play in the 1930s.

But, underlying and abetting the excitement, there is a somewhat deeper motivation at work. Recognizing it proceeds from foregrounding logical empiricism's commitment to the *unity of science*, a theme sounded without compromise in the *Wissenschaftliche Weltauffassung*:

The goal ahead is *unified* science. The endeavor is to link and harmonize the achievements of individual investigators in their various fields of science. From this aim follows the emphasis on *collective efforts*, and also the emphasis on what can be grasped intersubjectively; from this springs the search for a neutral system of formulae, for a symbolism freed from the slag of historical languages; and also the search for a total system of concepts. Neatness and clarity are striven for, and dark distances and unfathomable depths rejected. (Carnap et al. 1929/1983, 306)

Carnap was moved to emphasize the same theme some 30 years later:

In our discussions, chiefly under the influence of Neurath, the principle of the unity of science became one of the main tenets of our general philosophical conception. This principle says that the different branches of empirical science are separated only for the practical reason of division of labor, but are fundamentally merely parts of one comprehensive unified science. (Carnap 1963, 52)

With respect to psychology, though, unified science had particular resonance, for in the European context the social sciences as a whole had often been held out as an intellectual endeavor fundamentally *different* from the natural sciences. And this is a point Carnap emphasizes. The unity of science thesis, he continues,

must be understood primarily as a rejection of the prevailing view in German contemporary philosophy that there is a fundamental difference between the natural sciences and the *Geisteswissenschaften* (literally "spiritual sciences", understood as the sciences of mind, culture, and history, thus roughly corresponding to the social sciences and humanities). In contrast to this customary view, Neurath maintained the monistic conception that everything that occurs is a part of nature, i.e., of the physical world. I proposed to make this thesis more precise by transforming it into a thesis concerning language, namely, the thesis that the total language encompassing all knowledge can be constructed on a physicalistic basis. (ibid., 52)

According to the particularly German distinction between *Naturwissenschaften* and *Geisteswissenschaften*, the former, the natural or physical sciences, dealt with things which lacked meaning; they could therefore employ a method which made no use of understanding (*verstehen*), as a means to acquire knowledge about those objects. But the *Geisteswissenschaften*, or social sciences – particularly psychology – addressed themselves to intrinsically meaningful things, such as mental states or collective attitudes, and therefore required as a necessary part of their method an *understanding* of mental states, emotions, *Zeitgeists*, and so forth (see, e.g., Hempel 1935, 167–8). And Carnap's narrative makes it clear how the attention to psychology, and particularly the drive to show that psychology could be cast in physical terms, was, in the hands of the logical empiricists, simply the development of a rejection of the

Naturwissenschaften/Geisteswissenschaften distinction. Or, to put the point positively, and in logical empiricist terms, it was simply the result of pursuing the goal of linking and harmonizing the various fields of science and of rejecting "dark distances and unfathomable depths." Calls for clarity and sobriety aside, this was, it is worth noting, no dry academic debate. In an essay of Carnap's on psychology cast in physical language that we shall explore in more detail below, Carnap is moved to ask his reader to "make a special effort ... to retain the objectivity and openness of mind always requisite to the testing of a scientific thesis" (1932/1959, 168).

Finally, emphasis on the unity of science thesis and the attack on the *Naturwissenschaften/Geisteswissenschaften* divide provides us as well with an explanation of the relative *inattention* logical empiricism paid to the natural sciences other than physics – chemistry or biology, for example. For their objectivity or inter-subjectivity was not in question; instead, it rested comfortably on the established objectivity of physics. It would be several decades before issues of reduction, explanation, and their own home-grown conceptual problems fostered separable philosophies of, for example, biology or chemistry.

The unity of science thesis, and the challenge posed in the context of the *Geisteswissenschaften/Naturwissenschaften* debate, is certainly a critical factor in accounting for the interest logical empiricism displayed in psychology. But it does not exhaust the factors, and indeed, it may not, from a philosophical point of view, be the most significant factor. Central strands of the logical empiricist program were destined to make the science of psychology problematic for logical empiricism, largely *independent* of debates over the legitimacy of the *Naturwissenschaften/Geisteswissenschaften* divide. For at a very general level, behind even the unity of science thesis, the aim of the logical empiricists' epistemological project was to display the objective validity of the sciences – particularly relativistic physics, of course, but not *just* relativistic physics; all genuine sciences were candidates for a rational reconstruction aimed at making their status as objective knowledge plain. The logical empiricists had, however, judged two very traditional strategies for accomplishing this task unacceptable. A classic empiricist *reduction* of science to experience – a display of how all science was in the end simply an economical description of sense experience, in the manner of David Hume or Bertrand Russell – was regarded as unacceptable because experience itself, the "given," was private and subjective rather than public or objective. But an account of science which located its objectivity in something other than experience risked divorcing science from experience altogether, and this alternative the logical empiricists found equally unacceptable. The way out was to locate objectivity not in experience but in the *logical structure* of experience. For such structure was objective or, at least, intersubjective. It could be conveyed, shared, discussed, and refined. This approach to objectivity as intersubjectivity is at the heart of Carnap's *Aufbau* and informs much of his subsequent work. We find it clearly expressed as well in Albert Blumberg and Herbert Feigl's introduction of logical empiricism to the North American philosophical world, their 1931 *Journal of Philosophy* article "Logical Positivism: A New Movement in European Philosophy" (which, incidentally, introduced the term "logical positivism"). There Blumberg and Feigl argued that

[k]nowledge or the communicable expresses the formal structure but not the content of experience. For the immediately given is private, non-communicable. It can be pointed to by means of demonstratives like "this," "that," "here," "now," "I"; but assertions in which such words occur are not propositions in the strict sense. In other words, it is not the experienced qualitative content which is mirrored in any system of knowledge, but the formal structure or relations of the given. This becomes clear if we consider that the modifications of the world in which a consistent substitution of qualities (e.g. red for green and green for red) took place would leave the whole edifice of knowledge unchanged. For, although it may seem at first glance that "red," "hot," "bitter," etc., signify the immediately given qualities themselves, we see that knowledge, as distinguished from mere "listing" or "cataloguing," does not begin until we recognize relations of similarity or dissimilarity between experiences. Hence, from the point of view of knowledge (*Erkenntnis* as distinguished from *Erlebnis*) the essence of "red," etc., is not its experienced quâle, but its unique set of relations to other qualities. (ibid., 285–6)

Leaving aside the question of whether worlds are indeed empirically or epistemically equivalent under substitution of red for green and vice versa, it is clear that at the heart of this suggestion is the idea that what is communicated in the system of knowledge, what is intersubjective, is, emphatically, not experience, but the logical *form* of experience. Responding perhaps to the need to maintain a connection between knowledge and experience, Blumberg and Feigl are at pains not to omit reference to experience or the given altogether; the given can be pointed to, and indeed it is pointed to, by the terms in the atomic propositions in a system. "Knowledge," Blumberg and Feigl write, "though it communicates only the form of the given, nonetheless is based upon the content, for the words in the atomic propositions are definable only concretely through pointing to content. Knowledge expresses the form and points to the content" (288). What this "pointing to" does, however, apart from preserve reference to experience, is not clear.

This notion of objectivity as intersubjectivity, with the object of intersubjective agreement being the logical form of experience, encountered profound technical difficulties and proved ultimately unworkable (see Friedman 1999, Richardson 1998, and several of the essays in this volume). For present purposes, though, we will want to notice a feature of the approach that proved immediately problematic for logical empiricism's treatment of psychology, and yet for just this reason drew the attention of the logical empiricists to psychology and, it can be argued, of psychologists to logical empiricism.

To appreciate this problem, it helps to recall the notion, prevalent in the 1920s and 1930s but nearly antiquated today, that psychology is the science of human experience. Psychology, William James wrote in his 1892 textbook, was the *"description and explanation of states of consciousness as such"* (1).[3] The majority of American psychologists in the 1930s still subscribed to this idea, or something close to it (the obvious exception were the behaviorists, who took psychology to have behavior as its subject matter). Yet the general account of a science on offer from logical empiricism rendered that science intersubjective by, in effect, replacing the role played by experience in other, traditionally empiricist accounts of science with, instead, the logical *form* of the experience associated with that science. The logical empiricists avoided experience itself in favor of its logical form – for form, but not the content of experience itself, was communicable. And here arises the problem: how would such a

---

[3] James, in fact, takes himself to be quoting George Trumbull Ladd, but does not give a reference.

strategy of establishing objectivity work for a science *the very object of which was experience?* How specifically could a rational reconstruction of psychology do justice to psychology's rightful topic? In the course of an earlier debate within the Vienna Circle known as the protocol sentence debate, Moritz Schlick had worried that on the various accounts of science being offered by Carnap, and by Neurath, science would lose touch with experience. The problem we are considering here is this worry in its most acute form, for the science at issue is one that purports to be a science *of experience*.

Logical empiricist writings on psychology are sensitive to this issue and can then be seen not just as attempts to settle the *Geisteswissenschaften/Naturwissenschaften* debate in favor of unified science, but as attempts to fashion a coherent epistemological account of psychology, an endeavor that would have been called for even in the absence of heated debates over the unity of the natural and social sciences. This is the *problem of experience for logical empiricism's philosophy of psychology*, or, simply, *the problem of experience*. It is around just this problem that a good deal of the interaction between logical empiricism and psychology occurs in the 1930s; and it is in light of this problem, in conjunction with the logical empiricist emphasis on the unity of science, that we can best understand both logical empiricism's philosophy of psychology and its influence on psychology.

This story is in fact all the more interesting in that the logical empiricists were writing most extensively about psychology just as the movement itself was being translated, by way of emigration, into a cultural and scientific context in which the *Geisteswissenschaften/ Naturwissenschaften* debate was of far less import. When logical empiricism arrived in the United States in the course of the 1930s, it found American professional psychology marked by methodological debate between various schools of psychology and a collective desire for methodological directives, but largely absent the *Naturwissenschaften/Geisteswissenschaften* concerns that the logical empiricists felt compelled to engage in the European context. As a result, the themes the logical empiricists had pressed in their discussion of psychology – unity of science, anti-metaphysics, and physicalism – had a significantly different resonance in the ears of American psychologists, and the problem of experience, what might be identified as a more *internal* motivation for logical empiricism's approach to psychology, stood out starkly. Here, incidentally, is an instance in which the translation of logical empiricists' thought to a non-European context had an illuminating intellectual effect. Psychologists in the United States generally took the unity of psychology with the natural sciences as given, but they were acutely aware of the challenge inherent in actually providing an account of psychology which preserved its status as the study of human experience while simultaneously according it the objectivity of the natural sciences. With the *Geisteswissenschaften/Naturwissenschaften* debate set aside, that is, in the context of agreement on the unity of science, the ground was cleared considerably for fruitful interaction. The result, however, was not anything approaching a uniformly endorsed solution to the problem of experience. Rather, the upshot was a diverse collection of accounts of how psychology, understood as a science of experience, could be objective. Or, to put it another way, the result was a diverse collection of competing interpretations of experience.

As a way of illustrating its significance, I will explore three different, influential, and illuminating attempts to grapple with the problem of experience in the 1930s. I will consider first Rudolf Carnap's 1932 *Erkenntnis* essay, "Psychologie in physikalisher Sprache" (Psychology in Physical Language), Carnap's most sustained attempt to render psychology in physicalist language. I will then turn to Herbert Feigl's 1934 *Philosophy of Science* essay, "Logical Analysis of the Psycho-Physical Problem," and then finally to E. C. Tolman's 1935 *Philosophy of Science* essay, "Psychology versus Immediate Experience" (Tolman, it should be noted, was less a logical empiricist than a psychologist highly sympathetic to the program of logical empiricism). In the course of examining these accounts there will be some occasion for sideways glances at other related movements of interest in this regard, including radical behaviorism, psychophysics, and operationism. In conclusion, then, the legacy of logical empiricism for the philosophy of psychology will be considered.

RUDOLF CARNAP AND PSYCHOLOGY IN PHYSICAL LANGUAGE

Carnap's central claim in his "Psychology in Physical Language" is that the statements of a legitimate psychology, including statements about our own experience, can be translated into statements describing physical occurrences. Taking his argument for physicalism in his 1932 *Erkenntnis* article, "The Physical Language as the Universal Language of Science," as a "point of departure," Carnap aims to establish that "a definition may be constructed for every psychological concept which directly or indirectly derives that concept from physical concepts" (1932/1959, 167). Within the collection of sentences that comprises a science, Carnap distinguishes protocol from system sentences, the former serving as evidence for the latter. Taking up the distinction, we might express Carnap's position as follows: protocol sentences are about immediate experience, that is, the given, and the given is the proper topic of psychology. Protocol sentences can, however, be rendered as sentences about physical occurrences, and thus can be the topic of an objective science, or at least as objective a science as physics itself. Psychology, in short, can be an objective science of immediate experience.

A good portion of "Psychology in Physical Language" is taken up with showing that a particular sentence drawn from psychology, 'Mr. A is now excited', is equivalent to a statement in physical terms about A's physiology (or, more precisely, about physical dispositions A has in light of his physiology), and in responding to anticipated objections to this proposal, several of them rooted in the *Naturwissenschaften/Geisteswissenschaften* debate (see 1932/1959, 181ff.). For our purposes, the crucial discussion comes in section 7, when Carnap turns to statements about one's own mind, these being the protocol statements paradigmatically about "the given." Carnap has already noted that these statements have a distinct epistemic status, as compared to statements about other minds, and that "this distinction cannot be made among the sentences of intersubjective science," although it is "indispensable" "for the epistemic analysis of subjective, singular, sentences" (170). And here we can glimpse a difference between Carnap's view and the views of other physicalists, some of which we will examine below. For many physicalists, the construal of psychology as an objective science of experience involved no loss of epistemic distinctions – the subjective was not eliminated, but reconceptualized as physical. But on Carnap's account, it turns out, the physicalization of psychology deprives us of an epistemological distinction. And the loss, while not one we should mourn, is real.

Carnap begins his discussion of sentences about one's mind by reminding us of the distinction between system and protocol sentences in the example he considers. The distinction is important in this particular example because we have two sentences that look and sound the same, but are in fact distinct. We have the *system* sentence (uttered by A), 'I now am excited,' and the different *protocol* sentence (uttered by A as well, perhaps), 'I am now excited.' The difference between the two is epistemological: "the system sentence ... may, under certain circumstances, be disavowed, whereas [the] protocol sentence, being an epistemological point of departure, cannot be rejected" (191).

This suggests the following picture: a system sentence of psychology, specifically, about A's psychological state, rests epistemologically on protocol statements (A's and others'), and as all these statements, system and protocol, can be translated into statements solely about physical occurrences, the overall theory is objective. But as an account of Carnap's thinking about first person psychological reports, this picture is not quite accurate. A closer reading indicates that A's epistemic basis for the system sentence 'Now I am excited' is not in fact an orthographically identical *protocol* sentence, but a different protocol sentence altogether. Earlier, in evaluating an objection based upon an argument from analogy, Carnap is led to consider reports of one's own psychological state. There he argues that a sentence like 'I am now angry' is not the appropriate protocol sentence, for that sentence "does not adequately represent the state of affairs which is meant. It asserts that a certain property belongs to a certain entity. All that exists, however, is an experienced feeling of anger. This should [be] formulated as, roughly, 'now anger'" (177).

This point is not forgotten when Carnap comes to the section devoted to statements about one's own mind, for in the relevant place in the table Carnap provides to compare the epistemological situation for statements about one's own mind with statements about the minds of others, we find the sentence 'Now excited' entered as the protocol sentence for the system sentence (with respect to A) 'I am now excited.' This fact reflects a fundamental epistemological asymmetry between A and others with respect to statements about A's mind. And Carnap is sensitive to this asymmetry. For those other than A, the system statement about A's excitement rests not on A's protocol, 'now excited,' nor on the similar-sounding protocol sentence anyone other than A may accept, but, typically, on the protocol sentence which is brought about by A's utterance of the sentence 'I am now excited.' Carnap thus urges: "Generally speaking, a psychologist's spoken, written, or printed protocol sentences, when they are based on so-called introspection, are to be interpreted by the reader, and so figure in intersubjective science, *not chiefly as scientific sentences, but as scientific facts.*" The failure to appreciate this point of method, writes Carnap, is to a large extent "the source of epistemological confusion of contemporary psychology" (ibid., 195, emphasis in original). For our purposes, the relevant point is that on Carnap's account A's epistemological access to the sentence about A's own mind is different from the epistemological access had by A's peers. My excitement and the evidence for it are both objective and, indeed, physical, but *my* evidence for my excitement is inaccessible to my peers. My epistemological position is, as it were, privileged.

What are the immediate consequences of Carnap's full account of statements about one's own mind for the problem of experience? The asymmetry I've just outlined is, I believe, the asymmetry Carnap identifies early in the essay (but never returns to explicitly), when he notes that there is an epistemological difference between sentences about other minds and sentences about one's own mind which "cannot be made among the sentences of an inter-subjective science, all of which go over into physical statements, but which is 'indispensable' for the epistemological analysis of subjective, singular, sentences" (ibid., 170). We can draw this claim out a bit by making one clear point of comparison between Carnap's view and the more general logical empiricist orientation to psychology that we might have expected, according to which the psychologist is an observer in no better epistemological position than her peers, even when the object under observation is her own mental state. Although there is nothing in the points raised here to suggest that Carnap *cannot* maintain that the sentences of psychology can be translated into physical sentences, protocol sentences included, a form of the special access associated with immediate experience nevertheless persists in his 1932 account.

Carnap's later work, for example, his (1936/1937), reflects some development of Carnap's thought on the matter of experience, with his coming eventually to deny the asymmetry of first versus third person reports and to urge, alternatively, that all protocol sentences were intersubjective. Exactly how such a position could be reconciled with an account of psychology as a science of experience, though, remained problematic.[4]

HERBERT FEIGL ON THE PSYCHOPHYSICAL PROBLEM

We find a similar approach, with different emphases, in Herbert Feigl's 1934 "Logical Analysis of the Psychophysical Problem." The focus of Feigl's essay is the relation of the mental to the physical, and his central thesis is that the two are, in fact, identical: *"the strict identity of the 'mental' life with certain processes in the 'physical' world,"* Feigl writes, *"is not a matter of belief or Weltanschauung (dogmatic monism) but a truth capable of logical demonstration"* (420, emphasis in original). This result Feigl obtains by means of a verificationist account of cognitive, as opposed to emotive, meaning. Cognitive meaning, particularly cognitive *factual* meaning (Feigl allows for cognitive *formal* statements, such as comprise logic and mathematics), is subject to the "pragmatic formula" that Feigl locates in Charles Sanders Peirce (and, he adds, in Wittgenstein): *"if and only if assertion and denial of a proposition imply a difference capable of experiential test the proposition has a factual meaning"* (422). This criterion, he adds, "is the simple, impartial result of a comprehensive reflection upon how propositions are used in common life and in science. If we are to know what we are talking about we must have an idea under what conditions our statements would be true or false" (422).

The application of this criterion to the mind-body problem (the problem of the relation between the mental and the physical), if not the solution itself, is straightforward. In ascribing mentality to the (human) bodies around us, we can legitimately, that is, scientifically, be ascribing nothing more than physical properties: "to ascribe to our fellow men consciousness *in addition* to overt behavior and discoverable physiological processes implies ... a transcendence, an

---

[4] I thank Thomas Uebel for drawing my attention to Carnap's later work on this score.

introduction of empirically unverifiable elements" (424). And, following Carnap, Feigl takes ascriptions of a mental life *to ourselves* to be, when legitimate, no more than ascriptions of physical states.

This handling of the mind-body problem is, however, really a preliminary of sorts. Squaring off against what he rightly senses as the real and deeper issue, Feigl offers perhaps as clear a statement of the problem of experience as could be asked for. "If factual meaning depends on experiential verification," Feigl asks,

pray, *what is experience* and *whose* experience is referred to? Can we meaningfully assert the reality of the psychical (in the sense of immediate experience) and of the physical (in the sense of events in a spatio-temporal order)? Furthermore: Is immediate experience the subject matter of introspective psychology, and if so, how should we interpret its relation to the physical world, particularly to the physiological processes in nervous systems? *What then is the logical relation of psychology and physics?* Indeed, no respectable philosophy can afford to disregard these questions. (ibid., 428)

Feigl's answer depends upon distinguishing two notions of experience, the first, the logical, the "basis and raw material of all factual knowledge," and the second, biological: "a late product of organic evolution" (428). Feigl proceeds to characterize experience in the logical sense as a "language of elementary propositions, the language of data" (429); this is, clearly, the protocol language under a different name. On the basis of the language of data is constructed a second language, the physical language; physical objects are then shown to be logical constructs of experience in this first sense, and, as in Carnap's view, statements about them can be translated or reduced to the language of data, if need be.

On Feigl's view *only after* we have identified the protocol language and constructed physical objects on its basis can propositions or questions about experience in the second, biological, sense be sensibly forwarded or posed, and, indeed, these are then scientific claims or questions. *Only on* this basis, that is, can claims about external objects make sense. The first, and most important, step in solving the problem of experience for Feigl is to hold fast to this very insight:

What we must never forget is to take a definite stand. Either we pursue the task of *philosophy* i.e. *logical analysis*, or we are engaged in *science*. In the first case we are concerned with the reconstruction of empirical

knowledge in terms of immediate experience. Ontological transcendence
has no meaning here. ... In the second case we have accepted the level of
spatio-temporal constructs ... as our universe of discourse; and transcendence means ... something quite harmless, namely reference to objects
outside our skin. Only the confusions of both points of view is fatal.
(ibid., 431–2)

The balance of the solution consists in mapping the manner in
which psychology can and does talk of experience, that is, employ
the language of data, in a fully scientific, rather than a logical, mode.
This mode permits, for example, consideration of the question of
whose experience is being considered, the relation, that is, between
the experience and some physical body.

The use of both languages makes psychology highly susceptible to
confusing the logical endeavor, in which it is not engaged, with the
scientific one, in which it is, and this requires proportional caution on
the part of psychologists. And since the claims about experience can
be put in physical terms, psychology can take its place among the
other sciences. Thus Feigl arrives at a view not dissimilar to Carnap's:

The whole of introspective psychology as expressed in the language of data
can then be considered as a part of the physical language. The result of this is
not only that a system of hypothetical experiential propositions corresponds
to a single physical proposition; but if physicalism is correct, every singular
experiential proposition is also translatable into a complex physical proposition. To every proposition describing introspectively what, as we say, is
given as a datum of my consciousness, there would be a corresponding
proposition in physical language describing, as we say, the condition of my
nervous system. From the intersubjective point of view these two types of
proposition are only verbally different. (ibid., 436)

This would come to be one source for the "identity theory" of the
mind. Interestingly, the epistemic asymmetry, noted in our discussion of Carnap's view – the seemingly privileged perspective we each
have to our own experiences – Feigl relegates to the category of
emotive meaning (ibid., 440).

E. C. TOLMAN ON THE PROBLEM
OF EXPERIENCE

At first glance E. C. Tolman might seem an unusual choice to
consider in this context, for Tolman was a self-identified behaviorist,

and one of the most prominent of that second generation of behaviorists (after the first generation of Edward Thorndike, Jacques Loeb, Ivan Pavlov, and John Watson), which included B. F. Skinner and Clark Hull. And behaviorists, it was suggested above, were, by virtue of being behaviorists, *immune* to the problem of experience. Further, the 1935 essay of Tolman's to be considered, written upon his return from an eight-month visit to the Vienna Circle and addressed explicitly to the place of experience in psychology, begins with the following declaration:

I am a behaviorist. I hold that psychology does not seek descriptions and intercommunications concerning immediate experience per se. Such descriptions and attempts at direct intercommunications may be left to the arts and to metaphysics. Psychology seeks, rather, the objectively stateable laws and processes governing behavior. ... Even in the cases where the organism is oneself, these determining causal factors can and must – for the purposes of psychology – be stated objectively. It is true that in these latter instances, in which the animal in question is oneself, one may in one's rôle, not of a psychologist, but of an artist or a metaphysician, attempt to describe and convey to another man one's own facts of immediate experience. But such a description and report of immediate experiences ... will not, for the purposes of the psychologist, add anything essentially new to the picture. Experience *qua* experience, while of concern and interest to the man on the street, the philosopher and the poet, does not enter as such into the laws and equations of psychology, – in so far, at any rate, as psychology is to be considered as a science. (ibid., 356–7)[5]

Here Tolman has, it seems, completely rejected the notion that psychology has or ought to have experience as its topic, and rejected it on the grounds of objectivity: "experience *qua* experience ... does not enter ... into the laws and equations of psychology," he urges, because these laws must be "objectively stateable." How then could Tolman be understood to offer an account of psychology as the science of experience, when he so clearly denies exactly this?

Consider a second passage from Tolman's paper, four pages later. After rehearsing what he identifies as the "dualism" of "independent material objects" as opposed to "immediate sense data,"

---

[5] In a footnote in this passage, Tolman notes that he is using "the phrase 'immediate experience' to designate the immediately given pre-analytical complex as this appears to the naive man and before the subtleties of philosophical and scientific analysis have been applied to it."

Tolman indicates that he intends to abandon this conception of "two sets of metaphysical stuffs" for a new conception, one more "successful for a philosophy of science." Tolman will hold, he tells us,

that immediate experience just as it appears, contains quite as much objectivity as it does subjectivity. Immediate experience, as initially given, is not my private world or your private world. It is not something to be studied primarily by psychology. It is, rather, an initial, common matrix out of which both physics and psychology are evolved. It is the only tangible real that we have. Physics does not present another real behind that of immediate experience. Nor does psychology, as such, study this real of immediate experience in a more first hand way than does physics. Physics is a set of logical constructs – a set of rules and equations whereby we are aided in finding our way about from one moment of immediate experience to another. Further, and this purports to be the only new and specific contribution of this paper, psychology is, I shall argue, but another such set of logical constructs, another such set of rules and equations, which, when added to those of physics, will give us still further aid in finding our way about from one moment of experience to the next. (ibid., 359)

This, clearly, is no repudiation of immediate experience, nor is it a repudiation of psychology's aim to make immediate experience its object of study. What it is is the *objectification* of immediate experience – what we might think of as a proposal for a new way to think about experience, or, equivalently, a successor to that notion of experience which describes it as private, ineffable, and subjective.

Understanding Tolman's successor notion requires taking very seriously his proposal to do away with the "traditional dichotomy" between sense-data and a reality reflected by sense-data. What the replacement notion is, exactly, will be addressed in a moment; I want to note first that in appreciating Tolman's aim of replacing a subjective, private notion of experience with an objective, public one, we release ourselves from reading the first passage I quoted from Tolman's paper as contradicting the second. That first passage is in fact less a repudiation of experience than a repudiation of the notion that there is a science which studies anything inherently private or subjective; such things are best left to the "philosopher and the poet." But experience as Tolman wants us to understand it is "the only tangible real we have" and is indeed an object for psychology, albeit not *primarily* for psychology. Experience in this new sense is the object of physics as well and, we are led to believe, of every science. In sum Tolman's behaviorism amounted to the view that psychology, if it is to be a science, must be objective.

Recognizing Tolman's equivocation over the term "experience" resolves an apparent contradiction, then. But what of this new concept – how does it work, and how does Tolman build a conception of psychology around it? In his visit to Vienna, sparked most likely by encountering Schlick in Stanford, Tolman met and began a fruitful collaboration with Egon Brunswik, a perceptual psychologist and frequent visitor to the Vienna Circle (see, e.g., Tolman and Brunswik 1935). Brunswik had joined Karl Bühler's Psychological Institute in Vienna in 1927 and there developed an account of perception according to which agents "expected" or "intended" certain environmental "characters" with varying degrees of success. Brunswik's experiments on object constancy – our tendency to see an object as the same despite apparent changes in its color, shape, and so on – convinced Brunswik, and Tolman, that what was intended or expected – what was immediately experienced – was, typically, *not* a representation or image of an external object (what Tolman called a "perspective") but the external object itself, what Tolman called an "independent" (ibid., 360). Aspects of these ideas had been part of Tolman's thinking since his embrace of neorealism in the 1920s, and were present, albeit murkily, in Tolman's 1932 *Purposive Behavior in Animals and Men*. In 1934 he adopted Brunswik's ideas and terminology and used it as the basis for his successor notion of experience.

That notion, and Tolman's approach to the problem of experience, can be conveyed via three closely related points. First, for Tolman, perception, or intendings, are immediate, but they are all the same fallible. In Tolman's and Brunswik's terms, an intending can vary in terms of how successfully it "attains" or "achieves" its object. Second, psychology's aim is to arrive at the laws and equations which govern the intendings of humans and their relative successes; most of Tolman's paper is taken up, in fact, with an outline of the psychological laws he hoped he and others would eventually work out in detail. The third, and perhaps most important point, is that the objectivity of psychology as a science of experience is itself achieved on Tolman's account by the application of this theory of perception *to the psychologist*. Taken as an account of the activity of the psychologist's own scientific activity, this theory of perception implies that the intendings of others, not just one's own intendings, could themselves be immediately perceived. On this account, then, experience was the subject of intersubjective agreement and thus the proper basis for a science.[6]

This consideration of Tolman's approach to the problem of experience invites a brief glance at the approach to the same problem taken by some of Tolman's peers in the 1930s. S. S. Stevens, a Harvard psychophysicist just beginning his career when Tolman was starting his collaboration with Brunswik, was deeply convinced both that scientific knowledge was constituted by agreement (and that there-fore it was, necessarily, public and shared) and that experience was psychology's proper topic. These convictions led Stevens to define experience operationally, in fact, in terms of what he took to be the most fundamental element of behavior, discrimination, the "con-crete differential [reaction] of the living organism to environmental states, either internal or external" (1935, 518). The *experience*, then, upon which physical science is founded," Stevens wrote, is "nothing more than a term which ... denotes the sum total of the dis-criminatory reactions performed by human beings, for *to experience* is, for the purposes of science, *to react discriminatively*" (ibid., 521). And for psychologists satisfied neither with notions of experience proposed by Tolman or Stevens there was the option offered by the behaviorists Clark Hull or B. F. Skinner, both of whom urged of course that psychology do away with experience altogether and become a science of observable behavior. Since psychology was understood by neither Hull nor Skinner as a science of experience, neither of them faced the *problem of experience* faced by Tolman and Stevens. It is, I think, in light of this fact that we can understand Hull and Skinner's merely perfunctory engagement with logical empiricism, a fact well documented by Laurence Smith (1986).

CONCLUSION

In Carnap, Feigl, and Tolman we have then three initial, repre-sentative, and divergent attempts to grapple with the manner by which psychology, conceived as a science of experience, could attain

---

[6] For an extensive and illuminating discussion of Tolman's views see Smith (1986, chs. 3–5); for a discussion of Brunswik's views see Leary (1987).

the intersubjectivity found in other sciences and thus take the place logical empiricism had prepared for it. The history of the handling of this problem in subsequent decades, through to the end of the twentieth century, is a complicated one, several parts of which have not yet been told in any detail. On the one hand, the ascendancy of behaviorism through the 1930s, 1940s, and 1950s in psychology, combined with the attention garnered by debates over which of various forms behaviorism should take, directed attention far from the question of experience and its place in psychology. Psychophysics continued apace in these decades, but with far more emphasis on the relations (typically, the mathematical relations) between psychical phenomena and the physical stimuli taken to cause them than on the *relata* themselves (see Stevens 1951, 1973). The inattention to experience was supported by a steady relaxation of the logical empiricist criteria of verifiability and cognitive meaningfulness, and a corresponding emphasis on the epistemological legitimacy of theories tied tenuously to experience, both recounted in Hempel (1951) (see also Carnap 1963). By the late 1960s, neither the field of psychology nor the philosophy of science much resembled their 1930s instantiations, a fact often cited informally in explaining the reemergence, in the mid-1980s through to the present, of a cognitive science especially and explicitly interested in consciousness. This is in many ways the modern manifestation of the problem of experience of the 1930s. In this manner, and indeed quite unexpectedly, reflections on the part of logical empiricists and their fellow travelers about the possibility and means of an objective science of experience may prove relevant still.

10 Philosophy of Social Science in Early Logical Empiricism

The Case of Radical Physicalism

Philosophy of social science is unlikely to figure in many people's judgment as a field in which logical empiricism effected great progress. If anything, impressions run to the contrary. Considered in the right light, however, the riches of logical empiricist philosophy of social science were considerable. The trick is to find the proper lighting. Here the aim is to illuminate a much misunderstood early doctrine, not only for its intrinsic interest but also – alongside Chapters 3 and 11 but from a different angle – to highlight what was lost when central members of the Vienna Circle were marginalized in the heyday of orthodox logical empiricism.[1]

THE PLURALITY OF LOGICAL EMPIRICIST PHILOSOPHIES OF SOCIAL SCIENCE, BROADLY CONCEIVED

For current purposes virtually all post–World War II philosophy of social science must be neglected. The reason is by no means that there is no good work in the field during that time by logical empiricists.[2] Nor is the reason that in this period it is even more difficult to decide membership of the movement than in the previous one.[3] It is rather that no figures central in pre–World War II

---

[1] For a general survey of logical empiricist philosophy of social science, see Hempel (1969). For surveys of positivism in sociology see Giddens (1978) and Halfpenny (1982), of positivism in economics Caldwell (1982).

[2] For instance, there are C. G. Hempel's essays on social scientific typology and functional explanation; see chapters 7 and 11 of Hempel (1965).

[3] For instance, while he is clearly an exponent of analytical philosophy of social science, can Ernest Nagel be considered a logical empiricist? In other cases too,

logical empiricism in this field remained to continue their work after the war.[4] Given this discontinuity of personnel, the concentration here will lie on prewar logical empiricist philosophy of social science. Even so delimited, the field holds forgotten riches.

The impression that great progress cannot be diagnosed in this field depends very much on who is considered a logical empiricist. It is true that amongst the movements' central thinkers before World War II only Otto Neurath actively pursued a serious interest in the social sciences and worked on their metatheory.[5] Neurath, of course, hardly figures as a reference point for contemporary philosophy of social science other than as a positivist scarecrow.[6] Yet as soon as thinkers located by choice on the periphery of the movement are taken into account, we encounter the three distinct and highly original programs associated with Karl Menger, Felix Kaufmann, and Edgar Zilsel. With Menger we touch on the beginnings of rational choice theory, with Kaufmann on phenomenological sociology, with Zilsel on an early form of sociology of knowledge that embraced all the sciences and did not stop with consideration of their institutional aspects.[7] Each of these theorists made important early contributions to what nowadays are viewed as

---

inclusion would be imperialist and exclusion too harsh, as in the case of Herbert Simon. To be sure, the wish of Karl Popper – whose work on the subject was also first published only by 1945 – to be sharply distinguished from the logical empiricists shall be respected here, as in Hempel (1969, 164–5).

[4] Note that with the exception of his 1942 paper on lawlike explanation in history, Hempel's work in this area dates from the early 1950s onwards.

[5] On Neurath as a general theorist of social science see, besides Hempel (1969), Fleck (1982), Zolo (1989, 93–147), P. Neurath (1991), Uebel (1997).

[6] See, e.g., Dallmayr and McCarthy (1977, 8) who simply note without comment Neurath's notorious dismissal of empathy in social science as comparable in importance to a researcher's cup of morning coffee. For the judgment that logical empiricism remained "sterile" for the field of social science because of Neurath's dominance of the field, see Dahms (1997, 110). For the contrary judgment that Neurath had very little influence, see Giddens, who instead asserted: "The influence of the writings of the logical positivists has been assimilated into sociology in a much more important and pervasive way through a general acceptance of the model of scientific explanation developed in the phase of the devolution of logical positivism into positivistic philosophy" (1978, 255). By the latter phase is meant what I would call post–World War II orthodox logical empiricism.

[7] See Zilsel (1926; 2000), K. Menger (1934), Kaufmann (1936; 1944). On Neurath's and Frank's views on the sociology of knowledge, see Uebel (2000).

significant – in the case of rational choice theory, even dominant – paradigms of research in social science.[8]

So why not count the record of early logical empiricism in this area a success and the fount of contemporary glory? When each of these theorists made theoretical breakthroughs, they did so not as representatives of logical empiricism, but as "closely related" individual researchers and critics of what they perceived to be the standard position.[9] Short of discounting their self-image, Menger, Kaufmann, and Zilsel cannot be counted into the movement without reservations.[10] With reservations, however, the following can be asserted. Logical empiricism has a qualified record of success in the field of philosophy of social science. When taken in its extended breadth, early logical empiricism exhibited a remarkable plurality of philosophies of social science. Groundbreaking work on research paradigms not commonly associated with logical empiricism was undertaken by theorists on the periphery of the Vienna Circle, while at its center a subsequently neglected version of so-called physicalistic social science was being developed that challenged the

---

[8] For such judgments of contemporary relevance see, on Zilsel: Raven and Krohn (2000); on Kaufmann: Helling (1985), Zilian (1990), Dahms (1997); on Menger: Leonard (1998).

[9] Neurath (1930c/1981, 390) listed Kaufmann, K. Menger, and Zilsel among researchers "closely related" to the Vienna Circle, apparently in accordance with their wishes. The previous manifesto of 1929 listed Menger as member, Zilsel as closely related, and did not mention Kaufmann at all (Carnap, Hahn, and Neurath 1929 [1973, 317, 328]). Despite his regular attendance at Circle meetings, Kaufmann had declined Carnap's invitation to submit a publication list for the manifesto and figure there either as a member or as *nahestehend* because of his different views on the nature of the a priori (letter to Carnap, June 26, 1929, ASP RC 028–25–03, quoted in Zilian 1990, 20–1), while Menger had asked to be reclassified after the publication of that manifesto because of its quasi-political slant (Menger 1980, xviii). In his memoirs, Menger notes about Zilsel that he "attended only a few of the meetings and, for reasons unknown to me, wanted to be considered only as close to, and not as a member of the Circle" (1994, 67). Kaufmann also attended meetings of the *Geist-Kreis* around Friedrich Hayek and Ludwig Mises's seminars, so he may have wished to retain his neutrality.

[10] Compare Hempel, who stated: "Only one among the influential logical empiricists had a specialized knowledge of the social sciences: Otto Neurath", then noted some work by Carnap on "the logic of psychology and the social sciences", Frank's "perceptive observations about social and political factors affecting scientific inquiry", and work by Bergmann and Feigl on psychology (1969, 164). Hempel did not even mention Kaufmann, Menger, or Zilsel.

presumptions of the orthodox understanding of unified science as well as those of explicitly antipositivist critics.[11]

ANTIPOSITIVIST OPPOSITION TO SOCIAL SCIENCE IN UNIFIED SCIENCE

This chapter concentrates on the idea of social science in physicalist unified science. Antipositivist critics tend to speak as if the notion of a physicalist social science were a contradition in terms, with its supposed reductionism undercutting the distinctive explanatory dimension of social science. Some even saved themselves explicit argument to this conclusion and rest their case for dismissal with the mere mention of the idea of the "methodological unity of science", reserving argument for combatting still other aspects of "positivism".[12] When the grounds of the opposition are made explicit, however, one can see that it depends on a very specific understanding of the idea of the unity of science:

This ... ideal involved, in addition to methodological unity, a substantive unity, which is to be achieved by the systematic reduction of all sciences to one basic science, usually physics. Such a reduction (or rather, a series of reductions) can be achieved either by defining the concepts of one science (say, biology) in terms of those of another science (say, chemistry), or by deriving the laws and theories of the former from the latter. Thus ideally, we would have a hierarchy of sciences, beginning with physics, and proceeding through chemistry, biology, psychology and sociology, in which all are 'reduced' to the first. (Keat and Urry 1975/1982, 25–6)

---

[11] Note that my conception of the Circle's "periphery" here is narrower than Stadler's in (1997). Notably too, all of our protagonists were associated with the Vienna Circle, not the Berlin Society for Empirical Philosophy. Hempel (1969) also did not mention any theorist of the Berlin group.

[12] Thus Brian Fay, in his influential *Social Theory and Political Practice*, provided arguments only against the first three of the four characteristics of "positivist metatheory of social science": "For my purposes there are four essential features of this metatheory: first, drawing on the distinction between discovery and validation, its deductive-nomological account of explanation and concomitant modified Humean interpretation of the notion of 'cause'; second, its belief in a neutral observation language as the proper foundation of knowledge; third, its value-free ideal of scientific knowledge; and fourth, its belief in the methodological unity of the sciences" (1975, 13).

This chapter will argue that this particular understanding was by no means shared by all proponents of the program of unified science, least of all by Neurath, the most vocal proponent of physicalism.

It must be noted that many critics, especially those influenced by writings of the Frankfurt School, took themselves to possess other reasons for resistance against physicalist social science as well. With Vienna Circle philosophy in general maligned as the absolutization of "the impassive 'fact-finding' mechanism of science", what could be expected from its philosophy of social science but politically reactionary neutralism?[13] Here only the methodological aspect of Neurath's program can be discussed. But the political dimension cannot be ignored altogether, for it provided motivation for Neurath himself – importantly, one that runs contrary to that imputed by critics. Over and above the fact that the Vienna Circle's doctrine of unified science represented a self-conscious attempt to go against the trend of contemporary academic thought in Central Europe and furnished a nonmetaphysical program for the very widely perceived need to unify the ever more disparate individual sciences,[14] it must not be forgotten that the doctrine also served more specific ends.

Considered in its time and place, it is clear that Neurath's physicalist program was meant to provide a bulwark against the undemocratic and racist social doctrines that were gaining increasing currency in Central Europe in the 1920s and 1930s and that typically were hiding from scientific scrutiny – indeed, claiming a scientific mantle all of their own – under the guise of the separation of the human from the natural sciences, the split between 'Geistes-' and 'Naturwissenschaften'. As Neurath's writings indicate, this opposition ranged from the populist historical dilletantism of Oswald Spengler, through the increasingly self-consciously German

---

[13] The quote is from Horkheimer (1937/1972, 60–1) who initiated the stance still characteristic of Habermas with his slogan "That we disavow reflection is positivism" (1968/1972, vii). For the so-called positivism dispute in early 1960s German sociology, see Adorno (1969); for a detailed history of its precursors, including the unfortunate interaction between Horkheimer and Neurath, see Dahms (1994). While in the books cited above Fay and Keat and Urry clearly adopted the perspective of the Frankfurt School, Keat (1981) already expressed grave reservations about its antipositivist arguments. For a recent reassessment of the Horkheimer-Neurath dispute, see O'Neill and Uebel (2004).

[14] For the post–World War I discussions of the "crisis of science", see Ringer (1969, chs. 6–7).

sociology of the widely respected academic Werner Sombart, to the ever more explicit embrace of 'völkisch' fascism by the once merely ideosyncratically holist Othmar Spann.[15] But on this point we need not rely on Neurath himself. Independent contemporaries of Neurath's such as Karl Menger shared his judgment, and recent historians of the period such as Fritz Ringer have come to broadly similar conclusions concerning the precarious position of modernist theorists of society in interwar German academia (see Menger 1994, 177; Ringer 1969).

NEURATH'S 'INTERNAL' CRITICS: ZILSEL, MENGER, KAUFMANN

Zilsel, Menger, and Kaufmann shared this distinctly hygienic intention of Neurath's, but they also shared some of the antipositivist misgivings against the physicalist program. Neurath did his program no service, it must be said, by his all-too robust dismissal of everything suspectable of metaphysics. Moreover, it did not help, as Hempel once put it, that "Neurath's writings on the subject [of social science] often seem more like political manifestoes, like programs both for analysis and for action, than like carefully reasoned analytical studies" and that he remained "frustratingly vague on points of systematic detail" (1969, 166–7, 170).

Zilsel's criticism of the Vienna Circle in general has been summarized as labeling it an "empirical school without empirical research".[16] His criticism of Neurath is an instance of this. In his review of *Empirical Sociology* Zilsel criticized the lack of concrete social science examples: "in this 'empirical sociology' fertile empiricism withdraws behind logic" (1932, 93). Zilsel objected to the strategy by which the Circle sought to ensure the unity of science – this unity had to be shown, not decreed ex cathedra: "The discovery of laws would bring about a far more interesting unification of the sciences than the spatio-temporal universal

---

[15] See Neurath (1921) for his extensive critique of Spengler and his (1931) for his criticism of Sombart and Spann in the section "Metaphysical Countercurrents" not contained in the English translation but reviewed in P. Neurath (1991).

[16] Raven and Krohn (2000, xlv). The following two quotations from Zilsel (1932) and (1932a) use their translation. Elsewhere, translations of material where no translation are given in the bibliography are by the present author.

language" (1932a, 154). The unity of science could not be ensured by prescribing a physicalist language to be shared by all sciences, but only by finding actual laws that integrate the social sciences in law-governed natural science. Zilsel also rejected as a mistaken "asymmetry" the physicalist demand "that sociology dissolve and analyse its concepts all the way down to elementary observations, whereas physics is allowed its compound concepts" (1932, 92). In particular, physicalism was wrong to reject talk of internal mental states even when there are "empirical indicators" for them. Lastly, Zilsel rejected what he considered the impoverished conception of social scientific laws which physicalism bequeathed: "Are there not also functional connections and laws in sociology?" (ibid., 93). Zilsel's impatience with the relative lack of examples of empirical work is understandable, yet Neurath is not wholly defenseless here. Were programs like his wholly superfluous? Surely it cannot be expected of a philosophy of social science that it deliver what only social science itself can deliver. The telling points of Zilsel's criticism is rather his criticism of what he claimed were the limits of physicalism and his demand that unity of science be nomologically based.

Menger denounced what later he called "the rather loose employment of the word 'meaningless' which was especially rampant in the Circle in the years 1927–32" (1979, 14). He preferred to rest his own dismissal of metaphysical theories rather on the impossibility of establishing the objective validity of any answers that might be given to them: "While in full agreement with the well-founded criticism of known metaphysical theories, I could not join in the dogmatic rejection of metaphysics in the lump" (ibid.). This led him to reject the unified science program: "[A]part from an instinctive aversion to monistic schemes of any kind, I feared that the idea of a unified science might possibly lead to the exlusion a priori of potentially valuable objects or methods of study" (1994, 176). Moreover, he saw it as a futile exercise: "Those who speak of the unity of science ... seem to overlook the facts that the separation of science from other intellectual activities can be no more practicable and useful than that of particular sciences from one another" (1934/1974, 24). Menger's objection to the unified science program as overly rigid seems to scupper its central idea, but his implicit endorsement of Popper's criticism of the demarcation problem in this context suggests that he mistook the criterion of cognitive significance for a criterion of scientific probity, but they do not coincide (see Carnap 1963a, 877–9). This is not insignificant since at least in principle Menger applauded employing the idea of unified science to combat the ideological use of the separatist *Geisteswissenschaften*.

Kaufmann, finally, objected to the "over-extension" of the unity of science thesis due to the thesis of physicalism (1936, 139).[17] As a thinker deeply influenced by Husserl, he could not but object to determinations of cognitive probity that would rule out of bounds *Wesensschau*, the intuitive grasp of essences, and as well his conception of social science as "essentially" concerned with the interpretation of the actions of others required access to meanings (ibid., 167). Accordingly, he objected to physicalism, like behaviorism, that wrongly discounts "introspective experience" for the reason that it is intersubjectively uncontrollable and therefore unscientific because it is not open to external observation (ibid., 132, 137). By contrast, Kaufmann held that the statements by which psychological assertions can be controlled are not exclusively physicalistic ones, that is, about the behavior of physical bodies. But neither did it require a scientifically inexplicable process of empathy. What is required to afford control of statements arrived by empathy are "generalizations which concern empirical correlations between physical (outer) and psychological facts" – it is reliance on this type of correlations that "distinguishes the methods of natural science from those of *Geisteswissenschaft*" (ibid., 138). Two things are notable here. First, that Kaufmann's concept of *Geisteswissenschaft* does not have to postulate the radical separation of social science from natural science, but only stressed a methodological difference. Second, that the correlations whose employment accounts for that difference make an irreducible reference to psychological states and treat them not as names for behavioral dispositions but theoretical entities.

---

[17] Kaufmann's English version of his monograph (1944), which was radically rewritten (and his phenomenological sympathies toned down) in the attempt to build a bridge to Deweyan pragmatism, must be disregarded here, but it may be noted that the antiphysicalist argument of (1936) is preserved in basic outline in chapter XI of (1944).

The question of the validity of Kaufmann's criticisms thus turns on how reductive Neurath's physicalism is understood to be.[18]

DIFFERENT CONCEPTIONS OF PHYSICALISM AND UNITY OF SCIENCE

To evaluate these criticisms we must, first of all, clarify what was at stake when the so-called left wing of the Vienna Circle (Carnap, Neurath, Frank, Hahn) spoke of the unity of science.[19] Most generally, the issue concerned the relation between science and philosophy: in their view, a reconceptualization of both science and philosophy was required. Philosophy was to join science as its metatheory. Science retained its autonomy from speculative philosophy by recognizing that reflection about its own procedures, principles, and concepts belonged to itself as its metatheory. Neither did science remain merely positive, nor was all philosophy discarded. Philosophy was retained as metatheoretical reflection, even though its former claim to a separate source of knowledge was rejected most energetically. What remained of philosophy became one of two metatheoretical perspectives, either what Carnap called the "logic of science" or empirical theory of science, what Neurath called its "behavioristics".[20]

As regards the unification of the first-order sciences, different models were pursued in the Vienna Circle. Here we must reconstruct what Neurath meant when he spoke of social science "in the framework of physicalism". For Neurath the term "physicalism" denoted different conceptions of varying breadth. There is physicalism as a "comprehensive attitude" amounting to his anti-foundationalist epistemological naturalism; this cannot be

---

[18] This episode is of significance beyond the rather puzzling fact that these criticisms were published despite Neurath's patient efforts to show that they did not apply. For Kaufmann was, as noted, also a member of the Viennese Geist-Kreis, other members of which took themselves to be well informed about the goings on in the Circle because of his reports. One of these was Friedrich August Hayek, whose own criticisms of Neurath's physicalism perpetuated and radicalized Kaufmann's confusions (see Hayek 1942–4). For some discussion of criticisms by Hayek and Popper, see Uebel (2000a).

[19] By the designation "left wing" Neurath and Carnap distinguished those who opposed Wittgensteinian positions on the issues of verificationism and, later, metalinguistic discourse; see Carnap (1963, 57–8).

[20] See Carnap (1934/1937, § 72) and Neurath (1936b/1983, 149; 1936g/1983, 169).

discussed here but must be assumed as background.[21] But there remain the metalinguistic and the nomological theses of physicalism, physicalism as a thesis concerning the language of unified science and as a thesis concerning the nomological structure of unified science. (Respectively, in what relation do the terms and laws of the special sciences stand to those of physics?)

The first published use of the term 'unified science' (*Einheitswissenschaft*) appears to come in the collectively authored manifesto of 1929: "The scientific world conception is characterised not so much by theses of its own, but rather by its basic attitude, its points of view and direction of research. The goal ahead is *unified science*. The endeavour is to link and harmonise the achievements of individual investigators in their various fields of science" (Carnap, Hahn, and Neurath 1929/1973, 305–6). In his own publications of the time, Neurath was not much more specific than this. Unified science was "an interconnected system of formulations of lawlike connections between spatio-temporal processes" (1930b/1981, 369), "in which all concepts are formed in one way, in which on the basis of certain rules of control all assertions are reduced to individual experiences which everybody can check" (1929a/1981, 347). Since these were formulations in a newspaper article and in an abstract of a lecture, the lack of specificity is not surprising. Even so, one difference is already apparent. According to the manifesto, unified science was to follow the lead of the constitutive system of concepts on an auto-psychological basis developed in Carnap's *Aufbau* (compare Carnap, Hahn, and Neurath 1929/1973, 309, with Carnap 1928, §§ 4, 41). Neurath's phrase "individual experiences which everybody can check" suggests, however, that he was suspicious of the phenomenalist basis of Carnap's methodological solipsism and that he already worked towards what he soon called "'unified science' on a 'materialistic basis'" (1930b/1981, 369) by the time the manifesto was published. By 1931 he called "physicalism" the program of developing "the physicalistic unified language of unified science" which was "'intersubjective' and 'intersensual'" (1931c/1981, 408). Now, when Carnap went physicalist, this came to mean that this basic language abstracted from experiential qualities and intuitive conceptualizations of

---

[21] For a discussion of the interpretation of Neurath as a naturalistic epistemologist, pioneered by Haller and the later Hempel, see Uebel (1991a).

objects altogether and relied exclusively on quantitative measures applied to space-time coordinates (1932, 1934/1937, § 40). For Neurath, however, the basic physicalistic language was not that of mathematical physics (which for Carnap alone guaranteed objectivity), but an appropriately cleansed everyday language (1932). Therein lay a continuing difference; even later on, as we shall see, their ideas of the basic "thing-language" diverged.[22]

Nothing was said in these early days by either Carnap or Neurath about the internal nomological structure of unified science. The unity of science was rather discussed as a metalinguistic thesis. Still, the earliest formulations of physicalistic unified science give cause for misgivings. With social science located at the far end of the projected reductive genealogy of concepts, it remained entirely unclear how much of it could be retained as legitimate. Ultimately, however, the issue is whether these misgivings also tell against Neurath's mature conception of unified science. To this end Kaufmann's and some of Zilsel's criticisms will here be evaluated in terms of the metalinguistic and Menger's largely in terms of the nomological thesis of physicalism. The full evaluation of Zilsel's criticism requires still further detail (which will also involve C. G. Hempel). I begin by discussing Neurath's nomological thesis under the name of "encyclopedism".

NEURATH'S ENCYCLOPEDISM

Menger's fear that the idea of unified science meant the exlusion a priori of potentially valuable objects or methods of study questions whether there is room for diversity of methods and domain formation in unified science. This goes to the heart of Neurath's own distinctive understanding of the unity of science. Commonly associated with physicalism is indeed a very rigid conception of this unity, but this was not Neurath's view. What he was looking for was unity in diversity. Unified science encompassed inquiries of different orders (first and second order, to start with) and thereby retained what was retainable of philosophy. But what, then, was the internal structure of the unification of the first-order sciences?

---

[22] Neurath's and Carnap's understandings of physicalism have often been confused in as much as the latter was taken as more careful formulations of the former, as by Hempel (1969, 175ff.).

As outlined in the critical comment quoted in Section 2, the standard conception of the unity of science envisages this unity as a pyramid of reductively related disciplines with physics at the base. Accordingly it demands, at least in principle, the reduction of sociological laws to those of physics and the reduction of sociological concepts to those of physics. Here it must be noted that, at least since 1935, Carnap problematized the derivability of the laws of a special science from those of more general ones (1936, 69). Still in 1938, however, Carnap stated that "no scientific reason is known for the assumption that such a derivation should be in principle and forever impossible" (1938, 61), but he himself no longer pursued such a unity of laws. However, in the late 1950s, precisely the reductive program of unity by intertheoretic reduction was promoted "as a working hypothesis" by Paul Oppenheim and the young Hilary Putnam (1958), and their view became emblematic for orthodox logical empiricism and its "received view" of science generally.

Now consider Neurath. The preface of *Empirical Sociology* merely states:

All scientific statements can be connected with each other and constitute a uniform domain which comprehends only statements about observable states of affairs. For this the name *unified science* has been proposed. If one wishes to stress that in this way everything really becomes physics, then one may speak of physicalism. (1931/1981, 424)

More than one important distinction is elided here, but Neurath's thinking about these matters soon became clearer, and already in 1932 he rejected the pyramid model:

The development of physicalistic sociology does not mean the transfer of the laws of physics to living things and their groups, as some have thought possible. Comprehensive sociological laws can be found as well as laws for definite narrower social areas, without the need to be able to go back to the microstructure, and thereby to build up these sociological laws from physical ones. (1932a/1983, 75)

Two things are important here: the rejection of the postulate of the reducibility of the laws of social science to those of physics and the rejection of the postulate of methodological individualism (in one of its guises).

Systematically speaking, the rejection the reducibility of the laws of social science follows from the rejection of the reducibility of the individual terms of social science to those of physics. Even though he came to question term-by-term reduction, Neurath did not provide an argument to this effect. Yet significantly enough he also wrote: "One can understand the working of a steam engine quite well on the whole without surveying it in detail. And indeed, the structure of a machine may be more important than the material of which it consists" (1931/1973, 333). The explanatory kinds or principles invoked in social science need not be reducible to those concerning material constituents. By stressing this, Neurath quite plainly sought to allow for the possibility of functional and structural analyses and explanations that were being explored at the time in Durkheimian sociology and anthropology and had long been a mainstay of Marxist analysis. (How precisely legitimate forms of such explanations would go was another matter, of course.)

Neurath, this suggests, argued from the variety of explanatory principles to the nomological irreducibility of social science. When noting "the sociological laws found without the help of physical laws in the narrower sense must not necessarily be changed by the addition of a physical substructure discovered later" (1932a/1983, 75), he did not, therefore, invoke merely the distinction between the contexts of discovery and justification such that intertheoretic reductions of laws are required only in the latter (as may be suspected). Rather, he rejected the idea that such reductions were required even in the latter context. Indeed, he also declared cautiously that doubt existed whether they were even possible: "According to physicalism, sociological laws are not laws of physics applied to sociological structures, but they are also not unproblematically reducible to laws about atomic structures" (1932b, 106). By 1934, he stressed that "such reducibility is not a necessary consequence of the fact that in principle all terms and sentences belong to the same physicalist language" (1936d/1981, 762–3). Whatever Neurath's encyclopedic unity was, it was not a reductive hierarchy of laws.

A significant corollary must be mentioned here. Nomological antireductionism also has a still more specific dimension of relevance to social science, namely, the rejection of methodological individualism in its nomological sense.[23] Concerning sociological

---

[23] According to Hempel, Neurath "refrained from making any general claims on the realizability of the program of methodological individualism" (1969, 174).

laws Neurath wrote: "Naturally certain correlations result that cannot be found with individuals, with stars or machines. Social behaviourism establishes laws of its own kind" (1932a/1983, 75). Given the strenuous opposition to metaphysical social science in his *Empirical Sociology* (section V), where he explicitly opposed the invocation of the supra-individual entities that populated the rising *völkisch* ideologies, it is clear that Neurath did not aim to support ontological holism of any kind.[24] Rather, he stressed the nomological autonomy of sociology or any other social science by pointing to the irreducibility of their laws to those of psychology.

So much for the structure of encyclopedic unity: What about the methodological difference between the sciences? Neurath did not require that social science be conducted just like natural science. "The programme of unified science does not presuppose that physics can be regarded as an example for all the science to follow" (1937/1981, 788). As noted above, social science possesses distinctive principles of explanation and, as we shall see below, may also be oriented to nonuniversal generalizations. Such research may well be of a different kind from that aiming for universal laws. Neurath's recognition of methodological pluralism is also reflected in his stress that it would be mistake to hold social science to the standard achieved by physics and his admonition of colleagues in the unified science movement to also investigate sciences that do yet meet those exacting standards.

Sometimes one tends to prefer handling precise terms to such a degree that certain problems are avoided which are still structured less clearly. Certain phrases characteristic of the appreciation of art or of sociological considerations are thus discarded too quickly as being too vague and still too indeterminate and containing potentially metaphysical terms. But such incomplete reflexions often contain all the scientific results that so far achieved in this field and one should rather try to build on this. Of course, rigorous analysis by means of the logic of science is more satisfying when one turns to physics. (1936e/1981, 712)

To be sure, in *Foundations of the Social Sciences* Neurath reemphasized his monistic conviction that "procedure in all empirical

[24] Compare: "The object of history and economics are people, things and their arrangement" (Carnap, Hahn, Neurath 1929/1973, 315).

sciences is the same", but this simply expressed his empiricist outlook, for immediately he went on: "yet there are questions of degree: some techniques may be applied more frequently in one science than in another" (1944, 37).

In sum, the encyclopedic unity envisaged by Neurath did not require a reductive hierarchy of laws (either with physics or psychology at its base). Nor did he require a strong form of methodological monism. For Neurath, the claim of unified science was minimalist: "all laws of unified science must be capable of being linked with each other, if they are to fulfill the task of predicting as often as possible individual events or groups of events" (1932a/1983, 68). From this pragmatical base, Neurath's encyclopedism developed under its own name from the mid-1930s, characterized by the slogan "No system from above, but systematisation from below" (1936b/ 1983, 153). Or as he put it still 10 years later, "our scientific practice is based on local systematizations only, not on overstraining the bow of deduction" (1946/1983, 232).

Neurath's encyclopedism is decisive for assessing Menger's criticism of the idea of unified science as threatening undue rigidity: "The anticipation of a pyramid of non-overlapping sciences and subsciences hinders the free evolution of the sciences. We should regard the social sciences as a collection of a great many scientific units which can become combined in very different ways. That is real 'encyclopedism' within the unity of science movement" (Neurath 1939/1983, 211). If the integratability into the existing sciences is the criterion for membership in unified science, then Menger's qualms have found an answer. It was precisely the point of Neurath's encyclopedism to overcome conceptions of unified science that rendered it a restrictive "monistic scheme". (Menger's criticism was based only on the earliest formulations of the unified science program.) As for Zilsel's criticism of physicalism's overly rigid conception of social scientific laws, it must be noted again that Neurath allowed for functional laws (and suggested as much in *Empirical Sociology* itself).

NEURATH'S PHYSICALISM

When considering physicalism as a thesis concerning the language of unified science, it is particularly important to see the difference between Neurath and Carnap.

For Carnap early on, "physicalism" meant that every language of science, that is, the languages of all its different disciplines, can be translated into the language of physics. For him, the "physicalistic language" contained "not only physical terms (in the narrow sense) but also all the various special terminologies (of biology, psychology, sociology, etc.) understood as reduced by definitions to their basis in physical determinations" (1932b/1934, 95–6). Now, importantly, Carnap never intended physicalism to make an ontological claim. But just as importantly, by 1935 Carnap also learnt that the original criteria of translatability had been conceived of too narrowly: instead of eliminative definability of special terms, the physicalist language also had to countenance nonelimitative reducibility (1936, 1936/1937). Still later, he had to allow for free-floating theoretical terms, still more indirectly related to the observational base (1939). Originally, then, Carnap's physicalism required the complete translatability of the languages of all the sciences into that of physics, but this was gradually relaxed. With the recognition of noneliminative reducibility Carnap switched to the "thing-language" of "observable terms", special terms of physics too becoming reducible to it in this weakened sense (1936, 65; 1936/1937, 466–7).

Neurath's metalinguistic physicalism was linked closely to the criterion of empirical respectability, but already at an early stage he sought to allow for nonreductive forms of it: "Physicalism ... only makes pronouncements about what can be related back to observation statements *in some way or other*" (1931/1981, 425, italics added). For Neurath, meaningfulness was inextricably linked to the availability of intersubjective evidence: he rejected the possibility of private protocol languages already in 1931.[25] But what was the language in which such test procedures are formulated? On this point, some of Neurath's pronouncements make it difficult to distinguish his view from Carnap's. Thus still in late 1932 he wrote that "this unified language of unified science, which by and large can be derived from everyday language by certain alterations, is the language of physics" (1932a/1983, 62). The qualifications he introduced seemed only to concern the nature of the language of physics at the time: "What matters is that the concepts of unified science always share the fate of the fundamental concepts of physics" (ibid.;

---

[25] For reconstructions of the latter argument in context, see Uebel (1995).

cf. 1931/1981, 425). Again, however, Neurath's formulations soon became more careful:

What is first given to us is our historical ordinary language with a multitude of imprecise, unanalysed terms. We start by purifying this ordinary language of metaphysical components and thus arrive at the physicalist ordinary language. A list of forbidden words can serve us well in doing this. In addition, there is the physicalist language of advanced science that we can design to be free of metaphysics from the very start. It is at our disposal only for certain sciences, indeed only parts of sciences. (1932/1983, 93, trans. altered)

What Neurath did here – and this is a distinction he retained ever since – was to distinguish sharply between the language of physics proper and the "physicalistically cleansed" everyday language, the "universal slang" or "universal jargon" (ibid., 92; cf. 1941/1983, 214). His reasoning was that the testing of even the high-level theories of physics ultimately depends on formulations in that "physicalistically cleansed" everyday language. Virtually from the start, Neurath's conception of the physicalist language was not bound to the language of physics as such. And as his preferred schema for protocol statements indicates, his universal slang also differed from Carnap's later thing-language in admitting as primitive also perception terms attributable to persons but not to things (compare Neurath 1932 with Carnap 1936/1937, 12–13).

All along, then, physicalism did not represent for Neurath a logical condition on the relation of individual terms in the different disciplines of unified science to those of physics proper, but an epistemological condition on the admissability of whole statements into unified science.[26] Two points are notable here. The first is that from Neurath's physicalism did not follow what did follow from Carnap's in 1932: that all the individual terms admissable into unified science be definable in the terms of physical theory. Once Carnap demanded only that they be reducible to the thing-language of observable predicates – and given that a term's being reducible

[26] That Neurath took entire statements as units of analysis in the early 1930s is revealed by an anecdote in Carnap (1963, 58); still in his *Foundations of Social Science* Neurath stated that "whole sentences have to be translated into whole sentences" (1944, 7). This difference also anticipates disputes between Carnap and Quine.

meant "know[ing] how to use it on the basis of observations" (1936/1937, 467) – Neurath may well have considered the battle won (even though differences remained).[27] Clearly, Neurath meant to grant different disciplines – and so also the social sciences – what nowadays is called their conceptual autonomy.

Second, for Neurath, physicalism expressed the condition of empiricism. As we saw, Neurath's conception of testability was pretty informal, but what may appear as characteristic sloppiness on his part may just as well be counted as sagacious foresight. Given that the formalist project of delimiting the empirical criterion of meaning by providing precise conditions of necessity and sufficiency was never completed to general satisfaction, one may applaud his retention of in-principle testability as the hallmark of empirical discourse as based on an informal, exemplar-based understanding of the idea of testing. For him, metalinguistic physicalism did not follow from some foundational meaning theory, but rather was backed by the naturalistic resolve to start *in medias res*. Physicalistic statements are statements about "spatio-temporal structures" (1931/1981, 424). Only those statements are admissable that can be tested – or, as Neurath put it, "controlled" – by direct or indirect reference to intersubjectively available observational facts. What follows for physicalistic social scientific theories is simply that they too must allow for derivations that can be formulated in the everyday language speaking of spatio-temporal structures and can be tested as such.

Note that even though he spoke less carefully than Carnap, Neurath also sought to avoid ontological claims concerning the constitution of mental phenomena:

Physicalism encompasses psychology as much as history and economics; for it there are only gestures, words, behaviour, but no 'motives', no 'ego', no 'personality' beyond what can be formulated spatio-temporally. It is a separate task to ascertain what part of the traditional material can be expressed in the new strict language. Physicalism does not hold the thesis

---

[27] Neurath applauded Carnap's conception of "reduc[ing] all terms to well-known terms of the language of daily life" (1938a, 19; cf. 1937/1983, 176). It seems that given Carnap allowed perception terms to be reducible to the thing language (1936/37, 12), Neurath considered their disagreement negligible: perception terms were primitive terms in his universal slang.

that 'mind' is a product of 'matter', but that everything we can sensibly speak about is spatio-temporally ordered. (1931/1973, 325)

Here Neurath employed what Carnap called the potentially misleading "material mode of speech" (1932b/1934, 37–42) to characterize admissable languages in terms of their domain.[28] Even Neurath's rejection of ontological holism – his rejection of talk of *Volksgeist* and the like – need not be read as an ontological affirmation, but can be read as such a characterization of admissable languages by their domain. Languages that speak of supernatural forces or supraindividual agents simply will not be admitted into unified science for the reason that it is entirely unclear how such statements could be tested.

So Neurath's physicalism too was antireductionist in intent. Importantly, his adoption of the term "behaviorism" is also to be understood in this spirit: "There is no longer a special sphere of the 'soul'. From the standpoint advocated here it does not matter whether certain individual tenets of Watson, Pavlov or others are maintained or not. What matters is that only physicalistically formulated correlations are used in the description of living things, whatever is observed in these beings" (1932a/1983, 73). "Behaviourism" for Neurath meant simply the limitation to physicalistic statements, that is, to statements about human activities as taking place in space and time.[29] While he did not stress it early on, we may note that this includes talk of many of the 'intervening variables' which for the psychologists mentioned had become illegitimate.

---

[28] When Neurath claimed that "physicalism" represented the "heir" and "logically consistent development of materialism" (1932c/1981, 568), he similarly meant a materialism cleansed of ontological claims, seeking to uphold some continuity with the philosophical tradition that was historically dominant in the workers' movement (1931/1981, 467). By contrast, Neurath remarked about "sociology on a materialistic basis", that its main points can be communicated by a rendition of the materialistic conception of history (1931,1973, 363).

[29] Note that this is intended to be still wider than Hempel's reading: "In Neurath's science of behavioristics, statements about phenomena of consciousness and about mental processes would be replaced by statements about spatio-temporally localizable occurrences such as macroscopic behaviour (including gestures and speech acts) and about physiologically and physiochemically described processes in the brain and the central nervous system" (1969, 170–1). My point is that Neurath's universal slang does not require the replacement of physicalistically understood psychological termini of the everyday language.

Thus note not only that Neurath was open in principle to Freud's psychoanalysis – he headed a working group dedicated to the 'physicalization' of Freud's texts – but that his own theory of protocol statements makes explicit reference to intentional phenomena, not only via behaviorist circumlocutions like "speech thinking", but also directly via expressions like "thinking person" etc.[30]

This is not to deny that at some early stage Neurath may have flirted with a more traditional conception of behaviorism, but even then the intention was to make intentional phenomena amenable to nonmetaphysical theorizing.[31] Thus Neurath was happy to follow Carnap's liberalization of his earlier reductionist strictures, and from about 1936 Neurath tended to prefer the term 'behavioristics' for its presumably less restrictive associations (1936g/1983, 164; cf. 1944, 17, 51).[32] Then he also stated:

While avoiding metaphysical trappings it is in principle possible for physicalism to predict future human action to some degree from what people 'plan' or 'intend' ('say to themselves'). But the practice of individual and social behaviourism shows that one reaches far better predictions if one does not rely too heavily on these elements which stem from 'self-observation' but on others which we have observed in abundance by different means. (1936e/1981, 714)

In later years, Neurath made his antireductionist intention ever more explicit. Thus he noted that "statements of the type 'this entrance hall of a building thrills me' can be regarded as physicalist ones because they are observation statements" (1941/1983, 221) and pointed out that "[h]istorians of human social life are highly

---

[30] For Neurath on psychoanalysis see Neurath (1932a/1983, 80; 1939/1983, 210), Frenkel-Brunswick (1954), and Carnap (1963, 58). On the intentional load of his protocol statements see also Neurath (1936g/1983, 162–3) and discussion in Uebel (1993).

[31] Hempel rightly notes that "Neurath put mentalistic terms like 'mind' and 'motive' on the Index on the grounds that they tended to be construed as standing for immaterial agencies" (1969, 169).

[32] Hempel rightly notes also that Neurath did not "explicitly offer [a Rylean] kind of dispositional construal" of psychological terms – even though "[s]ome of his suggestions are strikingly suggestive and remind one of ideas that Gilbert Ryle was later to develop much more subtly and fully" (1969, 170, 169). For instance, Neurath's argument against hypostasizing the running of a watch (e.g., 1932a/1983, 73) appears to anticipate Ryle's objections to invoking Cartesian ghosts in the body machine.

interested in descriptive terms such as deal with the feeling-tone of persons, their devotion, their fear and hopes" (1944, 15).

It was in this inclusive sense that Neurath continued to expound a "social behaviorism" that, as he put it early on, "ultimately comprehends all sociology, political economy, history etc." (1932c/1981, 565). Once again, the way he discussed these matters early on were misleading. Thus he noted that sociology does not investigate just any old changes in human groups but that "it takes an interest in connections among stimuli that take place between individuals. Without analyzing these connections in detail it can sometimes under certain circumstances make statements about the overall behaviour of groups linked by stimuli, find laws and with their help make predictions" (1932a/1983, 75). Likewise, he stressed that sociology is an inquiry concerned with the "coherence" and development of social habits, of customs and institutions, and of their combination in large-scale structures (cf. 1931/1973, 371–403). Neurath's talk along such lines – "how far the theological teachings concerning the emancipation of slaves can be taken into account as 'stimulus' and how far as 'response'" (1932a/1983, 85) – is ambiguous. Here his nonreductive understanding of physicalism and "social behaviorism" become important. Were the latter a strict behaviorism that abjured any appeal to variables intervening between stimulus and response, its prospect to deliver sociologically relevant correlations would rightly be called into question. Thus later he noted explicitly: "We can discuss historical and sociological problems in all details without being forced to use the terms 'inner experience' and 'outer experience' or 'opposites' of equivalent scientific significance in forming boundary lines between sciences. That does not mean that we exclude what is called 'inner experience'" (1939/1983, 209). We may rightly be skeptical about the value of exclusive use of overtly behavioristic procedures and concepts, of course; the point here is that Neurath's physicalism was not limited to them.

Neurath's metalinguistic physicalism, at least in intention, was a partial form of what nowadays is called "nonreductive physicalism" (that is, minus the latter's unabashed 'metaphysical' dimension).[33] It allowed for the conceptual autonomy of the special sciences within

---

[33] Contemporary examples would be functionalists of varying stripes (Lewis, middle-period Putnam, Papineau) and anomalous monists (Davidson).

the framework of empiricism. Turning now to the criticisms of Neurath's idea of physicalist social science, we can readily see them rebutted. Menger's criticism focused on the supposed attempt, via the idea of unified science, to demarcate science from metaphysics by the meaning criterion, but as we saw, this was not Neurath's strategy. Kaufman's and some of Zilsel's objections also turn on an unduly restrictive view of what concepts physicalism allows and what not. With Neurath aiming for a version of nonreductive physicalism, Kaufmann's and Zilsel's antireductionist objections are also answered.

LAWS AND PREDICTIONS IN PHYSICALIST SOCIAL SCIENCE

Let me now turn to Zilsel's criticism that Neurath did not do enough to establish the unity of science thesis and that the unity of science should be based nomologically. Neurath's response and counter-criticism – as well as a similar criticism he made of Hempel – show that his concept of physicalist social science also escapes the very common antipositivist criticism that focused on the exclusive reliance on the deductive-nomological and inductive-statistical model of explanation.

Neurath recognized a variety of types of scientific generalizations and laws that it is the proper business of science to establish. We already noted Neurath's recognition of the possibility of functional laws. In addition, Neurath not only accepted deterministic and probabilistic laws (e.g., 1932a/1983, 68), but he also did not require that laws across the sciences be the same in their scope. When he spoke of "laws for definite narrower social areas" (ibid., 75) or "'social laws' which are valid for distinct social formations" (1931/1973, 371), he endorsed the view that generalizations in social science could range from universal laws to far more circumscribed specifications: "Let us not start from what one tends to call a 'law of nature', but those less demanding generalizations which are common in the social sciences. Results gained from a rather restricted range of examples are extended to a further set of cases that also are fairly restricted" (1937/1981, 788). Such limitations were not merely a temporal inconvenience, but a chronic condition of the social sciences: "Most sociological regularities that support the deduction of predictions are formulated in such a way that they are valid only for relatively complex structures of certain geographical regions and historical periods" (1936f/2004, 506). (On this point Neurath came into conflict with Carl Menger (father of Karl) and the school of Austrian economics – and later with Popper – who believed that all theoretical sciences had to aim exclusively for strict and universal rules.)

Now compare Zilsel. For him, historico-sociological laws were "macro-laws" like gas laws; they did not correspond to the micro-laws which describe the behavior of individual molecules. As such they are statistical and may pertain either to regularities of temporal succession (historical laws) or relations of simultaneity (sociological laws). Having given some examples, Zilsel noted that "all these 'laws' are yet incomplete in so far as only necessary but not sufficient conditions are given", indeed, that "all these historical 'laws' have to be considered as preliminary and more or less probable assertions only" (1942/2000, 205). So it may appear as if there did obtain, after all, wide agreement with Neurath. Where Neurath spoke of reducing the scope of social scientific laws, there Zilsel spoke of "general statistical laws of smaller groups" that "are less exact" (ibid., 202). Yet Neurath did not agree with Zilsel that the difference between historico-sociological and physical laws was due merely to the relative immaturity of the social sciences. To see the reason for this, note that late in his career Neurath focused increasingly on the phenomenon and the causes of unpredictability in the social sciences.

All along, of course, Neurath had been aware of two forms of unpredictability peculiar to the social sciences. First, there are events that cannot be predicted in all details without self-contradiction, like the publication of a novel, the emergence of an architectural idea, the discovery of a scientific formula, or a technical invention.[34] Second, Neurath stressed, as he had been doing since 1911 – long before Robert Merton or even W. I. Thomas[35] – the phenomon of reflexive (self-fulfilling or self-defeating) predictions: "But there is

[34] "[T]hrough making the prediction this man also makes the very statement of which he intended to say it will not be made sooner than in the next century": Neurath (1944, 29; cf. 1931/1973, 404–5; 1932a/1983, 88; 1936c/1981, 775–6).

[35] See, e.g., Neurath (1911/1998, 517; 1919/1973, 152; 1921/1973, 160). Compare Thomas (1928) and Merton (1936, 1948).

yet another limit to sociological predictions. They are, as products of an era, co-determinants of what they assert. ... The asserting and the denying prophet have become agents through their predictions, which does not mean that their forecast must always have a reinforcing character; it may happen that their influence is positively paralysing" (1931/1973: 404–5; cf. 1932a/1983, 88; 1936c/1981, 775; 1944, 28; 1946c/1983, 245–6). Significantly, Neurath did not claim that the phenomenon of reflexive predictions makes all prediction in the social science in principle impossible. Neurath's point is rather that while these phenomena can also have repercussions for the ability to make predictions in the natural sciences – "a decision told to others ... may lastly be connected with geological changes (building of dams, etc.), which may lastly be connected with an alteration of the orbit of the earth" (1944, 29) – in the social sciences they are of greater importance. Moreover, while he freely admitted that "in astronomy it makes no difference whether anybody writes a prediction down or not" (1944, 28), he rejected the idea that the phenomenon of reflexive predictions provided "confirmation of the view that mind and spirit have their special secrets" (1936c/1981, 775). Neurath was aware of the specific "problematic" (his quotation marks) of the social sciences: "Where language has to be regarded as an important social item and the flexibility and alterability of human societies have to be taken into account, new difficulties arise" (1944, 37–8). But his reaction to all these complications was not to call into doubt the concept of unified science, but to show what wide variety of scientific investigations it can encompass.

In addition, Neurath in the 1940s drew increasing attention to what he once called "unpredictability as something given in principle".[36] This unpredictability arises when it is unclear whether a

---

[36] Neurath to Carnap, September 29, 1943, p. 13 (RC 102–55–03 Archives of Scientific Philosophy, University of Pittsburgh). For the same idea in his publications see Neurath (1944, 28–30; 1946/1983, 232; 1946b/2004, 552; cf. 1946c/1983, 245–6). The idea itself was by no means new to him. Consider: "Sometimes a change in a sociological position may be predictable though the direction of the change cannot be known ... but this happens in physics too: a cone spinning on its top will fall, but which way cannot be predicted" (1931/1973, 362). All along, he castigated as "metaphysical" the "fiction" of proceeding "from an 'ideal forecast', from the Laplacean mind that knows all initial conditions and all formulas and thus can

situation is stable or unstable. A situation or an "aggregation", as Neurath put it, "may be called unstable if even a small variation in the initial state may bring about a tremendous difference in the state of the whole aggregation in question – 'tremendous' here from a sociological viewpoint".[37] The consequences for a purely nomologi-cal approach to social science are plain. It becomes very problematical indeed that it often must remain "an open question which social situations may be regarded as unstable", for when the aggregation is unstable "the behavior of human groups may be connected with some changes which appear 'by chance'" (1944, 28). It was precisely for this reason that Neurath opposed "the assumption of many social scien-tists that the behavior of masses is more easily predictable than the behavior of individuals", for "they sometimes mix up the behavior of the masses which may be regarded as average behavior of individuals and the behavior of masses which cannot be regarded as such behav-ior" (26; cf. 1946c/1983, 244–5).

It was against this background that Neurath accused Zilsel of continuing to hanker after the "systems assumption".[38] Was that fair? It certainly looks as if Zilsel's acquiescence into the peculiarity of socio-historical laws goes a long way towards Neurath's demand that the generalizations of the social sciences not be held to the same standard as physical laws. But Zilsel nevertheless asserted: "pre-diction will always stand as the ultimate test for a law" (1941, 206). If that were meant to demand the testability of each social scientific generalization by prediction, Zilsel would here demand what Neurath argued cannot be attained in quite a few of the discussions typical of the social sciences.

---

predict everything" (ibid., 404). "It is not an intrinsic property of a developed science that it should be able to predict any individual event" (1932a/1983, 77).

[37] His example was the following: "Let us imagine that we can predict that a certain unstably situated stone will roll down a slope from a pass but that there is no hypothesis which tells us why we should expect it to roll more to the right than to the left. If the tribes on the right-hand valley are threatened by this stone and an avalanche following the fall of this stone, the history of a continent may become different from the history of the same continent following a migration of tribes connected with the fall of an avalanche into the left-hand valley" (1944, 28).

[38] In letter from Neurath to Carnap, September 29, 1943, p. 13 (RC 102-55-03 Archives of Scientific Philosophy, University of Pittsburgh). In other respects, Neurath was favourably inclined towards Zilsel's work, for instance, his critique of the concept of genius (1931/1973, 388; 1941/1983, 223).

Yet another logical empiricist came in for Neurath's criticism for neglecting unpredictability. For Hempel (1942) history was subject to the schema of deductive-nomological explanation just as much as physics – even though so far it could produce only "explanation sketches" – and the symmetry of explanation and prediction applied here as well. Hempel's model of explanation was to hold across all of unified science. In correspondence, Neurath objected with some vehemence, ultimately accusing Hempel of commitment to "unpluralist 'ontological realism'".[39] Neurath asked not only what kind of social scientific laws there were that satisfied the condition Hempel accepted as a matter of course, namely, that they be strictly universal.[40] He also objected that, since sometimes the entire aggregation functions as "determining condition", acceptance of unpredictability forms an "essential part" of the project that is social science: "the explanation-sketch does not help us where unpredictability is at the [sic!] stake".[41] The very complexity of the situation renders any thought of having full cognitive control of all relevant elements illusory.

Neurath's criticism was only partly to the point. First of all, Hempel was not committed to historical laws as such. In history and sociology often "the universal hypotheses in question frequently relate to individual or social psychology, which somehow is supposed to be familiar to everybody through his everyday experience; thus, they are tacitly taken for granted" (1942 [1965, 236]). Second, Hempel recognized that "in general the initial conditions and especially the universal hypotheses ... cannot be unambiguously be supplemented" (ibid., 237–8). Third, Hempel noted that "those universal hypotheses to which historians explicitly or tacitly refer in offering explanations, predictions, interpretations, judgements of relevance etc. are taken from various fields of scientific research, in so far as they are not pre-scientific generalizations of everyday experience" (ibid., 242). As Hempel's

---

[39] Letter to Hempel, November 25, 1944 (Neurath papers, Vienna Circle Archive, Rijksarchief Noord-Holland, Haarlem, the Netherlands).

[40] Compare: "We have very fine studies on market correlations, but we do not know under what conditions these correlations remain valid. Certainly they do not remain valid where no markets exist" (1944, 30).

[41] Letter to Hempel, November 25, 1944, Neurath papers, Vienna Circle Archive, Rijksarchief Noord-Holland, Haarlem, the Netherlands.

considerations did remain "entirely neutral with respect to the problem of 'specifically historical laws'" (ibid.), Neurath's criticism seems overdone, but he focused on the fact that Hempel's account recognized only provisional exceptions to predictability. The inability of Hempel's concept of science to find room for unpredictability in principle meant that his model of deductive-nomological explanation, even of inductive-statistical explanation, appeared unacceptable for the social sciences. Since the peculiarities of the social sciences constituted for Neurath only gradual differences with the natural sciences, it follows that his rejection of Hempel's model of scientific explanation has still wider implications. Years before other counterexamples to the covering law model were discovered, Neurath dismissed its necessity, albeit on grounds that remained foreign to most of the later discussion.[42] To repeat, for Neurath unpredictability did not spell the end of empirical social science nor the end of the ideal of the unity of science. But it did confirm the futility of the rigid formalist conception of scientific explanation that dominated orthodox logical empiricism. as much as did the more or less sophisticated hierarchical conception of the unity of science.

To conclude, Neurath's later elaborations of his early pronouncements on physicalism and unified science reveal a position that sought to be sensitive to actual practice in the social sciences and avoid undue schematism. While Neurath himself shared some of the criticisms that can be found in antipositivist writers, he did not draw their conclusions, for, unlike them, he did not regard the doctrines attacked as essential to logical empiricism. Of course, the present survey has not yet established the overall viability of Neurath's conception of physicalist social science. To decide this, it is not enough that Neurath weathered the criticisms leveled against his conception already by Zilsel, Menger, and Kaufmann and that a major reason for thinking it incompatible with their own programs is removed. Still further exploration of relevant issues like the relation between physicalist and interpretive social science and the

---

[42] Neurath's opposition to the DN-model in the social sciences was also stressed in Reisch (2001, 207) and Uebel (1997, 180). Zolo (1986/1989, 97) attested to Neurath the rejection of the DN-model tout court, on the debatable grounds that Neurath recognized no universal statements at all.

possibility for "critical" physicalist social science is required. But it does appear notable that standard antipositivist criticisms fail against Neurath's encyclopedic alternative to the orthodox conception of unified science.[43]

---

[43] For helpful critical comments on previous versions I am indebted to Elisabeth Nemeth, John Preston, and Alan Richardson.

11 Logical Empiricism and the History and Sociology of Science

INTRODUCTION

Our image of logical empiricism has changed dramatically during the last two decades. One of the entrenched views proven wrong was that the logical empiricists were not interested in the historical and social context of science and of philosophy of science. Today we know that some of the most important members of the Vienna Circle (especially Neurath, Carnap, Frank, and Hahn) were perfectly aware of the fact that their efforts to elaborate a new philosophical conception of scientific knowledge were by no means "neutral" in respect to the social conditions and political struggles of the time. Carnap's foreword to *Der logische Aufbau der Welt* in 1928 and the Vienna Circle's manifesto of 1929 are only the best known examples. Yet it is not that easy to find explicit answers to the questions of which part history and sociology of science should play in the "orchestrated" unified science (to borrow an expression Neurath adopted) and how the relation between history and sociology of science and philosophy of science should be conceived. To reconstruct such an answer is the purpose of this chapter.

THE SOCIO-HISTORICAL DIMENSION OF EARLY LOGICAL EMPIRICIST PHILOSOPHY OF SCIENCE

One reason why the aspect of logical empiricism that concerns us here has escaped attention for so long is that the type of contextualization of science which Neurath, Frank and Zilsel intended did not fit very well into the twentieth-century debates through which the sociology of science defined itself as an autonomous

278

discipline. This holds for the debates in the 1920s and '30s about the sociologies of science developed by Max Scheler and Karl Mannheim just as much as for Robert Merton's, which dominated the international discussion in the 1940s and '50s. In both cases the subject matter of the new discipline was delimited against two competitors: first, against Marxist social theory and its materialist thesis that being determines consciousness; second, against philosophy (with similar arguments as in the dispute about psychologism prior to World War I).[1] The way in which the history and sociology of science was thematized by the early Logical Empiricists was at odds with those debates for they were concerned neither with the delimitation against Marxism nor with the differentiation of the disciplines of philosophy and sociology. By contrast, Hans Reichenbach's distinction between the "context of discovery" and the "context of justification" is nowadays standardly viewed as effecting the latter differentiation, even though it may be read to simply fix the difference between descriptive and normative judgments and thereby to facilitate a clarification of the relation between the two. Understood in this way Reichenbach's distinction finds a legitimate and indispensable place within both philosophy and sociology of science.[2]

Consider the relation to Marxism. Otto Neurath and Edgar Zilsel, members of the Social Democratic Workers Party since the end of World War I, explicitly related their conception of the sociology of science to the historically materialist framework of Marxist social theory. Each did so very much in his own way.

For Neurath, physicalism represented the logically clarified and so most contemporary form of materialism (Neurath 1931). For him Marxist social theory measured up to modern scientific standards much better than the "humanist" or *geisteswissenschaftliche* social theories of his day. From this perspective he defended Marxism against Mannheim's diagnosis that, given the "higher viewpoint" of the sociology of science, Marxist social theory represented but one one-sidedness among others. Neurath did not deny that, like any other conception of society, Marxism reflected the conditions under

---

[1] On the latter debate in the 1930s in Germany and Austria, especially about Mannheim, see Kusch (1999); on Neurath's and Frank's view of the sociology of knowledge, see Uebel (2000).

[2] See Reichenbach (1938, 3–4) and Stadler (2004) for discussion of this distinction in Logical Empiricism.

which certain social groups lived and that in this sense it represented an ideology. But he stressed that ideologies cannot be evaluated as to whether their standpoint is higher or lower but only as to whether their conceptions of society are scientific, whether they are logically consistent and empirically testable. Just that is what Marxist social theory was – a "strictly scientifically oriented view" – even though it was not the only possible one: "It is clear that already due to the insufficiency of our data it is possible to have several scientific theories about the course of history that do not contradict themselves. And it makes good sense to justify on sociological grounds the choice amongst the scientifically possible suppositions" (Neurath 1930/1981, 351).

So Marxism, for Neurath, is "one-sided" after all in that it develops certain hypotheses concerning history and the structure of the social order and tries to support these empirically but does not do the same with other hypotheses that logically are equally possible. This one-sidedness, however, is a characteristic of every theory whatsoever and for principled reasons cannot be avoided. (Neurath noted this as early as his 1913 publications.) Yet it is a special characteristic of sociology that it makes it possible for practitioners to analyze their own social standpoint from a sociological per-spective and on that basis make conscious decisions about the questions and assumptions that underlie their research. Moreover, this reflexivity not only is possible for sociologists, it also is demanded of them for scientific reasons: sociologists would neglect an essential aspect of their discipline if they failed to reflect their own social position.[3] Sociology is "a science that tries to make predictions but, as a matter of course, in so doing, takes account of the sociological standpoint of those who give statements and of the actions of those who contribute to the realizations of their own prophecies" (Neurath 1930/1981, 354). But these considerations are far from establishing a "higher viewpoint" (ibid., 351). On the contrary, they prompt sociologists to become aware of how much their own assertions form part of the social nexus they investigate, how they depend on and how they intervene in it. (Neurath had

---

[3] In the form of the demand for the "objectivization of the objectivizer" this idea assumes a comparably central role in the sociology of Pierre Bourdieu; see his (1984) and (1989).

long pointed out that social scientific predictions may work as "self-fulfilling prophecies", for instance, in his "Anti-Spengler" [1921/1973, 160].) Marxist sociology, for Neurath, possessed a much more enlightened attitude towards itself than Mannheim's. It recognized that sociologists do not "enjoy a kind of social extra-territoriality" (Neurath 1931/1973, 406) and that their knowledge claims therefore possess scientific validity only if they make explicit both the social determination of their hypotheses and the social consequences they possibly could have.

Edgar Zilsel also thought of his research into cultural history as an attempt to confirm in proper empirical fashion Marx's theory of history, which he deemed "extremely difficult and supportable only by the most careful investigations" (1931a/1992, 90). It was part of this project to investigate historically in which way scientific thinking is influenced by the class conflict. Yet despite the Marxist provenance of his concern Zilsel hardly referred to related debates within Marxism (see Fleck 1993, 504). One exception was his debate (1931) with the prominent Austro-Marxist, philosopher, and cofounder of the Viennese Sociological Society Max Adler, in which his critical attitude became apparent. Despite their political proximity Zilsel considered Adler's Kantian social theory more as an instance of idiosyncratic school philosophy than as a fruitful scientific perspective. Instead he valued all the more the essay of another Austro-Marxist, Otto Bauer's "Weltbild des Kapitalismus" (The Worldview of Capitalism, 1924). For Zilsel, this work (which so far has hardly ever been mentioned in the context of the debate about the sociology of science) managed to uncover precisely the broad sociological connections that are at issue in the sociology of science. The fact that academic philosophy took no cognizance whatsoever of this "probably most fruitful and comprehensive publication in the history of philosophy of the last few years" was for him an in itself most "instructive contribution to the sociology of science" (1929/1992, 42).

Zilsel had a very good eye for the limitations and often empty pretensions of contemporary academic philosophy, and he observed the world of science and academia from a sociological vantage point. In one original study that is instructive still today Zilsel showed that the main philosophical movements of his day, despite all differences between them, shared a certain complex of characteristics. This he labeled "school philosophy" and derived it from the social conditions under which university professors conduct philosophy. "They all strongly emphasize the separation of philosophy from the sciences and of the individual sciences from each other, they have a particular preference for taxonomies and formal investigations, they organize themselves into rather authoritarian 'schools', etc." (1931a/1992, 95).

Zilsel argued that the sharp separation of philosophy from the empirical sciences can be considered as a sociological phenomenon, and he thought it the task of a theory of history and society that builds on Marx to show that and how the intellectual struggles about this separation are related to the class struggles of their day. These forward-looking investigations enabled him to comment particularly instructively on the connection between the political and intellectual developments of his time.[4] Thus he analyzed the "philosophical foundations" of National Socialism according to Hitler's 1933 party congress address (Zilsel 1933) and provided a detailed description of the catastrophic consequences of the Nazi assumption for the sciences in Germany (1933 and 1933a, respectively). Before he fled in 1938, most of Zilsel's writings on the sociology of science were published in the Social Democratic monthly *Der Kampf*, a journal of considerable intellectual standards, which always, however, took itself to provide a forum for political rather than academic debate. He dedicated his large-scale 1926 study of the origin of the concept of the genius to the spirit which characterized the Viennese adult education institutes where he taught from 1922 to 1934. If his investigations should prove fruitful, they would show that, rather than at the university, "*living* science found a home in adult education" (1926, xxx).

As noted, the sociology of science of the 1920s and '30s defined itself by delimitation not only against Marxism but also against philosophy according to the example of the psychologism dispute. Here we must recall that the logical empiricists adopted a differentiated attitude towards the alleged alternative that structured this dispute. They accepted the view that the principles of logic and mathematics cannot be derived empirically, but they rejected the

---

[4] Zilsel developed *in nuce* the types of questions that more recently have been posed by Ringer (1969), Bourdieu (1984), and Charle (1990).

view that they were grounded either in a transcendent realm of ideas or in a priori laws of thought. Rather, following Poincaré, they regarded the logical and mathematical principles of science as conventions concerning the use of signs, as free creations of the human spirit subject to historical change (Frank 1949). Accordingly, the issue of the "historical and sociological relationships of scientific views" (Frank 1932/1998, 264) was recognized as important from early on but was pursued differently than in the contemporary debate about Mannheim's sociology of science. The point was not to derive scientific theories from the social being of scientists, but to make clear the criteria for their development of logical mathematical frameworks, which – and here the Logical Empiricists gave a new interpretation to the a priori of Kant – "must first be injected or transplanted into sensible nature before any properly empirical science of nature is then possible" (Friedman 1998, 248).

This issue was alien to Mannheim's sociology of science, originating in mathematics and natural science or, more precisely, in the philosophical reflections about the foundations of physics necessitated after the discoveries of the late nineteenth and early twentieth centuries had exploded the framework of Newtonian physics and Kantian epistemology. It was in utter contrast to Mannheim, who had exempted the exact sciences from his sociological relativization of their knowledge claims, that for the Logical Empiricists the historical relativization began precisely with what turned the natural sciences into exemplary exact sciences, namely, their mathematical framework. Their insight that in principle this framework can be chosen freely, and that in this sense it is arbitrary, thus was not owed to the external perspective of the sociologists but to philosophical analyses of the basic concepts of physics undertaken by mathematicians, natural scientists, and philosophers like Mach, Poincaré, Duhem, and Einstein.

Rudolf Carnap's "principle of tolerance" (1934, § 17) represents one consequence drawn from these developments and proposes a radically relativist concept of rationality that sounds much like a philosophical version of late-twentieth-century sociology of scientific knowledge (SSK). As Friedman has argued, it was therefore not Wittgenstein but Carnap who can be regarded as the guarantor of epistemological relativism. Unlike Carnap, Wittgenstein tried to describe "'the essence of language' – its function, its construction *from within* the very norms and practices he was describing" (Friedman 1998, 262). In this sense Wittgenstein shared the philosophical tradition's concern with the normative ideals of rationality.

At first the historical and sociological contextualization of science which Neurath, Frank, and Zilsel intended appears to be more closely related to the ideas of Carnap than Wittgenstein's. But already a second glance makes clear that the traditional philosophical concern "to take reflective responsibility ... for the normativity of our most fundamental cognitive categories" (ibid., 263) played an important role in their thinking as well. Frank even placed it in the very center of the entire project of Logical Empiricism – "the problem is to outline a method to handle our concepts 'responsibly'" (1950, 167) – and Neurath never stopped emphasizing that the ultimate justification of scientific concepts stems from exemplifying guiding ideas rooted in the practical life of active persons. (His simile of the sailors on the boat expresses this as well.) Just for this reason did both insist so strongly that only the scientists themselves were able to take responsibility for the norm-giving leading concepts and categories of science and not some independent philosophical authority (see Neurath 1936/1981, 695; cf. Uebel 2000b, 57 and 332). Yet here we see also the basic difference of Neurath, Frank, and Zilsel from the philosophical tradition. The cognitive practices to be justified are regarded as actions in space and time, history and society, by individuals and groups, and philosophical reflection about the norms guiding these actions does not lead us out of history altogether. Just that was the mistake of Kant's a priori. Knowledge in general and science in particular are social phenomena, and the philosophical attempt to clarify and justify their principles must be understood as part of the historical-social phenomenon we call science. Whoever wishes to take this seriously and tries to question the taken-for-granted character of our cognitive norms and inquire into their justification must reconstruct the "reflexive position" as a position in history and society.

This is precisely where the project of "unified science" comes in that Neurath and Frank valued so much. There they sought to create a forum for practitioners from the most different fields of science to undertake what is as unusual in science as it is in other areas of human activity: to render explicit the principles that guide actions and to inquire into their justification. Carnap's epistemic pluralism was intended to furnish the blueprint for a conceptual space that was open in principle and whose cohesion rested upon nothing but the will of the actors within it to achieve clarity about what justified the validity claims of their assertions. The reflective distance required would in such a space not spring from an autonomous philosophical position but arise from the opposition of the "pluriform" (Neurath's expression) questions and objects of scientific theorizing.[5] History and sociology of science assume a key role in this as the empirical complement to Carnap's conception of philosophy as the "science of possibilities".[6] They would complement the logical analysis of possible linguistic frameworks and analyze empirically the many paths that human thought really followed and still follows. For Zilsel too, such a combination would envigorate both philosophy and empirical science in all its fields (1932a, 152).

"LET US NOT LET GO OF THE GUIDING HAND OF HISTORY." (ERNST MACH)

Already for Ernst Mach it was impossible to separate the rational justification and historical reconstruction of scientific concepts. Progress in science was unthinkable without repeated glances backwards into the history of science, for the biggest obstacles to expanding our knowledge are those that we have created ourselves, the "auxiliary concepts". To be sure, they are an inevitable part of the fabric of knowledge, within and outside of science, and without them we would be unable to orient ourselves in the world. Long before we become aware of them we have employed them in ordering our experiences so as to render ourselves capable of action and survival. But we tend to misunderstand these concepts that we have created ourselves as representatives of an independent reality. This tendency towards hypostatization, however, we cannot overcome once and for all, but we must try to remember how we arrived at these concepts: "We are accustomed to call concepts metaphysical, if we have

---

[5] In this perspective, already "unified science" sought to take seriously those aspects of scientific knowledge which Helen Longino has emphasized under the rubric "sociality of knowledge" (1990; 2002).

[6] For the latter characterization of Carnap's philosophy see Mormann (2000, 210; 2005); for the compatibility of Carnap's "logic of science" and Neurath's "behaviouristics" see Uebel (2001).

forgotten how we reached them. One can never lose one's footing, or come into collision with facts, if one always keeps in view the path by which one has come" (Mach 1872/1911, 17).

For Neurath, Frank, and Zilsel, the large-scale historical study *The Science of Mechanics* was Mach's most important book. Its analysis of the central concepts of Newtonian physics showed how acquaintance with history can provide new avenues for current theorizing. Mach called his method "historical-critical". In the case of classical mechanics this method consisted in "consider[ing] anew the facts on which the law of inertia rests and which draws its limits validity and finally considers a new formulation" (1883/1960, 293). Such an employment of history starts from a current concern and is in this sense present-centered but by no means celebratory, for Mach's glance into history was not intended to provide ancestral legitimation for currently accepted views and perspectives. On the contrary, it was intended to rob these contemporary views of their seeming inevitability and to question the authority of the views we grew up in:

A view, of which the origin and development lie bare before us, ranks in familiarity with one that we have personally and consciously acquired and of whose growth we possess a very distinct memory. Such a view is never invested with that immobility and authority which those ideas possess that are imparted to us ready formed. We change our personally acquired views far more easily. (Mach 1896/1986, 5)

When Mach directs our attention to the fact that "history has made all", he did not mean to suggest that it pursues its course without our being able to intervene. Rather, led by "the guiding hand of history" we can learn to change our opinions and the circumstances under which we live. Whether we let go of it or not is up to us: "Let us not let go of the guiding hand of history. History has made all; history can alter all. Let us expect from history all" (Mach 1872/1911, 18).

This is also one of the most forceful moments in the thought of Otto Neurath. He too was convinced that history can help us to test and, if need be, change the conceptions that we were taught. In his own discipline of political economy as well it helped to replace traditional views with (once more in Mach's words) "a freer, fresher view, conforming to developed experience" (1886/1897, 24). To be sure, for Neurath this conviction still had another point, for it was from the start connected with the question of how historical research itself could be conducted scientifically.

Neurath completed his studies of political economy and economic history in Berlin with leading figures of the so-called Historical School.[7] In his dissertation he investigated the very different interpretations of Cicero's *De Officiis* up to the nineteenth century. In doing so Neurath showed that the use that is made of classical texts changes not only with altered social and economic conditions, but also in line with different conceptions of the course of history. Already in this context it becomes apparent that ideas and theories are not merely the effects of social conditions but also themselves causal factors in affecting these conditions. Ideas and theories have their own history which must be investigated comparatively if their role in a given historical situation is to be understood properly. His *Antike Wirtschaftsgeschichte* (Economic History of Antiquity) represents a real-world complement to the history of ideas of his dissertation. There Neurath compared historical forms of economic organization, not without first sketching the history of the research interests that had previously characterized the field. But Neurath also recalled the origin of economic science, very much in Mach's historical-critical sense, in his later economic writings so as to question its traditional auxiliary concepts (like the concept of *homo economicus*) or its increasingly narrow focus on market and price relations. To be sure, the conception of comparative studies of economic orders is derived from the Historical School, but only a few years after his doctorate he called on economists (in Mach's terms again) to reconsider the facts on which their assertions rested. The subject matter of economics comprises all the institutions and measures that can have an influence on the well-being of individuals and groups. Not only historically given, but also merely possible, institutions and measures had to be considered if the comparative approach was to become the core of a truly scientific economics.

In Neurath's work, history of science did not merely figure in reflexive use (as the history of his own discipline) but also as an independent pursuit. Theories should be subjected to the same principles of comparison as economic organizations. In two essays on the history of optics of 1915 Neurath complained that "[s]o far we

---

[7] For Neurath's intellectual and political biography see Lola Fleck (1996).

have not developed a special technique for the analysis of trains of ideas" (1916/1983, 13) and demanded that "[t]he historians of physics must arrange the views of physicists into groups in the same way as botanists, the plants, or chemists, the compounds" (ibid., 14). With the example of the various theories of light, Neurath showed that these can be considered as complexes of elementary assumptions (periodicity, Huyghens's principle, emission, interference) and that these complexes often were constituted in unexpected ways. Thus he found that Descartes was classified both as having produced a wave theory and a particle theory of light, in both cases for good reasons. Such "mixed theories", Neurath argued, were not unusual, and he proposed to draw consequence for theory classification generally. Theories were not to be characterized in terms of one element that is particularly salient today; instead, one had to make

uniform use of all elements of a theory for its characterisation. ... Early chemistry also first characterised compounds by individual elements that seemed especially important, whereas modern chemistry gives names to the compounds from which their composition becomes clear. The same would be of course possible in the field of the classification of theories. The theories would have to be dissected into their elementary components whose combination could then be fixed by a kind of formula. (1916/1983, 14–15)

Such analyses would reveal the true variety of the history of theories, unconstrained by the assumption that they are the creation of individual authors or representations of objects. Neurath's proposed "special technique for the analysis of trains of ideas" considers theories as relatively independent entities that stand in manifold relationships to the people who formulate them, the phenomena that they describe, and the conditions under which they are developed. Once we become aware of the multiplicity of possible combinations allowed by a limited number of elementary ideas, then those combinations that actually were developed appear in an unusual light. Then we realize that a number of most various circumstances determine which combination is being developed at a particular moment: the state of the scientific and technological development, social developments, political power relations, the working conditions of scientists.[8]

---

[8] In a 1978 lecture Michael Foucault once presented reflections on the history of knowledge that show a remarkable affinity with Neurath's approach; see Foucault (1990).

In this context Neurath also anticipated an idea that much later finds a central role in Pierre Bourdieu's theory of the "scientific field": that the frequent polarization of theoretical options into mutually exclusive alternatives is determined neither by logic nor empirical evidence but sociologically, by the efforts of protagonists to position themselves in their discipline (see Bourdieu 1975 and 1984): "Dichotomies, however, are not only crude intellectually, but also mostly the product of scientific pugnacity. One characterises the opponent as pungently as possible for the purpose of beating him down as forcefully as possible. At such occasions transitions are only troublesome. Thus dichotomies are a result of a warlike spirit" (Neurath 1916/1983, 15). The contrast between emission and wave theories of light for Neurath was an example of the "most primitive form of classification" of theories, dichotomies. He added: "there is an abundance of such dichotomies in all fields: realism – idealism, tariff – free trade, etc." And while he conceded that under certain circumstances "dichotomies, precisely through their deficiencies, have a stimulating effect on scientific life", he nevertheless warned: "Even if that were the case, they would be useful for science perhaps, but themselves unscientific" (ibid.).

By contrast, a scientific history of science would make "uniform use of all elements of a theory for its characterization" and thereby relativize the current alternatives, perhaps even call them into question. Neurath therefore had two aims. The first was to develop a method that can help to turn history of science into a science in its own right, where the analysis and combination of elementary ideas would only be a first step; the second would be to place the systems of hypotheses under investigation into the context of their time: "Our reference to a total world-view becomes a duty" (ibid., 30). Neurath's second aim was to draw our attention to the significant potential of history of science for present-day scientific progress if it were able to introduce standards of highest generality for the "analysis of trains of ideas". For only if we are aware that historically given theories are but special cases in a broad spectrum of thinkable possibilities will we be able to escape the lure of an illusory history of science determined by an inner logic to have arrived at our current theories. It is precisely the "mixed theories" ("the ill-famed group of 'eclectics'" [ibid., 16]) that resist easy classification in contemporary discussion that can help us to overcome false alternatives in our own thinking. Neurath's later analogy between magic and science was likewise meant to exemplify that the "ways of the scientific world-conception" do not always run as the grand historical narratives would have it. (His objections to Comte's positivism rested in his rejection of the image of science as the highest point of a stepwise development [1930/1983, 33].) For Neurath, work on the scientific conception of the world does not always build on the very latest achievements but sometimes approximates earlier phases. Since empirical testing played a greater role in magical practices than in later theologies, science is more closely related to magic than to Judeo-Christian theology and the metaphysics derived from it (ibid., 34).

"ALL SCIENTISTS ARE HISTORIANS TO A CERTAIN DEGREE." (OTTO NEURATH)

Neurath's point that the interpretation of a historical text also depends on the conception of history that is entertained is not too surprising in the context of his dissertation. In the discussions of the Vienna Circle he expanded his point to encompass scientific texts in general. His notorious proposal for the formulation of so-called protocol sentences renders observational statements as three-part relations (person, time, place) and thereby has history enter into physicalism (see Neurath 1932 and the discussion in Uebel 1993). In his critique of Popper's *Logic of Scientific Discovery* Neurath explained the advantage of his proposal:

Popper is of the opinion that it is "a widely spread prejudice that the statement, 'I see that the table here is white' has epistemologically greater merits than the statement, 'The table here is white'". ... For us such pro-tocol statements have the merit of greater stability. The statement "In the sixteenth century people saw fiery swords in the sky" can be retained whereas the statement "There were fiery swords in the sky" would have to be deleted. (1935/1983, 129)

It is important to note that Neurath did not claim that observations rendered in the form of his protocol statements are more stable because they fix upon what is physically given independently of the observer (a still common misunderstanding). Rather, they are more stable because, on the contrary, they explicitly mention the human agency under certain historical conditions. Brought in the form of the protocol statement, experiences may be related to others wherever and by whomever they were made and may in this fashion expand and alter the domain of experience that Neurath called "unified science". In the example of the so-called observations of the sixteenth century this means that they can be classified as "hallucinations" and thus contrast with "reality statements". But they become no less important for history. Neurath's proposed form of protocol statements accords all observation statements the same principled status of candidates for inclusion in unified science and aims to include as many of them as possible in its network of functional descriptions. At the same time it reminds us that every inclusion comes with an evaluation of its status (either as hallucination or lie or reality statement) and that this evaluation remains also in principle revisable. This renders evident that scientists are engaged in a permanent assessment of the history of knowledge – without, of course, being aware of it. Neurath even wrote that all scientists are "historians to a certain degree": they discuss "observation-statements made by eyewitnesses", compare them and decide which ones to accept or reject (1944, 13). For these discussions it is by no means irrelevant what conception of the history of theories one holds.

When Popper claimed that, in Neurath's words, "a theory which has been well corroborated can only be superseded by one of a higher level of universality; that is, by a theory which is better testable and which, in addition, contains the old, well-corroborated theory" (1935/1983, 130), he drew a picture of the progress of science that, Neurath argued, more careful considerations, like those by Duhem, had long rejected. Popper's conception prevents scientists from realizing that even the falsification of a hypothesis does not relieve them of the responsibility to consider the situation in its entirety:

We can very well imagine that a falsifying hypothesis that Popper would call 'confirmed' is pushed aside by a successful scientist because, on the basis of very serious general considerations, he deems it an impediment to the development of science that itself would show how this objection is to be refuted. ... It would be interesting to show what the defensive motions of the practitioners are in such cases. (ibid., 124)

Neurath sought to replace Popper's "pseudorationalism of falsification" with closer investigations of what scientists really do when confronted with a falsificating hypothesis: science had to become an empirical object not only of historical but also sociological and psychological research. What he called "the behavioristics of scholars" comprised both detailed investigations of the type of current laboratory studies and the history of forms "of cognitive cooperation" (1930/1981, 352).

Neurath's "behavioristics" did not exclude the inner life of people (thoughts, feelings, intentions) but rather included not only the published opinions of scientists but also "their 'internal speech' which is sometimes different", even their expectations (which he recognized as important) (1944, 43). The external perspective of Neurath's behavioristics has more in common with that of the ethnologist than the classical behaviorists. "We have fine questionnaires as far as preliterate tribes are concerned but hardly any when we try to ask sociologists how they themselves behave in arguing and writing" (ibid.). Even hypotheses should be considered as "social items" (ibid., 45), for they are, first, part of a collective undertaking and, second, they can have far-reaching social consequences: "The pursuit of sociology, of mathematics, of biology are activities like any other. Hence trends in scientific research are never socially neutral, although they do not always stand at the center of social struggle. As once astronomy and later biology were matters of annoyance, so today is sociology" (1931/1973, 403).

For Neurath, in contrast to Merton, it was not only the institutional setting of science that became its object but also its product, validated knowledge claims. Of course, Neurath would not have gone as far as those representatives of science studies who see in the logical and empirical justifications of scientific claims nothing but rhetorical strategies for the imposition of culturally and socially determined interpretations. Neurath did not explicitly employ Reichenbach's distinction of the contexts of discovery and justification, but he respected it, if only in so far as it destinguished descriptive and normative inquiries. His contributions to the protocol sentence debate discuss classical questions of the justification of knowledge claims. Yet they also show that he thought that such philosophical considerations remained incomplete or even became misleading if they were not complemented by the historical and sociological investigation of the phenomena at issue (see, e.g., 1934/1983, 104). In this sense, the reconstruction of the logico-linguistic structure of scientific theories on the one hand and their investigation as "social items" on the other were for Neurath complementary aspects of the same project of clarifying what it is that we do when we expand our empirical knowledge.

"SCIENCE IS NOT INEVITABLE; THIS QUESTION IS VERY FRUITFUL INDEED." (EDGAR ZILSEL)

Nowadays Edgar Zilsel is regarded as one of the twentieth-century pioneers of the sociology of science, but in philosophy his work is still little known. One reason may be that his views are not easy to categorize. He took seriously the philosophical tradition to a greater extent than customary in the Vienna Circle and engaged in empirical research more extensively than most of its members. (Compare his critical remarks in his 1932 review of Neurath's *Empirical Sociologie*.) Zilsel was both physicist and mathematician and a philosopher. He gained his Ph.D. in 1915 under Heinrich Gomperz with a work that sought to develop a theory of induction based on the law of large numbers. (See Hahn's 1917 critical review.) From the early 1920s onwards he engaged increasingly in historical research. His first published result was *Die Entstehung des Genie-begriffs* (The Origin of the Concept of Genius) of 1926.[9]

Already in 1918 Zilsel had published a study on the cult of the genius as form of pseudo-religion typical of the late nineteenth and early twentieth centuries. Still under the influence of Gomperz, Zilsel's approach there remained mainly psychological and philo-sophical. This orientation is not totally alien to the later study, but it is subsumed under the economic and sociological perspective of Marxist theory. Zilsel reconstructed the ideal of the genius as a "social phenomenon" with the intention to discover causal laws in the humanities. His interest centered on the question "which con-ceptions of superlative human beings are connected with which conditions of human society" (1926, 2). Zilsel's *Geniebegriff* offers a wealth of partly very unusual material. Its achievement consists in

[9] Zilsel submitted it for his *Habilitation* in philosophy at the University of Vienna, but it was rejected by the majority of committee. For more on this and the life and work of Zilsel see Dvorak (1981), Raven and Krohn (2000), Raven (2003).

attempting a historical reconstruction of European individualism (within which concepts such as reflection and formalization played a central role) and to combine this with a sociological analysis of the changes prompted by the development of capitalism. In doing so Zilsel employed social scientific statistics (of book production and reading behavior) to add to Marxist theory of history the theoretical dimension that Pierre Bourdieu later was to call the "struggle for the symbolic order". That dimension concerned the struggles about the ideas and schemata according to which the social order was interpreted and evaluated. Zilsel showed that the "evaluative stances" exhibited a "remarkable persistence" (1926, 35) and by no means always directly corresponded to economic reality. The class struggle was always also a struggle about the socially dominant evaluative stances. This point of view is of great importance too for the sociological explanation of the rise of modern science, which became Zilsel's large-scale project and of which he could realize certain fragments.[10]

According to Zilsel, between the thirteenth and sixteenth centuries three types of rationality can be discerned in Europe, each of them the product of certain social conditions: logic and classificatory thought at the universities, historical and linguistic knowledge at the courts of the rulers, and the technical and experimental knowledge of the engineers. The economy of early capitalism assigned increasing importance to the engineers without, however, granting them social ascendancy: their economic strength was a necessary but not a sufficient condition since the traditional disrespect of manual labor remained an obstacle. This disrespect was rather gradually weakened by a number of symbolic struggles, for instance, in the well-known dispute about whether painting (which required manual labor) could count as high art just like poetry. Only once the unquestioned dominance of the "literati" was broken did it become possible for "artist-engineers" to ascend socially and for the three types of rationality to become combined in the way that is characteristic for modern experimental and mathematical natural science.

Nowadays Zilsel's basic theses can be criticized from different perspectives. For instance, it is known today that the rise of modern

---

[10] Zilsel's essays on this topic were written and, in part, published during the time of his exile in the United States (1939–44) and have been collected in (Zilsel 2000).

science did not only depend on the breaking down of social barriers and the establishment of new forms of cooperation, but also on the erection of new barriers which excluded competing candidates for knowledge. Zilsel's conviction, moreover, that the enterprise of science was motivated not by the desire of individuals for fame and fortune (as he claimed for the humanists) but guided by the ideal of concern for the subject matter itself also appears today as a naïve idealization. Despite this, Zilsel's thesis has proved itself fruitful by contributing to the development of a new discipline of scientific research (and just that was Zilsel's own criterion for "living science"). In addition, one may surmise, however, that the rather unorthodox combination of perspectives that is so typical for Zilsel's work can stimulate research in the science of science still today. This certainly holds for philosophers concerned with the relation between philosophy and history and sociology of science.

On the one hand, Zilsel insisted (like the Vienna Circle) that philosophy had to orient itself by means of the recognition of physical and cultural-historical facts instead of "cut[ting itself] off from the fruitful ground of the individual sciences" (Zilsel in a letter of 1924 quoted in Raven and Krohn 2000, xliii). On the other hand, he addressed his logical empiricist friends without much success with the demand that a philosopher "concerned with fruitful empirical research" investigate what neither logic nor empirical science can investigate. Zilsel did not simply mean the clarification of the meaning of propositions in Schlick's sense, but rather Kantian concerns. For him, the Kantian a priori has a "defensible core" that could be separated from the pseudo-problems also pursued by Kant and the neo-Kantians. Carnap's radical analysis of the logical structure of language rather provided the very conditions to restate the old question of the "transcendental conditions of all experience" in a new and "nonoccult" fashion. Zilsel accepted Carnap's relativistic results but, unlike Carnap and Neurath, did not believe that the resultant problems could be answered by reference to "practice". Philosophers had to retain the question of how the many logically possible propositional systems were related to our experience as an explicitly theoretical question, for it remained very fruitful. "Kant's question really [is]: what conditions must be fulfilled for science to develop? Science is not inevitable; this question is very fruitful indeed" (1932a, 154).

The studies Zilsel published in the 1940s translate this philosophical question into a sociological one: what social conditions must be fulfilled for science to develop? But this did not mean that for him the philosophical question dissolved into a historical sociological one. Questions of great generality like this cannot be pursued in the individual sciences but pose themselves again and again. The point is rather to deal with them without abstracting from the concrete context of scientific research in which they emerge. An impressive example of such a combination of foundational philosophical reflection and scientific research can be found in Zilsel's own life-long concern with the concept of the causal law. His historical research sought to determine causal laws within the field of the humanities that were no different in principle from those of physics (this would contribute more to unified science, he thought, than the spatiotemporal universal [1932a, 154]). Yet to make clear wherein this principled similarity of all scientific laws consisted, one had to go back to the critical revision of the concept of law in modern physics, especially Ernst Mach's, "who with particular vehemence rejected the everyday causal conceptions for science. Due to him we know that the search for natural laws means unearthing functional connections between states, processes and natural events" (1927, 280). Applied to the humanities, Mach's insights would clarify the problem of historical laws and help avoid "sterile considerations" prompted by "vague conceptions of causation and law" (ibid., 286). In turn, historical-sociological research was to help clarify the concept of law in the natural sciences by isolating its cultural elements that always come into play when scientists try to determine the lawful connections between physical phenomena. Thus Zilsel showed in 1942 that the modern concept of natural law retains certain traces of both Judeo-Christian theology and jurisprudence and of the quantitative measures of the engineering in early capitalism, which were in turn connected with the ideals of order of political absolutism (see Zilsel 1942/2000, 96–122).

The historical and social relativization of scientific concepts and theories did not lead Zilsel to deny the universal validity of scientific knowledge. It led him instead to the only seemingly paradoxical insight that the universally valid claims of modern science could not have been achieved without certain economic, social, and political conditions having been fulfilled. Thus historical-sociological research does not dissolve the philosophical wonder about the very existence of science but rather makes available a framework within which the philosophical question after the grounds of its universal validity can be asked more precisely. Zilsel is to be believed when he wrote in 1924 that he conducted his historical research "in the hope of serving philosophy better than I would were I to cut it off from the fruitful ground of the individual sciences" (quoted in Raven and Krohn 2000, xliii). This was a way of turning the attention of philosophers to those very things that are taken for granted and do not stir philosophical reflection even though they are part of the cognitive practice, the standards of which they question or seek to legitimize:

We are only too inclined to consider ourselves and our own civilization as the natural peak of human evolution. From this presumption the belief originates that man simply became more and more intelligent until one day a few great investigators and pioneers appeared and produced science as the last stage of a one-line intellectual ascent. Thus it is not realized that human thinking has developed in many and divergent ways – among which one is the scientific. One forgets how amazing it is that science arose at all and especially in a certain period and under special sociological conditions. (Zilsel 1942a/2000, 7)

"EVERY ADVANCE TOWARDS LIBERALISM
IN GOVERNMENT AS WELL AS IN
SOCIETY AND RELIGION HAS BEEN
CONNECTED WITH THE ADVANCE OF
SEMANTICS." (PHILIPP FRANK)

While Zilsel's studies in sociology of science have found increasing numbers of readers ever since the 1970s, it remains the case that Philipp Frank's contributions to this topic remain largely neglected. One reason may lie in the fact that the discussion of so-called external factors of theory choice in science tended to focus on Thomas Kuhn and that similar considerations by Frank simply were forgotten.[11]

---

[11] Butts (2000, n. 8) tells the following story. "In 1954, Philipp Frank gave a lecture for the American Academy of Arts and Sciences. In the audience, seated side-by-side, were Tom Kuhn and Adolf Grünbaum. Frank was discussing change in science, progress in science. He stated that if one really wants to understand

Perhaps some reasons may lie also in the facts of the cold war (see the contribution by Reisch in this volume.) This is not unlikely inasmuch as Frank remained the only representative after the deaths of Zilsel and Neurath who stressed the cultural and political relevance of Logical Empiricism and continued to act as a public intellectual.[12] It is important here to note that Frank did not merely place science in its social context but also and especially the philosophy of science. He reconstructed the historical background of logical empiricism itself and stressed that the group which later was called the "first" Vienna Circle took its start very consciously from their own historical context and considered their own developing philosophy of science as a response to the cultural crisis of their day.[13]

After the demise of the mechanical worldview a philosophical theory was no longer available that was able to explain the basis on which natural science could claim objective validity even though it moved further and further away from everyday knowledge. In this they also saw the cause of the increasing superstition and irrationalism of their day. From the start, the task to develop a new

scientific progress, one should consider the example of a woman buying a dress. (These were more generous political times – political correctness meant something quite different than it means now. Senator McCarthy was finding communists everywhere.) The woman will look for a dress that fits properly the changes in her body that have taken place since the last dress was purchased, hopefully at the same time not distorting the good fit of other parts of her body. Thus there are two primary considerations: the dress must fit better than older ones in places that matter, and there must be a better overall fit. Of course some good fit might be lost in the attempt to satisfy the second consideration. So also in science we look for satisfaction of the two considerations, now applied to theories. Often a newly accepted theory has lost some of the explanatory power of its earlier rival. Examples are plentiful. The loss of explanatory power of a theory is now widely referred to as 'Kuhn loss'. Years later, shortly before his death, Adolf reminded Tom of Frank's remarks. Tom Kuhn was shocked. It is Adolf's view that Tom had absorbed the lesson offered by Frank, had repressed conscious memory of it, and had, by some mental trickery, called it into consciousness as his own idea. But now we know the truth: one of the fathers of scientific philosophy actually wrote Kuhn's *The Structure of Scientific Revolutions.*" Grünbaum also recalled this event during discussions at conferences in Vienna in 1991 and 2003.

[12] See Nemeth (2003). For Frank's apparent marginalization in the United States and the few scientists who continued philosophy of science in his sense (Robert S. Cohen, Marx Wartofsky, Gerald Holton, et al.) see Hardcastle and Richardson (2003, xvii–xxi).

[13] For the "first" Vienna Circle see Frank (1941; 1949), Haller (1985), and Uebel (2000b).

conception of scientific knowledge was viewed as a contribution to a cultural project that far transcended the field of philosophy of science itself.

According to Frank already in 1917, Mach's theory of knowledge had to be understood as an intervention in an ongoing cultural discussion. Mach's teaching that all of our concepts are but auxiliary concepts and should be recognized as such was an attempt to renew Enlightenment thinking with particular regard to natural science and to safeguard its social relevance. Precisely for this reason Mach's ideas always were controversial within and outside of science. Positivists were clearly party to such disputes, but often they themselves did not see what consequences these had on science itself. They overlooked that the passion with which scientists defend their views belongs to the nature of science: "the establishment of theories by the positivist wing has been made all too often in empty space, without connections with the total activity of mankind" (1932/1998, 14). Here Frank conceded some justification to Planck's critique of Mach, but he stressed that the impassioned defense of scientific theories was not to be read as expression of a deep metaphysical need. Rather the conflicts suffered, for instance, by Galileo showed that the disputes about a physical theory could well be connected with the political and social developments of the time. "Therefore there is no need to amplify the positivist conception of science by a metaphysical concept of truth but only by a more comprehensive study of the connections that exist between the activity of the invention of theories and the other normal human activities" (ibid.).

For Frank, the study of these sociological connections has a well-defined philosophical basis, namely, the insight that it is not always possible to tie the acceptance of a theory to logical and empirical criteria. This insight is the "most important prerequisite for understanding the role played by sociological factors in the acceptance of scientific doctrines" (1951a, 19). Whenever a scientific "draw" is reached between theories, then the authorities or other social powers will support those that tend to influence the behavior of people in a way that they find desirable:

It is important to learn that the interpretation of a scientific theory as a support of moral rules ... has played a role in all periods of history. This role probably can be traced back to a fact that is well known to modern students of anthropology and sociology. The conduct of man has always been shaped according to the example of ideal society, on the other hand, this ideal has been represented by the 'behavior' of the universe, which is, in turn, determined by the laws of nature, in particular, by physical laws. In this sense, the physical laws have always been interpreted as examples for the conduct of man, or, briefly speaking, moral laws. (1956, 19)

It was precisely this context that David Bloor focused upon when he picked up on the Durkheim-Mauss thesis "that the classification of things reproduces the classification of men" (1982, 267) and made it the basis of the Strong Program in the sociology of science.[14] Frank too thought that the idea "that human society is, in a way, a picture of the universe" (1957, 18) was applicable also to modern science. Still, in the twentieth century a number of very abstract scientific theories (e.g., the theory of relativity and quantum theory) were interpreted as either threats to or as in "support of moral rules" and therefore were considered highly controversial (1951, 155).

Of course, Frank also stressed that modern science altered the conditions for a moral interpretation of the order of nature in a most decisive way. The most important such alteration consisted not in that it drew a new picture of the universe but that it helped promote a new conception of human knowledge. Step by step, philosophical reflection about science came to reject the metaphysical claims that true knowledge uncovers the inner nature of being and that theories represent the pregiven order of existence. It showed rather that theories are due to the constructive power of the human mind to organize the world of experience. This perspective, first formulated by Kant, undercut all pretense to find in theories about the behavior of the universe recipes for individual and social human behavior (ibid., 121–4). Its place was taken by the idea of a continuous cognitive progress that finds its basis not in the order of nature but in the principles of human reason.

Twentieth-century philosophy of science continued this development but revised some central aspects. By stressing that theories are "freely invented" symbolic systems that are interpreted empirically, it created the basis for an interpretation of the progress

[14] For a brief comparison of the similarities and differences between Frank's and Neurath's approach and the Strong Programme see Uebel (2000, S144–9).

of science that did not appeal to unchanging principles of reason. From a philosophical perspective, scientific progress depends on a better understanding of the linguistic frameworks within which alone the concepts employed have a clear meaning (1951, 22–3). Wherever new experiences cannot be brought into congruence with antecedently formulated theories, scientists are forced to reflect on the relation between their concepts and the linguistic framework within which they are defined.[15] Viewed in this way, the continued expansion of human knowledge can be secured only by people who are prepared to analyze the linguistic frameworks within which they have formulated and justified their knowledge claims so far and, if needed, to develop richer languages that allow the theoretical comprehension of an enlarged stock of experiences. Which new experiences will be taken so seriously as to prompt the creation of new frameworks and which theories will be accepted does not depend on some intrinsic logic of discovery but on the manifold connections that exist between the inventors of theories and the "other normal human activities".

For all the closeness of his own thought to Kuhn's, however, Frank stressed different elements. For him the interpretation of the progress of science that twentieth-century philosophy of science made possible was something like a heuristic model with the help of which we can make visible that progress in society and politics also follows the example of "semantic progress".[16] In this sense natural science does provide a social ideal for Frank, but of course not one derived from nature but its own historically progressive practice. It is important that the role of furnishing an ideal does not accrue to science automatically. Frank was far from thinking that some kind of preestablished harmony obtained between scientific and social-political progress (as Popper and Merton would seem to suggest).[17] The most important contribution that science could make to social progress was not, after all, something that scientists

---

[15] For the relationship between "relativism" and "objectivity" in Frank see Nemeth (2003) and Stadler (2004).

[16] Frank analyzed examples from religion and ethics; see (1951, 26–7, 32, 42–3). For the antiracist arguments developed by Frank in this context see Uebel (2003, 103–6).

[17] On the historical context of the "confident connection between liberal democracy and science" in Merton's early writings see Richardson (2003, 76–8).

develop under all circumstances but only when science was taught and conducted in a particular way. This was the ability and pre-paredness to reflect on the guiding conceptions of one's own cog-nitive practice and to critically investigate their justification. In his contributions to the Conference on Science, Philosophy, and Reli-gion (collected in Frank 1951) Frank opposed the trend of the day and defended the view that science was not to be viewed, and taught, as a collection of facts or as specialized knowledge in sharply delimited disciplines or as an end itself. Young scientists should learn first of all to transgress disciplinary boundaries and to confront the philo-sophical questions that such transgressions inevitably give rise to, for instance, the question of what it means to prove a claim (see Nemeth 2003, 129).

From this perspective we can now attempt to spell out the phil-osophical point of the movement for which Frank worked many years as the director of the Institute for the Unity of Science. The point was systematically to create occasions at which scientists were enabled to perceive themselves as active agents, where they become aware that not all decisions that go into the acceptance of theories can be made on the basis of logical or empirical criteria and that therefore the attempt at conscious reflection about the basis of their scientific contention cannot limit itself to just these criteria. Rather, their self-reflection must seek to lay bare the manifold of norms by which the cognitive practice of science is connected to the social, cultural, and political world of their day.[18] Thus philosophy, history, and sociology of science must together become the decisive dimensions of a cognitive practice that takes seriously the insight that its own norms cannot be justified outside of history.

---

[18] Bourdieu's ideas of a "reflexive sociology" (1989) contain remarkable parallels to the program of unified science; on this see Broady 1996. His book *Sociologi och epistemologi. Om Pierre Bourdieus sociologi och den historiska epistemologin* (Stockholm, 1990) unfortunately remains untranslated.

Part Four: Logical Empiricism and Its Critics

12 Wittgenstein, the Vienna Circle, and Physicalism

A Reassessment

INTRODUCTION: THE "STANDARD ACCOUNT" AND ITS LIMITATIONS

The precise nature of Wittgenstein's relationship to the Vienna Circle has been much debated, and there are deep disagreements about the strengths and weaknesses of the different positions attributed to the principal protagonists. However, there has been a widespread consensus about the overall character of the encounter: the early Wittgenstein was an important influence on the founders of logical empiricism, and the later Wittgenstein one of its leading opponents. In other words, the "standard account" of Wittgenstein's relations with the Vienna Circle is that the early Wittgenstein was a principal source and inspiration for the Circle's formulation of its positivistic and scientific philosophy, while the later Wittgenstein was deeply opposed to the logical empiricist project of articulating a "scientific conception of the world."[1]

Earlier versions of this chapter were presented at UC Santa Cruz, the University of British Columbia, the University of Nebraska at Omaha, and the University of Iowa. I would like to thank the members of the audience at those events for their extremely helpful critical comments and suggestions. I am also very grateful to the editors of this volume for their comments on previous drafts.

[1] The first half of the standard account – concerning the influence of the *Tractatus* on the Vienna Circle – can be found in such canonical texts as the Circle's manifesto, first published in 1929, "The Scientific Conception of the World: The Vienna Circle" (Carnap, Hahn, and Neurath 1929), and Ayer's extremely influential expository account in *Language Truth and Logic* (Ayer 1936). For an authoritative recent exposition of the "standard account" from an orthodox Wittgensteinian perspective, see Hacker (1996, ch. 3) and Stern (1999) for a brief response.

In part, the success of the *Tractatus* as a canonical text for twentieth-century philosophy turns on the way it is open to such a wide variety of interpretations: as

However, this telegraphic summary of a complex and intricate relationship is at best only half-true and at worst deeply misleading. For it amounts to an oversimplified template that prevents our appreciating the fluidity and protean character of the philosophical dialogues that took place at the time, both between Wittgenstein and various members of the Vienna Circle, and among the logical empiricists over the value of Wittgenstein's contribution. Furthermore, Wittgenstein's own views changed rapidly and repeatedly during the 1920s and 1930s. Many of the participants in these discussions gave expression to a wide range of different views; taken out of context, their formulation of those views can easily strike a contemporary reader as clear anticipations of positions that are now standard items of philosophical terminology, such as physicalism, verificationism, or a use theory of meaning. Nevertheless, at the time those positions had not been articulated with anything like the degree of clarity that we now take for granted. In retrospectively identifying and attributing clear-cut positions, lines of influence, and axes of disagreement to Wittgenstein and his interlocutors in Cambridge and Vienna, it is very easy to read back our current understanding of familiar terminology and the associated distinctions into a time when those terms were used in a much more open-ended way.

A considerable distance separates contemporary discussion of physicalism from the use of this term in the early 1930s, despite the terminological similarities. While there is general agreement that physicalism requires that all significant languages are translatable into a physical language, there is considerable room for

the work of Russell's student, as a contribution to the philosophy of mathematics, or logic, as a work of positivist epistemology, as a contribution to ontology, as a book with an ethical point, as mystical, or as self-undermining nonsense. In Stern (2003), I argued for an alternative approach to the history of *Tractatus* reception, based on the proposal that we should attend to the conditions that made it possible for such a very wide variety of different approaches to *Tractatus* interpretation to have been in the forefront at different times since its publication in 1922. From that perspective, this chapter focuses on the initial reception of the *Tractatus* in Vienna. However, as soon as Wittgenstein began to talk to Schlick and his Circle, the relationship takes on at least two further dimensions: we have to consider the ways in which Wittgenstein responded to them, and we have to consider the ways in which their views changed over time. As soon as we zoom in to Vienna in the late 1920s, all of the issues that unfold piecemeal in the subsequent scholarly work on the topic are already in the air.

disagreement, both about what makes a language suitably physical as well as about what counts as a translation, or a reduction of one language to another. For present purposes, we need only consider the distance beween contemporary views about the nature of the translation involved. First, most current treatments are in terms of supervenience, an approach that was first popularized by Davidson (1970); previous debate was usually framed in terms of one form of reductionism or another. However, even classic type-type reductionism, often taken as the starting point for contemporary exposition, is first set out in Smart (1959), whose work also provided a point of departure for the emergence of functionalist token-token reductionism in the 1960s. The form of midcentury reductionism that most closely corresponds to the approach advocated by Carnap is the relationship of intertheoretic reduction, which was given its classic formulation by Nagel (1961). However, Nagel's systematic program of logically deriving one theory from another by means of bridge laws is far more sophisticated than Carnap's 1932 proposal, which amounted to little more than a series of examples of proposed physicalistic translations of problematic protocol statements.[2] While Carnap's paper was much more argumentative than Neurath's previous work on the topic, there was very little detailed analysis of the relationship between protocol statements and physical language. Indeed, at one point in his paper Carnap says that *"pseudo-questions are automatically eliminated"* (Carnap 1934a, 83; 1932b, 456, italics in original) by using the "formal mode" of speech. This is a concise summary of a *Tractatus*-inspired approach, namely, dissolving philosophical questions by clarifying syntax, in contrast with Carnap's mature view, also present in the same paper: namely, solving philosophical problems by means of an analysis of the relevant syntax and semantics. In other words, the "standard account" is not only far too simple to do justice to the historical phenomena; it is also anachronistic.[3]

---

[2] For a good introduction to the current literature on physicalism, see Stoljar (2005). For an introduction to what has become known as the "Received View" of scientific theories, and its evolution from Carnap's early formulations over the next quarter century or so, see Suppe (1977, 3–61).

[3] For further discussion of my objections to the "standard account," see Stern (2004, ch. 2) on the relationship between the *Tractatus* and the *Philosophical*

Published primary materials documenting the meetings, conversations, and correspondence from this period now provide us with a considerable quantity of information about Wittgenstein's contacts with the early logical empiricists; the last 20 years have seen a remarkable growth in the detail and sophistication of the philosophical and historical literature on this period.[4] However, very little of this scholarship has reached an audience beyond the relatively narrow circle of experts on early analytic philosophy and the history of early-twentieth-century philosophy of science. Because most scholars of the period have assumed that the framework provided by the standard account can accommodate the mass of new information concerning Wittgenstein's relationship with the early logical empiricists, the extent to which the new archival materials provide compelling grounds for rejecting the standard account put forward by the first and second generation of interpreters has rarely been appreciated. Furthermore, the animosity, competitiveness, and mutual misunderstanding that were important aspects of the debates between the principal figures has frequently been reproduced in the literature on this topic, instead of providing a topic for critical analysis. Indeed, most recent work on the history of this encounter is clearly identifiable as a defense of one or another of the original protagonists. It is precisely because the philosophical debates that took place in Vienna 70 or 80 years ago concerned the initial formulation of positions that are still debated today that contemporary readers are so ready to argue about the history of those debates. Yet for that very reason, it is often extremely difficult for us to appreciate the distance that separates twenty-first-century philosophy from the issues that engaged the founders of logical

---

Investigations, and Stern (2005) for a more polemical approach to the difficulties generated by talk of "early" and "late" Wittgenstein.

[4] The principal primary source for information on Wittgenstein's conversations with the Vienna Circle is Waismann (1967), which is based on Waismann's shorthand notes of meetings with Wittgenstein from 1929 to 1932. We do not have a comparable record of the content of their earlier meetings. Wittgenstein and Waismann (2003) provides a collection of verbatim transcriptions of dictations and discussions with Wittgenstein together with Waismann's redrafting of material provided by Wittgenstein, dating from 1928 to 1939. Among the most prominent books in the literature on Wittgenstein's relationship with the logical empiricists are: Baker (1988), Coffa (1991), Friedman (1999), Hacker (1996), Haller (1988), Hintikka and Hintikka (1986), McGuinness (2002), Stadler (2001).

empiricism, or the interpretive pitfalls that can lead us to turn that complex and multifaceted engagement into a simple story of progress from crude beginnings to contemporary philosophical sophistication. Indeed, some of the most important developments in the recent scholarship on the history of this period have been studies that have mapped out the role of post-Kantian conceptions of logic and experience in Carnap's *Aufbau* and the role of early-twentieth-century physics and engineering in Wittgenstein's *Tractatus*. (On the *Aufbau*, see Coffa 1985; 1991; Friedman 1999; Richardson 1998. On the *Tractatus*, see Hamilton 2001; 2001a; 2002; Hide 2004; Lampert 2003; Spelt and McGuinness 2001; Sterrett 2002. For a critical review of this literature, see Nordmann 2002.)

The aim of this chapter, in the spirit of this recent work on the history of early analytic philosophy, is to provide a broader perspective on the nature of the overall debate between Wittgenstein and his interlocutors in the Vienna Circle, starting from their own understanding of their respective positions. Those positions emerge more clearly, I believe, if we attend closely to the details of what they had to say at the time about specific areas of agreement and disagreement. Too often, the programmatic statements about the nature of their work that are repeated in manifestos, introductions, and elementary textbooks have occupied center stage in the subsequent secondary literature. Consequently, after a brief survey of the principal stages of Wittgenstein's relations with the Vienna Circle, we turn to a more detailed examination of a turning point in their relationship. That turning point is Wittgenstein's charge, in the summer of 1932, that a recently published paper of Carnap's, "Physicalistic Language as the Universal Language of Science," made such extensive and unacknowledged use of Wittgenstein's own ideas that Wittgenstein would, as he put it in a letter to Schlick, "soon be in a situation where my own work shall be considered merely as a reheated version or plagiarism of Carnap's."[5]

---

[5] Letter from Wittgenstein to Schlick, May 6, 1932; translation from Hintikka (1989/ 1996, 131): "Und nun werde ich bald in der Lage sein, daß meine eigene Arbeit als bloßer zweiter Aufguß oder als Plagiat der Carnapschen angesehen werden wird." While I will cite and make use of published translations of Wittgenstein's correspondence, the German text of all these letters is now available in Wittgenstein (2004), together with an extensive apparatus.

WITTGENSTEIN'S CONTACTS WITH
MEMBERS OF THE VIENNA CIRCLE:
A BRIEF CHRONOLOGY

We can distinguish three distinct phases in the development of
Wittgenstein's influence on the early logical empiricists. First, the
Vienna Circle repeatedly read and discussed the *Tractatus* in the
early and mid-1920s. The second phase, Wittgenstein's informal
conversations with Schlick and his friends in the late 1920s, began
when Schlick and Wittgenstein met in early 1927, and ended with
Wittgenstein's return to Cambridge at the beginning of 1929. Third,
there was a series of more formal meetings with Schlick and Waismann during 1929–34, with the aim of producing a book setting out
Wittgenstein's philosophy, which continued, in an attenuated form,
until Schlick's death in 1936.

1919–1926

In 1919 Wittgenstein was discharged from the Monte Cassino pris-
oner-of-war camp and finished his work on the book he had written
while he was a soldier in the Austro-Hungarian army. He returned
home to Vienna, convinced that he would do no more philosophical
work. After completing a teacher-training program, he spent the first
half of the 1920s teaching in small village schools in the region. In
1921 the first edition of the *Tractatus Logico-Philosophicus* was
published in German under the title *Logisch-philosophische
Abhandlung* (Logico-Philosophical Treatise) in the last volume of
Ostwald's journal *Annalen der Naturphilosophie*. The first Routledge edition, with the preface by Bertrand Russell and an English
translation by C. K. Ogden and Frank Ramsey, was published two
years later in 1923. Wittgenstein's career as a teacher ended in the
spring of 1926; in the summer of that year, he began work as an
architect on a house for his sister, Margarethe Stonborough, a project
that was to occupy him for the next two years. (For a much fuller
account of these years, see Monk 1990, chs. 8–10.)

In 1922 Moritz Schlick was appointed Professor of Natural Philosophy at the University of Vienna. That year, Hans Hahn, a
mathematician at the University, held a seminar, primarily focused
on Russell and Whitehead's *Principia Mathematica*, attended by

Schlick and Kurt Reidemeister, another mathematician, at which the *Tractatus* was discussed. In the fall of 1924, Schlick began an interdisciplinary discussion group, the Schlick Circle, which can, in retrospect, be seen as the beginning of the Vienna Circle. The group included Reidemeister, Hahn, Otto Neurath, his wife, Olga Hahn-Neurath, Felix Kaufmann, a legal theorist, Friedrich Waismann, Schlick's assistant and librarian, and Herbert Feigl, a student of Schlick's; it was joined by Rudolf Carnap during the second semester (Stadler 2001, 199). During the 1924–5 academic year, the Schlick Circle read a large part of the *Tractatus* aloud, discussing it "sentence by sentence" (Carnap 1963, 24). In December 1924 Schlick wrote to Wittgenstein, expressing his admiration for the *Tractatus* and asking for an opportunity to visit him and received a very friendly answer in January. (The letter is quoted in McGuinness's introduction to Waismann 1967, 13.) However, although Schlick wrote back a few days later, reaffirming his intention of visiting, it was not until April 1926 that he attempted to visit Wittgenstein, by which time Wittgenstein had given up his teaching position. Schlick's wife recalled that he approached the visit "as if he was preparing to go on holy pilgrimage ... he explained to me, almost with awesome reverence, that Wittgenstein was one of the greatest geniuses on earth" (letter from Blanche Schlick to Friedrich von Hayek, quoted and translated in Nedo 1983, 194 and 375). Subsequently, Schlick sent Wittgenstein some of his work and suggested a meeting with one or two other people to discuss logical problems, but did not receive a reply.

During this period, the Schlick Circle knew of Wittgenstein only as the author of the *Tractatus* and Russell's student. The principal ideas that they took from their readings of his book can be summed up under two headings. First, they were inspired by his focus on the nature of language, and the idea that the structure of language, and of the language of different areas of inquiry, could be analyzed by applying the tools provided by modern logic. Second, Wittgenstein's *Tractatus* offered an approach to logic which offered some hope of doing justice to the Kantian request that we give an account of the necessity of the truths of logic, and of the deep difference between truths of logic and truths about matters of fact, without giving up on a thorough-going empiricism, or invoking the problematic notion of synthetic a priori truth. One can read the *Tractatus* as proposing that logical truths, and perhaps even parts of mathematics, are true in virtue of meaning, and so analytic, in a suitably accommodating understanding of that term.

While parts of the *Tractatus* struck the Circle as very promising, and were seized upon for members' own work, other parts could not easily be accommodated to their positivistic program. Indeed, the *Tractatus* is open to a number of very different readings, depending on which parts of the text one regards as central, and which parts one considers peripheral.[6] From the first, Neurath was deeply suspicious of the ontology of facts with which the book begins, which struck him as a relic of traditional metaphysics, and the mysticism with which it concludes. Schlick and Waismann, who were enormously impressed by Wittgenstein, would soon take on the role of his representatives and interpreters within the Circle. Other members of the group, including Carnap, occupied the middle ground, prepared to learn from Wittgenstein, yet critical of many of his ideas, and especially what they considered to be the leading, yet deeply suspect, role of the "unsayable" in the *Tractatus*.

1927–1928

In February 1927 Mrs. Stonborough wrote to Schlick, explaining that while Wittgenstein felt unable to meet with a group to discuss the topics Schlick had proposed, he did think that "if it were with you alone ... he might be able to discuss such matters. It would then become apparent, he thinks, whether he is at present at all capable of being of use to you in this connexion" (quoted by McGuinness in the introduction to Waismann 1967, 14). Subsequently, Schlick was invited to lunch; his wife reported that he once again had the "reverential attitude of the pilgrim. He returned in an ecstatic state, saying little, and I felt I should not ask questions" (ibid.). While Wittgenstein told Engelmann, with whom he was collaborating on the building of his sister's house, that "each of us thought the other must be mad" in that first conversation, a series of meetings between the two of them soon followed at which they established a good mutual understanding (McGuinness, in the introduction to Waismann 1967, 15).

---

[6] For further discussion of the variety of different ways of reading the *Tractatus*, see Stern (2003).

By the summer of 1927, Waismann had become a regular participant in these meetings, and Carnap joined them on five occasions
that summer; Herbert Feigl and his fiancée, Maria Kaspar, were also
regular participants. Before their first meeting, Schlick warned
Carnap that he should be very restrained, avoiding debate and direct
questions: "the best approach, Schlick said, would be to let Wittgenstein talk and then ask only very cautiously for the necessary
elucidations" (Carnap 1963, 25).[7] When Carnap met Wittgenstein,
he saw that "Schlick's warnings were fully justified. ... His point of
view and his attitude towards people and problems, even theoretical
problems, were much more similar to those of a creative artist than
to those of a scientist; one might almost say, similar to those of a
religious prophet or a seer. ...[It] was as if insight came to him
through a divine inspiration, so that we could not help feeling that
any sober rational comment or analysis of it would be a profanation"
(Carnap 1963, 25–6). At that first meeting, Schlick, despite the
advice he had given Carnap beforehand, unfortunately brought up
the topic of Carnap's enthusiasm for Esperanto. Carnap was not
surprised that Wittgenstein was opposed, but he was surprised by his
vehemence. "A language which had not 'grown organically' seemed
to him not only useless but despicable" (Carnap 1963, 26). Afterwards, Carnap described Wittgenstein in his diary as "a very interesting, original, and attractive person."[8]

Wittgenstein had a number of further meetings with Schlick,
Waismann, and Feigl during 1927–8, although Carnap was away
from Vienna in the winter and did not rejoin the group. While we do
have some brief reports of what went on at the meetings that took
place between Wittgenstein, Schlick, "and a few carefully chosen
members of Schlick's Circle" (Monk 1990, 243), there is no detailed
record of what was said in their discussions, which covered topics

---

[7] Carnap's discussion there of Wittgenstein's influence on him and the Vienna Circle
(Carnap 1963, 24–9) is remarkably judicious.

[8] Carnap also characterized Wittgenstein as having an "artistic nature" (Künst-
lernatur), which McGuinness wry observes implies that he "has to be handled with
care" (McGuinness 1991/2002, 189). McGuinness's particularly informative
account of Wittgenstein's "Relations with and within the Circle" (1991/2002,
ch. 17) is unusual for the extent to which the author gives even-handed attention to
the views of the various parties involved. Carnap's diary notes for three of the
meetings in the summer of 1927 are quoted at greater length in Stadler (2001, 428).

such as the foundations of mathematics and of Ramsey's work on identity. Wittgenstein also read to them, once from Wilhelm Busch and another time from Rabindranath Tagore, with his back to the group "because he did not want to see their expressions as he read" (Feigl, quoted in McGuinness 2002, 189). Perhaps the principal lesson that the members of the Vienna Circle learned from these meetings was that Wittgenstein was not as unambiguously opposed to religion and metaphysics as they were. Carnap reports that prior to their meeting, "when we were reading Wittgenstein's book in the [Vienna] Circle, I had erroneously believed that his attitudes to metaphysics were similar to ours. I had not paid sufficient attention to the statements in his book about the mystical, because his feelings and thoughts in this area were too divergent from mine. Only personal contact with him helped me to see more clearly his attitude on this point" (Carnap 1963, 27).

Wittgenstein never attended a formal Thursday night meeting of the Schlick Circle. However, he did go to a lecture given by L. E. J. Brouwer, an eminent Dutch mathematician, on "Mathematics, Science, and Language" in March 1928 that was attended by other members of the Circle. According to Feigl, who spent several hours with Wittgenstein and Waismann in a café after the lecture, Wittgenstein had until then been reluctant to discuss philosophy, and had to be persuaded to go, but "it was fascinating to behold the change" that evening: "he became extremely voluble and began sketching ideas that were the beginning of his later writings ... that evening marked the return of Wittgenstein to strong philosophical interests and activities" (Feigl, quoted in Pitcher 1964, 8, n. 8).

1929–1936

In the autumn of 1928, Wittgenstein's work on his sister's house ended. In January 1929 he visited John Maynard Keynes in Cambridge and decided to stay on to do some further philosophical work. The eight-week academic terms allowed plenty of time for extensive visits to Vienna during the vacations. Early that year, Wittgenstein decided that he would meet only with Schlick and Waismann; with Wittgenstein's encouragement, Waismann planned to write a popular exposition of Wittgenstein's philosophy based on these discussions. Wittgenstein's own views were constantly changing and developing during these years, and with the possible exception of Waismann, most of his interlocutors were primarily interested in making use of his ideas for their own work. Each of these ideas takes on a wide variety of different forms, and formulations, in the hands of the figures who took part in this discussion. For instance, in his conversations with members of the Vienna Circle in the late 1920s, Wittgenstein introduced the notion of a principle of verification: the idea, roughly speaking, that the meaning of an empirical claim consists in what would confirm, or provide evidence for, that claim. Carnap's memoir speaks of "Wittgenstein's principle of verifiability" (Carnap 1963, 45); in 1930 both Moore and Waismann recorded Wittgenstein as saying that "the sense of a proposition is the way in which it is verified" (Moore, in Wittgenstein 1993, 59; Waismann 1967, 79), and further development of the view can be found in the contemporaneous *Philosophical Remarks*.[9] Later on, Wittgenstein would say that questions about verification are just one way of talking about how words are used (see, e.g., Wittgenstein 1953, I, § 353), but his earlier pronouncements are much more dogmatic.

Waismann's extensive and carefully dated notes of their meetings, the manuscripts based on his work with Wittgenstein, and the book that he ultimately wrote based on this collaboration provide us with a detailed record of various stages of their relationship (Waismann 1967; 1997; Wittgenstein and Waismann 2003; Baker 1979 is an extremely informative introduction to their relationship). The earlier material, a systematic digest of Wittgenstein's ideas, presumably provided the basis for Waismann's regular reports on Wittgenstein's views at the Vienna Circle's meetings, which, we are told, were prefaced by the disclaimer "I shall relate to you the latest developments in Wittgenstein's thinking but Wittgenstein rejects all responsibility for my formulations. Please note that" (Janik and Veigl 1998, 63).[10]

---

[9] See Wittgenstein (1964, §§ 59, 150, 160, 225, 232). For a valuable essay on Wittgenstein and the Vienna Circle on verification, which includes an appraisal of the previous literature on the topic, see Hymers (2005).

[10] Waismann also played the role of a representative of Wittgenstein's views in the papers he presented at international conferences in Prague (1929) and Königsberg (1930). This chapter of Janik and Veigl's book provides an informative discussion of how class and social status influenced the outcome of the subsequent controversy.

Waismann's work on the book can be divided into several distinct phases. During the first phase, from the late 1920s to 1931, he planned to write a comprehensive introduction to Wittgenstein's philosophy, incorporating the leading ideas of the *Tractatus* and Wittgenstein's more recent work into a systematic exposition. In 1930 Waismann's projected volume, *Logic, Language, Philosophy*, was advertised in *Erkenntnis* as the first volume in a series of books setting out the views of the Vienna Circle. However, Wittgenstein became increasingly unhappy with the plan, writing to Schlick on November 20, 1931, that he was "convinced that Waismann would present *many* things in a form *completely* different from what I take to be correct" (quoted by Baker in the preface to Wittgenstein and Waismann 2003, xxvii). Matters came to a head on December 9, when Wittgenstein met with Waismann to discuss "Theses," a summary of Waismann's interpretation of his philosophy. (The "Theses" are Appendix B of Waismann 1967, 233–61; they are discussed on pp. 182–6.) Characteristically, Wittgenstein repudiated not only the details of Waismann's exposition, but also its very title, insisting that none of his philosophy consisted in formulating theses (Waismann 1967, 183). It is this fundamental disagreement, or misunderstanding, that was to be the single biggest obstacle in Wittgenstein's attempts at collaboration with Waismann on a systematic exposition of his ideas, even when no more than a restatement of what Wittgenstein had said (Waismann 1967) or an arrangement of what Wittgenstein dictated to Waismann (Wittgenstein and Waismann 2003), for it still failed to capture the point of what Wittgenstein was trying to do with these ideas.

Wittgenstein criticized both the *Tractatus* and the "Theses" for their "dogmatism": they claim that a logical analysis of ordinary language into elementary propositions is possible, but do not carry it out.[11] Instead of conceiving of philosophy as a matter of searching for an analysis of our language, Wittgenstein now characterized it as a matter of clarifying our current grasp of language, in terms that anticipate some of his most famous later statements about the

---

[11] For further discussion of Wittgenstein's response to the *Theses* and "dogmatism," see Stern (1995, 101–4) and Stern (2004, 48).

nature of philosophy,[12] and connect them with the method recommended towards the end of the *Tractatus:*

As regards your Theses, I once wrote, If there were theses in philosophy, they would have to be such that they do not give rise to disputes. For they would have to be put in such a way that everyone would say, Oh yes, that is of course obvious. ... I once wrote, The only correct way method of doing philosophy consists in not saying anything and leaving it to another person to make a claim.[13] That is the method I now adhere to. (Waismann 1967, 183–4)

This breakdown led to a second phase, roughly from 1932 to 1934, during which Wittgenstein became a co-author of a book that would no longer provide an account of a modified Tractarian approach, but rather set out his new philosophy, largely in his own words, as dictated to Waismann. During this period Waismann also had access to much of Wittgenstein's work in progress, and they met frequently. However, this plan ultimately foundered towards the end of 1934, because Wittgenstein was, as Waismann put it in a letter to Schlick written in August of that year, "always following up the inspiration of the moment and demolishing what he has previously sketched out."[14] This led to a third phase, in which Wittgenstein withdrew from the project, leaving Waismann and Schlick to proceed with the book as they wished, and Waismann's regular meetings with Wittgenstein ceased. Subsequently, Wittgenstein broke off contact with Waismann, warned his students about Waismann's interpretation of his work, and even advised them not to attend Waismann's courses (Janik and Veigl 1998, 66). While Wittgenstein's connection with the Vienna Circle came to an end only with Schlick's murder in June 1936, it is unlikely that the other members of the Circle learned much about the development of Wittgenstein's work after the end of 1934.

---

[12] "If one wanted to establish *theses* in philosophy, no debate about them could ever arise, because everyone would be in agreement with them" (Wittgenstein 2005, § 89, 309). Cf. Wittgenstein (1953, § 128).

[13] McGuinness, who translated this passage, notes that this is a rough statement of *Tractatus* 6.53.

[14] Cited in Baker's introduction to Wittgenstein and Waismann (2003, xxvii); the preface provides more detailed information about the various stages of the book project.

WITTGENSTEIN AND CARNAP ON PHYSICALISM

In early May 1932, Wittgenstein received an offprint of Carnap's paper "Die physikalische Sprache als Universalsprache der Wissenschaft" (Physical Language as the Universal Language of Science; Carnap 1932b). Carnap's paper was translated into English by Max Black and published in 1934 as a small book under a new title: *The Unity of Science*. The shorter, more accessible, title was clearly a better choice for a popular book than the original scholarly title. However, Black did translate and rephrase the title of the paper inside the book, turning the original's talk of "physical language as the universal language of science" into "Physics as a Universal Science" (Carnap 1934a, 31). This choice of words is doubly flawed. First, the translation turns a title in the formal mode of speech – a claim about the grammar, or syntax, of our language – into one in the material mode – a claim about the world. Second, a crucial question left open by the talk of "physical language" – whether physical language is to be narrowly identified with the language of physics, or to be understood more broadly as any language that refers to physical objects – is resolved by the new translation in favor of the narrow reading.

The paper proved to be a turning point in the movement away from phenomenalistic analyses of scientific language: one of the first, and one of the most influential, papers arguing for the physicalistic thesis that any significant language must be translatable into an entirely physical vocabulary. While the paper is a defense of physicalism, the terms "physicalism" and *"Physikalismus,"* first used in print by Otto Neurath during the previous year, do not occur in Carnap (1932b), except in a footnote where he cites some of these works of Neurath's (Carnap 1934a, 74n; Carnap 1932b, 452n).[15] Although the thesis of physicalism is already stated in papers of Neurath's published in 1931, he provides very little by way of an argumentative defense of the thesis (Neurath 1931a; see also Neurath 1931c and 1931b). In the papers Neurath published that year, Neurath advocated materialism without metaphysics: "unified

---

[15] The former term occurs in the title of Neurath (1931b), the latter in the titles of (1931a) and (1932a). Because of an oversight, corrected in the English translation, Neurath (1931a) is not cited in the German original. Indeed, the citations were included only after Neurath complained to Carnap that an earlier draft did not acknowledge his contribution.

science on a materialistic basis," as Haller puts it (Haller 1989, 20). In other words, Neurath puts forward the view that there is only one kind of object: physical objects, the objects that are studied by the sciences. Carnap's main aim in his 1932 paper on physicalism was to put that view on a firm philosophical foundation, by showing how it could be articulated within a program of analysis of the structure of our language – what would soon be called "logical syntax," but which Carnap also spoke of as "metalogic."

Carnap makes extensive use of the distinction between the "material" and "formal" modes of speech: "The first speaks of 'objects,' 'states of affairs,' of the 'sense,' 'content' or 'meaning' of words, while the second refers only to linguistic forms" (Carnap 1934a, 38; Carnap 1932b, 435). A footnote attached to the end of that sentence promises that "A strictly formal theory of linguistic forms ('logical syntax') will be developed later." A sentence added to the footnote in the 1934 translation identifies "the book here announced" as *The Logical Syntax of Language*. However, the original German for the parenthetical phrase is not "logische Syntax," but "Metalogik," more naturally translated as "metalogic." In 1932 Carnap used the two more or less interchangably and had not yet settled on "logical syntax" as his preferred term; thus while the translation is linguistically odd, it does have a certain consistency.[16] Both terms would have attracted Wittgenstein's attention. Logical syntax is the Tractarian term for the rules of a sign-language that is "governed by *logical* grammar" (*Tractatus* 3.325; the expression is also used in 3.33, 3.334, 3.344, and 6.124), Wittgenstein's proposed replacement for Frege and Russell's goal of a *Begriffschrift*, or "conceptual notation." The term "metalogic" does not occur in Wittgenstein's earliest writing, but during 1931–3 he repeatedly speaks of it in dismissive terms: the first page of the *Big Typescript* states that "just as there is no metaphysics, there is no metalogic" (Wittgenstein 2005, 2; see also 3, 13, 158, 220, 223, 305). While it is debatable precisely what Wittgenstein meant by that term, it is clear that Wittgenstein rejects the very idea of metalogic, treating it as an expression of the idea that one can take up a "sideways on" stance

---

[16] Talk of "logical syntax" highlights the idea that Carnap proposed a systematic study of the structure of language; talk of "metalogic" draws our attention to the "second order" character of the project.

from which one can appraise the relationship between language and the world.[17]

Throughout the paper, Carnap draws our attention to the distinction between the material and the formal mode of speech, using a double column layout to simultanously set out problematic claims in both "modes." The paper proceeds by identifying a number of different languages. "Protocol language," or "primary language," is used to describe "directly given experience of phenomena" (material mode) or more carefully speaking, "statements needing no justification and serving as foundations for all the remaining statements of science"(formal mode) (Carnap 1934a, 45; 1932b, 438). The simplest statements in physical language are initially introduced as those that specify a "quantitatively determined property of a definite position at a definite time" (material mode) or attaching to "a specific set of co-ordinates ... a definite value or range of values of a coefficient of physical state" (formal mode) (Carnap 1934a, 52–3; 1932b, 441). Carnap qualifies this by acknowledging that future developments in physics may well lead to modifications, but maintains that all that matters for present purposes is that however it is modified, statements in protocol language will remain translatable into physical language. Most of the remainder of the paper is devoted to arguing that "every scientific statement can be translated into physical language" and responding to objections to his claim that "statements in protocol language ... can be translated into physical language" (Carnap 1934a, 76; 1932b, 453).

On May 6, 1932, very shortly after he had received Carnap's offprint, Wittgenstein wrote to Schlick, setting out his initial response. He expressed his concern that Carnap's use of his own unpublished work was so extensive that others would regard his own work, when it was eventually published, as no more than "a reheated version or plagiarism of Carnap's" (letter from Wittgenstein to Schlick, May 6, 1932; translation from Hintikka 1989/1996, 131). He went on to

---

[17] Hilmy (1987, ch. 2) argues that the rejection of "the metalogical" plays a central role in Wittgenstein's turn towards ordinary language in his post-*Tractatus* writings. Hilmy conjectures that Wittgenstein's principal target in his critique of metalogic is work written after the *Tractatus*, but before the first surviving post-*Tractatus* manuscripts, which date from the beginning of 1929.

express a strongly proprietorial approach to what he clearly regarded as the fruit of his own labor:

I see myself as drawn against my will into what is called "the Vienna Circle." In that Circle there prevails a community of property, so that I could e.g. use Carnap's ideas if *I wanted to* but he could also use mine. But I don't *want* to join forces with Carnap and to belong to a circle to which he belongs. If I have an apple tree in my garden, then it delights me and serves the purpose of the tree if my *friends (e.g. you & Waismann)* make use of the apples; I will *not* chase away thieves that climb over the fence, but I am entitled to resent that they are posing as my friends or alleging that the tree should belong to them jointly. (Letter from Wittgenstein to Schlick, May 6, 1932; translation based on Hintikka 1989/1996, 131)

For half a century, this controversy was not discussed in the literature on Wittgenstein and the Vienna Circle. Carnap did include a discussion of it in a draft of his intellectual autobiography, but it was not included in the published version. There he wrote that

Years later, some of Wittgenstein's students at Cambridge asked him for permission to send transcripts of his lectures to friends and interested philosophers. He asked to see the list of names, and then approved all but my own. In my entire life, I have never experienced anything similar to this hatred directed against me. I have no adequate explanation; probably only a psychoanalyst could offer one. (Carnap, quoted in Stadler 2001, 433–4)

After substantial excerpts from Wittgenstein's correspondence in 1932 with Schlick and Carnap on the topic were published in Nedo and Ranccheti (1983, 254–5, 381–2), Wittgenstein's accusations received the attention of a number of leading experts on the history of early analytic philosophy, including Coffa (1991, 407–8), Haller (1988a; 1989; 1990), Hintikka (1989), Hintikka and Hintikka (1986, 145–7), McGuinness (1985, 1991), Monk (1990, 324), Pears (1988, 302–3, 316), Stadler (1992; 2002, 429–48), and Uebel (1995). (For a longer list of authors who have discussed this priority dispute, see Uebel [1995, 348–9]; the paper provides a thorough review of the literature on the topic up to the mid-1990s.) However, Wittgenstein's *Prioritätstreit* with Carnap is far less well known than his falling out with Popper (Edmonds and Eidinow 2001), despite the fact that we know far more about the positions on either side in the Wittgenstein-Carnap controversy. Indeed, a couple of recent pieces on the origins of physicalism not only take it for granted that "the word *physicalism*, when introduced into philosophical conversation by Neurath and Carnap, seemed theirs to define" (Gates 2001, 251) but do not even mention Wittgenstein's claims (Gates 2001; Manninen 2003).

While Wittgenstein's initial letter to Schlick expressed his immediate outrage at what he considered the wholesale appropriation of his ideas, he did not further specify what he considered Carnap had stolen. Instead, Schlick took on the task. (See the discussion of this chronology in Hintikka 1989/1996, 134–5.) A little over two months later, Schlick wrote to Carnap, saying that he considered it "necessary to mention Wittgenstein by name, time and again when it comes to points specific to him and characteristic of his way of thinking, especially as he has himself published nothing for quite awhile and instead circulated his ideas orally" (letter from Schlick to Carnap, July 10, 1932; translation from Hintikka 1996, 134). Schlick listed the following points on which he considered an acknowledgement appropriate:

1. top of p. 433 (the nature of philosophy); [Carnap 1934a, p. 33]
2. bottom of p. 435 and following (ostensive defining does not lead us outside language); [Carnap 1934a, p. 39ff.]
3. top of p. 440 (the character of laws of nature, where hypotheses are characterized by means of their peculiar logical form, which differs from ordinary propositions); [Carnap 1934a, pp. 48–9]
4. furthermore the passages where pseudo-problems are eliminated by means of the "formal mode of speech" (p. 452, note, p. 456), for in fact this is after all W[ittgenstein]'s basic idea. [Carnap 1934a, footnote on p. 74; pp. 82–4] (Letter from Schlick to Carnap, July 10, 1932; translation from Hintikka 1989/1996, 134. I am responsible for adding the numbering and the cross-references to the English text.)

This list is our best evidence as to which parts of the paper Wittgenstein regarded as "stolen apples," as Hintikka puts it. But if we go back to Wittgenstein's first letter to Schlick, we can add a number of further charges to these particular points of alleged indebtedness:

5. the claim that physicalism is in the *Tractatus*;
6. the allegation that Carnap's work is so similar to Wittgenstein's that Wittgenstein would look as if he had taken his ideas from Carnap

Perhaps what is most striking about Wittgenstein's dispute with Carnap is the last item on this list: Wittgenstein's insistence that Carnap's work was so close to his own. For Wittgenstein's usual response to those who made use of his ideas in print, including Waismann's explicitly expository project, was to complain that his work had been misrepresented, or misunderstood.

However, assessing such a charge of unacknowledged intellectual indebtedness is a much more complex matter than it is in any case of petty theft or plagiarism. The criteria of identity for a conception of ostensive definition, the laws of nature, physicalism, or the nature of philosophy, are legitimate topics of philosophical debate in their own right. Given a suitably coarse-grained summary of Wittgenstein's and Carnap's positions on each of these topics, they are strikingly similar; given a suitably fine-grained reconstruction, the differences between them may seem much more important. Wittgenstein's defenders have highlighted the similarities; Carnap's defenders have emphasized their differences.

Not only is it extremely difficult to establish when one person has taken an idea from another, but even if one assumes, for the sake of argument, that those facts have been settled, the standards of appropriate behavior are much less clear-cut than they are in the case of taking an apple from someone else's tree, or using another's words without citation. Indeed, in this case, one could well argue that Wittgenstein, despite his protestations to the contrary, had effectively invited the Vienna Circle to make use of his ideas. For he had agreed to provide a steady stream of expository material to Waismann and Schlick, on the explicit understanding that Waismann would serve as his representative and devote his energies to writing a book setting out Wittgenstein's work. Thus, there is good reason to maintain that even if Wittgenstein's claims about the extent of Carnap's indebtedness had been entirely correct, his vehement request for a detailed acknowledgment would have been unjustified.

Furthermore, it is not unusual for a philosopher to be extremely sensitive about others using his work, yet much less ready to acknowledge his own use of another's ideas. Wittgenstein rarely referred to other philosophers' work in his own writings, and expressed a positively cavalier attitude towards such matters in the Preface to the *Tractatus*, where he wrote that the book gave no sources "because it is indifferent to me whether what I have thought has already been thought by another."[18] Surely, Carnap was equally indifferent about his sources when he sent his paper to Wittgenstein. Indeed, it was only after Neurath read an earlier draft of the paper and complained that his prior work on physicalism should be cited, work that he and Carnap had discussed at length for several years, that Carnap inserted the footnote referring to Neurath's previous publications on physicalism.[19]

Because the six complaints of Wittgenstein's listed above range from points of detail to very general questions of method, it will be helpful to arrange them into three broadly related groups. First, there are quite specific ideas which Wittgenstein alleges were taken from his own work (items 2 and 3). Second, there are very broad methodological considerations (items 1, 4, and 6). Finally, there is the intermediate-level claim that Carnap's physicalism is already in the *Tractatus*.

Consider first items 2 and 3, which are both relatively small and specific. Hintikka has little trouble showing that the passages on these topics in Carnap's paper, cited in Schlick's letter, are very close to a summary statement of Wittgenstein's own ideas at the time about ostension and hypotheses, as set out in his meetings with Schlick and Waismann at the time. Furthermore, Carnap could have heard such ideas summarized by Waismann in his presentations to the Vienna Circle (Hintikka 1989/1996, 139–41).[20] So it is not difficult to see how Wittgenstein could have taken umbrage over those passages. However, that hardly shows that Carnap did develop his own views out of what he had gleaned from Waismann rather than working out something like those ideas for himself, drawing on

---

[18] Wittgenstein's thoughts about influence and originality are much more complicated, and interesting, than this overly brief summary can convey. For further discussion of Wittgenstein's discussion of originality and talent, see Monk (1990), Stern (2000), McGuinness (2002).

[19] For a more detailed discussion of Neurath's priority claim, and its relationship to Wittgenstein's, see Uebel (1995, 334, 341–4).

[20] Hintikka's interpretation of the controversy is an exception to the generalization (see above) that Wittgenstein's defenders have stressed broad similarities between his work and Carnap's, while Carnap's defenders have pointed to detailed differences. Hintikka's reading of Wittgenstein's philosophy in the early 1930s is unusually Carnapian, and thus he finds more similarities in points of details than other interpreters.

related work by Poincaré and Reichenbach. It is precisely because what Wittgenstein had to say about the relationship between hypothesis, evidence, experience, and ostension in the years from 1929 to 1931 is not only a plausible development of the *Tractatus*, but is also a rational and plausible view, that it is unsurprising that others working on these questions might independently arrive at strikingly similar views. In a later letter to Schlick, Wittgenstein addressed these concerns: "Carnap has got his conception of hypotheses from me and again I have found this out from Waismann. Neither Poincaré nor Reichenbach could have the same conception, because they do not share my conception of propositions and grammar" (letter from Wittgenstein to Schlick, August 8, 1932. Nedo and Ranccheti 255, n. 20; Hintikka 1989/1996, 140).[21] Wittgenstein maintains here that Carnap's conception of hypotheses is the same as his own, because he claims that Carnap's conception of hypotheses is dependent on Wittgenstein's broader conception of the nature of language.[22] This leads us back to the methodological considerations we initially put to one side. Wittgenstein's more specific charges cannot be separated from broader concerns.

Because the question whether Carnap's conception of philosophy (1) and overall methods (4, 6) in the disputed paper is the same as (or similar enough) to Wittgenstein's is such a large one, it may well appear far more difficult to assess than the previous question about points of detail. Certainly, a full appraisal of the relationship between their respective philosophical programs is far beyond the scope of this chapter. However, the overall character of their relationship is actually considerably clearer than many of the details. For, as we have

---

[21] Earlier in the same letter, Wittgenstein claims that Carnap has forgotten a conversation in which Waismann reported to him Wittgenstein's conception of ostensive definitions.

[22] Hintikka supports Wittgenstein's charge by elaborating the analogies between the logic of Carnap's protocol sentences and Wittgenstein's treatment of elementary propositions circa 1929–31, and observes that there is a "remarkable similarity," because "for both of them, many singular propositions ... have to be confirmed indirectly by deriving them from directly verifiable propositions" (1989/1996, 141). However, one could well respond that the similarity is entirely unremarkable. Both philosophers were responding to the same predicament, which Ernst Tugendhat has called "veritative symmetry" and "epistemological asymmetry": my self-ascription of an experience and your ascription of that experience to me share the same truth-conditions, yet the grounds for our beliefs are radically different.

already seen, there can be no doubt that Carnap was deeply influenced by, and indebted to, Wittgenstein's overall approach to philosophy, a fact attested not only in his intellectual autobiography, but also in *The Logical Syntax of Language* (see Carnap 1934, xvi) and Max Black's introduction to the 1934 translation of the physicalism paper (Carnap 1934a, 16–20).[23] In particular, Carnap's project of setting out the logical syntax, or metalogic, of language is a direct descendent of the *Tractatus*'s goal of clarifying logical syntax. Of course, there are also important dissimilarities between their conceptions of syntax, and of philosophy. In particular, Carnap's careful and measured discussion of his relationship to Wittgenstein in *The Logical Syntax of Language* highlights two related points of principled disagreement: Carnap's rejection of Wittgenstein's view that syntax is inexpressible (and so can only be shown, not said), and his rejection of Wittgenstein's conception of philosophy as an elucidatory activity that cannot be formulated (see Carnap 1934, 282–4). However, we do not need to resolve the question of whether it is the similarities or differences between their respective philosophical positions that are more significant to defend Carnap from Wittgenstein's objections. For it is clear, I believe, that while Carnap's work is deeply influenced by Wittgenstein's, his insistence that the nature of philosophy, and the nature of language, can be made explicit does amount to a fundamental and far-reaching methodological disagreement. Carnap's indebtedness to Wittgenstein is comparable to Wittgenstein's debt to Russell and Frege, or Russell's debt to Frege. While there is scope for legitimate scholarly debate over the extent and nature of the debt, there can be no doubt that the influence was extremely important, yet it is also undeniable that there were also fundamental disagreements between them.

Let us now return to the question of the relationship between Wittgenstein's philosophy and Carnap's physicalism. In his reply to Schlick's letter setting out Wittgenstein's complaints, Carnap treated this as the crucial issue, saying that he did not mention Wittgenstein because "he has after all not dealt with the problem of

[23] Black's discussion of Wittgenstein's work in the preface must have been approved by Carnap, if not actually prompted by him and, like the material cited in the previous and the next note, can be seen as a response to Wittgenstein's criticism of Carnap's lack of attribution in the original paper. Black reads the *Tractatus* as phenomenalistic and contrasts it with Carnap's physicalism.

physicalism" (letter from Carnap to Schlick, July 17, 1932; translation from Hintikka 1989/1996, 133). Schlick sent a copy of Carnap's letter on to Wittgenstein, who wrote back that "It is not true that I have not dealt with the question of 'physicalism' (albeit not under this – dreadful – name) and with the same brevity with which the entire *Tractatus* is written" (letter from Wittgenstein to Schlick, August 8, 1932; translation based on Hintikka 1989/1996, 137).

In his defense, Carnap's interpreters have reiterated the point that Carnap himself made briefly in his earlier letter to Schlick: Wittgenstein had "not dealt with the problem of physicalism," at least in the terms in which Carnap and Neurath understood that problem. For there is a strong prima facie case that Wittgenstein never discussed physicalism. The term does not occur in the *Tractatus*. Indeed, it is never used anywhere in the entire corpus of Wittgenstein's writings.[24] However, the absence of the word is no more relevant to the question whether Wittgenstein dealt with physicalism in the *Tractatus* than the absence of that word from Carnap's own paper. While "Did the author of the *Tractatus* deal with the topic of physicalism in that book?" sounds at first like a straightforward preliminary question, it is not. For it turns on how we are to understand not only the topic of physicalism, but also how we are to understand what it is for something to be "in" the *Tractatus*. Because the book is so compressed, we need to consider not only what is explicitly stated there, but also the conclusions that its author expected readers to draw for themselves.[25]

In a recent discussion of these very questions, Cora Diamond rightly observes that the idea of a view's being "in" the *Tractatus* needs to be understood in a way that includes more than simply what is explicitly said there, while remaining distinct from the much broader category of

---

[24] A search for *"physicalism," "physikalisch,"* and their variants yields no results in the Bergen electronic edition of Wittgenstein's *Nachlass*, which includes not only the typescripts and manuscripts on which all his published works are based, but also a great deal of preparatory work (Wittgenstein 2000; the correspondence quoted here, in which the term does occur, is part of a separate database, Wittgenstein 2004).

[25] Wittgenstein would later say that "every sentence in the *Tractatus* should be seen as the heading of a chapter, needing further exposition" (Drury 1984, 159–60). Nevertheless, he was extremely reluctant to provide such exposition, even in response to Russell's explicit requests, insisting that it was a task that should be left up to the reader.

whatever can be inferred from it (Diamond 2000, 263). Her very plausible proposal is that we use "in the *Tractatus*" to cover "the conclusions Wittgenstein wants his readers to draw for themselves, the lines of thought he wants his readers to work through for themselves" (ibid.). Diamond gives this potentially open-ended proposal some specificity by suggesting that we need to think about what Wittgenstein expected Russell, in particular, to work out from his reading of the book. The main aim of Diamond's essay is to argue that an early version of the private language argument is "in the *Tractatus*." However, she does connect her exposition of a Tractarian critique of Russell's views on our knowledge of others' inner states with Wittgenstein's claim that physicalism is "in the *Tractatus*." Roughly speaking, Diamond draws the connection in the following way. The *Tractatus*'s treatment of logic requires that we give up the Russellian conception of objects of acquaintance as belonging to subjects, for the *Tractatus* requires that all languages must be intertranslatable, and the Russellian conception, because it is committed to the privacy of another's mental contents, does not satisfy this requirement. Once we draw this conclusion, "[w]e are left with the translatability into each other of experience-language and ordinary physical-world language: they are not about different objects. It was Carnap's picking up *that* point from the *Tractatus*, and making it central in his 1931 physicalism, that underlay Wittgenstein's accusation of plagiarism" (Diamond 2000, 279).[26] Diamond is right to stress the centrality of the idea that all languages are intertranslatable in the *Tractatus*. The idea of "language as the universal medium" as Hintikka calls it, is a crucial Tractarian commitment with far-reaching consequences. Indeed, this is one reason why the emergence of physicalism and of arguments against the possibility of a private language are so closely interconnected. For if a private language, a "language which describes my inner experiences and which only I myself can understand" (Wittgenstein 1953/2001, § 256), is possible, then the physicalist thesis that all languages are intertranslatable must be false.[27]

---

[26] Wittgenstein explictly states the principle of intertranslatability at 3.343.

[27] For further discussion of the multitude of private language arguments in the air at the time, see Uebel (1995, § 7), where he argues that in the early 1930s, *"different private language arguments were in play to support different conceptions of physicalism"* (343, italics in original). Indeed, Dejnozka (1991) argues that Russell had already offered a number of related private language arguments.

Nevertheless, physicalism, however broadly conceived, requires more than bare intertranslatability: it also involves a claim about the priority, or the primacy, of the physical. For both a Tractarian solipsist and an *Aufbau*-inspired phenomenalist could accept the thesis of the intertranslatability of physical and phenomenal languages and take it to be a step on the way to arguing, against the physicalist, that "the world is *my* world" (*Tractatus*, 5.62). Furthermore, Diamond's defense of Wittgenstein does not do justice to the point that Wittgenstein and Carnap have very different conceptions of physicalism.[28] Wittgenstein's physicalism in the early 1930s amounts to a commitment to the primacy of the objects we discuss in our ordinary language, while Carnap's physicalism turns on the primacy of the objects posited by the physical scientist.[29] My own view is that Wittgenstein had not arrived at the physicalist position concerning the primacy of physical language over phenomenal language when he wrote the *Tractatus*, but this much-debated question of *Tractatus* interpretation need not detain us here. (For further discussion, see Stern 1995, 3.4, 4.2.) What matters for our purposes are the views Wittgenstein put forward in the late 1920s and the early 1930s, views that he regarded as a natural development of the *Tractatus*.

Indeed, the most promising starting point for a balanced understanding of the deep affinities and differences between Carnap and Wittgenstein is to recognize that each of them had been working out the consequences of the Tractarian view that all languages must be intertranslatable. In the 1920s each of them had been attracted to a phenomenalistic, or phenomenological, analysis of both everyday and scientific language: the idea that one could specify a scheme of translation that would somehow enable one to translate everything

---

[28] For more detailed discussion of this point, see Uebel (1995). Uebel observes that McGuinness's Solomonic attempt to resolve the priority dispute by sharing the responsibility for developing physicalism between Wittgenstein, who "had given the impulse," Neurath, who "proclaimed the importance of the thing," and Carnap, who "began to work out the details" (McGuinness 1991/2002, 196) is untenable because "the thesis they sought to promote was not one but many" (Uebel 1995, 346).

[29] This is only a fast and loose material-mode summary; more careful exposition would call for use of the formal mode of speech. Note also that Carnap regarded physicalism as an empirical thesis, while Wittgenstein would presumably have treated it as a matter for philosophical elucidation.

one would ordinarily say about the world into talk of one's inner states. They both spoke of a primary language, for directly talking about immediate experience, and a secondary language, for talking about physical objects.

While the *Tractatus* has very little to say about the philosophy of mind and epistemology, a dualistic discussion of the relationship between "primary" mental world and a "secondary" physical world played a leading role in Wittgenstein's subsequent articulation of the book's main ideas. If we look at the first post-*Tractatus* manuscripts, begun almost immediately after his return to Cambridge in January 1929, we find him developing a whole metaphysics of experience, barely hinted at in the *Tractatus*. It was based on a fundamental distinction between two realms, the "primary" and the "secondary." The primary is the world of my present experience; the secondary is everything else: not only the "external world," but also other minds, and most of my mental life. He repeatedly made use of a cinematic analogy, comparing the primary, "inner" world to the picture one sees in the cinema, the secondary, "outer" world to the pictures on the film passing through the projector. However, by October of that year he decisively rejected this whole approach. He came to see that the primary and secondary were not two different worlds, but rather two different ways of talking, and he thought of philosophy as a matter of clarifying those uses of language. It was only after Wittgenstein repudiated the goal of a "primary language" or "phenomenological language" in October 1929 that he accepted the primacy of our ordinary physical language and so adopted a recognizably physicalist approach (for further discussion, see Stern 1995, 5.2).

As Wittgenstein had announced these physicalistic conclusions in his December 1929 meetings with Waismann and Schlick, it is easy to see why Wittgenstein was convinced that Carnap had taken his physicalism from Wittgenstein. However, there is good reason to believe that Neurath and Carnap had already taken the crucial steps towards the physicalistic standpoint earlier that year, because of conversations with Heinrich Neider, a student member of the Vienna Circle. Neider had argued that the two-language approach in Carnap's *Aufbau*, which gives equal weight to both phenomenal and physical language, is incoherent, because a solipsistic starting point cannot accommodate intersubjectively verifiable evidence statements: only a physicalistic language can do that. Consequently, basic evidence statements must be formulated in the physical language (see Haller and Rutte 1977, 29–30; Uebel 1995, 335ff.). Indeed, while a critique along these lines may well have played a crucial role in showing both Carnap and Neurath that a phenomenalistic language could not provide a satisfactory basis for a reconstruction of scientific knowledge, it was certainly not the first formulation of a physicalistic thesis by a member of the Vienna Circle. In fact, in 1935 Schlick persuaded Carnap, much to Carnap's embarrassment, that Schlick had already proposed, and argued for, a version of physicalism in his *General Theory of Knowledge* in 1918 (Schlick 1918, 295; see Uebel 1995, 345–6.). Of course, neither Neider's nor Schlick's physicalisms made use of the distinction between the material and formal modes of speech; but their attention to questions about mapping one mode of speech onto another does anticipate the more systematic approach to questions of translation one finds in Carnap and Wittgenstein's work in the early 1930s.

Oddly, while the leading parties in this dispute shared a basic commitment to the primacy of physicalistic language, and the view that all significant languages are translatable, there was a remarkable lack of mutual understanding between them, and deep disagreement about the nature of the doctrines they disputed. Three-quarters of a century later, we are so much more conscious of the differences that separated them than the points on which they agreed that it takes an effort of historical reconstruction to appreciate why Wittgenstein once feared that his own work would be regarded as a pale shadow of Carnap's.

13 Vienna, the City of Quine's Dreams

Having finished his doctorate in two years, W. V. O. Quine made a beeline for Vienna. This was 1932, and the object of his visit, Rudolf Carnap, had already gone on to Prague. After a few months of attending Moritz Schlick's lectures and meetings of the Vienna Circle, Quine too went on to Prague. He was not to return to Vienna for over 35 years, not, in fact, until he delivered "Epistemology Naturalized" (Quine 1969) as a lecture there in 1968. In the meantime Quine acquired, and indeed cultivated, a reputation for rejecting, some would say refuting, everything that was central to the new Viennese philosophy.

Here I want to challenge that picture. Quine did arrive in Vienna in 1932, but intellectually at least he never left. Quine tended to identify the Vienna Circle with Carnap. The Vienna that I am talking about is broader and more heterogeneous. Quine is rarely seen as a historian, but his historical picture of the Circle and of Carnap has been enormously influential, and his historical writing plays a crucial role in his argument for his nonhistorical views. Second, Quine's own views have direct Viennese antecedents, or if not, the arguments for them do. And finally, the views for which Quine was most famous were modified over the years, specifically in Carnap's direction. In short, Vienna remained the city of Quine's dreams; it was the home of his concerns, the source of his arguments, and the lodestar of his aspirations.

VIENNA

What I mean by "Vienna" of course is the Vienna Circle. And this is a broad and varied tradition. Naturally, the city has other long-standing and distinguished philosophical traditions. Generally, those traditions seem to have been of an empiricist sort, Aristotelian and

332

sometimes Thomist. That is not surprising, given the predominance of Catholicism. Brentano and his school were well established in Vienna (and in Poland), and I say that despite Brentano's having been born in Germany, leaving the priesthood, and spending most of his time in Vienna as privatdocent rather than as professor. But if we take Viennese philosophy so broadly as to include the whole Aristotelian tradition, then the idea that Quine fits somewhere in such a wide spectrum would hardly be worth considering.

Besides, the Vienna Circle is quite wide enough. Friedrich Stadler lists 19 thinkers as its "inner circle" and 18 (including Quine) as its "periphery" (Stadler 1997, 610–867). But a writer is counted as peripheral if they are primarily associated with centers outside Vienna, not necessarily because their views place them outside the mainstream of Circle thought. Reichenbach is not listed in the inner circle because he was in Berlin, but he not only co-edited *Erkenntnis*, the more or less official journal of the group, but he could also legitimately claim to be one of the primary intellectual leaders of the whole movement. Still, so as not to beg any questions, we may limit ourselves to the inner circle. It is, even so, a very wide group having many leaders with distinct points of view. Here one would have to mention Hans Hahn, Philipp Frank, and Otto Neurath from the so-called first Vienna Circle beginning as early as 1907. Add Schlick, who, along with Hahn, was one of the main institutional anchors at the university. Add also Carnap and Kurt Gödel, of course, who were influential despite not yet being well established. And add at least a half dozen more too. The point is that the Circle cannot be identified with a single individual.

I will not try to catalog their varied positions. Suffice it to say that they had little in common but a positive enthusiasm for science, and intense concern for its methodology, an interest in exploring the methodological issues through exact logical and mathematical means, especially the logic of *Principia Mathematica*, and (with some hesitation over the case of Gödel) a commitment to defending one or another version of a trenchant empiricism.

This is a pretty fair description of Quine's most basic commitments as well. I will not try to defend that claim here, but I shall discuss his most characteristic doctrines and arguments in a later section of this chapter. In the meantime we need to ask where the widespread identification of Vienna Circle doctrines with those of one man, namely, Carnap, came from. The answer clearly is Quine. With him, the identification is early and strong. In 1938 he wrote in a letter: "Last term I gave a course on 'Logical Positivism', which is to say 'Carnap'" (Quine 1990a, 239). There is nothing sinister in this. By 1938 Hahn and Schlick were dead. Neurath had been out of town during Quine's time in Vienna, so he met him only in 1939. Moreover, Neurath spent the war years in England and died in 1945, whereas Carnap came to the United States and was highly productive for decades thereafter. Small wonder, then, that Americans tended to follow Quine's lead in associating the Vienna Circle largely with Carnap.

Quine figures into the identification in another way, however. Quine is seriously underestimated as a historian. He never presents himself as such, even though he has written on a wide variety of recent philosophic figures. His importance has been twofold: (a) his historical reflections play a crucial role in the structure of his own arguments, and (b) that history as history has been *enormously* influential. I shall not try to demonstrate the first point here, but I will cite some examples. I am not thinking about Quine's just-so stories about, say, how reference came to be. Rather, I have in mind the historical discussions that are at the very heart of "Two Dogmas" (Quine 1951) and of "Epistemology Naturalized". If Quine's argument is to be persuasive, then the reader's perception of the available alternatives must be carefully shaped. So we are given a historical narrative in which Carnap emerges as the culmination of the development of empiricism. We are thus free to ignore all philosophers other than Carnap, and our perception of what Carnap is doing is likewise shaped. Never mind that the historical portrait of Carnap is inaccurate; my present point is that Quine is doing history and making it do the argumentative job he needs to have done. These two papers are among Quine's most important, and the historical narrative is crucial to the surrounding argument. These are striking but not isolated instances.

Turning to point b, Quine's histories have been enormously influential as histories. It is to Quine that we owe the widespread conviction that Carnap is some sort of British empiricist whose driving concern in the *Aufbau* (Carnap 1928) was the ontological reduction of science to an absolutely certain domain of sense data. By implication, this was the motivating idea behind the whole Circle.

Michael Friedman and Alan Richardson have convincingly shown that neither ontology nor absolute certainty was at the heart of the *Aufbau* and that his neo-Kantianism is not especially British (see especially Friedman 1987 and Richardson 1998). It is also to Quine that we owe the general impression that Carnap's discussion of analyticity is likewise motivated by the quest for certainty and that an analytic sentence is one that will be held true come what may. This is squarely at odds with Carnap's conventionalism, not to mention the broadly empirical pragmatism that Carnap sees at work in the change of conventions. Still, Quine's caricature is endlessly repeated by others. As a third and final example of Quine's influence consider the topic of naturalism. Surely, Quine's omission of any mention of Neurath has slowed the world's appreciation of their very considerable similarities, for Neurath too was a naturalist. In "Epistemology Naturalized" Carnap is again portrayed as the culmination of traditional British empiricism. Quine is a naturalist; Carnap is his foil. So what is Carnap supposed to be? A supernaturalist? Here and in later writings Quine himself gives many different versions of epistemological naturalism, versions that the subsequent philosophical literature has been at pains to sort out. For many, Quine's presentation effectively disguised the fact that in some of the most important senses Carnap too is a naturalist. He endorsed very seriously the idea that science and scientific results should everywhere inform philosophic work. He used Gestalt psychology in framing his *Aufbau* definitions. And throughout all his work, utility *in science* was the measure of philosophic merit. True, Carnap might balk at the wholesale "surrender of the epistemological burden to psychology" (Quine 1969, 75), but so would Quine, judging from his later writing. And so would many of his avowedly naturalistic readers. Yet the legend persists that Carnap would keep empirical science sealed off from philosophy. And it persists in no small degree because of the influence of Quine's historical picture.

So Quine should count as an important historian both because of the role of his histories with his own philosophic arguments and because of his widespread influence. Again, Quine never claims to be a historian and would no doubt insist on a sharp distinction between real philosophy and its history. No doubt many would agree, but my counter-suggestion is, to borrow a phrase from one of Quine's many friends, that such a distinction would be "an untenable dualism" (White 1950).

QUINE'S ANTECEDENTS

We have so far seen that Viennese philosophy (for our purposes, the Circle) is broader than might be supposed. And we have hypothesized about the source of the misapprehension. Now it is time to look directly at Quine's doctrines and arguments to see how they map, if at all, onto the broad contours of Vienna. I shall examine seven of his most characteristic doctrines and claim for each that, allowing for changes of idiom, it was held by central members of the Circle or else the argument that Quine offers for it is built from such Viennese raw material.

I must emphasize at the outset, however, that I do not claim that Quine *derived* his ideas from the Vienna Circle. In some cases that may be possible. But in others, perhaps in most, there is the likelihood of reinvention. In recent decades Quine was confronted by historians with the striking similarity of his views and Neurath's. Quine's response was to admit the similarity but to deny that he ever knew Neurath well or had read his work deeply. Indeed, he claimed, they did not meet until after Quine's basic ideas were formed. That does not preclude influence through third parties. But I see no reason not to take Quine's self-report here at face value. In any case, priority disputes are generally sterile (though entertaining at a sufficient distance). My concern is not with the origin of Quine's ideas but with their location in philosophic space.

In locating those ideas I do not mean to appraise them either. Quine was a great philosopher and enormously creative. I admire his work and think that it is worth disagreeing with. And sometimes I do. But I will not do so here. Besides, given my well-known fondness for the Viennese tradition under discussion, no one can accuse *me* of intending to diminish Quine's reputation by placing him in such good company.

The seven Quinean doctrines that I shall discuss are

1. The rejection of analyticity (and related notions such as meaning)
2. The indeterminacy of translation

3. Epistemological holism (the Quine-Duhem thesis)
4. Naturalized epistemology
5. Physicalism
6. Behaviorism
7. The immanence of truth, reference, and ontology

There are, of course, many other Quinean views from which to choose, and one must not think that Quine's philosophy can be reduced to these seven or even to any short list of doctrines. My claim, rather, is that these seven are important, representative, and central features of Quine's view and that locating them will tell us much about where Quine stands with respect to the Viennese tradition. Of the seven, the first two require extended discussion. This I will postpone for just a bit. The remaining five (3–7) can be dealt with more directly.

Epistemological holism is the idea that our hypotheses meet the tribunal of experience, not individually, but together; no single hypothesis is ever refuted but can be held come what may in the way of experience. The thesis is now so firmly associated with Quine that he is standardly given half the name along with Pierre Duhem. But Duhem's work was actively discussed even by the first Vienna Circle, and Rudolf Haller (1982, 1985) has made a case for calling it the Neurath thesis because Neurath embraced it so early and developed it so fully. Philipp Frank embraced it as well. So did Carnap. Consider this remark from *The Logical Syntax of Language*:

There is in the strict sense no refutation (falsification) of an hypothesis; for even when it proves to be L-incompatible with certain protocol-sentences, there always exists the possibility of maintaining the hypothesis and renouncing acknowledgment of the protocol-sentences. ... Further, it is, in general, impossible even to test a singular hypothetical sentence. In the case of a single sentence of this kind, there are in general no suitable L-consequences of the form of protocol-sentences; hence for the deduction of sentences of the form of protocol-sentences the remaining hypotheses must also be used. Thus *the test applies, at bottom, not to a single hypothesis but to the whole system of physics as a system of hypotheses* (Duhem, Poincaré). (Carnap 1934/1937, 318)

Epistemological holism seems to have been the common property of the whole left wing of the Vienna Circle. By the way, Quine says he added the citation to Duhem to "Two Dogmas" at Hempel's suggestion, but that in fact he did not previously know of Duhem's ideas. Well, he certainly read and reread *Logical Syntax*. Could Quine have skipped this page?

Concerning epistemological naturalism, it is sometimes hard to pin down exactly what the view is, either in Quine or in other writers. I suggested above that in at least some of the many senses Carnap is a naturalist. Fortunately, we need not worry about that here, for there is no longer any serious doubt that Neurath was a naturalist in any sense that Quine would want. Too much excellent historical work has been done in recent years to need further elaboration here. Thomas Uebel (1992) is utterly convincing that Neurath was a naturalist in many respects like Quine. In addition, Dirk Koppelberg (1990) locates Quine between Carnap and Neurath on this issue (and others), and Quine concedes at least the parallel with Neurath (also see Quine 1990, 212).

Physicalism need not detain us either, because it is well known that both Carnap and Neurath were physicalists. It is perhaps more surprising that Schlick was also. In fact, it seems to have surprised Carnap and Neurath when they discovered it (Uebel 1995). It may be asked whether physicalism is not a particular version of naturalism; certainly it is a particular version of the idea that what there is in the world is what contemporary science says there is. Both "physicalism" and "naturalism", I fear, cover a somewhat indefinite class of doctrines and attitudes, so a precise answer may not be possible. Either way it would not diminish the case that Viennese antecedents are there. Our concern was never to count the doctrines, but rather to see that they were at home in Vienna.

Much the same can be said about behaviorism. There are many different views, comprising at least "methodological" and "philosophical" (or "radical") types. The former is a claim about what counts as legitimate evidence in a proper social science. Quine is avowedly a behaviorist of this sort, though he is willing to bring neurophysiological claims to bear on some psychological questions. Carnap from the 1930s on also accepted the idea that in the social sciences including psychology and linguistics the evidence had to be public and hence behavioral. Neurath, too, emphasized the importance of public evidence, and his somewhat complex prescribed form for protocol sentences seems behavioristically acceptable. Whether Quine or any of the Vienna Circle were behaviorists of the more radical sort is contested ground onto which we need not venture here.

Quine's doctrine that truth, reference, and ontology are imma-
nent notions is just the idea that there is no higher tribunal than our
evolving theory, that is, science, for any of these things. To ask
whether it is true that snow is white is just to ask whether according
to our best theory snow is white. To ask whether *"Hund"* refers to
dogs is simply to ask whether *"Hund"* is mapped onto "dog" in our
chosen manual of translation (assuming that our translation pre-
serves the behavioral dispositions). To ask what the ontology of a
claim or theory is simply to ask what it says there is when it is
mapped onto our familiar idiom via some chosen manual. There is
no question to ask that is not relativized to some manual of translation. Similarly there is no question to ask about what there really
is apart from our best and evolving theory. Again, some say that the
immanence of these notions just is part of naturalism. Whether it is
or not, it does seem that Quine's stance here is what lies behind
Neurath's otherwise puzzling rejection of the notion of truth altogether. For that matter, Quine's stance is of a piece with Carnap's
(1950) rejection of external questions in "Empiricism, Semantics,
and Ontology".

At last we come to Quine's two most famous doctrines, the
rejection of analyticity and the indeterminacy of translation. Surely
there is no precedent for the latter. And while there were some
Viennese, such as Gödel, who rejected the claim that mathematics
was analytic and still more who differed in greater or lesser ways
from the particulars of Carnap's account, no one rejected the very
notion in the way that Quine did. Nevertheless, I shall contend,
Quine's arguments against analyticity and about translation are
thoroughly in keeping with mainstream Circle arguments. In
Vienna, he would have been completely at home.

First, analyticity: what does Quine think is wrong with it? It can
be defined in terms of other terms such as "meaning", "synonymy", and the like. But these other terms are defective as well and
in the same way. It can be defined, circularly, in terms of itself, but
that is unavailing. What we lack, he says, is "any tenable general
suggestion ... as to what it is to be an analytic sentence" (Quine
1963, 403). Where we have had generality, "there has been some
drastic failure such as tended to admit all or no sentences as analytic" (Quine 1963, 404). What is needed for a tenable general
account? The same sort of empirical meaningfulness that we find

for terms elsewhere in science. What would provide that? Suitable behavioral criteria. What Quine is in effect demanding for "analyticity" is that it satisfy the same sort of empirical criterion of meaningfulness that Carnap himself demanded of Heidegger. These demands for empirical criteria were a standard Viennese stock in trade, and there were numerous variations. Hempel discussed many of them, rather pessimistically, in two famous papers that came out about the same time as "Two Dogmas" (Hempel 1950, 1951). There is an irony, of course, in the fact that many who reject the whole Viennese verificationist strategy as wrongheaded from beginning to end also accept Quine's argument here that is based on it. Quine's demands, of course, are vastly more liberal than the complete verifiability criterion that had been considered early on, but they are virtually identical to Carnap's own mature requirements.

I cannot here trace the development of the argument, or evaluate it, or explain why Carnap at first failed to understand Quine's demands and later denied their appropriateness for his own work. I have tried to do that elsewhere (Creath 1990a, Introduction; 2004). By way of an aside, I will say that I think the demand for empirical criteria for analyticity is indeed legitimate and that it can be met. But even that is outside my present purpose, which is to urge that, though Quine's rejection of analyticity as unintelligible may not be standard Viennese fare, his fundamental argument for that rejection is. Indeed, Quine's argument is a standard version of the most famous (infamous?) gambit to be associated with the Vienna Circle, namely, verificationism. What is new is not the argument but the target.

Finally, among Quine's doctrines we can turn to the indeterminacy of translation. I will mention in passing that Carnap himself has what is in effect an indeterminacy of reference argument in *Meaning and Necessity*, fittingly, in a discussion of Quine (Carnap 1947, 100–6). Carnap even makes several of the moves that Quine was to make 13 years later. I have discussed this elsewhere (Creath 1990). Rather than exploring that here, I want to concentrate as I just did in my remarks on analyticity on the argument rather than the doctrine. This will not be easy because there is little consensus beyond Quine's own formulations as to what the doctrine is. At a minimum, indeterminacy is the idea that there will always be a multiplicity of manuals of translation that will accommodate all of the available data and all of the possible data that the linguist has to go on. So far this might be an underdetermination thesis, but Quine says more. What makes it indeterminacy rather than under-determination is the idea that there is no fact of the matter as to which of the manuals is the right one. If the exact formulation of the thesis is controversial, there is even less consensus, much less, about what the argument for it is. The problem is compounded because both the theses and the arguments for them shifted over the years. No full-scale analysis is possible here, so I shall instead look at a few schematic renderings of Quine's arguments that are prominent in the literature. They are offered by Dagfin Føllesdal, who is both knowledgeable about and sympathetic to Quine, and by Roger Gibson, to whose rendering Quine seems to have been given Quine's official approval. None of the arguments offered completely coincides with my own analysis of Quine, but that, I suppose, should *prima facie* count against me rather than them. I do not intend to evaluate these arguments or Quine's, merely to locate them.

Føllesdal gives two different arguments. The first he schematizes as:

Duhem plus Peirce yields indeterminacy. (Føllesdal 1973, 291)

By this he means that epistemological holism combined with Peirce's verificationist theory of meaning provides a sufficient argument for the indeterminacy of translation. No doubt there are subsidiary premises that would be required, but these two are the chief and controversial ones. Føllesdal himself has doubts about this first argument because he has doubts about the verificationism. Quine in a brief comment said that he still found the verificationism attractive. It just failed as an account of the meaning of individual sentences because, as his holism insists, sentences do not meet experience individually (Quine 1986, 155–6). Presumably, verificationism would still be able to help underwrite indeterminacy. In any case, as we have seen, the epistemological holism was common enough in Vienna. So was the verificationism, even as a theory of meaning and not just of meaningfulness.

Føllesdal's second argument (call it II) is not so easily schematized. Gibson sees II as depending centrally on the idea that simplicity operates differently in translation than it does in, say, physics. Quine says in reply that that is not his line and that simplicity considerations would not in any case be sufficient to secure indeterminacy (Quine 1986, 155). I see in Føllesdal's development of II a different central idea. Consider these two passages:

The entities that one should assume there to be, are those and only those that are assumed by one's theory of nature, i.e. those that seem needed to account for all the evidence in as simple a manner as possible. ... The problem with intensional entities is that they currently serve no such useful purpose, but belong in eddies that, as Quine has argued in "Two Dogmas of Empiricism", are completely separated from those parts of our theory of nature which help account for our experiences. (Føllesdal 1973, 293)

In the case of empirical theories, this failure of a pragmatic definition of truth did not deter us from defining truth (e.g. à la Tarski) in terms of our talk about the world. Why can we not do the same for translation? The answer is, I think, – and here we are at the crucial point of the whole argument – that the only entities we are justified in assuming are those that are appealed to in the simplest theory that accounts for all the evidence. These entities and their properties and interrelations are all there is to the world, and all there is to be right or wrong about. All truths about these are included in our theory of nature. In translation we are not describing a further realm of reality, we are just correlating two comprehensive language/theories concerning all there is. (Føllesdal 1973, 295)

In other words, what gets us from underdetermination to indeterminacy is previously having secured the rejection of analyticity, synonymy, and intensional entities generally. If this is indeed a crucial premise in Quine's argument for indeterminacy, then it casts doubt on the ability of indeterminacy to confirm further the rejection of analyticity et al. in any useful way. Moreover, if this is the crucial premise, then we have already discussed its Viennese roots.

Gibson rejects Føllesdal's two arguments as too epistemological and offers his own more ontological version. His too can be schematized as follows:

Naturalism plus physicalism yields indeterminacy. (Gibson 1988, 111)

Michael Friedman (1975) suggests further that behaviorism and verificationism might have to be assumed as well. That may be, but for my purposes it does not matter. All four of these (families of) views were utterly standard in our Vienna. The thesis of the indeterminacy of translation was no doubt new with Quine. But if one or another of these analyses of his argument for it is correct, then the building blocks of his argument are not new with Quine.

CHANGES

We have discussed Quine's most characteristic views, and I urged that either they or the arguments that Quine offers for them go back to Vienna. I now want to turn to some of the changes that Quine made over his long and productive life. Many of these changes amount to Quine's moving even closer to Carnap than we have seen so far. For reasons of space I cannot go into any detail, but even a quick look at a couple of examples is revealing.

Quine is perhaps most famous for his rejection of analyticity, but beginning with *Roots of Reference* (Quine 1974) he developed his own notion of analyticity. No, it was not quite Carnap's version nor embedded in Carnap's epistemology. But Quine did seem to think that it had suitable behavioral criteria, that it was not circular, that it provided for cases of essential predication such as "No bachelor is married" and for elementary logic as well. He insisted that it did not cover set theory and mathematics, though in fact large parts of elementary arithmetic would be covered. Even if mathematics did not come out as analytic in English under the new criterion, Carnap would have been very happy with this level of agreement. He was making proposals, not descriptions, and would have been satisfied to propose that English be modified.

If Carnap is known for advocating an analytic/synthetic distinction and hence in effect a two-tier system of epistemic appraisal, Quine is known for advocating a one-tier system. There are signs of change even here. Originally, logic, mathematics, essential predications are all in one system together with physics, sociology, and the myriad particular claims of everyday life. All were to be equally open to change in the face of recalcitrant evidence, all subject to the demands of simplicity and conservatism. Perhaps he was too hasty in suggesting that only the totality of belief could meet experience. The large chunk or "critical semantic mass" would do as well in meeting observation categoricals (a generality compounded of observables). In 1990 and 1992 Quine published *Pursuit of Truth*, where he wrote:

Over-logicizing, we may picture the accommodation of failed observation categoricals as follows. We have before us some set S of purported truths that was found jointly to imply the false categorical. ... Now some one or more of the sentences in S are going to have to be rescinded. We exempt some members of S from this threat on determining that the fateful implication still holds without their help. *Any purely logical truth is thus exempted, since it adds nothing to what S would logically imply anyway;* and sundry irrelevant sentences would be exempted as well. (Quine 1990b, 12, emphasis added)

Giving logic a different role in ordinary empirical testing amounts to a two-tier system. Of course, logic is still revisable, but it was for Carnap too. Now the only issue seems to be what to put in which tier.

This change to a two-tier approach was not a momentary aberration. It appeared in both editions of *Pursuit of Truth* (1990 and 1992), and it was clearly restated in an essay of 1995. There he said: "Treating observation categoricals as empirical checkpoints of scientific theory, in section I above, I evidently gave logic a role separate from the rest of science. If a set of theoretical sentences is tested by testing an observation categorical that is implied by the set, then surely the logic of that implication is no part of the tested set" (Quine 1995, 352).

There were dramatic changes as well in Quine's treatment of simplicity and in his willingness to allow an intralinguistic notion of synonymy. The latter would be an epistemic notion amounting to interchangeability *salva confirmatione*. It would take a fair amount of space to document and evaluate these changes, space that I do not have here. Suffice it to say that when added together the changes are substantial and in the direction of accommodation with Carnap. Of course, Quine retains a distinctive view, vibrant and original. Rather, as Quine changed, as every living thinker must, he moved not away from Vienna but closer to Carnap.

Earlier we saw that the Circle was not to be equated with Carnap. If the world too often made such an identification, this was probably in large measure because of Quine's own influence as a historian. We have seen as well that many of Quine's most notable doctrines either had clear antecedents in Vienna, or the building blocks of his arguments for them did. This in no way diminishes his originality. And we saw that as Quine's views changed, they moved closer to Carnap's in important ways. The discovery that, despite his more than 35-year absence, Quine was always at home in Vienna should cause neither him nor ourselves alarm. It is powerful testimony to the fruitfulness of those Viennese discussions so many decades ago. Vienna is an enchanting city; it exerts a powerful spell; and it is truly the city of Quine's dreams.

14 "That Sort of Everyday Image of Logical Positivism"

Thomas Kuhn and the Decline of Logical Empiricist Philosophy of Science

In the twenty-first century, no one is a logical empiricist.[1] There are, to be sure, more than a few philosophers whose work resembles in important ways the work of the logical empiricists, indeed, whose work, if it had been done in the 1950s, would be logical empiricist work. But, no one presents such work under the rubric "logical empiricism." Nor, really, could anyone plausibly attempt to do so – being a logical empiricist really is not a live option for a twenty-first-century philosopher.[2]

It is a matter of some historical and philosophical interest to think about why and how logical empiricism came to lose its status as a philosophical project to be pursued. After all, as this volume amply demonstrates, logical empiricism was a leading project in analytic philosophy in the not too distant past and, indeed, the preeminent project within certain branches of philosophy, such as philosophy of science. Something substantial must have happened for such a project to decline so importantly in influence that even

---

[1] I have learned many relevant things from many people that I have tried to synthesize in this essay. Special thanks must go to my co-editor, Thomas Uebel; no one else knows the trouble we've seen. I learned to read Kuhn with new eyes thanks to instruction from Steven Shapin and the late Stephen Straker. My enthusiasm for this project was recently revived thanks to encouragement and comments offered by my colleagues in the Vancouver Circle (aka the Verein Stephen Straker): John Beatty, Keith Benson, Sylvia Berryman, Robert Brain, Adam Frank, Piers Hale, Brandon Konoval, Margaret Schabas, Judy Segal – and our distinguished visitors, Ernst Hamm, Alison Li, and, especially, Simon Schaffer.

[2] Even as staunch a supporter of logical empiricism as Wesley Salmon was led to circumscribe his support for logical empiricism in phrases such as "the philosophical spirit that animated the protagonists of logical empiricism" (Parrini and Salmon 2003, 8).

346

the most technical work in areas such as confirmation theory or philosophy of physics cannot today be said to be examples of logical empiricist philosophy of science.

THE RECEIVED VIEW

If we limit our vision of logical empiricism to philosophy of science, there is a readily available story as to the decline and fall of logical empiricism. Logical empiricism had been the leading project in philosophy of science throughout the English-speaking world, especially in North America, from the early 1930s through the late 1950s. But, starting in the late 1950s, a number of alternative projects in philosophy of science arose. In 1959 Karl Popper's most important work in philosophy of science, his *Logik der Forschung* of 1935, was finally translated into English as *The Logic of Scientific Discovery* (Popper 1959). Despite the affinities of topic and method between Popper and the logical empiricists, Popper was a well-known and vocal critic of many aspects of the logical empiricist project, especially its inductivism and its eliminativism regarding metaphysical matters. Popper's philosophy offered a falsificationist and realist alternative to logical empiricism. Other versions of scientific realism, such as the critical realism of Wilfrid Sellars (Sellars 1963), were also being developed in the late 1950s and early 1960s. Other philosophers offered nonempiricist alternatives in philosophy of science, such as the "postcritical" philosophy of science developed in the 1950s by the chemist-turned-philosopher Michael Polanyi (Polanyi 1958). This account of scientific knowledge stressed the tacit knowledge encoded in the details of scientific practice and the commitment the scientist had to the truth of scientific claims – aspects of science that Polanyi explained in a quasi-phenomenological fashion. This turn to practice was also to be found in the work in the 1950s of Russell Hanson, whose *Patterns of Discovery* (Hanson 1958) seemed to make available, on psychological and Wittgensteinian grounds, a genuinely philosophical interest in and account of scientific discovery. This, of course, was understood to conflict with the logical empiricist strictures against dealing with "the context of discovery" in philosophy of science. Similarly, by the mid-1960s, founders of a new "semantic view of theories" were self-consciously arguing against an account of scientific theories as formal axiom systems that was associated with logical empiricism (Suppe 1972; 1977).

All these developments placed logical empiricism, more or less explicitly, in issue. All of them sought to go beyond logical empiricism in doctrine or method. All of them played a role in decreasing the dominance and, ultimately, influence of logical empiricism. But all of the philosophers and movements mentioned so far pale in significance when compared to Thomas Kuhn's historical philosophy of science as presented in his 1962 monograph *The Structure of Scientific Revolutions* (Kuhn 1962 [1996]). Indeed, it is Kuhn's "role for history" and the naturalistic and social setting for an account of the historical development of science that, more than any other factor, according to the standard and informal histories of philosophy of science, caused the decline and eventual overthrow of logical empiricism.[3]

It is easy to see why Kuhn's work would have been so effective in rendering logical empiricism problematic: Kuhn's account of science asks us to take the actual historical development of science as the primary explanandum of a philosophy of science. He claimed, moreover, that history so considered would lead to a "decisive transformation of the image of science by which we are possessed" (Kuhn 1962 [1996], 1). This image is connected to some views widely associated with the logical empiricists: scientific theorizing is inductive and cumulative; the individual scientist contributes only new discoveries and new theories to cover the available evidence, theories which are then tested and justified via explicit logical arguments that tie them to anticipated experimental results. Science is, also, isolated from other forms of culture: the scientist need not seek concepts from outside science in his scientific theorizing; science is autonomous and self-justifying. As against this view,

---

[3] *Structure* is one of the best-selling and most widely cited academic books of the second half of the twentieth century; thus, the outlines of Kuhn's philosophy are well known. Some relatively recent sympathetic accounts of his philosophy of science can be found, for example, in Nickles (2003), Sharrock and Read (2002), Bird (2000), Hoyningen-Huene (1993), and Horwich (1993). Unsympathetic accounts of Kuhn's views, contrasting them not to logical empiricism but rather to an idiosyncratically understood Karl Popper, can be found Fuller (2000; 2004); warning: these last must be heavily laden with salt to be palatable! Hollinger (2003) and Uebel (2003b) provide much needed salt regarding Fuller (2000).

Kuhn argued for several theses. First, the autonomy of science is evident only in times of normalcy, when scientific concepts and theories are not in crisis, and is vouchsafed even there more by implicit traditions of practice than by rigid rules of scientific logic. Moreover, in times when the paradigms of normal science are not actively under dispute, theories are not really tested against experimental evidence, in the sense that mismatches might lead to genuine overthrow of the theories. Mismatches have the status of problems to be solved – and solved according to the means that the paradigm itself posits. It is not the theory but the practitioner's status as a competent scientist that is in test. Most importantly, Kuhn posits an historical development of science that is punctuated by moments of revolutionary crisis and during which it is open to a scientist to seek conceptual help from any field. Thus, in times of revolution, the ordinary conditions of scientific rationality no longer operate, and the embeddedness of science in a larger cultural context becomes important for revolutionary closure.

An example might help clarify the point. A project in philosophy of science that, like logical empiricism, seeks sharply to distinguish between science and metaphysics and that wishes to specify precise logical relations between properly scientific theories and experience would have, it would seem, no truck with any historical account of the work of leading scientists that finds them motivated by metaphysical doctrine and employing such doctrine to both find and justify the theoretic claims they make. Yet Kuhn, even before *Structure*, often offered such accounts of heroes of the scientific revolution. His account of Johannes Kepler in *The Copernican Revolution* (Kuhn 1957, 209–19), for example, assimilates the three laws of planetary motion that are Kepler's continuing contribution to the science of astronomy to other Keplerian doctrines such as the model of the universe based on the six Platonic solids. Kuhn also argues that Kepler's derivation of the second law of motion – the law of equal areas – depended on his account of the sun's *anima motrix* as the causal agent in the motion of the planets. Most generally, Kuhn argues that Kepler's entire astronomical program is based in a metaphysical faith in mathematically expressed harmonies in nature; he writes:

Kepler's application of the faith in harmonies may seem naive, but the faith itself is not essentially different from that motivating bits of the best contemporary research. Certainly, the scientific attitude demonstrated in those of Kepler's "laws" which we have now discarded is not distinguishable from the attitude which drove him to the three Laws we now retain. Both sets, the "laws" and the Laws, arise from the same renewed faith in the existence of mathematical harmony that had so large a role in driving Copernicus to break with the astronomical tradition and in persuading him that the earth was, indeed, in motion. (Kuhn 1957, 219)

Here Kuhn seems at pains to illustrate the historical productivity of metaphysical doctrine in scientific research and to claim that such metaphysical doctrine continues to have a role to play in scientific research even today. Moreover, he wishes to deny that Kepler's actual work can be neatly divided into those scientifically acceptable bits leading to the Laws we still accept and the metaphysically tainted bits that we have rejected. The metaphysical doctrines motivated and gave shape to all of Kepler's work; a metaphysically purified Kepler would not have had the scientific achievements of the historical Kepler.

In light of such facts about Kuhn's account of science, *Structure* was from early on taken to have important consequences for the possibility of a philosophy of science prosecuted along the lines outlined by logical empiricism. As early as 1963, Mary B. Hesse, in a review of Kuhn's book for the history of science journal *Isis*, said this about Kuhn's work:

It cannot be disputed that this is the first attempt for a long time to bring historical insights to bear on the philosophers' account of science, and whatever the puzzles that remain to be solved, Kuhn has at least outlined a new epistemological paradigm which promises to resolve some of the crises currently troubling empiricist philosophies of science. Its consequences will be far-reaching. (Hesse 1963, 287)

Among those less positively disposed to Kuhn's work, there was also the suggestion from early on that logical positivism was a main target of Kuhn's book. Dudley Shapere's famous review of Kuhn's book (Shapere 1964) suggests that this is the case, and he makes the case quite explicitly in a subsequent paper (Shapere 1966) that frames a discussion of Kuhn and Paul Feyerabend under the general rubric "the revolt against positivism" (which is the title of the first section of the paper).

By 1976 logical empiricism was taken to be a thing of the past even within the professional organization of philosophers of science in North America, the Philosophy of Science Association (PSA). At the 1976 PSA meetings, Lindley Darden gave a talk on the "heritage" of logical positivism and spoke of the logical empiricists as the "grandparents" of those who entered philosophy of science after 1968 (Darden 1976, p. 1). Her entire paper was given over to assessing whether there was anything of value in the logical empiricist concerns with the theory-observation distinction, the discover-justification distinction, and the unity of science. Similarly, in the introduction to his anthology on scientific revolutions, Ian Hacking (1981) cited nine doctrines that constituted the "image of science" that Kuhn sought to reject. While carefully noting that no philosopher of science clearly adopted all nine doctrines, Hacking claimed the collection formed "a useful collage not only of technical philosophical discussion but also of a widespread popular conception of science" (Hacking 1981, 2) and illustrated his account by indicating which of the nine doctrines were most central to Popper, Carnap, and Hans Reichenbach. Substantially this view of Kuhn's relations to logical empiricism has entered into the collective unconscious of the community of professional philosophers of science.

RECENT DOUBTS REGARDING THE RECEIVED ACCOUNT OF KUHN AND LOGICAL EMPIRICISM

The story we have rehearsed so far has, in its broad outlines, a wide currency in the community of philosophers of science. In recent years, however, with the flowering of a substantial scholarly literature reassessing the projects of logical empiricism, questions have been raised regarding the adequacy of the story to account for some of the details of the reception of Kuhn's work in relation to logical empiricism. One way to motivate these new doubts is to raise a question: Can we not use the discovery/justification distinction (which, of course, Kuhn also argued against) to explain why the Kuhnian doctrines just rehearsed are not principled objections to logical empiricism? For example, what in Kuhn's account of Kepler as discussed above would a logical empiricist have to disagree with? It is an article of doctrine for the logical empiricists that any given scientist may use nonscientific theories in his or her work – Kepler, when setting out to discover his laws of planetary motion, is given a free hand. All that is asked is that the laws he enunciates have empirical content, as certainly the three laws we continue to accept (as idealizations) do. So, too, does his model of the solar system on the basis of the Platonic solids, but this model has, precisely because of its empirical content, been subsequently falsified. Similarly, Kepler's own argument for the Second Law might have appealed to the Sun's *anima motrix*, but what the Law *says* can be disentangled from the framework within which Kepler derived the Law. Indeed, this must be the case if the Law has survived into our times, since Kepler's own dynamics of planetary motion were denied by all the relevant subsequent theories of planetary motion, from Cartesian vortices to Newton's gravitation theory to Einstein's general theory of relativity. That true empirical generalizations are derivable from false theories is a truth about logic that no logical empiricist would ever wish to reject. Neither would a logical empiricist philosopher of science wish to deny that someone committed to a false theory might for theoretical reasons be interested in areas of study that yield firm and permanent empirical generalizations.

Indeed, the charge that a positivistic conception of science could not account for the creative activity of the scientist was well known to the logical empiricists – such arguments went right back into the nineteenth century. For example, Philipp Frank had, decades before 1962, responded to arguments offered by Max Planck to the effect that a Machian scientist would be unable to use the principle of economy of thought to generate scientific theories. Interestingly, in his arguments Planck cited scientists such as Copernicus, Kepler, and Newton and assigned a positive role in their theorizing to "their unshakeable belief – whether resting on an artistic, or on a religious basis – in the reality of their world picture" (Planck 1909, cited in Frank 1917/1949, 63). Planck, thus, argued that commitment to the truth of a metaphysical world picture was widely productive of good scientific theories and that if scientists had restricted themselves to what passes positivist muster, they would have been less productive of excellent science. Frank argued that, whatever the historical facts about the figures Planck cites, no phenomenalist positivist of a

Machian cast need be any less theoretically imaginative. Citing the theoretical work of James Clerk Maxwell, whom he takes to be a Machian, Frank writes: "One cannot say of him that such adherence in any way crippled the flight of his imagination; indeed, quite the opposite. The conception of the relative worthlessness of the theory in comparison to the phenomenon gives to the theorizing of such an investigator something especially free and imaginative" (1949, p. 63). While one might not be convinced by Frank's arguments, the point before us is that views that bear a family resemblance to aspects of Kuhn's views were well known to the logical empiricists decades before Kuhn came on the scene – and the logical empiricists did not think their views were substantially refuted by those alternatives.

We can deepen this sort of worry about the standard account when we remember that the logical empiricists as a group all rejected a naive inductivism that claims that scientific theory can be both expressed in observational languages and derived from observational results. Given that this is the case, we might wonder whether the methodical and accumulationist "image of science by which we are possessed" that Kuhn seeks to explode can be properly assigned to logical empiricism at all. Reichenbach had introduced the "context of discovery" exactly to allow for a sort of creative freedom in science to theorize in ways that went strictly beyond the observational evidence. The way in which theorizing went beyond the available evidence was a common theme in the reflections of the logical empiricists upon the revolutionary physics of their own times. In the case of Reichenbach, this creative freedom was part of an historical story that included the revolutionary astronomy of Copernicus and Kepler. As early as the 1920s, Reichenbach discussed the achievements of Copernicus, Kepler, and Newton in these terms: "The collection of facts is the starting point of investigation; but it does not mark its end. Only when an explanation comes like a bolt of lightning and melts separate ideas together in the fire of thoughtful synthesis, is that stage reached which we call understanding and which satisfies the seeking spirit" (Reichenbach 1927/1942, 12–13).

These facts about the views espoused by the logical empiricists can be augmented with certain facts regarding their historical relations to Kuhn and his project. First, none of the most important logical empiricists wrote early reviews of Kuhn's book in which they expressed deep disagreement with Kuhn; this contrasts importantly with the reaction of Popper and his followers, who famously argued with Kuhn quite publicly in 1965 (Lakatos and Musgrave 1970), as well as realists such as Shapere (1964). Moreover, in the 1950s, the relations between Kuhn and his fellow Harvard historians of science and the logical empiricists and their students are instances of cross-fertilization and, at times, collaboration; certainly the logical empiricists seemed to think that the new historians who worked with James B. Conant were giving accounts of the history of science that illustrated their philosophical points. Philipp Frank's protégé Gerald Holton teamed up with a protégé of Conant's and teaching colleague of Kuhn's, Duane Roller, to write the history of physics (Holton and Roller 1958) most approvingly cited in Carl Hempel's primer on logical empiricism *The Philosophy of Natural Science* (Hempel 1966). Hempel, in that book, also cited Conant's work as illustrating a doctrine about science that Hempel endorsed (Hempel 1966, 40): "A large-scale theory that has been successful in many areas will normally be abandoned only when a more satisfactory alternative theory is available – and good theories are difficult to come by." In the footnote to this sentence, directly after citing Conant's work as "illustrat[ing]" this point, Hempel makes his only reference in the book to Kuhn's *Structure*, saying only that Kuhn's book provides a "provocative general conception of the rise and fall of scientific theories" (Hempel 1966, 40). Kuhn (1964, 258–9) himself at least once presented his work on thought experiments as illustrating points made by Carnap and Hempel about concept introduction via reduction sentences.[4]

Considerations such as these begin to indicate that the relations between Kuhn's work and the projects of logical empiricism are more complicated than the standard story allows. Moreover, the complications can be multiplied. In 1991 George Reisch (Reisch 1991) finally raised to serious philosophical attention a curious fact about Kuhn's 1962 book – it had originally appeared as a monograph in the series *Foundations of the Unity of Science*. This series was the successor project to Otto Neurath's *International Encyclopedia of*

---

[4] A paranoid vision of Kuhn's relations to Conant are provided in Fuller (2000). We still await a more even-handed and accurate version of this key story.

Unified Science, and it was still being co-edited by Rudolf Carnap and Charles Morris. Thus, it was the logical empiricists themselves who brought *Structure* into the world. As Reisch discovered, Carnap wrote positive editorial letters to Kuhn, praising his book and finding points of contact between his views and Kuhn's. In the first letter, from 1960, Carnap seemed to indicate that he liked precisely the most importantly anticumulative part of Kuhn's conceptual apparatus, the way paradigms bring with them new systems of concepts. As Carnap wrote:

I am myself very much interested in the problems which you intend to deal with, even though my knowledge of the history of science is rather fragmentary. ... Among many other items I liked your emphasis on the new conceptual frameworks which are proposed in revolutions in science and, on their basis, the posing of new questions, not only answers to old problems. (Reisch 1991, 266)

A series of authors starting with Reisch and including John Earman (1993), Michael Friedman (1993; 1998; 2001; 2003), and Gurol Irzik (Irzik and Grunberg 1995; Irzik 2002; 2003) have argued that Carnap was not wrong in finding important similarities between his work and the work of Kuhn.

Perhaps the most important point of contact between the work of Carnap and Kuhn that has been suggested in this new literature is a structural similarity in their epistemological positions that has been most diligently explored by Michael Friedman. Friedman's work on the origins of logical empiricism has uncovered the importance for Carnap and Reichenbach, at least, of the notion of the relativized or variable a priori (Friedman 1999; this volume). This notion was first invoked in their early work on the methodology of physics and was something of a Kantian version of conventionalism. Within the work of Carnap, the general idea worked itself out as a sort of linguistic framework relativity of scientific knowledge: The analytic sentences that constitute a well-formed language serve to stipulate the empirical meanings of the terms for that language. Together with the formal principles of deductive logic and confirmation theory, these principles first induce a notion of logical consequence and, thus, confirmation and disconfirmation in light of experience. Thus, what can be said and known in science is relativized to a linguistic framework – a framework constituted by analytic sentences. These analytic sentences are thus the a priori preconditions of scientific knowledge for that language; but the multiplicity of possible languages indicates that the a priori is not understood here as the absolutely necessary or unchanging. Indeed, in his remarks on the development of science, Carnap suggested that revolutionary change in science occurred exactly when there was a change in the underlying language of science. Since the movement from one linguistic framework to another is not a change of probability weightings within a framework, there was no rule-governed rationality that could explain it. Thus, Carnap himself held that only practical considerations could be used in suggesting a change of language and that a change so affected would not be a proper topic of epistemology.

The connection with Kuhn might by now be evident. Substitute in this story "paradigm" for "linguistic framework," and you have a fairly good summary of Kuhn's views in *Structure*. Paradigms, like linguistic frameworks, constitute the conditions of scientific knowledge – scientific knowledge-making only unproblematically occurs when a paradigm is in hand. Paradigms set the standards of evidence, also, making a rational change of theory within a paradigm rationally intelligible. Scientific revolutions, however, involve change of paradigm and, thus, cannot rely on any intraparadigm notion of rationality. From the point of view of normal science, then, paradigm change in revolutionary science looks irrational. Revolution is affected, then, by "persuasion" rather than the standards of proof available within a scientific paradigm.

The parallels here can be deepened. As Friedman, Reisch, and, especially, Irzik and Grunberg have noted, Kuhn's vexed notion of incommensurability of paradigms finds a parallel in Carnap. The inability of one linguistic framework to express precisely what can be expressed in another is a feature of Carnap's metalogic. Indeed, Carnap had relied on such incompleteness of possible communication to explain features of debates such as the debates in the foundations of mathematics between intuitionists and classical mathematicians. Since the logical framework of intuitionism was weaker than that of the classical mathematicians, it made perfect sense within the intuitionist framework to say that portions of classical mathematics were meaningless – no sentence within the intuitionist language could capture the import of some classical theorems. Carnap abjured any absolutist conclusions from this, however: there were other languages within which all the theorems of classical mathematics could indeed be expressed. The choice among such languages was determined by what one wanted mathematics to do for one's science.

These connections between the work of Carnap and of Kuhn became increasingly visible in the early 1990s when Kuhn began to discuss his work in neo-Kantian terms. He claimed in his 1990 PSA address that his position was "a sort of post-Darwinian Kantianism," which he explained as follows: "Like the Kantian categories, the lexicon supplies preconditions of possible experience. But lexical categories, unlike their Kantian forebears, can and do change, both with time and with passage from one community to another" (1990, 104). But Kantianism with movable categories was, as we have noted, the philosophical point of view upon which Riechenbach and Carnap cut their teeth in the early 1920s. As Friedman (2003) has noted, moreover, a number of the historians of science that Kuhn cites as influences in the preface to *Structure* – among them Alexander Koyré, Anneliese Maier, Hélène Metzger, and Emile Meyerson – were themselves participants in or influenced by the same arguments among the neo-Kantians that influenced Carnap and Reichenbach. In his encyclopedia article on the history of science, Kuhn went so far as to claim that the proper historical attitude toward the technical work of scientists of the past was imbibed in the community of historians of science from philosophers, all from the neo-Kantian and Hegelian idealist traditions:

Partly it was learned from men like [Friedrich] Lange and [Ernst] Cassirer who dealt historically with people or ideas that were also important for scientific development. ([E. A.] Burtt's *Metaphysical Foundations of Modern Science* and [A. O.] Lovejoy's *The Great Chain of Being* were, in this respect, especially influential.) And partly it was learned from a small group of neo-Kantian epistemologists, particularly [Leon] Brunschvicg and Meyerson, whose search for quasi-absolute categories of thought in older scientific ideas produced brilliant genetic analyses of concepts which the main tradition in the history of science had misunderstood or dismissed. (Kuhn 1968, 108)

Lange and Cassirer were the two most historically sensitive members of the Marburg School of neo-Kantianism; Brunschwicg and

Meyerson were leading early-twentieth-century neo-Kantian philosophers in France; Burtt and Lovejoy were leading practitioners
of idealist intellectual history in the early-twentieth-century English-speaking world.

These facts suggest that there is something of a shared intellectual background out of which both the historical project of Kuhn and
the formal project of logical empiricism arose. Friedman (2003) has
argued persuasively that, indeed, the historical and the formal are
two ways to radicalize the insights about the conditions of objectivity that formed the locus of epistemological interest for the neo-
Kantians and led to their most important internal differences. One
might add that the relations among the historical and the formal –
and the complicated relations of both to the psychological – were
also important to the phenomenological tradition, especially after
Husserl's transcendental and, then, historical turns.

Our own historical puzzles, however, seem to be multiplying.[5]
For we have been lately arguing that there is a deep connection in the
concerns of Carnap's logical empiricism and Kuhn regarding the
conditions of the possibility of scientific knowledge. Yet we have
also noted that Kuhn was understood almost from the start to be
importantly changing the direction of philosophy of science by
rejecting fundamental features of logical empiricism. This is now a
genuine historical puzzle. The most pressing aspect of this puzzle is
this: why did logical empiricism have a reputation that was at odds
with some of the most fundamental commitments of at least one of
its leading practitioners?[6] This is a rather large historical question
for which answers are hard to find. We can approach the issue by first
asking one more fairly straightforward historical question: Did Kuhn

---

[5] Interestingly, both Reisch (1991) and Irzik and Grünberg (1995) end their papers on
Kuhn and Carnap by admitting that they have not told a story that explains logical
empiricism's decline or the role of Kuhn in it. Reisch's more recent work (2005,
this volume) offers an account of logical empiricism's decline but does not directly
address the question of Kuhn's role therein.

[6] I would not want to identify logical empiricism with Carnap's philosophy. The
puzzle is how the motivating features of several versions of logical empiricism
(Carnap, Reichenbach, and Schlick, at least) and the continuing features of
Carnap's philosophy could have been so hard to see at this point in the history of
philosophy of science. This is especially odd in the case of Kuhn, whose knowledge
of other versions of logical empiricism, say, Neurath's, seems to have been almost
nonexistent.

understand himself to be arguing against logical empiricism in *Structure*? If so, what did he take himself to be arguing against?

THE IMAGE OF SCIENCE BY WHICH WE ARE POSSESSED: LOGICAL EMPIRICISM?

Kuhn's opponent in *Structure* is a bit shadowy – it is an image of science, an image Kuhn does not carefully locate. In the first instance, the image of science as a cumulative discipline is, for Kuhn, an image to be found in science textbooks. Moreover, since the crucial feature of the image is science-as-cumulative, the primary issue that Kuhn has with the image is historiographical. Kuhn begins the book by discussing the tasks the image assigns to historians of science and how recent history of science had uncovered that these were uninteresting and misleading tasks to assign to an historian of science. The logical empiricists were not notably writers of science texts – such writers were and are primarily scientists – and the logical empiricists might be forgiven for thinking that the image of science argued against in chapter 1 of *Structure* was not one for which they bore primary responsibility.

Nevertheless, there are signs already in chapter 1 of *Structure* that Kuhn associated this image of science with logical empiricism. Kuhn argues already on page 7 that "scientific theory and fact are not categorically separable, except perhaps within a single tradition of normal-scientific practice." Later, it becomes clear that Kuhn understands logical empiricism to insist on a neutral observation language to be contrasted once and for all with a theoretical language (cf. Kuhn 1962 [1996], 125ff.). Thus, he understands his point about fact/theory relations to tell against a logical empiricist understanding of science. Similarly, at the end of chapter 1, Kuhn says, "I may even seem to have violated the very influential distinction between 'the context of discovery' and 'the context of justification'" (Kuhn 1962 [1996], 8). This indicates his awareness of the distinction as drawn in logical empiricism as well as his suspicion that his own view must violate the distinction.

Moreover, there are further signs that Kuhn associated logical empiricism with the image of science he meant to reject. Thus, for example, his account of the incommensurability of normal-scientific traditions that follow distinct paradigms is led off with an objection he associates with logical positivism to his claim that revolutions are necessary in science:

The most prevalent contemporary interpretation of the nature and function of scientific theory ... , closely associated with logical positivism and not categorically rejected by its successors, would restrict the range and meaning of an accepted theory so that it could not possibly conflict with any later theory that made predictions about some of the same natural phenomena. (Kuhn 1962 [1996], 98)

It is not absolutely clear what view of theories Kuhn meant to ascribe to logical positivism in this passage. I suggest, on the basis of his long example regarding Newtonian and Einsteinian dynamics, that the view is this: If a theory, T, makes accurate predictions regarding a range of phenomena, then any successor theory, T′, to T, that accurately predicts those very phenomena cannot be said to be semantically incompatible or incommensurable with T. This is because they both must have statements about those phenomena as logical consequences, and, moreover, using the verification principle, the meaning of scientific theories is given by those of its logical consequences that report on observable phenomena. The two theories might be inconsistent if they give different predictions for some other range of phenomena, but they cannot have the peculiar semantic characteristics theories within two distinct paradigms have on Kuhn's account. Thus, if revolutions involving incommensurability across the revolutionary divide are actual, then scientific theories cannot received their meaning via their relations to preserved observational consequences.[7]

We have already had occasion to doubt whether Kuhn's reading of logical empiricism was strictly correct. Our question now is what made it available for Kuhn to ascribe these views to logical empiricism. What did he understand by logical empiricism? An answer to this question can be found in an interview he gave in 1995. Here is an extraordinary passage of this interview:

[7] I doubt any genuine logical empiricist would have so employed the verification principle in the 1950s or 1960s – certainly a closer reading of the logical empiricist literature on bridge principles, theoretical terms, and so on might have convinced Kuhn that the logical empiricists did not hold a view that made nontranslatability between languages of science that overlapped in empirical content impossible.

One thing I realize I left out before, that should be filled in, and that is the question as to where I got the picture that I was rebelling against in *The Structure of Scientific Revolutions*. And that's itself a strange and not altogether good story. Not altogether good in the sense that I realize in retrospect that I was reasonably irresponsible. I had been, as I'd said, vastly interested, caught a real interest in philosophy in my freshman year, and then had no opportunity to pursue it – initially, at least. It turned out that after I graduated and went off to the Radio Research Laboratory, and indeed continuing most of the time that I was in Europe – I was no longer having school assignments and papers to write – I had what was basically a nine-to-five job; and I suddenly had time to read. And I started reading what I took to be philosophy of science – it seemed the natural place to be reading. And I read things like Bertrand Russell's *Knowledge of the External World*, and quite a number of others of the quasi-popular, quasi-philosophical works; I read some von Mises; I certainly read Bridgman's *Logic of Modern Physics*; I read some Philipp Frank; I read a little bit of Carnap, but not the Carnap that people later point to as the stuff that has real parallels to me. You know this article that recently appeared. It's a very good article. I have confessed a good deal of embarrassment about the fact that I didn't know it [the Carnap]. On the other hand, it is also the case that if I'd known about it, if I'd been into the literature at that level, I probably would never have written *Structure*. And the view that emerges in *Structure* is not the same as the Carnap view, but it's interesting that coming from what were partially different ... Carnap staying within the tradition had been driven to this – I had rebelled already and come to it from another direction, and in any case we were still different. But that was the state of affairs in my mind at the time I had this experience of being asked to teach in the Conant course. And it was against that sort of everyday image of logical positivism – I didn't even think of it as logical empiricism for a while – it was that that I was reacting to when I saw my first examples of history. (1995, 305–6)

Is Kuhn arguing against logical empiricism in the *Structure* according to this account? Well, he is manifestly not arguing against a sophisticated understanding of the mature work of Carnap, for example. He is arguing against an image of something he takes to be logical empiricism, something he read in quasi-popular books, something he got from a mixed bag of sources including Russell's logical atomism and Bridgman's operationalism. Moreover, the time period in question in the quotation is between his being drafted into the army in 1943 and 1947 or 1948 when he was asked by Conant to teach in the General Science Education Program. It was presumably an image of logical empiricism that Kuhn found no reason to become skeptical of or to investigate further in the ensuing 15 years until the publication of *Structure*. Moreover, it is an image of logical empiricism that must have been substantially similar to the image in the minds of many of his readers, who agreed with him that he had shown the poverty of logical empiricism.

This is a key fact for our understanding of the post-Kuhnian decline of logical empiricism: from the mid-1940s onward, logical empiricism was already possessed of an image that neither differentiated it from other analytic projects such as Russell's external world project nor was very sophisticated. We should not, in particular, forget that the logical empiricists, although often decried as the most professional of all philosophers and among the least enjoyable philosophers to read, wrote a large number of rather popular books, books in which they did not carefully differentiate their own projects from other projects and in which they certainly could not be accused of holding the most subtle and searching of philosophical positions. Reichenbach, for example, produced several popularizations from the 1920s and 1930s, *From Copernicus to Einstein* (Reichenbach 1927/1942) and *Atom and Cosmos* (1930a/1932), right through to his final book, *Rise of Scientific Philosophy* (Reichenbach 1951a). Similarly, Frank often wrote for a non-specialist audience and did so in ways that quite explicitly amalgamated logical empiricism to a variety of different philosophical schools such as pragmatism and operationalism. Any proper account of the reception of logical empiricist philosophy must, surely, start with an account of the works that were most widely read among the scholars like Kuhn.

Consider for a moment Frank's (1951) book *Relativity: A Richer Truth*. This little book began as his series of lectures at the New York conferences on science and religion in the 1940s. There Frank presents logical empiricism as philosophical program for understanding science that does not undermine values (the deepest worry about science among the religionists) and that draws upon insights from movements such as pragmatism and operationalism. Indeed, a reader of the book can find these other philosophical and methodological programs named in the very titles of the chapters. Moreover, Frank's book received prominent reviews in the philosophical journals, where it was roundly panned. Frank was routinely condescended to by his reviewers. A young Stephen Toulmin thought the book naive, writing "its sub-title would perhaps best be: Logical Empiricism told to Children" (Toulmin 1951, 181), while A. P. Ushenko used his review to condemn the whole of logical empiricism: "I am urging students to read the book on account of Part One ... because its simplicity and clarity of presentation exposes the inadequacy and confusion of the author's philosophical affiliations where the more technical writings are protected by a camouflage of symbolic notation or pedantic belaboring of detail" (Ushenko 1951, 587). These reviews of Frank's book suggest that there is something importantly amiss in the questions about logical empiricism before and after Kuhn that both the standard story and the new literature on the reappraisal of logical empiricism have taken for granted: Both stories presume that logical empiricism was an almost universal commitment of philosophers of science in North America in the 1940s and 1950s and thus date the decline of logical empiricism in North America to after Kuhn's work. It is, however, far from obvious in exactly what sense logical empiricism dominated American philosophy or even American philosophy of science in the 1940s and 1950s. Ushenko's review (1951, 587), for example, announces a "decline in this country [the United States]" of logical empiricism in 1951 – and this was the review of Frank offered in the single most important journal in philosophy of science in North America at the time, *Philosophy of Science*.[8] An open-minded reading of the reviews of Frank's book indicate that logical empiricism was not only not accepted, it was at least at times deeply resisted and even resented, by philosophers in the 1940s and 1950s. Kuhn's account of how easy it was to acquire a working image of logical empiricism in the popular literature and not be asked to deepen one's understanding of it in the next 15 years, even as he became a prominent historian of science, suggests a similar lesson: Logical empiricism looked from the outside like something rather different from how it looked on the inside, and at least some

---

[8] I do not know who would have agreed with Ushenko in 1951; my point is that such claims could be made without fuss in the pages of the leading philosophy of science journal in North America, a fact that works against any straightforward claim that logical empiricism dominated the scene in philosophy of science at the time.

philosophers of science as well as most, if not all, historians of science were well on the outside of logical empiricism.

These suspicions can be confirmed by looking at reviews of Reichenbach's *Rise of Scientific Philosophy* (1951a). This volume was also subjected to searching criticism and extraordinarily negative reviews almost immediately. Reichenbach was pilloried on all sides. In *Philosophy Review*, Norman Malcolm (1951) took up the ordinary language banner, denouncing Reichenbach's presuppositions (e.g., that science is the most successful form of knowledge – Malcolm prefers his knowledge that the quince is in blossom or that his cereal will taste flat without a bit of salt) and pretensions (especially his claim to be offering a scientific philosophy; his methods and his alleged results, according to Malcolm, are not those of science). The Hegelian Errol Harris takes Reichenbach to task for 13 lively and entertaining pages in *Philosophical Quarterly*, concluding unhappily: "the desert sands in which the river of philosophical thought is choked are the arid wastes of self-styled 'scientific philosophy'" (Harris 1951, 165). Most relevantly for the story of Kuhn, I. Bernard Cohen, his Harvard colleague at the time and a man who had been approached to write the history of science monograph in the *Encyclopedia* and had refused, was quite tartly dismissive of Reichenbach's whole project. The following quotation serves to illustrate of the tone of the review as a whole:

Reichenbach very generously admits, "I do not wish to belittle the history of philosophy; but one should always remember that it is history, not philosophy. Like all historical research, it should be done with scientific methods and psychological and sociological explanations." Since the armory of the "scientific philosopher" appears to include so many episodes from the history of science, I must admit to a prejudice in favor of having the facts correct to begin with, and I cannot see how the sociological and psychological explanations and the scientific methods have any point if this is not the case. ... It seems a pity that a work that contains so much about the history of science and that is devoted to replacing "error" by "truth" should itself attempt to find truth by repeating error. (Cohen 1951, 328, 329)

There can be no doubt that Cohen found reason to be suspicious of logical empiricist understandings of the history of science as they were displayed in semipopular books like *The Rise of Scientific*

Philosophy. As for *Philosophy of Science,* no review of *The Rise of Scientific Philosophy* ever appeared on its pages.[9]

Any accurate description, then, of the relations of Kuhn to logical empiricism must take into account the understandings of logical empiricism held by both Kuhn and his audiences in 1962 as well as the ways in which logical empiricism had been controversial both within and without professional philosophy for more than a decade by 1962. Thus, for example, my sketch in the opening pages of this chapter would need to expand to consider important con-troversies about logical empiricism from well before 1958. The "received view" of logical empiricism circa 1962 is a topic upon which little work has been done. This is not surprising. Nearly all work in the recent history of logical empiricism has been done by philosophers whose main concern has been to recover logical empiricism's self-understandings and for whom "the received view" of logical empiricism is a myth to be exploded. Moreover, we have no good theory of the dynamics of change in the history of philosophy in general – yet the decline of logical empiricism due, in part at least, to the reception of works critical of it, including Kuhn's book, is surely an episode for which we would need to have a decent dynam-ical account.

As a minor contribution to a future literature on this topic, I wish to suggest that Kuhn's work helped to make widespread and to stabilize the very image of logical empiricism it sought to argue against. It is worth remembering the complex and carefully worded statement of his relations to logical empiricism with which Kuhn ends chapter 1 of *Structure.* Speaking of the discovery/justification and theory/observable fact distinctions, Kuhn wrote:

Having been weaned intellectually on these distinctions and others like them, I could scarcely be more aware of their import and force. For many years I took them to be about the nature of knowledge, and I still suppose that, appropriately recast, they have something important to tell us. Yet my

---

[9] I reiterate that this is an exercise in reception studies: how was logical empiricism understood by those who read it in its semipopular forms? That there is an important place for history in the logical empiricism of, for example, Otto Neurath (see, e.g., Uebel 1991a) is not currently at issue, precisely because this seems not to have been importantly noticed by those who forged the "received view" of logical empiricism. The issue in reception studies for Neurath scholars is how his work disappeared from view.

attempts to apply them, even *grosso modo*, to the actual situations in which knowledge is gained, accepted, and assimilated have made them seem extraordinarily problematic. Rather than being elementary logical or methodological distinctions, which would thus be prior to the analysis of scientific knowledge, they now seem integral parts of a traditional set of substantive answers to the very questions upon which they have been deployed. (1962 [1996], 9)

This view of such distinctions as substantive answers to questions of the possibility of scientific knowledge opened for Kuhn the possibility that there are better answers that do not employ precisely these distinctions. What, then, is the evidence upon which any such new account would be given and upon which the accounts would be judged? Kuhn answers this directly: "If they are to have more than pure abstraction as their content, then that content must be discovered by observing them in application to the data they are meant to elucidate. How could history of science fail to be a source of phenomena to which theories about knowledge may legitimately be asked to apply?" (Kuhn 1962 [1996], 9).

While it is open to doubt whether the relation of the history of science to philosophy of science is appropriately conceived of as the relation of evidence to theory, there is little doubt that it was Kuhn's rhetorical question here that won the day. After the work of Kuhn and a few others (Hanson, Feyerabend), it became obvious to working philosophers of science that their work had a greater responsibility to historical accuracy and illumination than the accounts of the logic of science in logical empiricism were understood to have. Thus, Kuhn helped crystallize within the professional community of philosophers of science the very image of logical empiricism he sought to reject: after Kuhn it was taken for granted that logical empiricism was ahistorical in the deep sense of providing no illumination regarding the historical processes of the development of science. It is quite clear that it was the historical setting of Kuhn's philosophy of science that Hesse saw as early as 1963 as being a new "epistemological paradigm." Hacking presented this view in a typically plain fashion in the introduction to his 1981 anthology on scientific revolutions:

Perhaps the contrast between the image [of science in traditional philosophy of science, including logical empiricism] and Kuhn's [image of science] lies not so much in a head-on collision about specifics as in a different conception of the relation of knowledge and its past. The old image was ahistorical and used the history of science merely to provide examples of logical points. Kuhn ... think[s] that the contents of a science and its methods of reasoning and research are integrally connected with its historical development. (Hacking 1981, 3)

Hacking notes here both the historical nature of scientific reasoning and the lack of importance of merely "logical points" in Kuhn. This suggests that Kuhn not only succeeded in dislodging the particular topics associated in his mind and the minds of his readers in the 1960s with logical empiricism (a timeless, universal logic of induction or of explanation, say); he also succeeded in changing the methods and tools of philosophy of science. Readers of Kuhn's book found a philosophy of science that used tools from history of science, Gestalt and Piagetian genetic psychology, Wittgensteinian philosophy, sociology of knowledge and science, rhetoric, history of art, and other disciplines to attempt to explain and ground the vision of epistemic change at its heart. No one reading *Structure* in 1962 would think for a moment that a logical empiricist had written it. The way Kuhn's philosophy of science opened itself up to other disciplines certainly explains in part why those disciplines were receptive to it. But philosophers also found a new set of tools, concerns, and ways of thinking. This much is admitted by one of those authors who came by the early 1990s to see a strong link between Kuhn's philosophy and Carnap's, John Earman, who wrote this in the conclusion to paper arguing for such a link:

I was a distant student of Carnap and a close student of Kuhn. But the two seemed to me so different in style and concerns that I placed them in different parts of the philosophical firmament. Only now have I begun to appreciate how misguided my placement was and how much philosophy of science can be enriched by considering how the ideas of these two giants interact. (Earman 1993, 32)

No doubt there is much to gain by thinking through the mutual relations of the ideas of Kuhn and Carnap. The historical question of the early reception of Kuhn's work and its relation to the decline of logical empiricism must, however, be more interested in Earman's early sense that the two philosophers were very different. One of Earman's own terms here –"style" – seems especially important: Kuhn's

way of treating the rather Kantian questions he shared with Carnap
was historical, psychological, and social, all. His philosophy of science was in method and style importantly different from the logical
methods and dry analytic style for which the logical empiricists were
famous. A proper history of the reception of Kuhn's work will have to
investigate the persuasiveness of his literary style within the academic
world of the 1960s.

THE RELATION OF PHILOSOPHY OF SCIENCE TO ITS PAST

Recent research into logical empiricism has argued against the
"everyday image of logical positivism" that Kuhn assumed, argued
against, and helped make canonical. It is for this reason that contemporary researchers such as Michael Friedman and Bas van
Fraassen can invoke logical empiricism and find resources within it
exactly when concerning themselves with the historical dynamics
of science. In the 1960s, however, the project of logical empiricism
did not find an adequate voice to respond to Kuhn's "role for history." This essay suggests that in part this was due to a feeling
among those within logical empiricism that Kuhn's account did not
importantly disrupt their own – theirs was a technical, not an
everyday image of logical empiricism – and in part due to a very
widely shared view among Kuhn's other readers that his work had
importantly shown the poverty of logical empiricism (as they
understood it), both in content and in method.

In addition to suggesting that philosophers ought to be more well
attuned to the reception of their own work and more interested in
making it, if not popular, at least understandable and persuasive to a
larger audience, I would suggest two further points. First, work in
the reappraisal of logical empiricism has brought it more centrally
into the continuing discussions in philosophy of science about the
post-Kuhnian predicament: how to account for serious conceptual
change in science without succumbing to a hopeless version of
relativism. It is here that the structural similarities between Kuhn's
and Carnap's accounts are genuinely important – since they either
deepen the problem or suggest that maybe Carnapian resources
might somehow solve Kuhnian problems. Second, to echo Earman
in a somewhat more historical tone, in this ongoing conversation,

we would be equally helped by a newly historically rich and intellectually responsible literature on the work of Kuhn and other philosophers of science in the 1940s and 1950s who were not logical empiricists. A more detailed understanding of the philosophical landscapes of the recent past may reveal resources to use to resolve current philosophical problems.[10]

[10] I do not mean to suggest that no such work has appeared. For some recent excavation of the American context in philosophy of science in the postwar period, see Reisch (2005) and Howard (2003).

Bibliography

Adler, Mortimer. 1941. "God and the Professors." *Science, Philosophy and Religion: A Symposium*. New York: Conference on Science, Philosophy and Religion in Their Relation to the Democratic Way of Life.

Adorno, Theodor W., et al. 1969. *Der Positivismusstreit in der Deutschen Soziologie*. Frankfurt/Main: Luchterhand. Trans. as The Positivist Dispute in German Sociology. London: Heinemann, 1976.

Allen, Raymond B. 1949. "Communists Should Not Teach in American Colleges." *Educational Forum* 13, no. 4, 433–40.

Alston, William and George Nakhnikian (eds.). 1963. *Readings in Twentieth-Century Philosophy*. New York: Free Press of Glencoe.

Anonymous. 1925. *Die Technische Hochschule* 5.

Anonymous. 1927. *Vossische Zeitung*, June 30.

Anonymous. 1931. "Gesellschaft für empirische Philosophie." *Erkenntnis* 2, 310.

Anonymous. 1937. *Bohemia*, September 17.

Anonymous. 1937a. *Prager Tageblatt*, September 17.

Anscombe, G. E. M. 1971. *An Introduction to Wittgenstein's Tractatus*. London: Hutchinson University Library.

Aspect, A., J. Dalibard, and G. Roger. 1982. "Experimental Tests of Bell's Inequalities Using Time-Varying Analyzers." *Physical Review Letters* 49, 1804–7.

Aster, Ernst V. 1935. *Die Philosophie der Gegenwart*. Berlin: Walter de Gruyter.

Awodey, Steve and A. W. Carus. 2001. "Carnap, Completeness, and Categoricity: The *Gabelbarkeitssatz* of 1928." *Erkenntnis* 54, 145–72.

Awodey, Steve and A. W. Carus. 2003. "Carnap vs. Gödel on Syntax and Tolerance." In P. Parrini, W. C. Salmon, and M. H. Salmon (eds.), *Logical Empiricism: Historical and Contemporary Perspectives*. Pittsburgh: University of Pittsburgh Press, 57–64.

Awodey, Steve and A. W. Carus. 2004. "How Carnap Could Have Replied to Gödel." In Awodey and Klein (2004), 199–220.

Awodey, Steve and A. W. Carus. 2007. "The Quest for Analyticity: Carnap's Studies in Semantics." In R. Creath and M. Friedman (eds.), *The Cambridge Companion to Carnap*. Cambridge: Cambridge University Press.

Awodey, Steve and A. W. Carus. Forthcoming. "Carnap's Dream: Wittgenstein, Gödel and *Logical Syntax*," *Synthese*.

Awodey, Steve and Carsten Klein (eds.). 2004. *Carnap Brought Home: The View from Jena*. Chicago: Open Court.

Ayer, Alfred J. 1936. *Language, Truth and Logic*. London: Gollancz.

Ayer, Alfred J. 1957. "The Vienna Circle." In *Revolution in Philosophy*. London: Macmillan & Co., New York: St Martin's Press, 70–87.

Ayer, Alfred J. (ed.) 1959. *Logical Positivism*. Glencoe, IL: Free Press.

Baker, Gordon. 1979. "Verehrung und Verkehrung: Waismann and Wittgenstein." In Luckhardt (1979), 243–85.

Baker, Gordon. 1988. *Wittgenstein, Frege, and the Vienna Circle*. Oxford: Blackwell.

Barbour, J. and H. Pfister (eds.). 1995. *Mach's Principle: From Newton's Bucket to Quantum Gravity*. Basel: Birkhäuser.

Bauer, Otto. 1924. "Das Weltbild des Kapitalismus". In O. Jenssen (ed.) *Der lebendige Marxismus. Festschrift zum 70. Geburtstag von Karl Kautsky*. Jena: Thuringer Verlagsanstalt, 407–64. Excerpts trans. as "The World View of Organized Capitalism" in T. Bottomore and P. Goode (eds.), *Austro-Marxism*. Oxford: Clarendon Press, 1978, 208–17.

Bell, D. and W. Vossenkuhl. 1992. *Science and Subjectivity: The Vienna Circle and Twentieth Century Philosophy*. Berlin: Akademie.

Bell, J. 1964. "On the Einstein-Podolsky-Rosen Paradox." *Physics* 1, 195–200. Reprinted in Bell (2004), 14–21.

Bell, J. 1966. "On the Problem of Hidden Variables in Quantum Mechanics." *Reviews of Modern Physics* 38, 447–52. Reprinted in Bell (2004), 1–13.

Bell, J. 1982. "On the Impossible Pilot Wave." *Foundations of Physics* 12, 989–99. Reprinted in Bell (2004), 159–68.

Bell, J. 2004. *Speakable and Unspeakable in Quantum Mechanics*. 2nd ed. Cambridge: Cambridge University Press.

Beller, M. 1999. *Quantum Dialogue: The Making of a Revolution*. Chicago: University of Chicago Press.

Bergmann, Gustav. 1954. *The Metaphysics of Logical Positivism*. New York: Longmans, Green and Co.

Beuttler, Fred. 1997. "For the World at Large: Intergroup Activities at the Jewish Theological Seminary." In J. Wertheimer (ed.), *Tradition Renewed: A History of the Jewish Theological Seminary*. New York: The Seminary, 667–736.

Biletzki, Anat. 2003. *(Over)Interpreting Wittgenstein*. Dordrecht: Kluwer.

Bird, Alexander. 2000. *Thomas Kuhn*. Princeton: Princeton University Press.

Bird, G.H. 1995. "Carnap and Quine: Internal and External Questions." *Erkenntnis* 42, 41–64.

Bloor, David. 1982. "Durkheim and Mauss Revisited: Classification and the Sociology of Knowledge." *Studies in History and Philosophy of Science* 13, 267–97.

Blumberg, Albert and Herbert Feigl. 1931. "Logical Positivism: A New Movement in European Philosophy." *Journal of Philosophy* 28, 281–96.

Bohr, N. 1948. "On the Notions of Causality and Complementarity." *Dialectica* 2, 312–19.

Bonk, Thomas (ed.). 2003. *Language, Truth and Knowledge. Contributions to the Philosophy of Rudolf Carnap*. Dordrecht: Kluwer.

Boring, E.G. 1935. "The Relation of the Attributes of Sensation to the Dimensions of the Stimulus." *Philosophy of Science* 2(2), 236–45.

Born, M. 1949. *The Natural Philosophy of Cause and Chance*. Oxford: Oxford University Press.

Bourdieu, Pierre. 1975. "The Specificity of the Scientific Field and the Social Conditions of the Progress of Reason." *Social Science Information* 14, 19–47.

Bourdieu, Pierre. 1984. *Homo academicus*. Paris: Editions de Minuit.

Bourdieu, Pierre. 1989. "Towards a Reflexive Sociology. A Workshop with Pierre Bourdieu." Introduction and trans. by L. Wacquant. *Sociological Theory* 7, 26–63.7, 26–63 A shortened version in S.P. Turner (ed.), *Social Theory and Sociology*. Oxford: Blackwell, 1996, 213–28.

Bridgman, Percy W. 1927. *The Logic of Modern Physics*. New York: Macmillan.

Broady, Donald. 1997. "The Epistemological Tradition in French Sociology." In Jostein Gripsrud (ed.), *Rhetoric and Epistemology. Papers from a Seminar at the Maison des sciences de l'homme in Paris, September 1996*. Rhetoric-Knowledge-Mediation Working Papers No. 1, 1997. Department of Media Studies, University of Bergen, 1997.

Browder, F. (ed.). 1976. *Mathematical Developments Arising from Hilbert Problems. Proceedings in Pure Mathematics*, vol. 28. Providence, RI: American Mathematical Society.

Brunswik, E. 1937. "Psychology as a Science of Objective Relations." *Philosophy of Science* 4(2), 227–60.

Buckley, William F. 1951. *God and Man at Yale: The Superstitions of "Academic Freedom."* Chicago: Henry Regnery.

Butts, Robert E. 2000. "The Reception of German Scientific Philosophy in North America: 1930–1965." In *Witches, Scientists, Philosophers: Essays and Lectures.* Dordrecht: Kluwer.

Caldwell, Bruce. 1982. *Beyond Positivism. Economic Methodology in the 20th Century.* London: Routledge. Rev. ed. 1994.

Campbell, N.R. 1953. "The Structure of Theories." In H. Feigl and M. Brodbeck (eds.), *Readings in the Philosophy of Science.* New York: Appleton-Century-Crofts, 288–308.

Carnap, Rudolf. 1922. *Der Raum: Ein Beitrag zur Wissenschaftslehre.* Berlin: Reuther & Richard.

Carnap, Rudolf. 1923. "Über die Aufgabe der Physik und die Anwendung des Grundsatzes der Einfachstheit." *Kant-Studien* 28, 90–107.

Carnap, Rudolf. 1924. "Dreidimensionalität des Raumes und Kausalität." *Annalen der Philosophie und philosophischen Kritik* 4, 105–30.

Carnap, Rudolf. 1927. "Eigentliche und uneigentliche Begriffe." *Symposion* 1, 355–74.

Carnap, Rudolf. 1928. *Der logische Aufbau der Welt.* Berlin: Weltkreis. 2nd ed. Hamburg: Meiner, 1961 Trans. in Carnap (1967).

Carnap, Rudolf. 1928a. *Scheinprobleme in der Philosophie: Das Fremdpsychische und der Realismusstreit.* Berlin-Schlachtensee: Weltkries. Trans. by R. George as "Pseudoproblems in Philosophy" in Carnap (1967), 305–43.

Carnap, Rudolf. 1929. *Abriß der Logistik.* Vienna: Springer.

Carnap, Rudolf. 1930. "Die Mathematik als Zweig der Logik." *Blätter für deutsche Philosophie* 4, 298–310.

Carnap, Rudolf. 1930a. "Die alte und die neue Logik." *Erkenntnis* 1, 12–26. Trans. by I Levi as "The Old and the New Logic" in Ayer (1959), 133–46.

Carnap, Rudolf. 1931. "Die logizistische Grundlegung der Mathematik." *Erkenntnis* 2, 91–105. Trans. by E. Putnam and G. Massey as "The Logicist Foundation of Mathematics" in P. Benacerraf and H. Putnam (eds.), *Philosophy of Mathematics: Selected Readings.* 2nd ed. Cambridge: Cambridge University Press, 1983, 41–52.

Carnap, Rudolf. 1932. "Psychologie in physikalischer Sprache." *Erkenntnis* 3, 107–42. Translated by Frederic Schick and reprinted as "Psychology in Physical Language" in Ayer (1959), 165–98.

Carnap, Rudolf. 1932a. "Über Protokollsätze." *Erkenntnis* 2, 215–28. Trans. by R. Creath and R. Nollan as "On Protocol Sentences," *Nous* 21 (1987), 457–70.

Carnap, Rudolf. 1932b. "Die physikalische Sprache als Universalsprache der Wissenschaft." *Erkenntnis* 2, 432–65. Trans. as Carnap (1934a), with some revisions and a new author's introduction.

Carnap, Rudolf. 1934. *Logische Syntax der Sprache*. Vienna: Springer. Translated as Carnap (1937).

Carnap, Rudolf. 1934a. *The Unity of Science*. Trans. and ed. by Max Black. London: Kegan Paul, Trench, Trubner & Co Repr., with changes and corrections by Carnap, in Alston and Nakhnikian (1963), 393–424.

Carnap, Rudolf. 1935. *Philosophy and Logical Syntax*. London: Kegan Paul.

Carnap, Rudolf. 1936. "Von der Erkenntnistheorie zur Wissenschaftslogik." *Actes du Congrès international de philosophie scientifique*, vol. 1. Paris: Hermann, 36–41.

Carnap, Rudolf. 1936a. "Über die Einheitssprache der Wissenschaft. Logische Bemerkungen zum Project einer Enzyklopädie." *Actes du Congres Internationale de Philosophie Scientifique, Sorbonne, Paris 1935*, Facs. II, "Unité de la Science." Paris: Hermann, 60–70.

Carnap, Rudolf. 1936/37. "Testability and Meaning." *Philosophy of Science 3*, 419–71; 4, 1–40.

Carnap, Rudolf. 1937. *The Logical Syntax of Language*. Trans. by A. Smeaton. London: Kegan Paul Repr. Chicago: Open Court, 2002.

Carnap, Rudolf. 1938. "Logical Foundations of the Unity of Science." In Neurath et al. (1938), 42–62.

Carnap, Rudolf. 1939. "Foundations of Logic and Mathematics." *International Encyclopedia of Unified Science*, vol 1, no. 3. Chicago: University of Chicago Press.

Carnap, Rudolf. 1942. *Introduction to Semantics*. Cambridge, MA: Harvard University Press.

Carnap, Rudolf. 1945. "On Inductive Logic." *Philosophy of Science 12*, 72–97.

Carnap, Rudolf. 1945a. "The Two Concepts of Probability." *Philosophy and Phenomenological Research 5*, 513–32. Reprinted in H. Feigl and W. Sellars (eds.), *Readings in Philosophical Analysis*. New York: Appleton–Century–Crofts, 1949, 330–48.

Carnap, Rudolf. 1947. *Meaning and Necessity: A Study in Semantics and Modal Logic*. Chicago: University of Chicago Press.

Carnap, Rudolf. 1950. "Empiricism, Semantics, and Ontology." *Revue Internationale de Philosophie 11*, 20–40.

Carnap, Rudolf. 1950a. *Logical Foundations of Probability*. 2nd ed. 1962. Chicago: Chicago University Press.

Carnap, Rudolf. 1952. *The Continuum of Inductive Methods*. Chicago: Chicago University Press.

Carnap, Rudolf. 1956. "The Methodological Character of Theoretical Concepts." *Minnesota Studies in the Philosophy of Science 1*, 38–56.

Carnap, Rudolf. 1963. "Intellectual Autobiography." In Schilpp (1963), 3–84.

Carnap, Rudolf. 1963a. "Replies and Systematic Expositions." In Schilpp (1963), 859–1013.

Carnap, Rudolf. 1966. *Philosophical Foundations of Physics: An Introduction to the Philosophy of Science*. New York: Basic Books. Martin Gardner (ed.). Republished as *An Introduction to Philosophy of Science*. New York: Basic Books, 1974.

Carnap, Rudolf. 1967. *The Logical Structure of the World. Pseudoproblems in Philosophy*. Translated by R. George. Berkeley: University of California Press, 1967. Repr. Chicago: Open Court, 2003.

Carnap, Rudolf. 1968. "Inductive Logic and Inductive Intuition." In I. Lakatos (ed.), *The Problem of Inductive Logic*. Amsterdam: North Holland, 258–67.

Carnap, Rudolf, Hans Hahn, and Otto Neurath. 1929. *Wissenschaftliche Weltauffassung. Der Wiener Kreis*. Vienna: Wolf. Trans. as "The Scientific World-Conception. The Vienna Circle" in Neurath (1973), 299–318.

Cartwright, Nancy, Jordi Cat, Lola Fleck, and Thomas E. Uebel. 1996. *Otto Neurath: Philosophy between Science and Politics*. Cambridge: Cambridge University Press.

Carus, A. W. 1999. "Carnap, Syntax, and Truth." In J. Peregrin (ed.), *Truth and Its Nature (If Any)*. Dordrecht: Kluwer, 15–35.

Carus, A. W. 2004. "Sellars, Carnap, and the Logical Space of Reasons." In *Awodey and Klein* (2004), 317–56.

Cassirer, E. 1910. *Substance and Function*. Trans. by W. Swabey and M. Swabey. New York: Dover Publications, 1953.

Cat, Jordi. 1995. "The Popper-Neurath Debate and Neurath's Attack on Scientific Method." *Studies in History and Philosophy of Science* 26, 219–50.

Cat, Jordi, Hasok Chang, and Nancy Cartwright. 1996. "Otto Neurath: Politics and the Unity of Science." In P. Galison and D. Stump (eds.), *The Disunity of Science: Boundaries, Contexts, and Power*. Stanford: Stanford University Press, 347–69.

Charle, Christophe. 1990. *Naissance des 'intellectuels' 1880–1900*. Paris: Editions de Minuit.

Coffa, J. Alberto. 1979. "Elective Affinities: Weyl and Reichenbach." In W. Salmon (ed.), *Hans Reichenbach: Logical Empiricist*. Dordrecht: D. Reidel, 267–304.

Coffa, J. Alberto. 1985. "Idealism and the *Aufbau*." In N. Rescher (1985), 133–56.

Coffa, J. Alberto. 1991. *The Semantic Tradition from Kant to Carnap: To the Vienna Station*. L. Wessels (ed.). Cambridge: Cambridge University Press.

Cohen, I. Bernard. 1951. "The Eternal Search." *Scientific Monthly* 73, 328–9.

Cooney, Terry, A. 1986. *The Rise of the New York Intellectuals: Partisan Review and Its Circle*. Madison: University of Wisconsin Press.

Cornforth, Maurice. 1950. *In Defense of Philosophy: Against Positivism and Pragmatism*. New York: International Publishers.

Crary, Alice and Rupert Read. 2000. *The New Wittgenstein*. New York: Routledge.

Creath, Richard. 1990. "The Unimportance of Semantics." *PSA 1990*, vol. 2, Arthur Fine, et al. (eds.), East Lansing, MI: Philosophy of Science Association, 405–15.

Creath, Richard (ed.). 1990a. *Dear Carnap, Dear Van: The Quine-Carnap Correspondence and Related Work*. Los Angeles: University of California Press.

Creath, Richard. 2004. "Quine on the Intelligibility and Relevance of Analyticity." In R. Gibson (ed.), *The Cambridge Companion to Quine*. Cambridge: Cambridge University Press, 47–64.

Cushing, J. T. 1994. *Quantum Mechanics: Historical Contingency and the Copenhagen Hegemony*. Chicago: University of Chicago Press.

Dahms, Hans-Joachim. 1994. *Positivismusstreit. Die Auseinandersetzungen der Frankfurter Schule mit dem logischen Positivismus, dem amerikanischen Pragmatismus und dem kritischen Rationalismus*. Frankfurt/ Main: Suhrkamp.

Dahms, Hans-Joachim. 1997. "Felix Kaufmann und der Physikalismus." In Stadler (1997a), 97–114.

Dahms, Hans-Joachim. 2004. "*Neue Sachlichkeit* in the Architecture and Philosophy of the 1920s." In Awodey and Klein (2004), 357–75.

Dallmayr, Fred R. and Thomas A. McCarthy (eds). 1977. *Understanding and Social Inquiry*. Notre Dame, IN: University of Notre Dame Press.

Danneberg, Lutz, Andreas Kamlah, and Lutz Schäfer (eds.). 1994. *Hans Reichenbach und die Berliner Gruppe*. Braunschweig: Verlag Friedr. Vieweg & Sohn.

Danneberg, Lutz and Wilhelm Schernus. 1994. "Die Gesellschaft für wissenschaftliche Philosophie: Programm, Vorträge und Materialien." In Danneberg, Kamlah, and Schäfer (1994), 478–81.

Darden, Lindley. 1976. "The Heritage of Logical Positivism: A Reassessment." *PSA: Proceedings of the Philosophy of Science Association*, 1976, 2, 242–58.

Daum, Andreas. 1998. *Wissenschaftspopularisierung im 19. Jahrhundert: bürgerliche Kultur, naturwissenschaftliche Bildung und die deutsche Öffentlichkeit*. Munich: R. Oldenbourg Verlag.

Davidson, Donald. 1970. "Mental Events." Reprinted in Davidson, *Essays on Actions and Events*. Oxford: Oxford University Press, 1980.

Dejnozka, Jan. 1991. "Russell's Seventeen Private-Language Arguments." *Russell*, Summer, 11–35.

Dewey, John. 1938. "Unity of Science as a Social Problem." *International Encyclopedia of Unified Science*, vol. 1, no. 1. Chicago: University of Chicago Press, 29–38.

Dewey, John. 1939. "Theory of Valuation." *International Encyclopedia of Unified Science*, vol. 2, no. 4. Chicago: University of Chicago Press.

Dewey, John. 1943. "Anti–Naturalism in Extremis." *Partisan Review* 10, 24–39.

Dewey, John and Horace Kallen (eds.). 1941. *The Bertrand Russell Case*. New York: Viking Press.

Diamond, Cora. 2000. "Does Bismarck Have a Beetle in His Box? The Private Language Argument in the *Tractatus*." In Crary and Read (2000), 262–92.

Dieks, D. 1987. "Gravitation as a Universal Force." *Synthese* 73, 381–97.

Dierker, Egbert and Karl Sigmund (eds.). 1998. *Karl Menger, Ergebnisse eines Mathematischen Kolloquiums*. Vienna: Springer.

Drury, M. O'C. 1984. "Conversations with Wittgenstein." In Rhees (1984), 98–171 and 218–25.

Dubislav, Walter. 1929. "Joseph Petzoldt in Memoriam." *Annalen der Philosophie* 8, 289–95.

Dubislav, Walter. 1933. *Naturphilosophie*. Berlin: Verlag Junker und Dünnhaupt.

Ducasse, C. J. 1959. "A Statement from the President to the Members of the Philosophy of Science Association." *Philosophy of Science* 26, 171.

Duhem, Pierre. 1906. *La Théorie Physique, son Objet et sa Structure*. Paris: Editions Rivière.Paris: Editions Rivière German trans. by Friedrich Adler as *Ziel und Struktur der physikalischen Theorien*. With a foreword by Ernst Mach. Leipzig: Johann Ambrosius Barth, 1908 English trans. as *The Aim and Structure of Physical Theory*. Princeton: Princeton University Press, 1991.

Dvorak, Johann. 1981. *Edgar Zilsel und die Einheit der Erkenntnis*. Vienna: Löcker.

Earman, John. 1972. "Notes on the Causal Theory of Time." *Synthese* 24, 74–86.

Earman, John. 1974. "An Attempt to Add a Little Direction to 'The Problem of the Direction of Time.'" *Philosophy of Science* 41, 15–47.

Earman, John. 1989. *World Enough and Space-Time*. Cambridge, MA: MIT Press.

Earman, John. 1993. "Carnap, Kuhn, and the Philosophy of Scientific Methodology." In P. Horwich (1993), 9–36.

Earman, John. 1995. *Bangs, Crunches, Whimpers, and Shrieks: Singularities and Acausalities in Relativistic Spacetimes*. New York: Oxford University Press.

Edel, Abraham. 1961. "Science and the Structure of Ethics." *International Encyclopedia of Unified Science*, vol. 2, no. 3. Chicago: University of Chicago Press.

Edmonds, David and John Eidinow. 2001. *Wittgenstein's Poker. The Story of a Ten-Minute Argument between Two Great Philosophers*. London: Faber and Faber.

Ehlers, J., F. Pirani, and A. Schild. 1972. "The Geometry of Freefall and Light Propagation." In L. O'Raifeartaigh (ed.), *General Relativity: Papers in Honour of J. L. Synge*. Oxford: Clarendon Press, 63–84.

Ehrenfest, P. and T. Ehrenfest. 1911. "Begriffliche Grundlagen der statischen Auffassung in der Mechanik." *Encyklopädie der mathematischen Wissenschaften, mit Einschluss ihrer Anwendungen*, Bd. 4, 1–90. Trans. by M. Moravcsik as *The Conceptual Foundations of the Statistical Approach in Mechanics*. New York: Dover Publications, 1990.

Einstein, Albert. 1905. "Zur Elektrodynamik bewegter Körper." *Annalen der Physik* 17, 891–921. Reprinted in Einstein (1989), 275–315. Trans. as "On the Electrodynamics of Moving Bodies" in J. Stachel (ed.), *Einstein's Miraculous Year*. Princeton: Princeton University Press, 1998, 123–60.

Einstein, Albert. 1916. "Die Grundlage der allgemeinen Relativitätstheorie." *Annalen der Physik* 49, 769–822. Reprinted in Einstein (1996), 284–337. Also issued as a *separatim*, *Die Grundlage der allgemeinen Relativitätstheorie*. Leipzig: J. Barth. Trans. as "The Foundation of the General Theory of Relativity" in Lorentz et al.(1923), 111–64.

Einstein, Albert. 1917. "Kosmologische Betractungen zur allegemeinen Relativitätstheorie." *Preußische Akademie der Wissenschaften (Berlin). Sitzungberichte. Physikalisch-Mathematische Klasse*, 142–52. Reprinted in Einstein (1996), 540–52. Trans. as "Cosmological Considerations on the General Theory of Relativity" in Lorentz et al. (1923), 175–88.

Einstein, Albert. 1921. "Geometrie und Erfahrung." *Preussische Akademie der Wissenschaft. Physikalisch-mathematische Klasse. Sitzungsberichte*, 123–30. Issued separately in augmented form as Einstein (1921a). Expanded and trans. as "Geometry and Experience" in G. Jeffrey and W. Perrett (eds.), *Sidelights on Relativity*. London: Methuen, 1923, 27–55.

Einstein, Albert. 1921a. *Geometrie und Erfahrung*. Berlin: Springer.

Einstein, Albert. 1952. "Relativity and the Problem of Space." In Einstein (1961), Appendix V. New York: Crown Publishers, 135–57.

Einstein, Albert. 1955. "Bemerkungen zu den in diesem Band vereinigten Arbeiten." In Paul A. Schilpp, *Albert Einstein als Philosoph und Physiker*. Stuttgart: Verlag W. Kohlhammer, 493–511.

Einstein, Albert. 1961. *Relativity: The Special and General Theory*. 15th ed. New York: Crown. Trans. by R. W. Lawson. First published in 1917.

Einstein, Albert. 1989. *The Collected Papers of Albert Einstein*. Vol. 2. J. Stachel (ed.). Princeton: Princeton University Press.

Einstein, Albert. 1996. *The Collected Papers of Albert Einstein*. Vol. 6. A. Kox, M. Klein, and R. Schulmann (eds.). Princeton: Princeton University Press.

Einstein, Albert. 2002. *The Collected Papers of Albert Einstein*. Vol. 7. M. Janssen, R. Schulman, J. Illy, C. Lehner, and D. K. Buchwald (eds.). Princeton: Princeton University Press.

Einstein, A., B. Podolsky, and N. Rosen. 1935. "Can Quantum-Mechanical Description of Physical Reality Be Considered Complete?" *Physical Review* 47, 777–80.

Fay, Brian. 1975. *Social Theory and Political Practice*. London: Allen & Unwin.

Feigl, Herbert. 1934. "Logical Analysis of the Psychophysical Problem: A Contribution of the New Positivsm." *Philosophy of Science* 1, 420–45.

Feigl, Herbert. 1950. "Existential Hypotheses: Realist versus Phenomenalistic Interpretations." *Philosophy of Science* 17, 35–62.

Feigl, Herbert. 1950a. "De Principiis non Disputandum ...? On the Meaning and the Limits of Justification." In M. Black (ed.), *Philosophical Analysis*. Ithaca, NY: Cornell University Press, 119–56. Reprinted in Feigl (1980), 237–68.

Feigl, Herbert. 1956. "Some Major Issues and Developments in the Philosophy of Science of Logical Empiricism." *Minnesota Studies in the Philosophy of Science* 1, 3–37.

Feigl, Herbert. 1959. "Philosophical Tangents of Science." In Feigl and Maxwell (1959), 1–15.

Feigl, Herbert. 1969. "The Wiener Kreis in America." In D. Fleming and B. Bailyn (eds.), *The Intellectual Migration: Europe and America 1930–1960*. Cambridge, MA: Harvard University Press, 630–73. Repr. in Feigl (1980), 57–94.

Feigl, Herbert. 1970. "The 'Orthodox' View of Theories: Remarks in Defense as Well as Critique." *Minnesota Studies in the Philosophy of Science* 4, 3–15.

Feigl, Herbert. 1980. *Inquiries and Provocations: Selected Writings 1929–1974*. R. S. Cohen (ed.). Dordrecht: Reidel.

Feigl, Herbert and Grover Maxwell (eds.). 1959. *Current Issues in the Philosophy of Science*. New York: Holt, Reinhart and Winston.

Festa, Roberto. 1999. "Bayesian Confirmation." In M. C. Galavotti and A. Pagnini (eds.), *Experience, Reality, and Scientific Explanation*. Dordrecht: Kluwer, 55–88.

Feyerabend, Paul K. 1958. "Reichenbach's Interpretation of Quantum Mechanics." *Philosophical Studies* 9. Reprinted in his Philosophical Papers, vol. 1. New York: Cambridge University Press, 236–46.

Feyerabend, Paul K. 1970. "Against Method: Outline of an Anarchistic Theory of Knowledge." In Michael Radner and Stephen Winokur (eds.), *Analyses of Theories and Methods of Physics and Psychology. Minnesota Studies in the Philosophy of Science*, vol. VI. Minneapolis: University of Minnesota Press 1970, 17–130.

Fine, A. 1982. "Hidden Variables, Joint Probability, and the Bell Inequalities." *Physical Review Letters* 48, 291–5.

Fine, A. 1996. *The Shaky Game: Einstein, Realism and the Quantum Theory*. 2nd ed. Chicago: University of Chicago Press.

Fleck, Christian. 1993. "Marxistische Kausalanalyse und funktionale Wissenschaftssoziologie: ein Fall unterbliebenen Wissenstransfers." In Haller and Stadler (1993), 501–24.

Fleck, Lola. 1982. "Otto Neurath's Beitrag zur Theorie der Sozialwissenschaften." In F. Stadler (ed.), *Arbeiterbildung in der Zwischenkriegszeit*. Vienna: Löcker, 100–3. Trans. as "Otto Neurath's Contribution to the Theory of the Social Sciences" in Uebel (1991), 203–8.

Fleck, Lola. 1996. "A Life between Science and Politics." In Cartwright et al. (1996), 7–88.

Frenke-Brunswick, Else. 1954. "Psychoanalysis and the Unity of Science." *Proceedings of the American Academy of Arts and Sciences* 80, 271–350.

Føllesdal, Dagfinn. 1973. "Indeterminacy of Translation and Under-determination of the Theory of Nature." *Dialectica* 27, 289–301.

Foucault, Michel. 1990. "Qu'est-ce que la critique? (critique et 'Aufklärung')." *Bulletin de la Société française de Philosophie* 84, 35–63. Trans. as *Was ist Kritik?* Berlin: Merve, 1992.

Frank, Philipp. 1917. "Die Bedeutung der physikalischen Erkenntnistheorie Ernst Machs für das Geistesleben unserer Zeit." *Die Natur-wissenschaften* 5, 65–72. Trans. as "The Importance for Our Times of Ernst Mach's Philosophy of Science" in Frank (1941), 54– 103, and Frank (1949), 90–121.

Frank, Philipp. 1930. "Was bedeuten die gegenwärtigen physikalischen Theorien für die allgemeine Erkenntnislehre?" *Erkenntnis* 1, 126–57.

Trans. as "Physical Theories of the Twentieth Century and School Philosophy" in Frank (1949), 90–121.

Frank, Philipp. 1932. *Das Kausalgesetz und seine Grenzen*. Vienna: Springer. Trans. by M. Neurath and R. Cohen as *The Law of Causality and Its Limits*. Dordrecht: Kluwer, 1998.

Frank, Philipp. 1932a."Naturwissenschaft." In R. Dittler, G. Joos, et al. (eds.), *Handwörterbuch der Naturwissenschaften*, Zweite Auflage, Band 7. Jena: Gustav Fischer, 149–58.

Frank, Philipp. 1934. "Hans Hahn." *Erkenntnis* 4, 315–16.

Frank, Philipp. 1935. *Das Ende der mechanistischen Physik*. Vienna: Gerold & Co. Trans. as "The Fall of Mechanistic Physics" in B. McGuinness (ed.), *Unified Science*. Dordrecht: Reidel, 1987, 110–30.

Frank, Philipp. 1936. "Die philosophischen Missdeutungen der Quantentheorie." *Erkenntnis* 6. Trans. as "Philosophical Misinterpretations of Quantum Theory" in Frank (1949), 158–71.

Frank, Philipp. 1938. "Bemerkungen zu E. Cassirer: Determinismus und Indeterminismus in der moderne Physik." *Theoria* 4, 70–80. Trans. as "Determinism and Indeterminism in Modern Physics" in Frank (1949), 172–85.

Frank, Philipp. 1941. *Between Physics and Philosophy*. Cambridge, MA: Harvard University Press.

Frank, Philipp. 1946. "The Foundations of Physics." *International Encyclopedia of Unified Science* vol 1, no. 7. Chicago: University of Chicago Press.

Frank, Philipp. 1949. *Modern Science and Its Philosophy*. Cambridge, MA: Harvard University Press.

Frank, Philipp. 1949a. "Einstein, Mach, and Logical Positivism." In Schilpp (1949), 271–86.

Frank, Philipp. 1950. "Comments on Realistic versus Phenomenalistic Interpretations." *Philosophy of Science* 17, 166–9.

Frank, Philipp. 1951. *Relativity-A Richer Truth*. London: Jonathan Cape.

Frank, Philipp. 1951a. "The Logical and Sociological Aspects of Science." *Proceedings of the American Academy of Arts and Sciences* 80, 16–36.

Frank, Philipp. 1956. (ed.) *The Validation of Scientific Theories*. Boston: Beacon Press.

Frank, Philipp. 1957. *Philosophy of Science: The Link between Science and Philosophy*. Englewood Cliffs, NJ: Prentice Hall. Repr. Westport, CT: Greenwood, 1974.

Friedman, Michael. 1975. "Physicalism and the Indeterminacy of Translation." *Nous* 9, 353–74.

Friedman, Michael. 1987. "Carnap's *Aufbau* Reconsidered." *Noûs* 21, 521–45. Repr. in Friedman (1999), ch. 5.

Friedman, Michael. 1992. "Epistemology in the *Aufbau*." Synthese 93, 15–57. Repr. in Friedman (1999), ch. 6.

Friedman, Michael. 1993. "Remarks on the History of Science and the History of Philosophy." In P. Horwich (2003), 37–54.

Friedman, Michael. 1997. "Helmholtz's *Zeichentheorie* and Schlick's *Allgemeine Erkenntnislehre*: Early Logical Empiricism and Its Nineteenth-Century Background." *Philosophical Topics* 25, 19–50.

Friedman, Michael. 1997a. "Carnap and Wittgenstein's *Tractatus*." In Tait (1997), 19–36. Repr. Friedman (1999), ch. 9.

Friedman, Michael. 1998. "On the Sociology of Scientific Knowledge and Its Philosophical Agenda." *Studies in History and Philosophy of Science* 29, 239–71.

Friedman, Michael. 1999. *Reconsidering Logical Positivism*. Cambridge: Cambridge University Press.

Friedman, Michael. 2000. "Hempel and the Vienna Circle." In J. Fetzer (ed.), *Science, Explanation, and Rationality: Aspects of the Philosophy of Carl G. Hempel*. Oxford: Oxford University Press, 39–64.

Friedman, Michael. 2000a. *A Parting of the Ways: Carnap, Cassirer, and Heidegger*. Chicago: Open Court.

Friedman, Michael. 2001. *Dynamics of Reason: The 1999 Kant Lectures at Stanford University*. Stanford, CA: CSLI.

Friedman, Michael. 2002. "Geometry as a Branch of Physics: Background and Context for Einstein's 'Geometry and Experience.'" In D. Malament (ed.), *Reading Natural Philosophy: Essays in the History and Philosophy of Science and Mathematics to Honor Howard Stein on His 70th Birthday*. Chicago: Open Court.

Friedman, Michael. 2002a. "Kant on Science and Experience." In C. Mercer and E. O'Neill (eds.), *The History of Early Modern Philosophy: Essays in Honor of Margaret Dauler Wilson*. London: Blackwell.

Friedman, Michael. 2003. "Kuhn and Logical Empiricism." In T. Nickles (2003), 19–44.

Fuchs, Margot. 2003. *Georg von Arco (1869–1940). Ingenieur, Pazifist, Technischer Direktor von Telefunken*. Diepholz: GNT–Verlag.

Fuller, Steven. 2000. *Thomas Kuhn: A Philosophical Fable for Our Times*. Chicago: University of Chicago Press.

Fuller, Steven. 2004. *Popper vs. Kuhn: The Struggle for the Soul of Science*. New York: Columbia University Press.

Galavotti, Maria Carla. 2003. "Kinds of Probabilism." In P. Parrini, W. C. Salmon, and M. H. Salmon (eds.), *Logical Empiricism: Historical and Contemporary Perspectives*. Pittsburgh: University of Pittsburgh Press, 281–303.

Galavotti, Maria Carla. 2005. *A Philosophical Introduction to Probability*. Stanford: CSLI. Publications.

Galison, Peter. 1990. "Aufbau/Bauhaus: Logical Positivism and Architectural Modernism." *Critical Inquiry* 16, 709–52.

Galison, Peter. 1996. "Constructing Modernism: The Cultural Location of *Aufbau*." In Giere and Richardson (1996), 17–44.

Gates, Gary. 2001. "Physicalism, Empiricism, and Positivism." In Carl Gillett and Barry Loewer (eds.), *Physicalism and Its Discontents*. Cambridge: Cambridge University Press, 251–67.

Gibson, Roger, F., Jr. 1988. *Enlightened Empiricism: An Examination of W. V. Quine's Theory of Knowledge*. Tampa: University of South Florida.

Giddens, Anthony. 1978. "Positivism and Its Critics." In T. Bottomore and R. Nisbet (eds.), *History of Sociological Analysis*. London: Heinemann, 237–86.

Giere, Ronald. 1988. *Explaining Science: A Cognitive Approach*. Chicago: University of Chicago Press.

Giere, Ronald and Alan Richardson (eds.). 1996. *Origins of Logical Empiricism*. Minnesota Studies in the Philosophy of Science, vol. 16. Minneapolis: University of Minnesota Press.

Gillies, Donald. 1998. "Confirmation Theory." In D. M. Gabbay and P. Smets (eds.), *Handbook of Defeasible Reasoning and Uncertainty Management Systems*, vol. 1. Dordrecht: Kluwer, 135–67.

Glymour, Clark. 1980. *Theory and Evidence*. Princeton: Princeton University Press.

Gödel, Kurt. 1949. "An Example of a New Type of Cosmological Solution of Einstein's Field Equations." *Reviews of Modern Physics* 21, 447–50.

Gödel, Kurt. 1995. "Is Mathematics Syntax of Language?" (two versions). In K. Gödel, *Collected Works, Vol. III: Unpublished Essays and Lectures*. Oxford: Oxford University Press, 334–63.

Goldfarb, Warren. "The Philosophy of Mathematics in Early Positivism." In Giere and Richardson (1996), 213–30.

Goldfarb, Warren and Thomas Ricketts. 1992. "Carnap and the Philosophy of Mathematics." In Bell and Vossenkuhl (1992), 61–78.

Goldstein, S. 1998. "Quantum Theory without Observers-Part Two." *Physics Today*, April, 38–42.

Gomperz, Heinrich. 1939. *Interpretation. Logical Analysis of a Method of Historical Research*. Den Haag: Van Stockum & Zoon. (Library of Unified Science, Monograph Series, Science 8/9).

Good, Irving John. 1965. *The Estimation of Probabilities. An Essay on Modern Bayesian Methods*. Cambridge, MA: MIT Press.

Good, Irving John. 1983. *Good Thinking*. Minneapolis: University of Minnesota Press.

Goodman, Nelson. 1955. *Fact, Fiction, and Forecast*. 2nd ed. London: Athlone Press; Indianapolis: Bobbs-Merrill Co., 1965.

Goodman, Nelson and Willard van Orman Quine. 1947. "Steps toward a Constructive Nominalism." *Journal of Symbolic Logic* 12, 97–122.

Gordon, Elizabeth. 1953. "The Threat to the Next America." *House Beautiful*, April.

Gruen, William. 1939. "What Is Logical Empiricism?" *Partisan Review* 6, 64–77.

Grünbaum, Adolf. 1973. *Philosophical Problems of Space and Time*. 2nd ed. Dordrecht: Reidel.

Haack, Susan. 1977. "Carnap's *Aufbau*: Some Kantian Reflexions." *Ratio* 19, 170–6.

Habermas, Jürgen. 1968. *Erkenntnis und Interesse*. Frankfurt/Main: Suhrkamp. Trans. as *Knowledge and Human Interests*. London: Heinemann, 1972.

Hacker, Peter. 1996. *Wittgenstein's Place in Twentieth Century Analytic Philosophy*. Cambridge: Blackwell.

Hacking, Ian (ed.). 1981. *Scientific Revolutions*. Oxford: Oxford University Press.

Hacohen, Malachi H. 2000. *Karl Popper. The Formative Years, 1902–1945. Politics and Philosophy in Interwar Vienna*. Cambridge: Cambridge University Press.

Hahn, Hans. 1917. "[Review] E. Zilsel, Das Anwendungsproblem, Leipzig, Barth, 1916." *Monatshefte für Mathematik und Physik* 28, Literaturberichte 37–8.

Hahn, Hans. 1929. "Empirismus, Mathematik, Logik." *Forschungen und Fortschritte* 5. Reprinted in H. Hahn, *Empirismus, Logik, Mathematik*. Frankfurt/Main: Suhrkamp, 1988, 55–65. Trans. by H. Kaal as "Empiricism, Mathematics and Logic" in Hahn (1980), 39–42.

Hahn, Hans. 1930. *Überflüssige Wesenheiten (Occams Rasiermesser)*. Vienna: Artur Wolf Verlag.

Hahn, Hans. 1930a. "Die Bedeutung der wissenschaftlichen Weltauffassung, inbesondere für Mathematik und Physik." *Erkenntnis* 1, 96–105. Trans. by H. Kaal as "The Significance of the Scientific World View, Especially for Mathematics and Physics" in Hahn (1980) 20–30.

Hahn, Hans. 1933. "Die Krise der Anschauung." *Krise und Neuaufbau*, 41–64. Trans. by H. Kaal as "The Crisis in Intuition" in Hahn (1980), 73–102.

Hahn, Hans. 1933a. *Logik, Mathematik und Naturerkennen*. Vienna: Gerold and Co. Trans. by H. Kaal as "Logic, Mathematics, and Knowledge of Nature" in B. McGuinness (ed.), *Unified Science*. Dordrecht: Kluwer, 1987, 24–45.

Hahn, Hans. 1980. *Empiricism, Logic, and Mathematics: Philosophical Papers*. B. McGuiness (ed.). Dordrecht: Reidel.

Hahn, Hans et al. 1931. "Diskussion zur Grundlegung der Mathematik." *Erkenntnis* 2, 135–49. Trans. by J. W. Dawson Jr. as "Discussion of the Foundations of Mathematics," *History and Philosophy of Logic* 5 (1984), 111–29.

Halfpenny, Peter. 1982. *Positivism and Sociology: Explaining Social Life*. London: Allen & Unwin.

Haller, Rudolf. 1979. *Studien zur österreichischen Philosophie. Variationen über ein Thema*. Amsterdam: Rodopi.

Haller, Rudolf. 1982. "Das Neurath-Prinzip." In F. Stadler (ed.), *Arbeiterbildung in der Zwischenkriegszeit*. Vienna: Österreichisches Gsellschafts- und Wirtschaftsmuseum, 79–87. Trans. as "The Neurath Principle: Its Grounds and Principles" in Uebel (1991), 117–29.

Haller, Rudolf. 1985. "Der erste Wiener Kreis." *Erkenntnis* 22, 341–58. Trans. as "The First Vienna Circle" in Uebel (1991), 95–108.

Haller, Rudolf. 1988. *Questions on Wittgenstein*. Lincoln, Nebraska: University of Nebraska Press.

Haller, Rudolf. 1988a. "Was Wittgenstein a Neopositivist?" In Haller (1988), 27–43.

Haller, Rudolf. 1989. "Wittgenstein and Physicalism." *Critica* 21, no. 63, 17–32.

Haller, Rudolf. 1990. "Was Wittgenstein a Physicalist?" In Hintikka (1990), 68–81.

Haller, Rudolf and Heiner Rutte. 1977. "Gespräch mit Heinrich Neider." *Conceptus*, 28–30.

Haller, Rudolf and Friedrich Stadler (eds.). 1993. *Wien–Berlin–Prag. Der Aufstieg der wissenschaftlichen Philosophie*. Vienna: Verlag Hölder-Pichler-Tempsky.

Halliwell, J.J., J. Pérez-Mercader, and W.H. Zurek (eds.). 1994. *Physical Origins of Time Asymmetry*. Cambridge: Cambridge University Press.

Hamilton, Kelly. 2001. "Wittgenstein and the Mind's Eye." In James C. Klagge (ed.), *Wittgenstein: Biography and Philosophy*. Cambridge: Cambridge University Press, 53–97.

Hamilton, Kelly. 2001a. "Some Philosophical Consequences of Wittgenstein's Aeronautical Research." *Perspectives on Science*, 9, 1–37.

Hamilton, Kelly. 2002. "Darstellungen in the *Principles of Mechanics* and the *Tractatus*." *Perspectives on Science* 10, 28–68.

Hanson, Norwood Russell. 1958. *Patterns of Discovery*. Cambridge: Cambridge University Press.

Hardcastle, Gary and Alan Richardson (eds.). 2003. *Logical Empiricism in North America*. Minneapolis: University of Minnesota Press.

Harris, Errol E. 1951. "Scientific Philosophy." *Philosophical Quarterly* 2, 153–65.

Hartshorne, C. 1934. "The Parallel Development of Method in Physics and Psychology." *Philosophy of Science* 1, 446–59.

Hayek, Friedrich August. 1942–4. "Scientism and the Study of Society." *Economica* 9, 267–91; 10, 34–63; and 11, 27–39. Repr. as Part 1 of *The Counter-Revolution in Science. Studies on the Abuse of Reason.* New York: Free Press, 1952

Hayek, Friedrich A. 1944. *The Road to Serfdom.* Chicago: University of Chicago Press.

Hecht, Hartmut and Dieter Hoffmann. 1982. "Die Berufung Hans Reichenbachs an die Berliner Universität." *Zeitschrift für Philosophie* 30, 651–62.

Hecht, Hartmut and Dieter Hoffmann. 1987. "Naturphilosophie im Verständnis der Berliner Gesellschaft für wissenschaftliche Philosophie." In *Naturphilosophie und Wissenschaftsentwicklung im 19. und 20. Jahrhundert, Greifswalder Philosophische Hefte* 5, 93–9.

Hecht, Hartmut and Dieter Hoffmann. 1991. "Die Berliner Gesellschaft für wissenschaftliche Philosophie. Naturwissenschaften und Philosophie zu Beginn des 20. Jahrhunderts in Berlin." *NTM – Zeitschrift für Geschichte der Naturwissenschaft, Technik und Medizin* 28, 43–59.

Hecht, Hartmut and Dieter Hoffmann. 1991a. "The Berlin Society for Scientific Philosophy as Organizational Form of Philosophizing in the Medium of Natural Science." In William, R. Woodward and Robert, S. Cohen (eds.), *World Views and Scientific Discipline Formation.* Dordrecht: Kluwer, 75–88.

Heidelberger, Michael and Friedrich Stadler (eds.). 2003. *Wissenschaftsphilosophie und Politik/Philosophy of Science and Politics.* Vienna: Springer.

Heisenberg, Werner. 1927. "Über den anschaulichen Inhalt der quantentheoretischen Kinematik und Mechanik." *Zeitschrift für Physik* 43, 172–98. Trans. by J. Wheeler and W. Zurek in Wheeler and Zurek (eds.), *Quantum Theory and Measurement.* Princeton: Princeton University Press, 1983, 62–84.

Helling, Ingeborg. 1985. "Logischer Positivismus und Phänomenologie: Felix Kaufmanns Methodologie der Sozialwissenschaften." In H.-J. Dahms (ed.), *Philosophie, Wissenschaft, Aufklärung. Beiträge zur Geschichte und Wirkung des Wiener Kreises.* Berlin: de Gruyter, 237–56.

Helmer, Olaf and Paul Oppenheim. 1945. "A Syntactical Definition of Probability and Degree of Confirmation." *Journal of Symbolic Logic* 10, 25–60.

Hempel, Carl Gustav. 1935. "Analyse Logique du Psychologie." *Revue des Synthèse* 10, 27–42. Reprinted in translation (by Wilfred Sellars) as "The Logical Analysis of Psychology," in C. G. Hempel, *Selected Philosophical Essays*, R. Jeffrey (ed.) Cambridge: Cambridge University Press, 2000, 165–80

Hempel, Carl Gustav. 1935a. "On the Logical Positivists' Theory of Truth." *Analysis* 2, 49–59. Repr. in Hempel (2000) 22–36.

Hempel, Carl Gustav. 1942. "The Function of General Laws in History." *Journal of Philosophy* 39, 35–48. Repr. in Hempel (1965), 231–44.

Hempel, Carl Gustav. 1945. "Studies in the Logic of Confirmation." *Mind* 54, 1–26, 97–121. Reprinted in Hempel (1965), 3–46, with a "Postscript," 47–51.

Hempel, Carl Gustav. 1950. "Problems and Changes in the Empiricist Criterion of Meaning." *Revue Internationale de Philosophie* 11, 41–63. Repr. in combination with Hempel (1951) and a postscript in Hempel (1965), 101–23.

Hempel, Carl Gustav. 1951. "The Concept of Cognitive Significance: A Reconsideration." *Proceedings of the American Academy of Arts and Sciences* 80, 61–77. Repr. in combination with Hempel (1950) and a postscript in Hempel (1965), 101–23.

Hempel, Carl Gustav. 1958. "The Theoretician's Dilemma." *Minnesota Studies in the Philosophy of Science* 2, 37–99. Repr. in Hempel (1965), 173–226.

Hempel, Carl Gustav. 1960. "Inductive Inconsistencies." *Synthèse* 12, 439–69. Reprinted in Hempel (1965), 54–79.

Hempel, Carl Gustav. 1963. "Implications of Carnap's Work for the Philosophy of Science." In Schilpp (1963), 685–709.

Hempel, Carl Gustav. 1965. *Aspects of Scientific Explanation and Other Essays in the Philosophy of Science*. New York: Free Press.

Hempel, Carl G. 1966. *Philosophy of Natural Science*. Upper Saddle River, NJ: Prentice–Hall.

Hempel, Carl Gustav. 1969. "Logical Positivism and the Social Sciences." In P. Achinstein and S. F. Barker (eds.), *The Legacy of Logical Positivism*. Baltimore: John Hopkins University Press, 163–94. Repr. in Hempel (2001), 253–75.

Hempel, Carl Gustav. 2000. *Selected Philosophical Essays*. R. C. Jeffrey (ed.), Cambridge: Cambridge University Press.

Hempel, Carl Gustav. 2001. *The Philosophy of Carl G. Hempel*. J. H. Fetzer (ed.) Oxford: Oxford University Press.

Hempel, Carl Gustav and Paul Oppenheim. 1945. "A Definition of 'Degree of Confirmation.'" *Philosophy of Science* 12, 98–115. Reprinted in Hempel (2000), 135–61.

Hentschel, Klaus. 1990. *Die Korrespondenz Petzoldt-Reichenbach. Zur Entwicklung der wissenschaftlichen Philosophie in Berlin*. Berlin: Verlag Sigma.

Herberg, Will. 1954. "Why They Became True Believers." Review of G. Almond, *The Appeals of Communism* (Princeton: Princeton University Press, 1954). *The New Leader*, December 13, 12–14.

Hesse, Mary. 1963. Untitled review of Kuhn, *The Structure of Scientific Revolutions*. *Isis* 54, 286–7.

Hesse, Mary. 1974. *The Structure of Scientific Inference*. Berkeley: University of California Press.

Hide, Øystein. 2004. "Wittgenstein's Books at the Bertrand Russell Archives and the Influence of Scientific Literature on Wittgenstein's Early Philosophy." *Philosophical Investigations* 27, no. 1, 68–91.

Hilbert, David. 1899. *Die Grundlagen der Geometrie*. Berlin: de Gruyter.

Hilbert, David. 1901. "Mathematical Problems, Lecture Delivered before The International Congress of Mathematicians at Paris in 1900." In Browder (1976), 1–34.

Hilbert, David. 1916. "Die Grundlagen der Physik: Erste Mitteilung." *Königliche Gesellschaft der Wissenschaften zu Göttingen. Mathematisch-physikalische Klasse. Nachrichten 1916*, 407. Quoted after T. Sauer, "Hilbert's Axiomatic Foundations of Physics." In M. Heidelberger and F. Stadler (eds.), *History of Philosophy of Science: New Trends and Perspectives*. Dordrecht: Kluwer, 2002, 225–37.

Hilbert, D. and W. Ackermann. 1928. *Grundzüge der theoretischen Logik*. Berlin: Springer.

Hilmy, S. Stephen. 1987. *The Later Wittgenstein: The Emergence of a New Philosophical Method*. New York: Blackwell.

Hintikka, Jaakko. 1966. "A Two-Dimensional Continuum of Inductive Methods." In J. Hintikka and P. Suppes (eds.), *Aspects of Inductive Logic*. Amsterdam: North-Holland, 113–32.

Hintikka, Jaakko. 1989. "Ludwig's Apple Tree: Evidence concerning the Philosophical Relations between Wittgenstein and the Vienna Circle." In W. L. Gombocz et al. (eds.), *Traditionen und Perspektiven der analytischen Philosophie. Festschrift für Rudolf Haller*. Vienna: Holder-Pichler-Tempsky, 187–202.Vienna: Holder-Pichler-Tempsky, 187–202 Repr. in *Ludwig Wittgenstein: Half-Truths and One-and-a-Half Truths (Selected Papers, Volume 1)* Dordrecht: Kluwer, 1996.

Hintikka, Jaakko. 1990. *Language, Knowledge, and Intentionality: Perspectives on the Philosophy of Jaakko Hintikka*. Leila Haaparanta, Martin Kusch, and Ikka Niiniluoto (eds.). *Acta philosophica Fennica*, vol. 49. Helsinki: Philosophical Society of Finland.

Hintikka, Jaakko. 1998. "Ramsey Sentences and the Meaning of Quantifiers." *Philosophy of Science* 65, 289–305.

Hintikka, Merrill B. and Jaakko Hintikka. 1986. *Investigating Wittgenstein.* Oxford: Blackwell.

Hoffmann, Dieter. 1993. "Die Berliner Gesellschaft für empirische/ wissenschaftliche Philosophie." In Haller and Stadler (1993), 386–401.

Hoffmann, Dieter. 1994. "Die Geschichte der Berliner Gesellschaft für empirische/wissenschaftliche Philosophie." In Danneberg, Kamlah, and Schäfer (1994), 21–32.

Hoffmann, Dieter. 2004. "Die Remigration von (Natur) Wissenschaftlern in die DDR: das Beispiel der Physiker Martin Strauss, Fritz Lange und Klaus Fuchs." In Norman Fuchsloch, Sabine Schleiermacher, and Rudi Seising (eds.), *Wissenschaft in der Sowjetischen Besatzungszone/DDR: Organisationsformen, Inhalte und Realitäten.* Husum: Matthiesen Verlag.

Hollinger, David A. 2003. "Paradigm's Lost." *Social Epistemology* 17, 183–5.

Holton, Gerald. 1993. *Science and Anti-Science.* Cambridge, MA: Harvard University Press.

Holton, Gerald. 1993a. "From the Vienna Circle to Harvard Square: The Americanization of a European World Conception." In Friedrich Stadler (ed.), *Scientific Philosophy: Origins and Development.* Dordrecht: Kluwer, 47–74.

Holton, Gerald and Duane, H. D. Roller. 1958. *Foundations of Modern Physical Science.* Reading, MA: Addison-Wesley.

Hook, Sidney. 1940. "The New Medievalism." *The New Republic,* October 28.

Hook, Sidney. 1941. "The General Pattern." In Dewey and Kallen (1941), 185–210.

Hook, Sidney. 1943. "The New Failure of Nerve." *Partisan Review* 10, 2–23.

Hook, Sidney. 1947. "The Future of Socialism." *Partisan Review* 14, 23–36.

Hook, Sidney. 1950. "Communists in the Colleges." *The New Leader,* May 6, 16–18.

Hook, Sidney. 1953. *Heresy, Yes–Conspiracy, No.* New York: John Day.

Hook, Sidney. 1953a. "Indoctrination and Academic Freedom." *The New Leader,* March 9, 2–4.

Horkheimer, Max. 1937. "Der neueste Angriff auf die Metaphysik." *Zeitschrift für Sozialforschung* 6, 4–51. Trans. as "The Latest Attack on Metaphysics" in Horkheimer, *Critical Theory.* New York: Seabury Press, 1972, 132–87.

Horwich, Paul (ed.). 1993. *World Changes: Thomas Kuhn and the Nature of Science.* Cambridge, MA: MIT Press.

Hosiasson-Lindenbaum, Janina. 1940. "On Confirmation." *Journal of Symbolic Logic* 6, 133–48.

Howard, Don. 1984. "Realism and Conventionalism in Einstein's Philosophy of Science: The Einstein-Schlick Correspondence." *Philosophia Naturalis* 21, 616–29.

Howard, Don. 2003. "Two Left Turns Make a Right: On the Curious Political Career of North American Philosophy of Science at Midcentury." In Hardcastle and Richardson (2003), 25–93.

Hoyningen-Huene, Paul. 1993. *Reconstructing Scientific Revolutions: Thomas Kuhn's Philosophy of Science*. Chicago: University of Chicago Press.

Hutchins, Robert M. 1936. *The Higher Learning in America*. New Haven, CT: Yale University Press.

Hutchins, Robert M. 1954. "Are Our Teachers Afraid to Teach?" *Look* 18, 27–9.

Hymers, Michael. 2005. "Going around the Vienna Circle: Wittgenstein and Verification." *Philosophical Investigations* 28, no. 3, 205–34.

Irzik, Gürol. 2002. "Carnap and Kuhn: A Belated Encounter." In M. Gardenfors, J. Wolenski, and K. Kijina-Placek (eds.), *In the Scope of Logic, Methodology, and Philosophy of Science*, vol. 2. Dordrecht: Kluwer, 603–60.

Irzik, Gürol. 2003. "Changing Conceptions of Rationality: From Logical Empiricism to Postpositivism." In P. Parrini, W. C. Salmon, and M. H. Salmon (eds.), *Logical Empiricism: Historical and Contemporary Perspectives*. Pittsburgh: University of Pittsburgh Press, 325–46.

Irzik, Gürol and T. Grünberg. 1995. "Carnap and Kuhn: Arch Enemies or Close Allies?" *British Journal for the Philosophy of Science* 46, 285–307.

Isaacson, D. 1992. "Carnap, Quine, and Logical Truth." In Bell and Vossenkuhl (1992), 100–30.

Jacoby, Russell. 1987. *The Last Intellectuals*. New York: Basic Books.

James, William. 1892. *Psychology: Briefer Course*. New York: Henry Holt and Company.

Jammer, M. 1974. *The Philosophy of Quantum Mechanics: The Interpretations of Quantum Mechanics in Historical Perspective*. New York: John Wiley.

Janik, Allan and Hans Veigl. 1998. *Wittgenstein in Vienna: A Biographical Excursion through the City and Its History*. New York: Springer.

Janis, Allen. 2002. "Conventionality of Simultaneity." *The Stanford Encyclopedia of Philosophy* (fall 2002 ed.). Edward N. Zalta (ed.), http://platostanford.edu/archives/fall2002/entries/spacetime–con-vensimul/.

Jeffrey, Richard C. 1965. *The Logic of Decision*. 2nd ed. 1983. Chicago: University of Chicago Press.

Jeffrey, Richard C. 1992. *Probability and the Art of Judgment*. Cambridge: Cambridge University Press.

Jeffrey, Richard C. 1995. "Carnap's Voluntarism." In D. Prawitz, B. Skyrms, and D. Westerståhl (eds.), *Logic, Methodology, and Philosophy of Science IX*. Amsterdam: North-Holland, 847–66.

Joergensen, Joergen. 1951. *The Development of Logical Empiricism*. Chicago: University of Chicago Press.

Jones, Roger. 1979. "Causal Anomalies and the Completeness of Quantum Theory." In W. Salmon (ed.), *Hans Reichenbach: Logical Empiricist*. Dordrecht: Reidel, 567–604.

Kaempffert, Waldemar. 1937. "Toward Bridging the Gaps between the Sciences." *New York Times Book Review*, August 7, 2.

Kaempffert, Waldemar. 1938. "Sciences to Be Unified through a Common Language." *New York Times*, February 14.

Kaila, Eino. 1930. *Der logische Neupositivismus: Eine kritische Studie*. Turku: Annales Universitatis Aboensis.

Kallen, Horace. 1940. "The Meanings of 'Unity' among the Sciences." *Educational Administration and Supervision* 26, 81–97.

Kallen, Horace. 1946. "The Meanings of 'Unity' among the Sciences, Once More." *Philosophy and Phenomenological Research* 6, 493–6.

Kallen, Horace. 1946a. "Reply." *Philosophy and Phenomenological Research* 6, 515–26.

Kallen, Horace. 1946b. "An Annotation to the Annotation." *Philosophy and Phenomenological Research* 6, 528–9.

Kallen, Horace. 1946c. "Postscript: Otto Neurath, 1882–1945." *Philosophy and Phenomenological Research* 6, 529–33.

Kamlah, Andreas. 1989. "Erläuterungen." In Reichenbach (1989), 371–454.

Kamlah, Andreas. 1991. "The Causal Relation as the Most Fundamental Fact of the World. Comments on Hans Reichenbach's Paper: The Space Problem in the New Quantum Mechanics." *Erkenntnis* 35, 49–60.

Kamlah, Andreas. 1992. "Hans Reichenbachs Beziehung zum Wiener Kreis." In Hans-Joachim Dahms (ed.), *Philosophie, Wissenschaft, Aufklärung. Beiträge zur Geschichte und Wirkung des Wiener Kreises*. Berlin: Verlag Walter de Gruyter, 221–36.

Kaplan, David. 1975. "Significance and Analyticity." In Jaako Hintikka (ed.), *Rudolf Carnap: Logical Empiricist*. Dordrecht: Reidel, 87–94.

Kaufmann, Felix. 1936. *Methodenlehre der Sozialwissenschaften*. Vienna: Springer. Repr. 1999.

Kaufmann, Felix. 1944. *Methodology of the Social Sciences*. Oxford: Oxford University Press.

Keat, Russell. 1981. *The Politics of Social Theory*. Chicago: University of Chicago Press.

Keat, Russell and John Urry. 1975. *Social Theory as Science*. London: Routledge, Kegan & Paul. 2nd ed. 1982.

Kegley, Charles. 1959. "Reflections on Philipp Frank's Philosophy of Science." *Philosophy of Science* 26, 35–40.

Kemeny, John and Paul Oppenheim. 1952. "Degree of Factual Support." *Philosophy of Science* 19, 307–24.

Klingaman, William K. (ed.). 1996. *Encyclopedia of the McCarthy Era*. New York: Facts on File.

Koppelberg, Dirk. 1990. "Why and How to Naturalize Epistemology." In R. Barrett and Roger Gibson (eds.), *Perspectives on Quine*. Cambridge, MA: Basil Blackwell, 200–11.

Kraft, Viktor. 1912. *Weltbegriff und Erkenntnisbegriff. Eine Erkenntnis-theoretische Untersuchung*. Leipzig: Johann Ambrosius Barth.

Kraft, Viktor. 1950. *Der Wiener Kreis*. Vienna: Springer Verlag.Vienna: Springer Verlag Trans. By A. Pap as *The Vienna Circle*. New York: Philosophical Library 1953.

Kraft, Viktor. 1974. "Popper and the Vienna Circle." In Schilpp (1974), 185–204.

Kretschmann, E. 1917. "Über den physikalischen Sinn der Relativitäts-postulate: A. Einsteins neue und seine ursprüngliche Relativitäts-theorie." *Annalen der Physik* 53, 575–614.

Krohn, Wolfgang and Diederick Raven. 2000. "The 'Zilsel Thesis' in the Context of Edgar Zilsel's Research Programme." *Social Studies of Science* 30.

Kuhn, Thomas S. 1957. *The Copernican Revolution*. Cambridge, MA: Harvard University Press.

Kuhn, Thomas S. 1962. "The Structure of Scientific Revolutions." *International Encyclopedia of Unified Science*, vol. 2, vol no. 2. Chicago: University of Chicago Press 3rd ed., 1996.

Kuhn, Thomas S. 1964. "A Function for Thought Experiments." Reprinted in T. Kuhn, *The Essential Tension*. Chicago: University of Chicago Press, 1977, 240–65.

Kuhn, Thomas S. 1968. "History of Science." Reprinted in T. Kuhn, *The Essential Tension*. Chicago: University of Chicago Press, 1977, 105–26.

Kuhn, Thomas S. 1990. "The Road since *Structure*." Reprinted in J. Conant and J. Haugeland (eds.), *The Road since Structure*. Chicago: University of Chicago Press, 2000, 90–104.

Kuhn, Thomas. S. 1995. "A Discussion with Thomas S. Kuhn." Reprinted in J. Conant and J. Haugeland (eds.), *The Road since Structure*. Chicago: University of Chicago Press, 2000, 255–323.

Kuipers, Theo A. F. 1997. "The Carnap-Hintikka Programme in Inductive Logic." In M. Sintonen (ed.), *Knowledge and Inquiry. Essays on Jaakko*

Hintikka's Epistemology and Philosophy of Science (Poznan Studies in the Philosophy of Science and the Humanities vol. 51). Amsterdam: Rodopi, 87–99.

Kuipers, Theo A. F. 2000. *From Instrumentalism to Constructive Empiricism*. Dordrecht: Kluwer.

Kusch, Martin. 1999. "Philosophy and Sociology of Knowledge." *Studies in History and Philosophy of Science* 30, 651–85.

Lakatos, Imre and Alan Musgrave (eds.). 1970. *Criticism and the Growth of Knowledge*. Cambridge: Cambridge University Press.

Lampert, Timm. 2003. "Psychophysical and Tractarian Analysis." *Perspectives on Science* 11, no. 3, 285–317.

Leary, D. 1987. "From Act Psychology to Probabilistic Functionalism: The Place of Egon Brunswik in the History of Psychology." In M. Ash and W. Woodward (eds.), *Psychology in Twentieth-Century Thought and Society*. Cambridge: Cambridge University Press, 1987, 115–42.

Lee, D. (ed.). 1980. *Wittgenstein's Lectures, Cambridge 1930–1932, From the Notes of John King and Desmond Lee*. Chicago: University of Chicago Press.

Lenin, Vladimir I. 1908. *Materialism and Empirio-Criticism*. Trans. by David Kvitko with Sidney Hook, 1927. New York: International Publishers Repr. 1972.

Leonard, Robert. 1995. "From Parlor Games to Social Science: von Neumann, Morgenstern and the Creation of Game Theory, 1928–1944." *Journal of Economic Literature* 33, 730–61.

Lewis, David. 1970. "How to Define Theoretical Terms." *Journal of Philosophy* 67, 427–46.

Longino, Helen. 1990. *Science as Social Knowledge: Values and Objectivity in Scientific Inquiry*. Princeton: Princeton University Press.

Longino, Helen. 2002. *The Fate of Knowledge*. Princeton: Princeton University Press.

Lorentz, H., A. Einstein, H. Minkowski, and H. Weyl. 1923. *The Principle of Relativity*. London: Meuthen, 1923; repr. New York: Dover, n.d. Trans. by W. Perret and G. B. Jeffrey of Das *Relativitätsprinzip*. Vierte Auflage. Leipzig: B. G. Teubner.

Lübbe, Hermann. 1965. *Säkularisierung. Geschichte eines ideenpolitischen Begriffs*. Munich: Verlag Alber Freiburg.

Luckhardt, C. G. (ed.). 1979. *Wittgenstein: Sources and Perspectives*. Hassocks, Sussex: Harvester.

Mach, Ernst. 1872. *Die Geschichte und die Wurzel des Satzes von der Erhaltung der Arbeit*. 2nd ed. Leipzig: Barth, 1909. Trans. *History and*

Root of the Principle of the Conservation of Energy. Chicago: Open Court, 1911.

Mach, Ernst. 1883. *Die Mechanik in ihrer Entwicklung. Historisch-kritisch dargestellt*. Leipzig: Barth. 7th ed. 1912. Trans. *The Science of Mechanics. A Critical and Historical Account of Its Development*. La Salle, IL: Open Court, 1960.

Mach, Ernst. 1886. *Die Analyse der Empfindungen und das Verhältnis des Physischen zum Psychischen*. Jena: Gustav Fischer. Trans. *Contributions to the Analysis of the Sensations*. La Salle, IL: Open Court, 1897.

Mach, Ernst. 1896. *Die Prinzipien der Wärmelehre. Historisch-kritisch entwickelt*. Leipzig: Barth. 2nd ed. 1900. Trans. as *Principles of the Theory of Heat. Historically and Critically Elucidated*. Dordrecht: Kluwer, 1986.

Mach, Ernst. 1922. *Die Analyse der Empfindung*. Jena: Gustav Fischer Verlag.

Mach, Ernst. 1965. *Erkenntnis und Irrtum*. Darmstadt: Wissenschaftliche Buchgesellschaft.

Malament, David. 1977. "Causal Theories of Time and the Conventionality of Simulataneity." *Noûs* 11, 293–300.

Malcolm, Norman. 1951. Untitled Review of Reichenbach (1951a). *Philosophical Review* 60, 582–6.

Malisoff, William M. 1946. "A Science of the People, by the People and for the People." *Philosophy of Science* 13, 166–9.

Manninen, Juha. 2003. "Towards a Physicalistic Attitude." In Stadler (2003c), 133–50.

Margenau, H. 1941. "Metaphysical Elements in Physics." *Reviews of Modern Physics* 13, 176–89.

Margenau, H. 1950. *The Nature of Physical Reality. A Philosophy of Modern Physics*. New York: McGraw-Hill.

Maxwell, James Clerk. 1876. *Matter and Motion*. London: Society for Promoting Christian Knowledge. Repr. New York: Dover, 1953.

McCumber, John. 2001. *Time in the Ditch: American Philosophy and the McCarthy Era*. Evanston, IL: Northwestern University Press.

McGill, V.J. 1936. "An Evaluation of Logical Positivism." *Science & Society* 1, 45–80.

McGuinness, Brian (ed.). 1987. *Unified Science: The Vienna Circle Monograph Series*. Originally edited by Otto Neurath. Dordrecht: Reidel.

McGuinness, Brian. 1988. *Wittgenstein: A Life. Young Ludwig, 1889–1921*. London: Duckworth.

McGuinness, Brian. 1985. "Wittgenstein and the Vienna Circle." *Synthese* 64. Repr. in McGuinness (2002), 177–83.

McGuinness, Brian. 1991. "Wittgensteins Beziehungen zum Wiener Kreis." In *Jour Fixe der Vernunft. Der Wiener Kreis und die Folgen.* W. Hochkeppel (ed.). Vienna: Holder-Pichler-Tempsky, 108–26. Trans. as "Relation with and within the Vienna Circle" in McGuinness (2002), 184–200.

McGuinness, Brian. 2002. *Approaches to Wittgenstein: Collected Papers.* London: Routledge.

Mehlberg, H. 1936. "Essai sur la théorie causale du temps." *Studia Philosophica* 1, 119–260. Trans. as "An Essay on the Causal Theory of Time" in *Time, Causality, and the Quantum Theory: Studies in the Philosophy of Science*, vol. 1. Dordrecht: Reidel, 1980.

Menger, Karl. 1933. "Die neue Logik." *Krise und Neuaufbau*, 94–122.

Menger, Karl. 1934. *Moral, Wille und Weltgestaltung. Grundlegung zur Logik der Sitten.* Vienna: Springer. Trans. as *Morality, Decision and Social Organization.* Dordrecht: Reidel, 1974.

Menger, Karl. 1979. "Logical Tolerance in the Vienna Circle." In Menger, *Selected Papers in Logic and Foundations, Didactics, Economics.* Dordrecht: Reidel.

Menger, Karl. 1980. "Introduction." In Hans Hahn, *Empiricism, Logic and Mathematics. Philosophical Papers.* Brian F. McGuinness (ed.), IX–XVIII. Dordrecht: Reidel.

Menger, Karl. 1994. *Reminiscences of the Vienna Circle and the Mathematical Colloquium.* Brian McGuinness, Louise Golland and Abe Sklar (eds.). Vienna Circle collection vol. 20. Dordrecht: Kluwer.

Merton, Robert. 1936. "The Unintended Consequences of Purposive Social Action." *American Sociological Review* 1, 894–904.

Merton, Robert. 1948. "The Self-fulfilling Prophecy." *Antioch Review* 8, 193–210. Repr. in Merton, *Social Theory and Social Structure.* Glencoe, IL: Free Press, 1949.

Monk, Ray. 1990. *Ludwig Wittgenstein. The Duty of Genius.* New York: Viking Penguin.

Mormann, Thomas. 2000. *Rudolf Carnap.* Munich: C. H. Beck.

Mormann, Thomas. 2005. "Geographie des Wissens und der Wissenschaften: Von der Encyclopédie zur Konstitutionstheorie." In E. Nemeth and N. Roudet (eds.), *Paris – Wien: Enzyklopädien im Vergleich.* Vienna: Springer, 33–64.

Morris, Charles. 1937. Logical Positivism, Pragmatism, and Scientific Empiricism. Paris: Hermann.

Morris, Charles. 1942. *Paths of Life: Preface to a World Religion.* Chicago: University of Chicago Press.

Morris, Charles. 1942a. "Empiricism, Religion, and Democracy." In L. Bryson (ed.), *Science, Philosophy, and Religion: Second Symposium*. New York, 213–41.

Morris, Charles. 1946. "The Significance of the Unity of Science Movement." *Philosophy and Phenomenological Research* 6, 508–15.

Morris, Charles. 1948. *The Open Self*. New York: Prentice-Hall.

Morris, Charles. 1960. "On the History of the International Encyclopedia of Unified Science." *Synthese* 12, 517–21.

Mühsam, H. 1927. "Renaissance des Positivismus." *Vossische Zeitung*, March 4.

Mulder, Henk L. 1968. "Wissenschaftliche Weltauffassung. Der Wiener Kreis." *Journal of the History of Philosophy* 6, 368–90.

Naess, Arne. 1936. *Erkenntnis und wissenschaftliches Verhalten*. Oslo: J. Dybwad.

Naess, Arne. 1993. "Logical Empiricism and the Uniqueness of the Schlick Seminar: A Personal Experience with Consequences." In Stadler (ed.), *Scientific Philosophy*, 11–26.

Nagel, Ernest. 1936. "The Meaning of Probability." *Journal of the American Statistical Association* 31, 10–26.

Nagel, Ernest. 1939. "Principles of the Theory of Probability." *International Encyclopedia of Unified Science*, vol. 1, no. 6. Chicago: University of Chicago Press.

Nagel, Ernest. 1939a. "Probability and the Theory of Knowledge." *Philosophy of Science* 6, 212–53.

Nagel, Ernest. 1943. "Malicious Philosophies of Science." *Partisan Review* 10, 40–57.

Nagel, Ernest. 1952. Review of Cornforth (1950). *Journal of Philosophy* 49, 648–50.

Nagel, Ernest. 1956. "Impressions and Appraisals of Analytic Philosophy in Europe." In Nagel, *Logic without Metaphysics and Other Essays in the Philosophy of Science*. Glencoe, IL: Free Press.

Nagel, Ernest. 1961. *The Structure of Science*. New York: Harcourt, Brace, and World.

Natorp, P. 1910. *Die logischen Grundlagen der exakten Wissenschaften*. Leipzig: Teubner.

Nedo, Michael and Michele Ranchetti. 1983. *Ludwig Wittgenstein. Sein Leben in Bildern und Texten*. Frankfurt/Main: Suhrkamp.

Neurath, Otto. 1906/08. "Zur Anschauung der Antike über Handel, Gewerbe und Landwirtschaft. (Cicero, de officiis I, c. 42)." *Jahrbücher für Nationalökonomie und Statistik* 32, 577–606 and 34, 145–205; repr. in Neurath (1998), 25–109.

Neurath, Otto. 1909. *Antike Wirtschaftsgeschichte.* Leipzig/Berlin: Teubner; repr. in Neurath (1998), 137–221.

Neurath, Otto. 1911. "Nationalökonomie und Wertlehre, eine systematische Untersuchung." *Zeitschrift für Volkswirtschaft, Sozialpolitik und Verwaltung* 20, 52–114. Repr. in Neurath (1998), 470–518.

Neurath, Otto. 1913. "Die Verirrten des Cartesius und das Auxiliarmotiv (Zur Psychologie des Entschlusses)." *Jahrbuch der Philosophischen Gesellschaft an der Universität zu Wien 1913.* Trans. "The Lost Wanderers and the Auxiliary Motive (On the Psychology of Decision)" in Neurath (1983), 1–12.

Neurath, Otto. 1915. "Prinzipielles zur Geschichte der Optik." *Archiv für Geschichte der Naturwissenschaften und der Technik* 5. Trans. as "On the Foundations of the History of Optics" in Neurath (1973), 101–12.

Neurath, Otto. 1916. "Zur Klassifikation von Hypothesensystemen (Mit besonderer Berücksichtigung der Optik)." *Jahrbuch der Philosophischen Gesellschaft an der Universität zu Wien 1914 und 1915*, 39–63. Trans. as "On the Classification of Systems of Hypotheses (With Special Reference to the Optics)" in Neurath (1983), 13–31.

Neurath, Otto. 1919. "Die Utopie als sozialtechnische Konstruktion." In *Durch die Kriegswirtschaft zur Naturalwirtschaft.* Munich: Callwey. Trans. "Utopia as a Social Engineer's Construction." In Neurath (1973), 150–55.

Neurath, Otto. 1921. *Anti-Spengler.* Munich: Callwey. Excerpts trans. as "Anti-Spengler" in Neurath (1973), 158–213.

Neurath, Otto. 1929. "Bertrand Russell, der Sozialist." *Der Kampf* 22. Repr. in Neurath (1981), 337–43.

Neurath, Otto. 1929a. "Wissenschaftliche Weltauffassung." *Arbeiterzeitung* (Vienna), October 13, 29. Repr. in Neurath (1981), 345–7.

Neurath, Otto. 1930. "Bürgerlicher Marxismus." In *Der Kampf* 23. Repr. in Neurath (1981), 349–421.

Neurath, Otto. 1930a. "Wege der wissenschaftlichen Weltauffassung." *Erkenntnis* 1, 106–25. Trans. as "Ways of the Scientific World-Conception" in Neurath (1983), 32–51.

Neurath, Otto. 1930b. "Einheitswissenschaft und Marxismus." *Erkenntnis* 1, 75. Repr. in Neurath (1981), 369.

Neurath, Otto. 1930c. "Historische Anmerkungen." *Erkenntnis* 1, 311–14. Repr. in Neurath (1981), 389–92.

Neurath, Otto. 1931. *Empirische Soziologie.* Vienna: Springer. Excerpts trans. as "Empirical Sociology" in Neurath (1973), 317–421.

Neurath, Otto. 1931a. "Physikalismus." *Scientia* 50, 297–303. Trans. as "Physicalism" in Neurath (1983), 52–7.

Neurath, Otto. 1931b. "Physicalism: The Philosophy of the Vienna Circle." *The Monist* 41, 618–23. Reprinted, with minor corrections, in Neurath (1983), 48–51.

Neurath, Otto. 1931c. "Weltanschauung und Marxismus." *Der Kampf* 24, 447–51. Repr. in Neurath (1981), 407–12.

Neurath, Otto. 1932. "Protokollsätze." *Erkenntnis* 3, 204–14. Trans. as "Protocol Statements," in Neurath (1983), 91–9.

Neurath, Otto. 1932a. "Soziologie im Physikalismus." *Erkenntnis* 2, 393–431. Trans. as "Sociology in the Framework of Physicalism" in Neurath (1983), 58–90.

Neurath, Otto. 1932b. "Das Frendpsychische in der Soziologie." [Unsigned abstract.] *Erkenntnis* 3, 105–6.

Neurath, Otto. 1932c. "Sozialbehaviorismus." *Sociologicus* 8, 281–8. Repr. in Neurath (1981), 563–9.

Neurath, Otto. 1933. *Einheitswissenschaft und Psychologie. Einheitswissenschaft*, vol. 1. In R. Haller and H. Rutte (eds.), *Gesammelte philosophische und methodologische Schriften*. Vienna: Hölder-Pichler-Tempsky, 1981, 423–527.

Neurath, Otto. 1934. "Radikaler Physikalismus und 'wirkliche Welt.'" *Erkenntnis* 4, 346–62. Trans. as "Radical Physicalism and the 'Real World,'" in Neurath (1983), 100–14.

Neurath, Otto. 1935. "Pseudorationalismus der Falsifikation." *Erkenntnis* 5, 353–65. Trans. as "Pseudorationalism of Falsification" in Neurath (1983), 121–31.

Neurath, Otto. 1936. *Le développement du Cercle de Vienne et l'avenir de l'empirisme logique*. Actualités Scientifiques et Industrielles, No. 290, Paris: Hermann & Cie. Trans. as "Die Entwicklung des Wiener Kreises und die Zukunft des Logischen Empirismus" in Neurath (1981), 673–702.

Neurath, Otto. 1936a. "Einzelwissenschaften, Einheitswissenschaften, Pseudorationalismus." *Actes* 1936 1: *Philosophie scientifique et empirisme logique*, 57–64. Repr. in Neurath (1981), 703–9. Trans. as "Individual Sciences, Unified Science, Pseudorationalism" in Neurath (1983), 132–8.

Neurath, Otto. 1936b. "L'encyclopédie comme 'modèle.'" *Revue de Synthèse* 12, 187–201. Trans. as "Encyclopedia as 'Model'" in Neurath (1983), 145–58.

Neurath, Otto. 1936c. "Drei Diskussionbeiträge." *Actes du Huitième Congrès Internationale de Philosophie à Prague, 2–7 Septembre 1934*, Orbis, Prague, 157 f., 244 f., 390. Repr. in Neurath (1981), 775–69.

Neurath, Otto. 1936d. "Einheitswissenschaft." *Actes du Huitième Congrès Internationale de Philosophie à Prague, 2–7 Septembre 1934,* 139–41. Repr. in Neurath (1981), 761–4.

Neurath, Otto. 1936e. "Mensch und Gesellschaft in der Wissenschaft." *Actes du Congres Internationale de Philosophie Scientifique, Sorbonne, Paris, 1935. II. L'Unite de la Science.* Paris: Hermann. Repr. in Neurath (1981), 711–17.

Neurath, Otto. 1936f. "Soziologische Prognosen." *Erkenntnis* 6, 398–405. Trans. in Neurath (2004), 506–12.

Neurath, Otto. 1936g. "Physikalismus und Erkenntnisforschung." *Theoria* 2, 97–105, 234–37. Trans. as "Physicalism and the Investigation of Knowledge" in Neurath (1983), 159–71.

Neurath, Otto. 1937. "Prognosen und Terminologie in Physik, Biologie, Soziologie." *Travaux de IXeme Congrès Internationale de Philosophie. IV. L'Unite de la Science: La Methode et les Methodes.* Paris: Hermann. Repr. in Neurath (1981), 787–94.

Neurath, Otto. 1937a. "Unified Science and Its Encyclopedia." *Philosophy of Science* 4, 265–77. Repr. in Neurath (1983), 172–82.

Neurath, Otto. 1938. "Die neue Enzyklopädie." In *Zur Enzyklopädie der Einheitswissenschaft* 6. Den Haag: Van Stockum & Zoon, 6–16.

Neurath, Otto. 1938a. "Unified Science as Encyclopedic Integration." In *International Encyclopedia of Unified Science* I/1. Chicago: University of Chicago Press, 1–27.

Neurath, Otto. 1939. "The Social Sciences and Unified Science." *Journal of Unified Science (Erkenntnis)* 9, 244–8. Repr. in Neurath (1983), 209–12.

Neurath, Otto. 1941. "Universal Jargon and Terminology." *Proceedings of the Aristotelian Society* 41, 127–48. Repr. in Neurath (1983), 213–29.

Neurath, Otto. 1944. "Foundations of the Social Sciences." *International Encyclopedia of Unified Science,* vol. 2, no. 1. Chicago: University of Chicago Press, 1–51.

Neurath, Otto. 1945. "Germany's Education and Democracy." *Journal of Education* 77, no. 912.

Neurath, Otto. 1945a. [Review of Hayek 1944.] *London Quarterly of World Affairs,* January, 121–2. Repr. in Neurath (2004), 546–8.

Neurath, Otto. 1946. "Orchestration of the Sciences by the Encyclopedism of Logical Empiricism." *Philosophy and Phenomenological Research* 6, 496–508. Repr. in Neurath (1983), 230–42.

Neurath, Otto. 1946a. "For the Discussion: Just Annotations, Not a Reply." *Philosophy and Phenomenological Research* 6, 526–8.

Neurath, Otto. 1946b. "After Six Years." *Synthese* 5, 77–82. Repr. in Neurath (2004), 549–55.

Neurath, Otto. 1946c. "Prediction and Induction." In Neurath (1983), 243–6.

Neurath, Otto. 1973. *Empiricism and Sociology.* Trans. and ed. by M. Neurath and Paul Foulkes. Marie Neurath and Robert S. Cohen (eds.). Dordrecht: Reidel.

Neurath, Otto. 1981. *Gesammelte philosophische und methodologische Schriften.* R. Haller and H. Rutte (eds.). Vienna: Hölder-Pichler-Tempsky.

Neurath, Otto. 1983. *Philosophical Papers: 1913–1946.* Trans. and ed. by R. S. Cohen and M. Neurath. Dordrecht: Reidel.

Neurath, Otto. 1998. *Gesammelte ökonomische, soziologische und sozialpolitische Schriften.* R. Haller and U. Höfer (eds.) Vienna: Hölder-Pichler-Tempsky,

Neurath, Otto. 2004. *Economic Writings. Selections 1904–1945.* T. E. Uebel and R. S. Cohen (eds.). Dordrecht: Kluwer.

Neurath, Otto et al. 1938. *Encyclopedia and Unified Science.* Foundations of Unified Science, vol. 1, no. 1. Chicago: University of Chicago Press.

Neurath, Otto, Rudolf Carnap, and Hans Hahn. 1929. *Wissenschaftliche Weltauffassung: Der Wiener Kreis.* Vienna: Wolf. Trans. as "The Scientific Conception of the World: The Vienna Circle" in Neurath (1973), 299–319.

Neurath, Otto, Rudolf Carnap, and Charles Morris (eds.). 1955. *Foundations of the Unity of Science.* 2 vols. Chicago: University of Chicago Press.

Neurath, Otto and J. A. Lauwerys. 1945. "Plato's Republic and German Education." *Journal of Education* 77, nos. 907, 910, 913.

Neurath, Paul. 1991. "Sociological Thought with Otto Neurath." In Uebel (1991), 209–22.

Nickles, Thomas (ed.). 2003. *Thomas Kuhn.* Cambridge: Cambridge University Press.

Niiniluoto, Ilkka. 1987. *Truthlikeness.* Dordrecht: Reidel.

Niiniluoto, Ilkka. 1998. "Verisimilitude: The Third Period." *British Journal for the Philosophy of Science* 49, 1–29.

Nordmann, Alfred. 2002. "Another New Wittgenstein: The Scientific and Engineering Background of the Tractatus." *Perspectives on Science* 10, 356–84.

Norton, J. 1984. "How Einstein Found His Field Equations, 1912–1915." *Historical Studies in the Physical Sciences* 14, 253–316.

Norton, J. 1985. "What Was Einstein's Principle of Equivalence?" *Studies in History and Philosophy of Science* 16, 203–46.

Norton, J. 1993. "General Covariance and the Foundations of General Relativity: Eight Decades of Dispute." *Reports on Progress in Physics* 56, 791–858.

Oeser, Erhard. 2003. *Popper, der Wiener Kreis und die Folgen*. Vienna: WUV.

Ohmann, O. 1930. "Joseph Petzoldt zum Gedächtnis." *Archiv für die Geschichte der Mathematik und Naturwissenschaften und Technik* 13, 199–214.

O'Neill, John and Thomas Uebel. 2004. "Horkheimer and Neurath: Restarting a Disrupted Debate." *European Journal of Philosophy* 12, 75–105.

Oppenheim, Paul and Hilary Putnam. 1958. "The Unity of Science as Working Hypothesis." In H. Feigl, G. Maxwell, and M. Scriven (eds.), *Minnesota Studies in the Philosophy of Science* 2. Minneapolis: University of Minnesota Press, 3–36.

Papineau, D. 1996. "Theory-Dependent Terms." *Philosophy of Science* 63, 1–20.

Parrini, Paolo and Wesley Salmon. 2003. "Introduction." In P. Parrini, M. C. Salmon, and W. C. Salmon (eds.), *Logical Empiricism: Historical and Contemporary Perspectives*. Pittsburgh: University of Pittsburgh Press, 1–9.

Pasteur, Paul and Friedrich Stadler (eds.). 2004. *Exil et retours d'exil*. Rouen. (Austriaca 56/2003).

Pauli, Wolfgang, Jr. 1947. Review of Reichenbach (1944). *Dialectica* 1, 176–8.

Pears, David. 1988. *The False Prison*, vol. 2. Oxford: Clarendon Press.

Peckhaus, Volker. 1994. "Von Nelson zu Reichenbach. Kurt Grelling in Göttingen und Berlin." In Danneberg, Kamlah, and Schäfer (1994), 53–73.

Petzoldt, Helga. 1984. "Zu einigen Problemen der philosophischen Lehre an deutschen technischen Hochschulen im 19. Jahrhundert." In Kovacs, Gizella, and Siegfried Wollgast (eds.), *Technikphilosophie in Vergangenheit und Gegenwart*. Berlin: Akademie-Verlag.

Petzoldt, Joseph. 1891. "Maxima, Minima und Ökonomie." *Vierteljahrsschrift für wissenschaftliche Philosophie*, 5–78.

Petzoldt, Joseph. 1926. "Komplex und Begriff." *Zeitschrift für Psychologie* 99, 74–101.

Petzoldt, Joseph. 1927. "Rationales und empirisches Denken." *Annalen der Philosophie und philosophische Kritik* 6, 145–60.

Pitcher, George. 1964. *The Philosophy of Wittgenstein*. Englewood Cliffs, NJ: Prentice-Hall.

Planck, Max. 1933. *Wege zur physikalischen Erkenntnis*. Leipzig: Hirzel Verlag.

Poincaré, Henri. 1908. *Science et Methode*. German translation, Leipzig: Teubner 1914.

Polanyi, Michael. 1958. *Personal Knowledge: Towards a Post-Critical Philosophy*. London: Routledge and Kegan Paul.

Popper, Karl R. 1934. *Logik der Forschung*. Vienna: Springer. Trans. and enlarged as Popper (1959).

Popper, Karl R. 1952. *The Open Society and Its Enemies*. London: Routledge & Kegan Paul.

Popper, Karl R. 1959. *The Logic of Scientific Discovery*. New York: Basic Books.

Popper, Karl R. 1974. "Intellectual Autobiography." In P. A. Schilpp (ed.), *The Philosophy of Karl Popper*. La Salle, IL: Open Court, vol. 1, 3–141.

Popper, Karl R. 1979. *Die beiden Grundprobleme der Erkenntnistheorie*. T. E. Hansen (ed.). Tubingen: Mohr.

Potter, M. 2000. *Reason's Nearest Kin: Philosophies of Arithmetic from Kant to Carnap*. Oxford: Oxford University Press.

Proust, Joelle. 1989. *Questions of Form: Logic and the Analytic Proposition from Kant to Carnap*. Minneapolis: University of Minnesota Press.

Psillos, St. 2000. "Rudolf Carnap's 'Theoretical Concepts in Science.'" *Studies in the History and Philosophy of Science* 31, 151–72.

Quine, Willard van Orman. 1948. "On What There Is." *Review of Metaphysics* 2, 21–38. Reprinted in Quine (1953), 1–19.

Quine, Willard van Orman. 1951. "Two Dogmas of Empiricism." *Philosophical Review* 60, 20–43. Reprinted in Quine (1953), 20–46.

Quine, Willard van Orman. 1953. *From a Logical Point of View*. New York: Harper.

Quine, Willard van Orman. 1957. "The Scope and Language of Science." British Journal for the Philosophy of Science 8, 1–17. Reprinted in *The Ways of Paradox and Other Essays*. New York: Random House, 1966, 215–32.

Quine, Willard van Orman. 1960. *Word and Object*. Cambridge, MA: MIT Press.

Quine, Willard van Orman. 1963. "Carnap and Logical Truth." In Schilpp (1963), 385–406.

Quine, Willard van Orman. 1969. "Epistemology Naturalized." In *Ontological Relativity and Other Essays*. New York: Columbia University Press, 69–90.

Quine, Willard van Orman. 1974. *Roots of Reference*. La Salle, IL: Open Court, 78–80.

Quine, Willard van Orman. 1986. "Reply to Roger F. Gibson, Jr." In L. Hahn and P. Schilpp (eds.), *The Philosophy of W. V. Quine*. La Salle, IL: Open Court, 155–7.

Quine, Willard van Orman. 1990. "Comment on Koppelberg." In R. Barrett and R. F. Gibson (eds.), *Perspectives on Quine*. Cambridge, Mass: Basil Blackwell, 212.

Quine, Willard van Orman. 1990a. Letter to Rudolf Carnap of February 4, 1938. In Creath (1990a), 239–44.

Quine, Willard van Orman. 1990b. *Pursuit of Truth*. Cambridge, MA: Harvard University Press.

Quine, Willard van Orman. 1995. "Reactions." In P. Leonardi and M. Santambrogio (eds.), *On Quine: New Essays*. Cambridge: Cambridge University, 347–61.

Raven, Diederick. 2003. "Edgar Zilsel in America." In Hardcastle and Richardson (2003), 129–47.

Raven, Diederick and Wolfgang Krohn. 2000. "Edgar Zilsel: His Life and Work." In Zilsel (2000), xix–lix.

Redhead, M. J. K. 1994. *From Physics to Metaphysics*. Cambridge: Cambridge University Press.

Reichenbach, Hans. 1916/1917. "Der Begriff der Wahrscheinlichkeit für die mathematische Darstellung der Wirklichkeit." Published in 4 parts in *Zeitschrift für Philosophie und Philosophische Kritik*, Bd. 161–3.

Reichenbach, Hans. 1920. *Relativitätstheorie und Erkenntnis Apriori*. Berlin: Springer. Translated by M. Reichenbach as *The Theory of Relativity and A Priori Knowledge*. Los Angeles: University of California Press, 1965.

Reichenbach, Hans. 1921. "Erwiderung auf H. Dinglers Kritik an der Relativitätstheorie." *Physikalische Zeitschrift* 22, 379–84.

Reichenbach, Hans. 1922. "Der gegenwärtige Stand der Relativitätsdiskussion." *Logos* 10, 316–78. Trans. by M. Reichenbach as "The Present State of the Discussion on Relativity" in Reichenbach (1978), vol. 2, 3–47.

Reichenbach, Hans. 1922a. "La signification philosophique de la théorie de la relativité." *Revue Philosophique de la France et de Étranger* 94, 5–61.

Reichenbach, Hans. 1924. *Axiomatik der relativistischen Raum-Zeit-Lehre*. Braunschweig: Vieweg. Translated by M. Reichenbach as *Axiomatization of the Theory of Relativity*. Los Angeles: University of California Press, 1969.

Reichenbach, Hans. 1925. "Die Kausalstruktur der Welt und der Unterschied zwischen Vergangenheit und Zukunft." *Bayerischen Akademie der Wissenschaften zu München, Sitzungsberichte der mathematisch-naturwissenschaftliche Abteilung*, 133–75. Trans. by E. Schneewind as "The Causal Structure of the World and the Difference between Past and Future" in Reichenbach (1978), vol. 2, 81–119.

Reichenbach, Hans. 1927. *Von Kopernikus bis Einstein*. Trans. as *From Copernicus to Einstein*. New York: Philosophical Library, 1942.

Reichenbach, Hans. 1928. *Philosophie der Raum-Zeit-Lehre*. Berlin: de Gruyter. Translated, with omission of an appendix, as Reichenbach (1958).

Reichenbach, Hans. 1929. "Ziele und Wege der physikalischen Erkenntnis." In *Handbuch der Physik*, vol. 4, Allgemeine Grundlagen der Physik. Berlin: Springer, ch 1, 1–80. Trans. by E. Schneewind as "The Aims and Methods of Physical Knowledge" in Reichenbach (1978), vol. 2, 120–225.

Reichenbach, Hans. 1929a. "Stetige Wahrscheinlichkeitsfolgen." *Zeitschrift für Physik* 53, 274–307.

Reichenbach, Hans. 1930. "Probleme und Denkweisen der gegenwärtigen Physik." *Deutsche Rundschau* July/August 1930.

Reichenbach, Hans. 1930a. *Atom und Kosmos*. Trans. as *Atom and Cosmos*. London: Allen and Unwin, 1932.

Reichenbach, Hans. 1930b. "Kausalität und Wahrscheinlichkeit." *Erkenntnis* 1, 158–88. Trans. in part by M. Reichenbach as "Causality and Probability" in Reichenbach (1978), vol. 2, 333–44.

Reichenbach, Hans. 1931. *Ziele und Wege der heutigen Naturphilosophie*. Leipzig: Verlag Felix Meiner.

Reichenbach, Hans. 1931a. "Der physikalische Wahrheitsbegriff." *Erkenntnis* 2, 156–71. Trans. by E. Schneewind as "The Physical Concept of Truth" in Reichenbach (1978), vol. 1, 343–55.

Reichenbach, Hans. 1932. "Die Kausalbehauptung und die Möglichkeit ihrer empirischen Nachprüfung." *Erkenntnis* 3, 32–64. Trans. by M. Reichenbach as "The Principle of Causality and the Possibility of Its Empirical Confirmation" in Reichenbach (1978), vol. 2, 345–71.

Reichenbach, Hans. 1935. *Wahrscheinlichkeitslehre*. Leyden: Sijthoff. Translated, with augmentation and omissions, by E H. Hutton and M. Reichenbach as *The Theory of Probability*. Berkeley: University of California Press, 1949 Reprinted 1971.

Reichenbach, Hans. 1936. "Logistic Empiricism in Germany and the Present State of Its Problems." *Journal of Philosophy* 33, 141–60.

Reichenbach, Hans. 1938. *Experience and Prediction*. Chicago: University of Chicago Press.

Reichenbach, Hans. 1944. *Philosophic Foundations of Quantum Mechanics*. Berkeley: University of California Press.

Reichenbach, Hans. 1946. "Reply to Ernest Nagel's Criticism of My Views on Quantum Mechanics." *Journal of Philosophy* 43, 239–47.

Reichenbach, Hans. 1948. "The Principle of Anomaly in Quantum Mechanics." *Dialectica* 2, 337–50.

Reichenbach, Hans. 1951. *Der Aufstieg der wissenschaftlichen Philosophie.* Berlin-Grunewald: Herbig.

Reichenbach, Hans. 1951a. *The Rise of Scientific Philosophy.* Berkeley: University of California Press.

Reichenbach, Hans. 1956. *The Direction of Time.* Berkeley: University of California Press.

Reichenbach, Hans. 1958. *The Philosophy of Space and Time.* Trans. by M. Reichenbach and J. Freund. New York: Dover.

Reichenbach, Hans. 1978. *Selected Writings, 1909–1953.* M. Reichenbach and R. S. Cohen (eds.). 2 vols. Dordrecht: Reidel.

Reichenbach, Hans. 1979. "Der gegenwärtige Stand der Relativitätsdiskussion." In Reichenbach, *Gesammelte Werke, Band 3.* Braunschweig/Wiesbaden: Friedr. Vieweg & Sohn.

Reichenbach, Hans. 1989. *Gesammelten Werke, Band 5: Philosophische Grundlagen von Quantenmechanik und Wahrscheinlichkeit.* Braunschweig/Wiesbaden: Vieweg.

Reichenbach, Hans. 1991. "The Space Problem in the New Quantum Mechanics." *Erkenntnis* 35, 29–47. Trans. of an unpublished manuscript ca. 1926 by M. Reichenbach.

Reisch, George A. 1991. "Did Kuhn Kill Logical Empiricism?" *Philosophy of Science* 58, 264–77.

Reisch, George A. 1994. "Planning Science: Otto Neurath and the International Encyclopedia of Unified Science." *British Journal for the History of Science* 27, 153–75.

Reisch, George A. 1995. "A History of the International Encyclopedia of Unified Science." Unpublished Ph.D. dissertation, University of Chicago, 1995.

Reisch, George A. 1997. "Epistemologist, Economist ... and Censor? On Otto Neurath's Infamous Index Verborum Prohibitorum." *Perspectives on Science* 5, 452–80.

Reisch, George. 2001. "Against a Third Dogma of Empiricism: Otto Neurath and 'Unpredictability in Principle.'" *International Studies in the Philosophy of Science* 15, 199–210.

Reisch, George A. 2003. "Disunity in the International Encyclopedia." In Hardcastle and Richardson (2003), 197–215.

Reisch, George. 2005. *How the Cold War Transformed Philosophy of Science: To the Icy Slopes of Logic.* Cambridge: Cambridge University Press.

Rescher, Nicholas (ed.). 1985. *The Heritage of Logical Empiricism.* Lanham, MD: University Press of America.

Rescher, Nicholas. 1997. "H$_2$O: Hempel–Helmer–Oppenheim, An Episode in the History of Scientific Philosophy in the 20th Century." *Philosophy of Science* 64, 334–60.

Rey, Abel. 1907. *La Theorie de physique chez les physiciens contemporains.* Paris. German trans. Leipzig: Klinkhardt 1908.

Rhees, R. (ed.). 1984. *Recollections of Wittgenstein.* New York: Oxford University Press. Revised edition; previously published as *Ludwig Wittgenstein: Personal Recollections.* Oxford: Blackwell, 1981.

Richardson, Alan. 1990. "How Not to Russell Carnap's *Aufbau.*" *PSA 1990,* vol. 1, 3–14.

Richardson, Alan. 1992. "Logical Idealism and Carnap's Construction of the World." *Synthese* 93, 59–92.

Richardson, Alan. 1996. "From Epistemology to the Logic of Science: Carnap's Philosophy of Empirical Knowledge in the 1930s." In Giere and Richardson (1996), 309–32.

Richardson, Alan. 1998. *Carnap's Construction of the World: The Aufbau and the Emergence of Logical Empiricism.* Cambridge: Cambridge University Press.

Richardson, Alan. 2003. "Tolerance, Internationalism, and Scientific Community in Philosphy: Political Themes in Philosophy of Science, Past and Present." In Heidelberger and Stadler (2003), 65–90.

Ricketts, T. 1994. "Carnap's Principle of Tolerance, Empiricism, and Conventionalism." In P. Clark and B. Hale (eds.), *Reading Putnam.* Oxford: Blackwell, 176–200.

Ricketts, T. 1996. "Pictures, Logic, and the Limits of Sense in Wittgenstein's Tractatus." In H. Sluga and D. G. Stern (eds.), *The Cambridge Companion to Wittgenstein.* Cambridge: Cambridge University Press, 59–99.

Ricketts, T. 1996a. "Carnap: From Logical Syntax to Semantics." In Giere and Richardson (1996), 231–50.

Ringer, Fritz. 1969. *The Decline of the German Mandarins. The German Academic Community, 1890–1933.* Cambridge, MA: Harvard University Press.

Robb, A. A. 1914. *A Theory of Space and Time.* Cambridge: Cambridge University Press.

Rozeboom, W. 1960. "A Note on Carnap's Meaning Criterion." *Philosophical Studies* 11, 33–38.

Russell, Bertrand. 1940. *An Inquiry into Meaning and Truth.* London: Allen and Unwin.

Russell, Bertrand and Alfred N. Whitehead. 1910–13/1925–7. *Principia Mathematica.* 2nd ed. Cambridge: Cambridge University Press.

Rutherford, James F. 1960. "Discussion: Frank's Philosophy of Science Revisited." *Philosophy of Science* 27, 183–5.

Ryckman, T. A. 1994. "Weyl, Reichenbach and the Epistemology of Geometry." *Studies in the History and Philosophy of Modern Physics* 25, 831–70.

Ryckman, T. A. 1996. "Einstein *Agonists*: Weyl and Reichenbach on Geometry and the General Theory of Relativity." In Giere and Richardson (1996), 165–209.

Ryckman, T. A. 2002. "Two Roads from Kant: Cassirer, Reichenbach and General Relativity." In P. Parrini, M. L. Salmon and W. C. Salmon (eds.), *Analytical and Continental Origins of Logical Empiricism: Contemporary Perspectives and Appraisals*. Pittsburgh: University of Pittsburgh Press.

Ryckman, T. A. 2005. *The Reign of Relativity: Philosophy in Physics 1915–1925*. New York: Oxford University Press.

Salmon, Wesley C. 1975. "Confirmation and Relevance." In G. Maxwell and R. M. Anderson (eds.), *Induction, Probability, and Confirmation (Minnesota Studies in the Philosophy of Science VI)*. Minneapolis: University of Minnesota Press, 3–36.

Salmon, Wesley C. 1979. "The Philosophy of Hans Reichenbach." In W. C. Salmon (ed.), *Hans Reichenbach: Logical Empiricist*. Dordrecht: Reidel, 1–84.

Salmon, Wesley C. 1991. "Hans Reichenbach's Vindication of Induction." *Erkenntnis* 35, 99–122.

Salmon, Wesley, C. 1999. "The Spirit of Logical Empiricism: Carl G. Hempel's Role in Twentieth-Century Philosophy of Science." *Philosophy of Science* 66, 333–50.

Satzinger, Helga. 1998. *Die Geschichte der genetisch orientierten Hirnforschung von Cecile und Oskar Vogt (1875–1962, 1870–1959) in der Zeit von 1895 bis ca. 1927*. Stuttgart: Deutscher Apotheker-Verlag.

Sauer, Werner. 1985. "Carnaps 'Aufbau' in Kantianischer Sicht." *Grazer Philosophische Studien* 23, 19–35.

Sauer, Werner. 1987. "Carnaps Konstitutionstheorie und das Program der Einheitswissenschaft des Wiener Kreises." *Conceptus* 21, 233–45.

Saunders, Frances S. 1999. *The Cultural Cold War: The CIA and the World of Arts and Letters*. New York: New Press.

Schilpp, Paul Arthur (ed.). 1963. *The Philosophy of Rudolf Carnap*. La Salle, IL: Open Court.

Schilpp, Paul Arthur (ed.). 1974. *The Philosophy of Karl Popper*. 2 vols. La Salle, IL: Open Court.

Schlick, Moritz. 1910. "Das Wesen der Wahrheit nach der modernen Logik." *Vierteljahrsschrift für wissenschaftliche Philosophie und*

Soziologie 34, 386–477. Trans. by P. Heath as "The Nature of Truth in Modern Logic" in Schlick (1979), vol. 1, 41–103.

Schlick, Moritz. 1917. *Raum und Zeit in der gegenwärtigen Physik*. Berlin: Springer. 3rd ed. 1920, 4th ed. 1922. Trans. by H. Brose from the 3rd ed. as *Space and Time in Contemporary Physics*. Oxford: Oxford University Press, 1920. Expanded to include changes in the 4th ed. by P. Heath. In H. Mulder and B. van de Velde-Schlick (eds.), *Moritz Schlick: Philosophical Papers*, vol.1. Dordrecht: Reidel, 1979, 207–69.

Schlick, Moritz. 1917a. "Raum und Zeit in der gegenwärtigen Physik." *Die Naturwissenschaften* 5, 161–7, 177–86.

Schlick, Moritz. 1918. *Allgemeine Erkenntnislehre*. Berlin: Springer. 2nd ed. 1925. Trans. by A. Blumberg from the 2nd ed. as General Theory of Knowledge. La Salle, IL: Open Court, 1985.

Schlick, Moritz. 1920. "Naturphilosophische Betrachtungen über das Kausalprinzip." *Die Naturwissenschaften* 8, 461–74. Translated by P. Heath as "Philosophical Reflections on the Causal Principle," in Schlick (1979), vol. 1, 295–321.

Schlick, Moritz. 1922. *Raum und Zeit in der gegenwärtigen Physik. Vierte Auflage*. Berlin: J. Springer. Trans. by H. Brose and P. Heath as *Space and Time in Contemporary Physics*. In Schlick (1979), vol. 1, 207–69.

Schlick, Moritz. 1925. *Allgemeine Erkenntnislehre. Zweite Auflage*. Berlin: Springer. Trans. as Schlick (1985).

Schlick, Moritz. 1930. "Die Wende der Philosophie." *Erkenntnis* 1, 4–11. Trans. by P. Heath as "The Turning Point in Philosophy" in Schlick (1979), vol. 2, 154–60.

Schlick, Moritz. 1931. "Die Kausalität in der gegenwärtigen Physik." *Die Naturwissenschaften* 19, 145–62. Trans. by P. Heath as "Causality in Contemporary Physics" in Schlick (1979), vol. 2, 176–209.

Schlick, Moritz. 1932. "Positivismus und Realismus." *Erkenntnis* 4, 1–31. Trans. by P. Heath as "Positivism and Realism" in Schlick (1979), vol. 2, 259–84.

Schlick, Moritz. 1935. "De la relation entre les notions psychologiques et les notions physiques." *Revue des Synthese* 10, 5–26. Trans. as "On the Relation between Psychological and Physical Concepts" in Schlick (1979), vol. 2, 420–36.

Schlick, Moritz. 1979. *Moritz Schlick: Philosophical Papers*. H. L. Mulder and B. van de Velde-Schlick (eds.). 2 vols. Dordrecht: Reidel.

Schlick, Moritz. 1985. *General Theory of Knowledge*. Trans. by A. Blumberg of Schlick (1925). La Salle, IL: Open Court.

Schramm, Alfred. 1993. "Zwei Theorien der Induktion – Reichenbach und Carnap." In R. Haller and F. Stadler (eds.), *Wien-Berlin-Prag. Der*

Aufstieg der wissenschaftlichen Philosophie. Vienna: Hölder-Pichler-Tempsky, 538–54.

Schrecker, Ellen W. 1986. *No Ivory Tower: McCarthyism and the Universities*. New York: Oxford University Press.

Scott, Stephen. 1987. "Enlightenment and the Spirit of the Vienna Circle." *Canadian Journal of Philosophy* 17, 695–710.

Seiler, Martin and Friedrich Stadler (eds.). 1994. *Heinrich Gomperz, Karl Popper und die österreichische Philosophie*. Amsterdam: Rodopi.

Sellars, Wilfrid. 1963. *Science, Perception, and Reality*. New York: Humanities Press.

Shapere, Dudley. 1964. Untitled Review of Kuhn (1962). *Philosophical Review* 73, 383–94.

Shapere, Dudley. 1966. "Meaning and Scientific Change." In R. G. Colodny (ed.), *Mind & Cosmos: Essays in Contemporary Science & Philosophy*. Pittsburgh: University of Pittsburgh Press, 41–85.

Sharrock, Wes and Rupert Read. 2002. *Kuhn*. Oxford: Blackwell.

Shimony, Abner. 1984. "Contextual Hidden Variables Theories and Bell's Inequalities." *British Journal for the Philosophy of Science* 35, 25–45.

Shimony, Abner. 1992. "On Carnap: Reflections of a Metaphysical Student." *Synthèse* 93, 261–74.

Simons, Peter. 2004. "Open and Closed Culture: A New Way to Divide Austrians." In Chrudzimski and Humer (eds.), *Phenomenology and Analysis: Essays on Central European Philosophy*. Frankfurt: Ontos Verlag, 11–32.

Sklar, L. 1993. *Physics and Chance: Philosophical Issues in the Foundations of Statistical Mechanics*. New York: Cambridge University Press, 1993.

Sluga, Hans and David Stern (eds.). 1996. *The Cambridge Companion to Wittgenstein*. Cambridge: Cambridge University Press.

Smart, J. J. C. 1959. "Sensations and Brain Processes." Reprinted in D. Rosenthal (ed.), *Materialism and the Mind-Body Problem*. Indianapolis: Hackett, 1987.

Smith, L. 1986. Behaviorism and Logical Positivism: A Reassessment of the Alliance. Stanford, CA: Stanford University Press.

Soames, S. 2003. *Philosophical Analysis in the Twentieth Century*, vol I: *The Dawn of Analysis*. Princeton: Princeton University Press.

Spelt, P. D. M. and Brian McGuinness. 2001. "Marginalia in Wittgenstein's Copy of Lamb's *Hydrodynamics*." In Gianluigi Oliveri Liveri (ed.), *From the Tractatus to the Tractatus and Other Essays*. Vol. 2. *Wittgenstein Studien*. Frankfurt: Peter Lang, 131–47.

Stachel, John. 1989. "Einstein's Search for General Covariance, 1912–1915." In D. Howard and J. Stachel (eds.), *Einstein and the History of General Relativity (Einstein Studies,* vol. 1). Boston: Birkhäuser, 63–100. Based on a paper circulating privately since 1980.

Stachel, John. 1993. "The Meaning of General Covariance: The Hole Story." In J. Earman et al. (eds.), *Philosophical Problems of the Internal and External Worlds: Essays on the Philosophy of Adolf Grünbaum.* Pittsburgh: University of Pittsburgh Press, 129–60.

Stadler, Friedrich. 1981. "Spätaufklärung und Sozialdemokratie in Wien 1918–1938." In Franz Kadrnoska, ed., *Aufbruch und Untergang. Österreichische Kultur zwischen 1918 und 1938.* Vienna, 441–73.

Stadler, Friedrich. 1982. *Vom Positivismus zur Wissenschaftlichen Weltauffassung.* Vienna: Löcker Verlag.

Stadler, Friedrich. 1990. "Richard von Mises – Wissenschaft im Exil." In R. v. Mises, *Kleines Lexicon des Positivismus.* Frankfurt/Main: Suhrkamp-Verlag, 7–51.

Stadler, Friedrich. 1992. "Wittgenstein und der Wiener Kreis – zwischen Rezeption und Plagiat." In *Philosophie, Psychoanalyse, Emigration: Festschrift für Kurt Rudolf Fischer.* Vienna: WUV Universitätsverlag, 398–414.

Stadler, Friedrich (ed.). 1993. *Scientific Philosophy: Origins and Developments.* Dordrecht: Kluwer.

Stadler, Friedrich. 1997. *Studien zum Wiener Kreis. Ursprung, Entwicklung und Wirkung des logischen Empirismus im Kontext.* Frankfurt/Main: Suhrkamp. Trans. as Stadler (2001).

Stadler, Friedrich (ed.). 1997a. *Phänomenologie und Logischer Empirismus. Zentenarium Felix Kaufmann (1895–1949).* Vienna: Springer.

Stadler, Friedrich. 2001. *The Vienna Circle: Studies in the Origins, Development, and Influences of Logical Empiricism.* Trans. by Camilla Nielson et al. Vienna: Springer.

Stadler, Friedrich. 2003. "The 'Wiener Kreis' in Great Britain: Emigration and Interaction in the Philosophy of Science." In Edward Timms and Jon Hughes (eds.), *Intellectual Migration and Cultural Transformation. Refugees from National Socialism in the English Speaking World.* Vienna: Springer, 15–180.

Stadler, Friedrich. 2003a. "Transfer and Transformation of Logical Empiricism." In Hardcastle and Richardson (2003), 216–33.

Stadler, Friedrich (ed.). 2003c. *The Vienna Circle and Logical Empiricism. Re-Evaluation and Future Perspectives.* Dordrecht: Kluwer.

Stadler, Friedrich (ed.). 2004. *Österreichs Umgang mit dem Nationalsozialismus. Die Folgen für die naturwissenschaftliche und humanistische Lehre.* Vienna: Springer. (In collaboration with Eric Kandel, Walter Kohn, Fritz Stern, and Anton Zeilinger.)

Stadler, Friedrich. 2004a. "Induction and Deduction in the Philosophy of Science: A Critical Account since the *Methodenstreit.*" In F. Stadler (ed.), *Induction and Deduction in the Sciences*. Vienna Circle Institute Yearbook, No. 11 Dordrecht: Kluwer, 1–15.

Stadler, Friedrich and Peter Weibel (eds.). 1995. *The Cultural Exodus from Austria*. 2nd rev. & enlarged ed. Vienna: Springer.

Stalker, Douglas (ed.). 1994. *Grue!* La Salle, IL: Open Court.

Stein, H. 1992. "Was Carnap Entirely Wrong, after All?" *Synthese* 93, 275–95.

Stern, David G. 1995. *Wittgenstein on Mind and Language*. Oxford: Oxford University Press.

Stern, David G. 1996. "The Availability of Wittgenstein's Philosophy." In Sluga and Stern (1996), 442–76.

Stern, David G. 1999. Review of Hacker (1996). *Philosophical Review* 108, 449–52.

Stern, David G. 2000. "The Significance of Jewishness for Wittgenstein's Philosophy." *Inquiry* 43, 383–402.

Stern, David G. 2003a. "The Methods of the *Tractatus*: Beyond Positivism and Metaphysics?" In P. Parrini, M. L. Salmon, and W. C. Salmon (eds.), *Logical Empiricism: Historical and Contemporary Perspectives* Pittsburgh, Pittsburgh University Press, 125–56.

Stern, David G. 2004. *Wittgenstein's* Philosophical Investigations: *An Introduction*. Cambridge: Cambridge University Press.

Stern, David G. 2005. "How Many Wittgensteins?" In A. Pichler and S. Säätelä (eds.), *Wittgenstein: The Philosopher and His Works*. Working Papers from the Wittgenstein Archives at the University of Bergen no. 17. Bergen: Wittgenstein Archives at the University of Bergen, 164–88.

Sterrett, Susan. 2002. "Physical Pictures: Engineering Models circa 1914 and in Wittgenstein's *Tractatus.*" In M. Heidelberger and F. Stadler (eds.), *History of Philosophy of Science: New Trends and Perspectives*. Dordrecht: Kluwer, 121–35.

Stevens, S. S. 1935. "The Operational Definition of Psychological Concepts." *Psychological Review* 42, 517–27.

Stevens, S. S. 1951. "Mathematics, Measurement, and Psychophysics." In S. S. Stevens (ed.), *Handbook of Experimental Psychology*. New York: Wiley and Sons, 1–49.

Stoljar, Daniel. 2005. "Physicalism." *The Stanford Encyclopedia of Philosophy* (winter 2005 edition), Edward N. Zalta (ed.). http://plato.stanford.edu/archives/win2005/entries/physicalism/.

Strauss, Martin. 1963. "Hans Reichenbach und die Berliner Schule." *NTM–Zeitschrift für Geschichte der Naturwissenschaft, Technik und Medizin*. Beiheft 1963, 268–78. Trans. as "Hans Reichenbach and the Berlin School" in Strauss, *Modern Physics and Its Philosophy*. Dordrecht: Kluwer, 1972, 273–85.

Suppe, F. 1972. "What's Wrong with the Received View on the Structure of Scientific Theories?" *Philosophy of Science* 39, 1–19.

Suppe, F. (ed.). 1974. *The Structure of Scientific Theories*. Urbana: University of Illinois Press.

Suppe, Frederick. 1977. *The Structure of Scientific Theories*. 2nd ed. Urbana. IL: University of Illinois Press.

Suppes, Patrick. 1966. "A Bayesian Approach to the Paradoxes of Confirmation." In J. Hintikka and P. Suppes (eds.), *Aspects of Inductive Logic*. Amsterdam: North-Holland, 198–208.

Tait, William W. (ed.). 1997. *Early Analytic Philosophy: Frege, Russell, Wittgenstein: Essays in Honor of Leonard Linsky*. Chicago: Open Court.

Thiel, Christian. 1984. "Folgen der Emigration deutscher und österreichischer Wissenschaftstheoretiker und Logiker zwischen 1933 und 1945." *Berichte zur Wissenschaftsgeschichte* 7, 227–56.

Thomas, W. I. and D. S. Thomas. 1928. *The Child in America: Behavior Problems and Programs*. New York: Knopf. Excerpts repr. in E. H. Volkart , Social Behavior and Personality. Contributions of W. I. Thomas to Theory and Social Research. New York: Social Science Research Council, 1951.

Thurm, Volker and Elisabeth Nemeth (eds.). 2003. *Wien und der Wiener Kreis. Orte einer unvollendeten Moderne. Ein Begleitbuch*. Vienna: Facultas/WUV.

Time. 1939. (Author not given.) "Unity at Cambridge." *Time*, September 18, 72–73.

Tirala, Lothar S. 1936. "Einweihungsvortrag." In A. Becker (ed.), *Naturforschung im Aufbruch: Reden und Vorträge zur Einweihungsfeier des Philip-Lenard-Instituts der Universität Heidelberg am 13. und 14. Dezember 1935*. Munich: Verlag Lehmann, 48–67.

Tolman, E. C. 1932. *Purposive Behavior in Animals and Men*. New York: Century Company.

Tolman, E. C. 1934. "Psychology versus Immediate Experience." *Philosophy of Science* 2, 356–80.

Tolman, E. C. and Brunswik, E. 1935. "The Organism and the Causal Texture of the Environment." *Psychological Review* 42, 43–77.

Torretti, R. 1983. *Relativity and Geometry*. Oxford: Pergamon Press.

Toulmin, Stephen. 1951. Untitled Review of Frank (1951). *Philosophical Quarterly* 1, 180–81.

Uebel, Thomas E. (ed.). 1991. *Rediscovering the Forgotten Vienna Circle: Austrian Studies on Otto Neurath and the Vienna Circle*. Dordrecht: Kluwer.

Uebel, Thomas E. 1991a. "Neurath's Programme for Naturalistic Epistemology." *Studies in History and Philosophy of Science* 22, 623–46.

Uebel, Thomas E. 1992. *Overcoming Logical Positivism from Within: The Emergence of Neurath's Naturalism in the Vienna Circle's Protocol Sentence Debate*. Amsterdam: Rodopi.

Uebel, Thomas E. 1993. "Neurath's Protocol Statements: A Naturalistic Theory of Data and Pragmatic Theory of Theory Acceptance." *Philosophy of Science* 60, 587–607.

Uebel, Thomas E. 1995. "Physicalism in Wittgenstein and the Vienna Circle." In K. Gavrolgu et al. (eds.), *Physics, Philosophy, and the Scientific Community: Essays in the Philosophy of Science and Mathematics in Honor of Robert S. Cohen*. Dordrecht: Kluwer, 327–56.

Uebel, Thomas E. 1997. "Sozialwissenschaft auf physikalistischer Grundlage im Wiener Kreis." In H.-J. Sandkühler (ed.), *Philosophie und Wissenschaften. Formen und Prozesse ihrer Interaktion*. Frankfurt/Main: Peter Lang, 169–92.

Uebel, Thomas E. 1998. "Enlightenment and the Vienna Circle's Scientific World-Conception." In A. Rorty (ed.), *Philosophers on Education: Historical Perspectives*. London: Routledge, 418–38.

Uebel, Thomas E. 2000. "Logical Empiricism and the Sociology of Knowledge: The Case of Neurath and Frank." *Philosophy of Science* 67 (Proceedings), S138–50.

Uebel, Thomas E. 2000a. "Some Scientism, Some Historicism, Some Critics: Hayek's and Popper's Critiques Revisited." In M. W. F. Stone and J. Wolff (eds.), *The Proper Ambition of Science*. London: Routledge, 151–73.

Uebel, Thomas E. 2000b. *Vernunftkritik und Wissenschaft: Otto Neurath und der erste Wiener Kreis*. Vienna: Springer.

Uebel, Thomas E. 2001. "Carnap and Neurath in Exile: Can Their Disputes Be Resolved?" *International Studies in the Philosophy of Science* 15, 211–20.

Uebel, Thomas E. 2003. "History of Philosophy of Science and the Politics of Race and Ethnic Exclusion." In Heidelberger and Stadler 2003, 91–118.

Uebel, Thomas E. 2003a. "Philipp Frank's History of the Vienna Circle: A Programmatic Retrospective." In Hardcastle and Richardson 2003, 149–69.

Uebel, Thomas E. 2003b. "The Poverty of 'Constructivist' History and Policy Advice." *Social Epistemology* 17, 307–16.

Uebel, Thomas E. 2004. "Carnap, the Left Vienna Circle, and Neopositivist Antimetaphysics." In Awodey and Klein (2004), 247–77.

Ushenko, A. P. 1951. Untitled Review of Frank (1951). *Philosophy and Phenomenological Research* 11, 587–90.

van Fraassen, Bas C. 1970. *An Introduction to the Philosophy of Space and Time.* New York: Random House.

van Fraassen, Bas C. 2002. *The Empirical Stance.* New Haven, CT: Yale University Press.

von Mises, Richard. 1928. *Wahrscheinlischkeit, Statistik und Wahrheit.* Vienna: Springer. Trans. as *Probability, Statistics and Truth*, 1939. 2nd enlarged ed. by Hilda Geiringer. New York: Dover, 1957.

von Mises, Richard. 1939. *Kleines Lehrbuch der Positivismus.* Den Haag. Trans. by J. Bernstein and R. G. Newton as *Positivism.* Cambridge, MA: Harvard University Press, 1951.

von Neumann, J. 1932. *Mathematische Grundlagen der Quantenmechanik.* Berlin: Springer. Trans. by R. T. Beyer as *Mathematical Foundations of Quantum Mechanics.* Princeton: Princeton University Press, 1955.

Waismann, Friedrich. 1930. "Logische Analyse der Wahrscheinlich-keitsbegriff." *Erkenntnis* 1, 228–48. Translated by H. Kaal as "A Logical Analysis of the Concept of Probability" in B. Mc Guinness (ed.), *Philosophical Papers.* Dordrecht: Reidel, 1977, 4–21.

Waismann, Friedrich. 1967. *Wittgenstein und der Wiener Kreis: Gespräche.* Frankfurt/Main: Suhrkamp. Trans. by J. Schulte and B. McGuinness as *Wittgenstein and the Vienna Circle. Conversations Recorded.* B. McGuinness (ed.). Oxford: Blackwell, 1979. (Same pagination.)

Waismann, Friedrich. 1997. *The Principles of Linguistic Philosophy.* 2nd ed.; 1st ed. 1965. Basingstoke, Hampshire: Macmillan.

Wartofsky, M. W. 1982. "Positivism and Politics: The Vienna Circle as a Social Movement." In R. Haller (ed.), *Schlick und Neurath – Ein Symposion (Grazer Philosophische Studien*, 16/17). Amsterdam: Rodopi, 79–101.

Weinberg, J. K. 1936. *An Examination of Logical Positivism.* London: Kegan Paul; New York: Harcourt Brace.

Weyl, H. 1921. *Raum-Zeit-Materie. Vierte* Auflage. Berlin: J. Springer. Trans. by H. L. Brose as *Space-Time-Matter.* London: Meuthen, 1923. Repr. New York, Dover, 1953.

White, Morton G. 1950. "The Analytic and Synthetic: An Untenable Dualism." In S. Hook (ed.), *John Dewey: Philosopher of Science and Freedom.* New York: Dial Press, 316–30.

Winnie, J. 1977. "The Causal Structure of Space-Time." In J. Earman et al. (eds.), *The Foundations of Space-Time Theories*. Minneapolis: University of Minnesota Press, 134–205.

Wittgenstein, Ludwig. 1922. *Tractatus Logico-Philosophicus*. With an introduction by Bertrand Russell. London: Kegan Paul. 2nd ed., 1933.

Wittgenstein, Ludwig. 1953. *Philosophical Investigations*. Trans. by G. E. M. Anscombe. G. E. M. Anscombe and R. Rhees (eds.). Oxford: Blackwell. 2nd ed., 1958. Rev. ed., 2001.

Wittgenstein, Ludwig. 1958. *The Blue and Brown Books. Preliminary Studies for the Philosophical Investigations*. References are to the *Blue Book* or *Brown Book*. 2nd ed., 1969. Oxford: Blackwell.

Wittgenstein, Ludwig. 1964. *Philosophical Remarks*. First published as *Philosophische Bemerkungen*, German text only. R. Rhees (ed.). Oxford: Blackwell. 2nd ed., trans. by R. Hargraves and R. White. Oxford: Blackwell, 1975.

Wittgenstein, Ludwig. 1993. *Philosophical Occasions*. James Klagge and Alfred Nordmann (eds.). Indianapolis: Hackett.

Wittgenstein, Ludwig. 2000. *Wittgenstein's Nachlass: The Bergen Electronic Edition*. Oxford: Oxford University Press.

Wittgenstein, Ludwig. 2004. *Briefwechsel Innsbrucker elektronische Ausgabe*. Monika Seekircher, Brian McGuinness, and Anton Unterkircher (eds.). Charlottesville, VA: Intelex Past Masters.

Wittgenstein, Ludwig. 2005. *The Big Typescript*. C. G. Luckhardt (ed.). Oxford: Blackwell.

Wittgenstein, Ludwig and Friedrich Waismann. 2003. *The Voices of Wittgenstein: The Vienna Circle*. Gordon Baker (ed.). Trans. Gordon Baker et al. London: Routledge.

Wohlstetter, Albert and Morton White. 1939. "Who Are the Friends of Semantics?" *Partisan Review* 6, 50–57.

Zabell, Sandy. 1997. "Confirming Universal Generalizations." In D. Costantini and M. C. Galavotti (eds.), *Probability, Dynamics and Causality*. Dordrecht: Kluwer, 127–44.

Zilian, H. G. 1990. *Klarheit und Methode: Felix Kaufmanns Wissenschaftstheorie*. Amsterdam: Rodopi.

Zilsel, Edgar. 1916. *Das Anwendungsproblem. Ein philosophischer Versuch über das Gesetz der großen Zahlen und die Induktion*. Leipzig: Ambrosius Barth.

Zilsel, Edgar. 1918. *Die Geniereligion. Ein kritischer Versuch über das moderne Persönlichkeitsideal mit einer historischen Begründung*. Vienna. 2nd ed. Frankfurt: Suhrkamp, 1990.

Zilsel, Edgar. 1926. *Die Entstehung des Geniebegriffs. Ein Beitrag zu Ideengeschichte der Antike und des Frühkapitalismus*. Tübingen: Mohr.

Zilsel, Edgar. 1927. "Über die Asymmetrie der Kausalität und die Einsinnigkeit der Zeit." *Die Naturwissenschaften* 15, 280–6.

Zilsel, Edgar. 1929. "Philosophische Bemerkungen." *Der Kampf* 22, 178–86. Repr. in Zilsel (1992), 31–44.

Zilsel, Edgar. 1930. "Soziologische Bemerkungen zur Philosophie der Gegenwart." *Der Kampf* 23, 410–24.

Zilsel, Edgar. 1931. "Materialismus und marxistische Geschichtsauffassung." *Der Kampf* 24, 68–75. Repr. in Zilsel (1992), 77–87.

Zilsel, Edgar. 1931a. "Partei, Marxismus, Materialismus, Neukantianismus." *Der Kampf* 24, 213–20. Repr. in Zilsel (1992), 88–98.

Zilsel, Edgar. 1932. Review of Neurath (1931). *Der Kampf* 25. Repr. in Zilsel (1992), 145–49.

Zilsel, Edgar. 1932a. "Bemerkungen zur Wissenschaftslogik." *Erkenntnis* 3, 143–61.

Zilsel, Edgar. 1933. "SA philosophiert." *Der Kampf* 26. Repr. in Zilsel (1992), 153–66.

Zilsel, Edgar. 1933a. "Das Dritte Reich und die Wissenschaft." *Der Kampf* 26. Repr. in Zilsel (1992), 167–78.

Zilsel, Edgar. 1941. "Physics and the Problem of Historico-Sociological Laws." *Philosophy of Science* 8(4), 567–79.

Zilsel, Edgar. 1942. "The Genesis of the Concept of Physical Law." *Philosophical Review* 51, 245–79. Repr. in Zilsel (2000), 96–122.

Zilsel, Edgar. 1942a. "The Sociological Roots of Science." *American Journal of Sociology* 47, 544–62. Repr. in Zilsel (2000), 7–21.

Zilsel, Edgar. 1992. *Wissenschaft und Weltanschauung. Aufsätze 1929–1933*. Karl Acham (ed.). Vienna.

Zilsel, Edgar. 2000. *The Social Origins of Modern Science*. Diederick Raven, Wolfgang Krohn, and Robert S. Cohen (eds.). Dordrecht: Kluwer.

Zolo, Danilo. 1986. *Scienza e Politica in Otto Neurath. Milano: Petrivelli*. Rev. ed. Trans. as *Reflexive Epistemology: The Philosophical Legacy of Otto Neurath*. Dordrecht: Kluwer, 1989.

Index